Reflections of a Mormon Historian

Reflections of a Mormon Historian

Leonard J. Arrington on the New Mormon History

Essays by
Leonard J. Arrington

Edited by
Reid L. Neilson and Ronald W. Walker

THE ARTHUR H. CLARK COMPANY
Norman, Oklahoma
2006

The Arthur H. Clark Company
2800 Venture Drive
Norman, OK 73069-8216

Library of Congress Catalog Card Number 2006011340
ISBN 0-87062-348-6
ISBN 978-0-87062-348-6

Library of Congress Cataloging-in-Publication Data

Arrington, Leonard J.
Reflections of a Mormon historian : Leonard L. Arrington on the new Mormon history / essays by Leonard J. Arrington ; edited by Reid L. Neilson and Ronald W. Walker.
p. cm.
Includes bibliographical references and index.
ISBN 0-87062-348-6 (hardcover : alk. paper)
1. Church of Jesus Christ of Latter-Day Saints—History. 2. Mormon Church—History. 3. Mormon History Association. 4. Arrington, Leonard J. I. Neilson, Reid Larkin. II. Walker, Ronald W. (Ronald Warren), 1939– III. Title.
BX8611.A79 2006
289.3072'2—dc22
2006011340

The paper in this book meets the guidelines for permanence and durability of the Committee on Production Guidelines for Book Longevity of the Council on Library Resources. ∞

To Marilyn Rish Parks

Contents

Foreword

I WAS THE LUCKIEST GIRL in the Logan Utah Tenth Ward of the Church of Jesus Christ of Latter-day Saints. As tradition would have it, once a year our primary class participated in a "daddy-daughter date." Each girl brought her dad to the church house and there enjoyed an evening of food, group games, and friendly competition among the "couples."

My father, Leonard Arrington, always participated in the activities of the evening with gusto. The formal ways and dignified behavior usually associated with being a university professor and highly respected historian were set aside for the evening. For a couple of hours he was my special date, and we had a grand time.

As we played "I have a little doggie, and he won't bite you . . . ," Dad gave his all, with exaggerated gestures and a huge smile on his face. As we did a little Virginia Reel, Dad whirled his gleeful partner as if we had practiced our spins for hours. And I could hardly contain myself when we began competing against other fathers and daughters in a series of word games. We won, hands down, of course! One thing for certain: once the activity was over, we would leave the church house hand and hand, and the two of us would skip all the way home, which for us was less than a block. My memories of those evenings, while more than forty years old, are as fresh and clear as if they occurred last night.

I have long since decided that children rarely have a very accurate view of what their parents' lives are really like. Few young people know in detail how their father or mother earns a living or maintains a household, let alone the details of their parents' private victories and defeats. For me, the essays of this book, carefully read, contribute a great deal to having a much broader understanding of my father.

It was only a few years after those precious daddy-daughter dates that my father was called to serve as Church Historian of the LDS Church. And it was a few years after that event that I finally began to understand something of the intellectual world my father inhabited. At the time I had no idea what the late-night clickity-clack that I heard coming through my bedroom wall from Dad's study was all about. I went to bed every night for years with the rhythmic sound of Dad's manual typewriter lulling me to sleep.

While he was busy helping to found the Mormon History Association, I was happy to have him critique or edit my English essays. While he was reconciling in his own mind faith and history, my brother Carl was simply delighted to have Dad as his Little League baseball coach. And, while Dad was busy adding to one of the most impressive and voluminous bibliographies the West has ever seen, James could count on Dad to be near the front of any audience that gathered to see a school theater production in which James performed.

Leonard touched many lives for good. Fortunately, Dad was blessed with a wife who was totally committed to raising a family and supporting her husband in his profession. Grace deserves far more credit for Dad's remarkable career than she generally receives. Grace died in 1982, and thus missed many opportunities in more recent years to be with Dad when he received prestigious awards, plaques, and two honorary doctoral degrees. After her passing, Dad married Harriet Horne, yet still made every effort to maintain a loving and close relationship with his children and grandchildren. Looking back, we all agree on one thing—our father was highly successful in balancing an extremely busy professional career with his role as husband and father.

The Arrington family is grateful to Reid L. Neilson and Ronald W. Walker for their efforts in preparing important selections from Leonard's essays for publication. The essays in this book are important in that they allow us to look into the heart and soul of the man behind that over-worked typewriter.

While family and friends knew Leonard well enough to predict what music he would put on the stereo at home, which meal he would order at a restaurant, and what flavor of Aggie Ice Cream he preferred, this book takes readers deeper than that—much, much deeper. It helps us explore the mind and the soul of the man who was not only the best of mentors and the first non–General Authority in more than a century to be entrusted with the calling of LDS Church Historian, but who was also, throughout his life, the dearest of friends, as well as a loyal brother, husband, and father. Oh, what I would give for just one more "daddy-daughter" date.

Susan Arrington Madsen
Hyde Park, Utah

Preface

EACH OF US KNEW LEONARD ARRINGTON DIFFERENTLY. For Reid L. Neilson, the encounter began six months before Arrington's death in 1999. His parents had given him a copy of *Adventures of a Church Historian*, to celebrate his twenty-sixth birthday.[1] The next morning, after spending much of the night reading, he had "fire in his bones." Arrington's autobiography *was* an adventure.

Then, there was Arrington's passing and funeral. At the time, Reid was vacationing with his family in Park City, Utah. His father saw the obituary and encouraged him to attend the services. Reid went, as this was his last opportunity "to meet" the celebrated dean of Mormon history. Carol Madsen, an Arrington colleague and Neilson family friend, welcomed him to the service, which was heavily populated by senior historians. Madsen later recorded the encounter. "As I sat in the chapel shortly before the funeral services for our beloved friend and historian," she wrote.

> I was surprised to see a young student whom I knew from Brigham Young University. He was studying business, but he harbored a deep love for Mormon history. . . . I asked him what had brought him to the funeral, thinking he had probably had some special contact of his own with Leonard, as so many others have had. He said he had never met Leonard but felt compelled to attend his funeral because Leonard was for him the cornerstone of the Mormon historical enterprise, and he wanted to pay his own personal respects to the man who had engendered such a love of Mormon history in him.
>
> That brief incident suggests to me the breadth of influence Leonard had on both the nature of Mormon historical writing and on those engaged in doing it. His work and his great gift of outreach were indeed beacons, drawing scholars from all fields, as well as would-be historians and family chronicles to his work and his words.[2]

Reid was that young business student. Arrington was a beacon for so many, as Madsen said, even to those he never met.

Several years have passed since that incident. Reid is now a Ph.D. candidate in religious studies at Arrington's alma mater—the University of North Carolina at Chapel Hill. As he goes about his graduate training in the Tar Heel State, his thoughts have often turned to Arrington, wondering if they may have sat in the same classrooms, walked identical brick paths, and struggled with similar questions. Although unsure about buildings and walkways, Reid has come to think that in some small way they share many of the same historical interests and hopes.

Ronald W. Walker had another young scholar experience, which in his case resulted in an enduring relationship with Arrington. Just out of graduate school, Ron had read *Great Basin Kingdom*, his great opus, and reverenced from afar.[3] It was quite exciting, then, when Arrington telephoned to ask him to come to his office: he had read one of Ron's graduate-school papers and wanted to get acquainted. Always outgoing and interested in others, Arrington quickly put him at ease. In time, Arrington even offered him one of the summer-term fellowships that the LDS Historical Department was handing out at the time. Several years later, Ron joined Arrington's staff, and over the course of time, their relationship went beyond professional things. They became friends.

ALTHOUGH WE COME TO THIS PROJECT with different perspectives and experience, we are united by our mutual interest in Arrington and the issues that he raised during the flowering of Mormon history. It is unlikely that Arrington, even with his sense of mission, saw what would become of his ideas. Now, a half-century since the publication of his *Great Basin Kingdom*, the writing of LDS history flourishes. Part of this can be seen by taking inventory: A recent bibliography of Mormon secondary literature, *Studies in Mormon History*, lists more than fifteen thousand titles, about half of which were written during Arrington's lifetime and many of which fell under his influence.[4]

That influence can best be explained by Arrington's life. By bloodline, as the material in the book suggests, he was a descendant of farmers from North Carolina. On the other hand, by religious heritage, he grew out of the religious and social idealism of the Mormon pioneer tradition. The Great Depression further shaped him. "I intended to learn to be a good farmer," he said of his first months at the University of Idaho at Moscow, Idaho.[5] Although this ambition fell before the prospect of an academic career, something of the small farmer of the eighteenth- and nineteenth-century American rural ideal always remained with him. He was drawn to "little people"—and to the hope of improving society. The ideas that shaped his writing had to do with practical and concrete things, yet they were also full of idealism.

There was also a spiritual dimension, which was best captured by a story that Arrington told about himself. During the winter of 1949–50, several years after serving a stint in World War II, he returned to North Carolina to complete his Ph.D. course work. While sitting in an alcove of the university library, full of feeling and ideas about his research, he had one of those "defining moments" that he sometimes spoke of. He would later remember the event as a "peak experience"—a feeling of ecstasy that "transported me to a higher level of consciousness." It was as though the divine was confirming his sense of mission. "Whatever my talents and abilities—and I have never pretended that they were extraordinary—an invisible higher power had now given me a commission," he later wrote. "I knew that God expected me to carry out a research program of his peoples' history and to make available that material to others. . . . My experience was a holy, never-to-be-forgotten encounter."[6]

The essays in this volume are a combination of these strains. They are full of practical ideas and ideals—they are "to-do lists" about how to approach the thinking and writing of history—and how, implicitly, society might be improved. Also running through the essays is Arrington's quiet quest to understand life's higher purposes. Not surprisingly, the historical movement that he helped to found—the New Mormon History—is likewise a halfway house between the secular and the religious. The annual meetings of the Mormon History Association and periodicals such as *Brigham Young University Studies*, *Dialogue: A Journal of Mormon Thought*, and the *Journal of Mormon History* epitomize the approach. This collection chronicles Arrington's determination to walk the middle way.

As this collection goes to press, we sense a new spirit rising. Increasingly, the study of the Mormon past is less historical and more inter-cultural. The change is seen in the talk about the development of "Mormon Studies" programs at Claremont, Utah State University, and Utah Valley State College. It is seen in the new interest of Mormon topics by Oxford, North Carolina, Columbia, Cambridge, and other prestigious university presses. Recent academic conferences on Mormonism at the University of Durham (1999), Yale University (2003), Claremont Graduate University (2004 and 2005), and the U.S. Library of Congress (2005) offer hope that the study of the LDS past is becoming less parochial. Mormonism as an academic discipline is moving beyond the birthing stages that Arrington's essays foreshadow.[7]

We present these essays, then, because of their content—what they have to say about the writing of the Mormon past—but also because they are historical documents about the progress of Mormon studies. They are prologue to what is becoming and brim with issues that continue to challenge Mormon historians. As such, these essays will interest readers of the Mormon past as well as its future writers. Together, we have selected fourteen of Arrington's essays for publication, several previously unpublished, which we have organized into three parts: "Arrington as Historian," "Reflections on Mormon History," and "Mormon Historical Writing."

The first section is biographical and includes Arrington's reflections on his own career. Essays in this section include "Historian as Entrepreneur: A Personal Essay," "Reflections on the Founding and Purpose of the Mormon History Association," and "The Founding of the LDS Church Historical Department." These essays provide a tour of Arrington's personal and professional life: his Idaho upbringing and university training; the start of his career; the establishment of the organization of history buffs and professionals that has done so much to shape recent Mormon historical writing; and the recounting of those tumultuous years, when as the first professional historian to be chosen to produce official Church history, he labored through the tugs and controversy of his job. This section also includes the essay "Myth, Symbol, and Truth," which provides an interior view of the man. Here, Arrington chronicles his response to the ultimate questions of his time and culture. What about religion—and Christianity? And what about Mormonism? This essay reveals him to be a "believer," who found meaning and worth in his religious tradition. Clearly, Arrington was not just a historian of Mormonism, but a *Mormon* historian.

Five essays on the meaning and value of Mormon history comprise the second section. These pieces have a wide range of format and message and are full of Arrington advice and cajoling. To begin with, "The Search for Truth and Meaning in Mormon History" sets out an argument for a more inclusive history, which despite the passage of twenty-five years since its publication has the freshness of counsel that has been only partly realized; his identification of five biases, or inclinations, of Mormon history writing remains a bill of indictment that future scholars must answer. Published here for the first time, "Clothe These Bones: The Reconciliation of Faith and History" is Arrington's invited attempt to give a sermon at the June 1978 History Division retreat held on Ensign Peak, Salt Lake City, Utah. After discussing many of the challenges and opportunities facing Mormon historians, he calls on his colleagues to breathe life into the dry bones of the past. Next, in "Personal Reflections on Mormon History," Arrington asserts the value of Mormon heritage. In his view, the rich humanity of the Mormon past, at least implicitly, is a call for similar virtue today. In another previously unpublished essay, "The Questing Spirit in Mormon History," he chronicles late nineteenth- and early twentieth-century LDS intellectual trajectories, including the exodus of Mormon students to universities beyond the Great Basin Kingdom. Arrington suggests that the same questing spirit that fueled higher education and the acquisition of knowledge in early Mormonism continues unabated to this day. The final piece in this section presents Arrington in twilight. Several years before his death, he proposed an annual lecture on Mormon history, and he provided the inaugural presentation, "Faith and Intellect as Partners in Mormon History." Quite typically, he argues for the symbiotic relationship of faith and intellect, the spirit and the mind, and makes the case for Joseph Smith, Eliza R. Snow, Brigham Young, Emmeline B. Wells, and George Q. Cannon as exemplars.

The last section is about Mormon history as history, or historiography, which is the study of historical writing. In "Scholarly Studies of Mormonism in the Twentieth Century" Arrington describes how the writing of Mormon history moved from nineteenth-century apologetics, argument, and curiosa to twentieth-century systematic and scholarly study. Although an optimist, he could not overlook Mormonism's lack of sweeping narratives, good biographies, and specialized studies of the more recent LDS past. Notwithstanding, "The Intellectual Tradition of the Latter-day Saints" reminds readers that Mormonism has its own intellectual tradition, embodied by such great thinkers as Orson Pratt, B. H. Roberts, Sterling McMurrin, Lowell Bennion, and Hugh Nibley, some of whom wrote history. Arrington was also concerned with the lack of solid international Church histories. In summer 1980, he traveled to Hawaii to give the keynote address of the Mormon Pacific Historical Society's inaugural conference. In the essay "On Writing Latter-day Saint History," he suggests the "heretical" idea that local LDS histories are more important than general histories, given the globalization of Mormonism. Appearing here for the first time, "The Marrow in the Bones of History: New Directions in Historical Writing" is Arrington's address to the Western University Press Association. He argues that intimate, first-person accounts of daily life provide the real marrow in the bones for historical writing. Moreover, Mormon history and its historians are fortunate to have the Church's vast archives and plentiful primary sources. Finally, "The Writing of Latter-day Saint History: Problems, Accomplishments and Admonitions" centers on the question of writing religious history and proposes a five-part periodization for understanding Mormon historiography.

Arrington's essays do not stand alone. Ron Walker's "Mormonism's 'Happy Warrior': Appreciating Leonard J. Arrington," written as a memorial shortly after his death, serves as our prologue. This essay chronicles Arrington's personal and professional life, describing how a young student, hopeful for a life as an Idaho chicken farmer, came to climb the heights of Mormon historical writing. It also offers a preliminary evaluation of Arrington's legacy and of that of the New Mormon History. The other bookend to our collection—the concluding essay in the collection—comes from David J. Whittaker, one of the more prolific bibliographers of the Mormon guild. Whittaker's essay, "Leonard James Arrington (1917–1999): A Bibliography," catalogues Arrington's prodigious writing by book, monograph, pamphlet, article, and by other miscellaneous writing. He also provides an updated listing of historical writing about Arrington. These bibliographies make clear that by virtue of volume and by quality, Arrington was virtually a one-man historical school.

WE THANK ARRINGTON'S PUBLISHERS for their permission to reprint his essays. Where possible and appropriate, we have dropped all bibliographic citations to the endnotes and added additional explanatory notes, while leaving the text unchanged despite obvious overlaps. We also express our warm debt to Susan Arrington Madsen and to the other trustees of the Leonard J. Arrington Foundation for their support. The Arrington Foundation asserts its right to control the rich collection of Arrington material, published and unpublished, and at each stage of our work, the Arrington family cooperated and offered advice about our project. The library at Utah State University allowed us to reprint the Arrington chronology from the Arrington collection register. We thank Amanda Midgley Borneman for source-checking the essays. Lastly, we thank our wives, Shelly and Nelani, who endured our late night puttering at the computer, and for our many historical colleagues who encouraged this book, including members of the Joseph Fielding Smith Institute for LDS Church History at Brigham Young University (1980–2005). That organization has now lapsed, but its influence upon this book and so many others is an indication of its past, important work.

When all is said and done, these essays are a historical record of one the LDS Church's leading intellectuals of the twentieth century—a record of Arrington and his thinking. He was our mentor. We wish him honor.

REID L. NEILSON
Chapel Hill, North Carolina

RONALD W. WALKER
Provo, Utah

PREFACE NOTES

1. Leonard J. Arrington, *Adventures of a Church Historian* (Urbana and Chicago: University of Illinois Press, 1998).
2. Carol Cornwall Madsen, "The Voices of Memory," *Journal of Mormon History* 25 (spring 1999): 100.
3. Leonard J. Arrington, *Great Basin Kingdom: An Economic History of the Latter-day Saints, 1830–1900* (Cambridge, Mass.: Harvard University Press, 1958).
4. James B. Allen, Ronald W. Walker, and David J. Whittaker, *Studies in Mormon History, 1830–1997: An Index Bibliography* (Urbana and Chicago: University of Illinois Press, 2000).
5. Arrington, *Adventures of a Church Historian*, 22.
6. Arrington, *Adventures of a Church Historian*, 28–29.
7. Many of these recent developments are traced in Ronald W. Walker, David J. Whittaker, and James B. Allen, with a contribution by Armand L. Mauss, *Mormon History* (Urbana and Chicago: University of Illinois Press, 2001), 68–98; and Philip Barlow, "Jan Shipps and the Mainstreaming of Mormon Studies," *Church History* 73 (June 2004): 412–26.

Mormonism's "Happy Warrior"
Appreciating Leonard J. Arrington

by Ronald W. Walker

Who is the happy warrior? Who is he
That every man in arms should wish to be?
—William Wordsworth[1]

THE PHONE RANG. Picking up the receiver, I heard my secretary's voice telling me of an incoming call. "Brother Walker," she said, "Grover Cleveland is on the phone and wants to speak with you."

At the time, I was working at the Salt Lake City headquarters of the Church Education System, where things were pretty serious. The formal ways of the place and the idea that a dead U.S. president was telephoning put me off balance—considerably.

Then I heard the cheery and distinctive rasp voice of Leonard J. Arrington. "Ron, this is Grover Cleveland," he said. "How would you like to come to work for us?" I was laughing too hard to reply.

During the next few weeks, Grover Cleveland's calls continued until I took the job with the historical department. My secretary, an able worker but not much of a historian, never broke the cipher.

Leonard Arrington was fun. Another time, several of us were eating at the Hotel Utah Coffee Shop. Leonard announced that he would order the dessert. "We want lemon chess pie," he told the waiter, who clearly was confused by the order. Minutes later, he returned to say that he had never heard of lemon chess pie. Nor did the restaurant have any.

Leonard's voice rose. "We want lemon chess pie," he said. "Go look for it and you'll find it." Leonard was smiling broadly as if he was aware of a great secret. The rest of us, confused like the waiter, inched down in our chairs.

Two more times, the waiter came to our table empty-handed, and two more times Leonard sent him back to the kitchen.

Then, without fanfare, the lemon chess pie suddenly appeared, and our discomfort turned to relief and total laughter. To complete Leonard's triumph, as we ate our delicious dessert, the chef came out of the kitchen to see how we were doing. "Do you like the pie?" he asked.

I never learned why lemon chess pie was such a state secret at the coffee shop—nor how Leonard came to discover it. In this, Leonard kept his own counsel.

Things were not always so happy. A year after I was hired at the LDS Historical Department, I told Leonard I was quitting due to a dispute over policy. I thought the matter serious.

Leonard closed his office door, and we talked. For the first time, I learned how deeply he cared about me personally. It was a quality that almost everyone who knew Leonard sooner or later discovered. The incident became a turning point in our relationship.

Leonard showed this same personal interest when reading our early draft manuscripts written at the Historical Department. "This is good," he would say to us young historians, even about a journeyman piece of work. Leonard wanted to encourage us, but there was another reason for his attitude. It was his way of saying that we should not unduly fuss with a draft but that we should get our writing into the marketplace as soon as possible. For truly superior work, Leonard's reaction was a little bit different. "This is *really* great," he might say. Those of us who worked with Leonard learned to listen for his adverbs and adjectives and especially for hints in his voice. Pause, shadow, and inflection meant everything.

I had Leonard reading my manuscripts long after we left the History Division and long after his formal retirement. It was a matter of friendship, and I admired his judgment. Shortly before his death, I was once more on the telephone. "Would you have time to read four essays that I have written for an upcoming book?" I asked.

Leonard thought that he might get to them in a couple of weeks, and I dropped them by his house.

That same evening Leonard was on the phone to say that he had read the first of the essays and thought that it was "great." A couple hours later came a similar call about the second essay. And the next day, there was another call, and on the second day, still another one. When I later picked up the four essays, it was clear that he had read every sentence. He had circled many typos and offered several important ideas about rephrasing and new sources. Of more personal meaning, he had put aside his own work to read my manuscript.

Leonard often sent a letter of congratulation a day or two after an article appeared in print—often before I was even aware a piece had been published. These letters were often handwritten on his personal, light-brown stationery. While these letters meant a great deal to me and made me feel that he had a personal interest in my work, I am sure that most Mormon writers were similarly honored by Leonard's correspondence. He was in the "business" of encouraging the historical enterprise, whether or not he always agreed with the argument of an article or book.

Of course, he had his own ideas about how history should be written. His ideas, in fact, helped to determine how Mormon history was written during the last part of the twentieth century. According to Leonard, the Mormon past should be investigated in human or naturalistic terms, yet without rejecting Mormonism's divinity.[2] He wanted a middle way, between the extremes of defending or attacking faith claims—the reason for being for most nineteenth-century and even a great deal of twentieth-century writing. Leonard was not the only LDS historian who adopted this neutral stance in his writing, but because of his personality and the quality of his work, his name because inseparably connected with what became increasingly known as the New Mormon History.[3]

The New Mormon History of course had many variations, but it was characterized by a restrained religious voice, an academic style of writing, and a search for understanding the Mormon past for its own sake and indirectly the understanding of self: A strong sense of self-discovery existed among Leonard and other New Mormon History writers. They wanted to learn more about their inherited belief and how that belief fit into the modern world of ideas.

Leonard described the path that led him to his work. He went from "chicken farmer to agriculture major; from agriculture to economics; from regional economics to Western economic history; and finally from Western history to Mormon studies."[4] After growing up on his family's irrigated Idaho farm and graduating from the University of Idaho in 1939, Leonard studied at the University of North Carolina at Chapel Hill. This last experience introduced him to the southern agrarian writers of the post–World War I era, whose influence was pivotal. He felt a "burning in my bones" to do for the American West what Odum, Vance, Heath, and others had done for southern regionalism.[5]

Two men further refined Leonard's sense of mission. The first was Richard T. Ely, whose 1903 essay in *Harper's Monthly* had launched the work of the early twentieth-century Mormon regionalists. In 1939 Leonard met Ely in Philadelphia at the annual convention of the American Economic Association. I "felt it [was] a gift of heaven that I could talk with this short, pink-cheeked, boyish-faced man, who had influenced two generations of economists and economic policy," Leonard later wrote.[6] Ely plied his young acquaintance with stories about the Mormon contribution to western settlement—stories that affected Leonard deeply. Later Leonard modestly reported that his Ph.D. dissertation was "merely an extension" of Ely's pioneering work.[7]

The other figure who helped direct Leonard's professional interest was Mormon apostle John A. Widtsoe. After completing his coursework at Chapel Hill and serving in World War II as a youthful Allied Controller of the Central Institute of Statistics during the American occupation of Italy, Leonard returned to the Intermountain West in 1946, accepting a teaching position in economics at Utah State University in Logan, Utah. Hoping to get his professional bearings, he sought Widtsoe's advice. The former president of Utah State University and the University of Utah urged the young scholar to narrow his interest in western regionalism to Mormon country. There, Widtsoe perceptively argued, Leonard would find a unified cultural region ideal to his ambition. Not the least of its advantages, Mormon regionalism had abundant and largely untapped historical resources.[8]

The late 1940s and early 1950s were busy for Leonard. He increasingly gained access to the rich but previously restricted sources of the LDS Archives in Salt Lake City. In Logan, he joined Utah State faculty member S. George Ellsworth, LDS Institute of Religion teacher Eugene E. Campbell, and another Institute of Religion faculty member, Wendell O. Rich, in monthly study sessions in which the men read papers, many later published, on Mormon culture and history. Ellsworth was especially helpful in introducing Leonard to the methods and standards of historical writing. Then, in 1951, Leonard began to publish in such scholarly journals as *Rural Sociology*, *Journal of Economic History*, *Economic History Review*, *Western Humanities Review*, *Pacific Historical Review*, and *Business History Review*.[9] This early work culminated in the publication of *Great Basin Kingdom: An Economic History of the Latter-day Saints, 1830–1900*, a watershed in the writing of the New Mormon History.[10] The book summarized the sociological and economic literature produced by such rural agrarians as Lowry Nelson and Nels Anderson.[11] More important, it contained Leonard's own meticulous and path-breaking research. The result was a fresh and detailed view of Mormon pioneering (despite the book's expansive subtitle, it focused on the Utah era). At the same time, the book reached a larger audience by being a case study of "modern" economic planning. Here Leonard suggested that the Mormons' Great Basin Kingdom, more than eighty years before the New Deal or the Fair Deal, was the agent in a vast enterprise of centralized decision-making and regulation. Moreover, the theocracy's social ideas of homogeneity, equality, and unity coincided with many of the values urged by Richard Ely, the southern agrarians, and New Deal planners. Leonard's book was a part of the intellectual and liberal *Zeitgeist* of its times.

The book made explicit Leonard's views about how Mormon history, as religious history, should be written. According to an important passage in the book's preface:

> The true essence of God's revealed will, if such it be, cannot be apprehended without an understanding of the conditions surrounding the prophetic vision, and the symbolism and verbiage in which it is couched. . . . A naturalistic discussion of "the people and the times" and of the mind and experience of Latter-day prophets is therefore a perfectly valid aspect of religious history, and, indeed, makes more plausible the truths they attempted to convey. While the discussion of naturalistic causes of revelations does not preclude its claim to be revealed or inspired of God, in practice it is difficult, if not impossible, to distinguish what is objectively "revealed" from what is subjectively "contributed" by those receiving the revelation.[12]

It was not that Leonard denied the hand of providence in the unfolding of Mormon events. Rather, he felt uncertain and unwilling to identify it, and so scrupulous was his restraint that some Mormon readers, unused to scholarly writing, assumed that *Great Basin Kingdom* was written either by a non-Mormon or an anti-Mormon. In another passage, Leonard suggested the difficulty of writing religious history. "The professional in us fights against religious naiveté," he wrote, while "the "religionist in us fights against secular naiveté—believing too little. And if this internal warfare weren't enough, we have a similar two-front war externally—against non-Mormons who think we LDS historians believe too much, and against super-Mormons who think we believe not enough."[13] Leonard's cautious approach to writing religious history—his willingness to give natural explanations, his restrained religious voice, and his attempt to find a "middle ground" between the extremes of secular and religious feeling—became hallmarks of the new Mormon writing.

His career launched, Leonard came to regard himself not only as an individual scholar but as a "historical entrepreneur."[14] This new role meant coordinating team efforts and often collaborating with graduate students and colleagues to produce a series of articles and monographs, mostly on western economic history. It also meant mentoring. Several Church authorities, impressed with Leonard's professionalism and LDS sympathy, urged Leonard to assist the rising generation of historical scholars.[15]

In 1965 Leonard played a leading role in organizing the Mormon History Association (MHA); he also served as its first president. The association was an outgrowth of informal discussion sessions that Leonard and other LDS historians had held at various regional and national professional meetings. Three years later, the MHA began to hold an annual meeting independent of other associations, and within fifteen years the MHA had between seven and eight hundred members, both Mormon and non-Mormons.[16]

As a "historical entrepreneur," Leonard also played a role in the reorganization of the LDS Church Historian's Office (CHO). In January 1966, President N. Eldon Tanner, a counselor in the First Presidency of the Church, interviewed Leonard about possible reforms at the CHO. Several years later, Leonard was a member of a committee of historians that advised the CHO to establish a continuing liaison with the historical community, to build a professional staff, to collect new material, to fund research grants for non-CHO personnel, and most important, to begin an ambitious, multivolume publishing program.[17] These suggestions helped to address the growing concern that the Church Historian's Office was not meeting its scriptural obligation to keep "a record . . . among you" (D&C 21:1; 47:1; 69:2–3; 85:1). Since the publication of B. H. Roberts's multivolume *Comprehensive History of the Church* in 1930, the CHO had not published new material. Nor had the CHO's policy of restricting access to its material encouraged non-affiliated historians to write Church history.

In January 1972, Leonard's role was greatly enlarged. In a precedent-breaking move, President Tanner, acting in behalf of the First Presidency, called Leonard to the office of LDS Church Historian, the first non–General Authority to serve in this position. "We are under obligation to write our history for the benefit of the generations to come, and we want it done in a thoroughly professional way," Tanner explained.[18]

At the time of his selection, Leonard was fifty-four years old. He had published widely and had served as president of the Agricultural History Society, Western History Association, and the Mormon History Association. Although his appointment was coupled with a half-time professorship at Brigham Young University, where he also served as director of the Charles Redd Center for Western Studies, in future years his teaching and research duties would increasingly be displaced by overseeing the work of others. However, there was a compensating advantage: as Church Historian he could use the research and writing of his associates to enhance his own writing projects.

Embarking on his new assignment, Leonard once more tried to steer a middle course. In August 1972, he wrote in his diary:

> As a result of yesterday's meeting with the First Presidency I have been thinking and praying about my calling as Church Historian. . . . On the one hand, I am the Church historian and must seek to build testimonies, spread the Word, build the Kingdom. On the other hand, I am called to be a *historian*, which means that I must earn the respect of professional historians. What I write must be craftsmanlike, credible, and of good quality. This means that I stand on two legs—the leg of faith and the leg of reason. . . . May the Lord bless me to be honest, frank, and fearless, when I must be honest, frank, and fearless; and may He bless me to be diplomatic and understanding when those qualities are required![19]

Leonard's new assignment placed him in charge of the History Division, a newly created section of the renamed LDS Historical Department assigned the responsibility of writing history. Leonard and his superior at Church headquarters, Elder Alvin R. Dyer, set high goals for the History Division, several of which had been discussed in previous conversations.[20] The program included publishing a sixteen-volume history of the Church that would mark Mormonism's 150-year anniversary in 1980. Leonard and Dyer also saw the need for a new one-volume treatment of Church history and proposed two different books: a narrative history designed for Church members and another, a topically arranged and analytical volume for more academically minded Mormons and non-Mormons. Other parts of the publishing program that soon emerged at the History Division included a "Heritage Series" featuring important diaries and documents; an oral history program; the publication of articles for scholarly journals and Church periodicals; and such miscellaneous projects as biographies of Church leaders, gender studies, local and regional history, and histories addressing "aspects of ordinary life."[21] It was, of course, an agenda for an entire generation of scholarship.

To meet these goals, Leonard chose two assistants who were active in the new history movement, James B. Allen and Davis Bitton. In addition, the History Division at its high tide had eleven, full-time "historical associates"—younger historians beginning their careers.[22] Further expanding its resources, the History Division granted more than five dozen $1,000 grants, many to men and women fresh from graduate school who produced a rich harvest of published articles and books.[23]

During its ten-year history, the History Division completed an impressive tally of work. Its oral-history program interviewed 800 people in almost 1,500 interviews. Edyth Romney transcribed 3,000 Church documents filling more than 50 volumes. The History Division staff wrote more than 350 articles, book chapters, and published reviews, 70 of which appeared in Church periodicals.[24] Still more significant, the History Division published 20 books, several of major importance.

Leonard contributed in a major way to these History Division publications. He wrote or coauthored almost five dozen articles and eight monographs or books. Among the latter was *Building the City of God: Community and Cooperation among the Mormons*, which he wrote based on an unpublished manuscript by the deceased Feramorz Y. Fox and with principal researcher and writer Dean L. May.[25] The book clarified the Mormons' communitarian "united order movement" of the 1870s. Also, Leonard joined with collaborator Davis Bitton to write *The Mormon Experience: A History of the Latter-day Saints*.[26] Analytical and interested in themes and ideas, this book was designed for the academically minded Mormon and non-Mormon reader and, as such, displayed a sensitive ear to current academic trends. Its topically arranged chapters gave generous treatment to such themes as Mormon and

Native American relations, to the history of LDS women, and to the cultural diverseness of nineteenth-century Mormon immigrants. It also spoke of the Church's "creative adjustment" and "reinvigoration" during the twentieth century. In short, here was a sophisticated and readable book that placed Mormonism in the mainstream of contemporary culture. It was religious history in the best sense of the phrase.

During his years at LDS headquarters, Leonard also completed several family commemorative biographies, some of which he had earlier begun at Utah State University. One of the best of these was *Charles C. Rich: Mormon General and Western Frontiersman*, which gave the history of the LDS apostle who directed Church colonization in southern California and later in the Bear Lake region on the Utah-Idaho border.[27] Leonard followed this volume two years later with *From Quaker to Latter-day Saint: Bishop Edwin D. Woolley*.[28] This book detailed the life of the long-standing bishop of Salt Lake City's Thirteenth Ward, one of the most prominent congregations of the pioneer era. Other commemorative biographies written by Leonard during the History Division era included books on Utah governor William Spry and industrialist David Eccles.[29]

Despite the outward success of the History Division, all was not well. Some General Authorities disapproved of the kind of history being produced at Church headquarters. In 1976, Ezra Taft Benson, president of the Quorum of Twelve Apostles, warned against humanizing Church leaders. Such an approach minimized God's ruling hand and undermined "our prophetic history," Benson thought. Moreover, Benson objected to the neutral language employed by some of the historians. Scholarly expressions like "experimental systems," "communal life," "communitarianism," and "Christian primitivism" seemed too unfamiliar to Mormon traditional history and possibly a violation of it.[30]

Apostle Boyd K. Packer was also concerned with the History Division's writing. His address "'The Mantle is Far, Far Greater Than the Intellect'" cautioned historians about telling too much. Packer wanted a more sympathetic, spiritual, and partisan history. "We are at war with the adversary," he reminded Church members.[31] The views of Benson and Packer seemed to be supported by a widely circulated University of Utah honor's thesis written by Richard Marshall. Marshall saw the threat of "secularism" in such events as the organization of the Mormon History Association and the professionalism of the Historical Department.[32] While Marshall's analysis was preliminary and by no means sophisticated, it had the effect of confirming the growing doubts about the historical community.

As signs of disapproval accelerated, I recall almost a surreal atmosphere at the History Division. Leonard, wishing to keep us younger historians on task and our morale at reasonable levels, tried to maintain an outward confidence. "We continue to hear good reports," he would tell us. "Our work is respected." Such declarations became increasingly threadbare in the face of the History Division's declining fortunes. A half-dozen years into the enterprise, the staff was downsized. Arrington's scriptural title of Church Historian was exchanged for a more bureaucratic one. Still more tellingly, the flagship sixteen-volume, sesquicentennial series that Leonard had boosted was canceled; Church leaders honored author contracts and gave permission for the outside publication of ongoing volumes, but they wanted no further connection with the project. In 1980, Leonard and a core of seven historians were administratively transferred to Brigham Young University, where we became members of the newly created Joseph Fielding Smith Institute for LDS Church History. Two years later in 1982, all of us maintained offices at BYU, and our physical move was complete. In a related move, administrators of the Historical Department Archives restricted access to the Church's collection and took steps to control the publication of past and ongoing research completed at the archives.[33]

In announcing the transfer of the History Division's staff, Church President Spencer W. Kimball put the best face on the Church's decision. "The stature, objectivity, and effectiveness of our fine professional historians will be enhanced by association with the Church's university," Kimball said.[34] It was true that BYU offered Leonard and the rest of us a more congenial home than Church headquarters with its ecclesiastical and public-relations style of management. However, it was also true that the move indicated a longing on the part of many Church authorities for more traditional, faith-promoting history. "Our great experiment in Church-sponsored history has proved to be, if not a failure, at least not an unqualified success," the usually ebullient Leonard privately wrote. He was particularly distressed that the collapse of the History Division might renew the charge of critics that historical writing and faith were incompatible.[35] As always Arrington stood between two fires and felt the heat of each.

From 1980 to 1986, Leonard served as director of BYU's Joseph Fielding Smith Institute for LDS Church History, retiring from the university in 1987. But his heart was not in it. Perhaps part of the problem was his distaste for driving from his home in Salt Lake City to Provo, particularly in winter. Whatever the reason, Leonard met his classes, maintained office hours, and directed the staff. But most of his energies went into writing, which was done at his Salt Lake City home.

The result was another crown jewel, Leonard's *Brigham Young: American Moses*, the first full-scale, modern biography of Mormonism's second Church president.[36] In writing this book, Leonard took advantage of the research that he and others had completed at the Church Historical Department. Already in hand were a series of articles, monographs, and edited works dealing with Young that were drawn from primary documents never previously used by historians.

The result was a historian's biography, full of detail, with an emphasis on Young's life and times. However, the book also sought to reveal Young's character. Navigating between the public opinion extremes of Young as saint and Young as sinner, Leonard found a man of complexity ("He shared with most public men the subtleties of policy that give every appearance of duplicity, yet he acted again and again in ways that could have been fueled only by deep sincerity"[37]). Using this formula, Leonard produced a favorable and sympathetic portrait of Mormonism's pioneer leader.

It earned him the prestigious David W. and Beatrice C. Evans Biography Award. It also secured him his third Mormon History Association Best Book award; the two previous ones were awarded to him and his coauthors for *Building the City of God* and *The Mormon Experience.* During his career, Leonard also received two MHA Best Article awards: "The Search for Truth and Meaning in Mormon History," published in *Dialogue: A Journal of Mormon Thought*,[38] and, coauthored with John Haupt, "Intolerable Zion: The Image of Mormonism in Nineteenth-Century American Literature," which ran in *Western Humanities Review*.[39] Moreover, Leonard received two honorary doctorates, the Utah State Historical Society's Distinguished Service Award, the Utah Council for the Humanities Governor's Award, and the appointment as Fellow to the Society of American Historians. These and a dozen and a half other awards made him the most honored Mormon historian of his generation.

His retirement from Brigham Young University did not slow his work. From 1987 to his death in 1999, not counting reissues of several earlier articles and books, Leonard wrote five encyclopedia articles, nineteen magazine articles, eighteen scholarly articles, and more than a half-dozen books. These "post-retirement" books included a two-volume history of the state of Idaho and four biographies: Charles Redd, W. W. Clyde, Harold Silver, and Madelyn Cannon Stewart Silver.[40] He was particularly pleased with the Madelyn Silver volume, which appeared only two and a half months before his death. ("One of the first major biographies of an LDS woman," he said enthusiastically.)

Perhaps the most important of his last books was his memoir, *Adventures of a Church Historian*.[41] Speaking as a historian whose life had come to embody the intellectual currents of his Church, Leonard produced a book larger than himself. It told the story of his life as a churchman, university teacher, administrator who worked with Church leaders and sometimes dueled with them, defender of historical movement that he came to lead, and chronicler of a troubled historiographical past.[42]

Leonard will be remembered for his economic history of the LDS

Church and the American West, but his influence was important in other areas, too: especially women's history, common people's history, and biography. And his influence will be extended by the large majority of younger writers in the field, who like me, felt Leonard's interest. While in some cases our historical approaches and interests became different than Leonard's, still, many of us, if unconsciously, sensed that our professional universe continued to revolve around Leonard. Whatever our differences, he was our mentor.

How will his legacy be viewed? It is only fair to say that, even in a commemorative essay such as this, at the end of his life, voices were being raised against his style of history. Mormon traditionalists, for example, had only grudging praise for his work and more often criticism. This growing conservative critique proceeded along several fronts. During the 1970s and 1980s, religious educators repeated the concerns of Elder Benson and Elder Packer, but because many of them isolated themselves by publishing in nonrefereed publications and by participating in professional groups of their own making, their voice was at the intellectual margins.[43]

More substantive were conservative academics led by some BYU political scientists. In their view, the New Mormon History was a form of secularism; and to prove their point, they claimed that the New Mormon History authors were guilty of employing loose working assumptions that were drawn, perhaps unconsciously, from nineteenth-century positivism.[44] This criticism went beyond a debate about methods and philosophy. It implicitly sought to reestablish a faith story that in its most extreme form was an antihistorism.[45]

The New Mormon History historians did not have to go beyond their own ranks to hear criticism. For example, historian Charles S. Peterson argued that the new history had proven to be a dead end. Despite its moderate spirit of "acquiescence and well-being," it had failed to gain the support of LDS leaders; it is true that not a single Mormon leader spoke publicly in its favor. Likewise, Peterson believed that it had failed to engage the interest of mainstream American historians—perhaps because the New Mormon History, despite Leonard's hope for moderation and the middle way, was "too defensive" and "assertive" and therefore, to some non-Mormons historians, too idiosyncratic. Without the support of the Mormon Church and isolated from its peers, the New Mormon History, Peterson argued, had failed as an important intellectual movement. He laid the blame on the book that began it, Leonard's *Great Basin Kingdom*. While acknowledging the book's strengths, Peterson believed that it had created an "exceptionalist" history that in the long run had been self-defeating; following its example, New Mormon historians wrote "Mormon history" for Mormons instead of engaging a broader audience. Peterson exaggerated to make his point, claiming that *Great Basin Kingdom* began and ended the New Mormon History as an influential historical movement.[46]

Another critic, Roger D. Launius, was concerned about the "ghettoization" of Mormon scholars. Like Peterson, Launius believed that Mormon studies had become too provincial and urged a new research agenda more in line with mainstream historical study—more work involving race, ethnicity, class, and gender and an avoidance of traditional Mormon topics that focused on Church origins, lineal development, and elites. Launius believed that, after more than forty years of writing, the New Mormon History was suffering a "deceleration" of energy and creativity and hoped that his recommendation might provide a new stimulus.[47]

While we are too close to Leonard's career and to the writing of the New Mormon History to make final judgments about this criticism, some tentative remarks may be in order. No one could question the mass of the recent work. From the end of World War II to 1995, or about the time *Great Basin Kingdom* was issued to the present, historians of Mormonism wrote more than 100 unpublished reports and task papers; almost 1,000 honors theses and masters' theses; over 430 Ph.D. dissertations; almost 6,000 articles and chapters in books; and about 1,700 books. As important as the 9,000 titles written since 1950 was its quality. The New Mormon History enlarged and changed almost every topic of LDS history; and despite the reproaches of some critics, the best of it helped

American regionalists and students of religion understand Mormonism better.

What lies ahead? Years after Leonard's death, the New Mormon History remains full of energy and has the promise of much new writing. No doubt the next decade or two will continue the flow of articles and books in Leonard's middle-way mold. Yet even with this prospect, the critics have a point. The New Mormon History has not captured a large audience and is not likely to; at the century's end, rank-and-file Mormons prefer historical fiction and popular film to the emotionally aloof history that is being written. Some of the new history writers, self-absorbed by their quest for roots, produce narrow and lifeless history. (Self-analysis and ennui are usually partners.) Moreover, the practitioners of the New Mormon History are "graying," to use Launius's phrase. New and midcareer historians are becoming few as young men and women, warned off by the collapse of the History Division, choose other careers and specialties. Who in the future will bear the historical standard?

So far, critics of the New Mormon History have been few and hesitant (most did not attack Leonard directly—it is hard to attack a community icon), but they may signal the beginning of the end of one intellectual movement and the start of something new. Perhaps as Leonard's generation passes from the scene, future historians will reflect the current two-fold criticism of the New Mormon History movement. On the one hand, we may have a more faithful, devout, less detached, even scriptural history—the kind suggested by the Church's conservative leaders and intellectuals. On the other hand, answering critics like Peterson and Launius, some future historians may also create a historiography more in line with mainstream American history writing: secular, hard-headed, professional, interdisciplinary, and multidimensional history that may have little appeal for most Church members. Still more likely, future writing will assume patterns that at the moment we cannot see.

Whatever the future, we can be certain about Leonard's influence. His work and the work of those whom he inspired left the Mormon historical landscape greatly enriched. His presence hovered over much of the recent work, providing many Church members with a past that reinforced their belief and faith. For them, Leonard helped make Mormonism intellectually respectable. For others, Leonard's work brought the discovery of heritage.

When Leonard died, the accolades were generous. Davis Bitton, his old History Division colleague, called him "the single most important historian of Utah and the Mormons in the 20th century" and added "there wasn't any [major historian] in the 19th century."[48] The Church-owned *Deseret News* ran an editorial that aimed at reconciliation and stressed his personal worth. "Arrington was a unique blend of a keen and inquisitive mind, impeccable integrity and guileless sense of self and others," the newspaper said. He "never forgot his roots as an Idaho farm boy and maintained a refreshing, self-effacing manner and straightforward writing style. . . . His cheerful and animated demeanor earned him friends and admirers across bounds and borders."[49]

My own view is similar, both about Leonard's gifts as a historian and his delight as a person. I have often thought he was best described by Wordsworth's "The Happy Warrior," although the poet's ideal man was too Victorian to fit Leonard properly. Still, other phrases of Wordsworth worked. Leonard was a "generous spirit" who labored "good on good to fix" and who owed to "virtue every triumph that he knows." And the poem's ending describes my friend as well as capturing a personal aspiration:

> And, while the mortal mist is gathering, draws
> His breath in confidence of Heaven's applause:
> This is the happy warrior; this is he
> That every man in arms should wish to be.[50]

Prologue Notes

1. Stephen Gill, ed., *William Wordsworth: The Major Works* (New York: Oxford University Press, 2000), 320–22. See "Character of the Happy Warrior."
2. Leonard J. Arrington, "Scholarly Studies of Mormonism in the Twentieth Century," *Dialogue: A Journal of Mormon Thought* 1 (spring 1966): 28. The essay is reprinted in chapter ten of this volume.
3. The phrase "New Mormon History" apparently first appeared in print in the late 1960s when Moses Rischin, then Fulbright Professor of History at University of Upp-

sala in Sweden, spoke of a "most exciting" development in the writing of Mormon history. According to Rischin, Mormonism's new generation of historians seemed willing to put aside Mormon "persistent cohesiveness," its "Old Testament concreteness," and its "cultural isolation" for a new kind of historical writing that was "at home among the *avant garde* Gentiles." See Moses Rischin, "Beyond the Great Divide: Immigration and the Last Frontier," *Journal of American History* 55 (June 1968): 49, and his "The New Mormon History," *The American West* 6 (March 1969): 49. For other early uses of the phrase, see Robert A. Rees, "'Truth Is the Daughter of Time': Notes Toward an Imaginative Mormon History," *Dialogue* 6 (autumn–winter 1971): 15–22, and Robert B. Flanders, "Some Reflections on the New Mormon History," *Dialogue* 9 (spring 1974): 34–41. It was Flanders's essay that especially popularized the phrase for Mormon readers.

4. Leonard J. Arrington, "Historian as Entrepreneur: A Personal Essay," *Brigham Young University Studies* 17 (winter 1977): 194. The essay is reprinted in chapter one of this volume.
5. Arrington, "Historian as Entrepreneur," 195–97; see also Leonard J. Arrington, "In Praise of Amateurs," *Journal of Mormon History* 17 (1991): 11–45.
6. Leonard J. Arrington, *Adventures of a Church Historian* (Urbana and Chicago: University of Illinois Press, 1998), 26.
7. Arrington, *Adventures of a Church Historian*, 26.
8. Arrington, "Historian as Entrepreneur," 196–98.
9. See David J. Whittaker, comp., "Leonard James Arrington, 1917–99: A Bibliography," *Journal of Mormon History* 25 (fall 1999): 41–56. An updated version of the essay is reprinted in the epilogue of this volume.
10. Leonard J. Arrington, *Great Basin Kingdom: An Economic History of the Latter-day Saints, 1830–1900* (Cambridge, Mass.: Harvard University Press, 1958).
11. E. E. Ericksen, "The Psychological and Ethical Aspects of Mormon Group Life" (Ph.D. diss., University of Chicago, 1918); Lowry Nelson, *The Mormon Village: A Pattern and Technique of Land Settlement* (Salt Lake City: University of Utah Press, 1952); and Nels Anderson, *Desert Saints* (1942; reprint, Chicago: University of Chicago Press, 1966). Nelson's work had been published as pamphlet-length articles twenty to twenty-five years earlier. Arrington was also influenced by such scholars as Hamilton Gardner, "Cooperation Among the Mormons," *Quarterly Journal of Economics* 31 (May 1917): 461–99, and "Communism Among the Mormons," *Quarterly Journal of Economics* 37 (November 1922): 134–74; Joseph A. Geddes, "The United Order among the Mormons (Missouri Phase)" (Ph.D. diss., Columbia University, 1924); Feramorz Y. Fox, "Cooperation Among the Mormons" (Master's thesis, University of California, 1912) and "The Mormon Land System: A Study of the Settlement and Utilization of Land Under the Direction of the Mormon Church" (Ph.D. diss., Northwestern University, 1932); and Thomas Lynn Smith, "A Sociological Analysis of Some of the Aspects of Rural Religious Culture as Shown by Mormonism" (Master's thesis, University of Minnesota, 1929).
12. Arrington, *Great Basin Kingdom*, ix.
13. Leonard J. Arrington, "Reflections on the Founding and Purpose of the Mormon History Association, 1965–1983," *Journal of Mormon History* 10 (1983): 101. The essay is reprinted in chapter two of this volume.

14. Arrington, "Historian as Entrepreneur," 200.
15. Arrington, "The Founding of the LDS Church Historical Department, 1972," *Journal of Mormon History* 18 (fall 1992): 41–47. The essay is reprinted in chapter three of this volume.
16. Between 1976 and 1991, MHA membership averaged 736, hitting a peak of 1,042 during the LDS sesquicentennial year of 1980. See Patricia Lyn Scott, James E. Crooks, and Sharon G. Pugsley, "'A Kinship of Interest': The Mormon History Association's Membership," *Journal of Mormon History* 18 (spring 1992): 155, 170.
17. Impressed by Arrington, Tanner authorized the historian to regard his historical work as the "equivalent in importance to other major [church] assignments you have held." Quoted in Arrington, "The Founding of the LDS Church Historical Department," 41–46.
18. Arrington, "The Founding of the LDS Church Historical Department," 47–48.
19. Leonard J. Arrington, Diary, 8 August 1972, copy in Leonard J. Arrington Archives, Merrill Library, Utah State University. See also Arrington, *Adventures of a Church Historian*, 94.
20. For an expression of Dyer's enthusiasm, see Alvin R. Dyer, "The Future of Church History," *Ensign* 2 (August 1972): 58–61.
21. "History Is Then—and Now: A Conversation with Leonard J. Arrington, Church Historian," *Ensign* 5 (July 1975): 8–13.
22. These included Maureen Ursenbach Beecher, Bruce D. Blumell, Jill Mulvay Derr, Ronald K. Esplin, Richard L. Jensen, Gordon Irving, Dean C. Jessee, Glen M. Leonard, Dean L. May, Carol Cornwall Madsen, D. Michael Quinn, Gene A. Sessions, and Ronald W. Walker. For a brief sketch of the History Division's associates, see the preface to *Celebrating the LDS Past: Essays Commemorating the 20th Anniversary of the 1972 Founding of the LDS Church Historical Department's "History Division"* (Provo, Utah: Joseph Fielding Smith Institute for Church History, 1992), xi–xv.
23. Even a partial list of "fellows" is impressive: Paul L. Anderson, Danel W. Bachman, Dale Beecher, Lowell C. (Ben) Bennion, Alfred L. Bush, Lawrence C. Coates, Rebecca Cornwall (Bartholomew), Richard O. Cowan, Eugene England, Peggy Fletcher (Stack), B. Carmon Hardy, Scott Kenney, John S. McCormick, Melodie Moench (Charles), Jill Mulvay (Derr), Max H. Parkin, Richard Sherlock, Susan Staker, David J. Whittaker, and Linda P. Wilcox.
24. Arrington, "The Founding of the LDS Church Historical Department," 54–55; Arrington, "Historian as Entrepreneur," 207. Davis Bitton, "Ten Years in Camelot: A Personal Memoir," *Dialogue* 16 (autumn 1983): 20–33, lists the History Division's publications.
25. Leonard J. Arrington, Feramorz Y. Fox, and Dean L. May, *Building the City of God: Community and Cooperation among the Mormons* (Salt Lake City: Deseret Book, 1976).
26. Leonard J. Arrington and Davis Bitton, *The Mormon Experience: A History of the Latter-day Saints* (New York: Alfred A. Knopf, 1979).
27. Leonard J. Arrington, *Charles C. Rich: Mormon General and Western Frontiersman* (Provo, Utah: Brigham Young University Press, 1974).
28. Leonard J. Arrington, *From Quaker to Latter-day Saint: Bishop Edwin D. Woolley* (Salt Lake City: Deseret Book, 1976).

29. William L. Roper and Leonard J. Arrington, *William Spry: Man of Firmness, Governor of Utah* (Salt Lake City: Utah State Historical Society and University of Utah Press, 1971) and Leonard J. Arrington, *David Eccles: Pioneer Western Industrialist* (Logan: Utah State University Press, 1975).
30. Ezra Taft Benson, "God's Hand in Our Nation's History," *1976 Devotional Speeches of the Year* (Provo, Utah: Brigham Young University Press, 1977), 314, 313, and Ezra Taft Benson, *The Gospel Teacher and His Message* (Salt Lake City: The Church of Jesus Christ of Latter-day Saints, 1976), 11–12. Benson's criticism was apparently aimed at passages in *Building the City of God and The Story of the Latter-day Saints*, a book coauthored by James B. Allen and Glen M. Leonard.
31. Boyd K. Packer, "The Mantle is Far, Far Greater than the Intellect," BYU *Studies* 21 (summer 1981): 264, 268.
32. Richard Stephen Marshall, "The New Mormon History" (Senior honors project summary, University of Utah, 1977).
33. For an insider's view, see Bitton, "Ten Years in Camelot."
34. As quoted in Arrington, "The Founding of the LDS Church Historical Department," 54.
35. Statement in my possession. See also Arrington, *Adventures of a Church Historian*, 149–50.
36. Leonard J. Arrington, *Brigham Young: American Moses* (New York: Alfred A. Knopf, 1985),
37. Arrington, *Brigham Young: American Moses*, xvi.
38. Leonard J. Arrington, "The Search for Truth and Meaning in Mormon History," *Dialogue: A Journal of Mormon Thought* 3 (summer 1968): 56–66. The essay is reprinted in chapter five of this volume.
39. Leonard J. Arrington and John Haupt, "Intolerable Zion: The Image of Mormonism in Nineteenth-Century American Literature," *Western Humanities Review* 22 (summer 1968): 243–60.
40. Leonard J. Arrington, *History of Idaho*, 2 vols. (Moscow and Boise: University of Idaho Press and Idaho State Historical Society, 1994); Leonard J. Arrington, *Utah's Audacious Stockman: Charlie Redd* (Logan and Provo: Utah State University Press and The Charles Redd Center for Western Studies, Brigham Young University, 1995); Leonard J. Arrington, *W. W. Clyde, The Builder* (Salt Lake City: Devonshire Press, 1999); Leonard J. Arrington and John R. Alley Jr., *Harold F. Silver: Western Inventor, Businessman, and Civic Leader* (Logan: Utah State University Press, 1992); and *Madelyn Cannon Stewart Silver: Poet, Teacher, Homemaker* (Salt Lake City: Publishers Press, 1998).
41. Leonard J. Arrington, *Adventures of a Church Historian* (Urbana: University of Illinois Press, 1998).
42. Before embarking on his memoir, Arrington produced several preliminary essays: "Historian as Entrepreneur," 193–209; "Recalling a Twin Falls Childhood," *Idaho Yesterdays* 25 (winter 1982): 31–40; "Why I Am a Believer," *Sunstone* 10, no. 1 (1985): 36–38 (The essay is reprinted in chapter four of this volume.); and *A Soldier in North Africa and Italy, 1943–1946: A Pictorial History* (Salt Lake City: Historian's Press, 1995).
43. For an illustration and defense of this position, see Keith W. Perkins, "Why Are We Here in New England? A Personal View of Church History," *Regional Studies in Latter-day Saint Church History*, edited by Donald Q. Cannon (Provo, Utah: Depart-

ment of Church History and Doctrine, Brigham Young University, 1988), 1–13. Also see Joe J. Christensen, "The Value of Church History and Historians: Some Personal Impressions," *Proceedings of the Church Education System Church History Symposium* (Provo, Utah: Brigham Young University Press, 1977): 12–17, and Robert Millet, "How Should Our Story Be Told?" in *To Be Learned Is Good If* . . . , edited by Robert Millet (Salt Lake City: Bookcraft, 1987), 1–8.

44. For a sampling of these critiques, see David E. Bohn: "No Higher Ground: Objective History Is an Illusive Chimera," *Sunstone* 8 (May–June 1983): 26–32; "Our Own Agenda: A Critique of the Methodology of the New Mormon History," *Sunstone* 14 (June 1990): 45–49; "The Larger Issue," *Sunstone* 16 (February 1994): 45–63; and "Unfounded Claims and Impossible Expectations: A Critique of New Mormon History," in *Faithful History: Essays on Writing Mormon History*, edited by George D. Smith (Salt Lake City: Signature Books, 1992), 227–61. See also Neal W. Kramer, "Looking for God in History," *Sunstone* 8 (January–March 1983): 15–17; Gary F. Novak, "Naturalistic Assumptions and the Book of Mormon," *BYU Studies* 30 (summer 1990): 23–40; Louis C. Midgley, "The Challenge of Historical Consciousness: Mormon History and the Encounter with Secular Modernity," in *By Study and Also by Faith: Essays in Honor of Hugh Nibley on the Occasion of his 80th Birthday*, edited by John M. Lundquist and Stephen D. Ricks (Salt Lake City: Deseret Book and Foundation for Ancient Research and Mormon Studies, 1990): 2:502–51; M. Gerald Bradford, "The Case of the New Mormon History: Thomas G. Alexander and His Critics," *Dialogue* 21 (winter 1988): 143–50.

45. The neotraditionalist criticism was weakened by a zest for controversy that at times seemed as personal as it was professional. Moreover, none of the neotraditionalists attempted to write history; and as a result, their criticism remained abstract and theoretical. On the few occasions that the critics cited books that they admired, historians were left wondering if a playful sense of irony was at work. See Kramer, "Looking for God in History," 15–17. On one item, however, the critics certainly erred: Neither Arrington nor most of the new Mormon historians advocated "scientific" or "objective history," a nineteenth- and early twentieth-century chimera long abandoned by the profession.

46. Charles S. Peterson, "Beyond the Problems of Exceptionalist History," in *Great Basin Kingdom Revisited: Contemporary Perspectives*, edited by Thomas G. Alexander (Logan: Utah State University Press, 1991), 143, 148.

47. Roger D. Launius, "The 'New Social History' and the 'New Mormon History': Reflections on Recent Trends," *Dialogue* 27 (spring 1994): 109–27. See also Roger D. Launius, "From Old to New Mormon History: Fawn Brodie and the Legacy of Scholarly Analysis of Mormonism," in *Reconsidering No Man Knows My History: Fawn M. Brodie and Joseph Smith in Retrospect*, edited by Newell G. Bringhurst (Logan: Utah State University Press, 1996), 197–99, and Roger D. Launius, "Mormon Memory, Mormon Myth, and Mormon History," *Journal of Mormon History* 21 (spring 1995): esp. 23–24.

48. Peggy Fletcher Stack, "Leonard Arrington, LDS Historian, Intellectual, Dies," *Salt Lake Tribune* (12 February 1999): B-1, B-5.

49. *Deseret News* (17 February 1999), Internet version.

50. First published as Ronald W. Walker, "Mormonism's 'Happy Warrior': Appreciating Leonard J. Arrington," *Journal of Mormon History* 25 (spring 1999): 113–30.

Chronology

2 July 1917	Leonard James Arrington is born on a farm near Twin Falls, Idaho, the third child of Noah Wesley and Edna Grace Corn Arrington
1917–35	Lives with his family in Twin Falls, Idaho
September 1931	Purchases one hundred hens and six roosters and began raising chickens for study and for sale
1931–35	Participates in the Future Farmers of America (FFA) association
October 1934	Attends the national FFA convention in Kansas City as Idaho's FFA president
Spring 1935	Attends the national officers' meeting of the FFA in Washington, D.C.
May 1935	Graduates from high school
September 1935	Travels to Moscow, Idaho, to attend the University of Idaho
1935–39	Studies first agriculture and then agricultural economics at the University of Idaho
June 1939	Graduates with high honors from University of Idaho
September 1939	Travels to Chapel Hill, North Carolina, to begin graduate work at the University of North Carolina in economics. Also begins teaching his own classes at the university after receiving a Kenan Teaching Fellowship
December 1939	Attends his first professional conference, the annual convention of the American Economic Association in Philadelphia, Pennsylvania, and meets Richard T. Ely, founder of the association

First published as "Leonard James Arrington Chronology," Leonard J. Arrington Papers Register, Utah State University Library.

Winter–Spring 1941	Becomes an economics instructor at North Carolina State College 1941–42 in Raleigh, taking classes as well as teaching for the winter and spring quarters of 1941, the summer session, and the entire 1941–42 school year
October 1941	Meets Grace Fort, a Wake Forest, North Carolina, girl who worked in Raleigh, North Carolina, at a birthday party given by Ruth Partridge
4 January 1942	Is appointed Branch President of the newly created Raleigh branch of the Church of Jesus Christ of Latter-day Saints
Fall 1942	Begins working with the Office of Price Administration in Raleigh as a price analyst
March 1943	Is drafted into the United States Army and goes to Fort Bragg, North Carolina, for training
24 April 1943	Marries Grace in Raleigh
29 July 1943	Sails to North Africa for his military assignment as part of a World War II Italian prisoner-of-war processing company
September 1944	Is relocated to Bagnoli, Italy, outside of Naples
November 1944	Assigned to serve as the American representative of the Istituto Centrale di Statistica (Institute of Statistics) to gather statistics for the rehabilitation of the Italian economy, published as *Censuses and Surveys for the National Reconstruction* (1945)
December 1945	Travels back to America
January 1946	Reunites with Grace and is discharged from the army
Winter–Spring 1946	Teaches economics at North Carolina State College and Meredith College and proposes to his Ph.D. committee that he write his dissertation on the economics of Mormonism
July 1946	To aid his research for his dissertation, Leonard accepts a teaching position with Utah State Agricultural College in economics, and moves with Grace to Logan, Utah
17 December 1948	Leonard and Grace's first child, James Wesley, is born
1949–50	Returns to North Carolina and completes his language exam, course work, and oral and written exams for his Ph.D. in economics

Winter 1950	Has a "peak experience" in North Carolina's university library where a feeling of ecstasy about Mormon history convinces him that God has given him a commission to carry out a research program of Mormon history and to make that history available to others
March 1951	Makes a presentation on Mormon economic history to the Mormon Seminar, which enables him to develop a theme for his dissertation: the consistent applications of antebellum policies in the Great Basin while the nation was adopting a more individualistic and freewheeling capitalism
September 1951	Meets with William Mulder, assistant editor of the *Western Humanities Review*, who convinces him to submit articles for publication
13 September 1951	Carl Wayne is born
Winter 1951–52	Writes his dissertation while on six months' leave from Utah State Agricultural College
March 1952	Returns again to North Carolina and successfully defends his dissertation, thereby acquiring a Ph.D. in economics with economic theory and economics–rural sociology as his fields
1954	Submits his dissertation to the Committee on Research in Economic History, a Cambridge, Massachusetts, non-profit organization "incorporated to encourage inquiry and publication in the field of economic history," for publication
25 August 1954	Susan Grace is born
1956–57	Receives a year's fellowship at the Henry E. Huntington Library and Art Gallery in San Marino, where he revises and expands his dissertation
1957	Resubmits his dissertation to the Committee on Research in Economic History, which arranges for its publication by Harvard University Press
1958	*Great Basin Kingdom: An Economic History of the Latter-day Saints* is published
1958–59	Receives a Fulbright Scholarship and serves as Fulbright Professor of American Economics at the University of Genoa and elsewhere in Italy
1961	Becomes Second Counselor in the Utah State University Stake Presidency

Spring 1962	Presents the Faculty Honor Lecture at Utah State University on the Japanese-American World War II Relocation Camp at Topaz, Utah
1963	Is notified that *Great Basin Kingdom* has been placed in the president's library in the White House, becoming the only book dealing with the history of the Mountain West in that library
1963	Gives two lectures on the Mormons as part of the University of Texas's television series of addresses on the history of American civilization, funded by the Ford Foundation
1963	Becomes a charter member of the Western History Association, which is organized in Santa Fe, New Mexico
9 September 1965	Along with thirteen other persons, organizes the Mormon History Association
28 December 1965	Attends the first meeting of the Mormon History Association and is elected first president of that organization
1966	Publishes *Beet Sugar in the West: A History of the Utah-Idaho Sugar Company*
1966	Receives the Charles Redd Humanities Award from the Utah Academy of Sciences, Arts, and Letters
1966–67	Serves as Visiting Professor of History at the University of California at Los Angeles to replace John Walton Caughey, editor of the *Pacific Historical Review*
October 1967	Is elected vice president and president-elect of the Western History Association
December 1967	Is elected vice president and president-elect of the Agricultural History Society
Spring 1969	Receives approval, along with S. George Ellsworth, from Utah State University to sponsor a scholarly journal for the Western History Association
May 1969	Receives the David O. McKay Humanities Award from Brigham Young University
October 1969	Receives approval from the Western History Association to become editor of the newly created *Western Historical Quarterly*

10 October 1969	Presents his presidential address to the Western History Association, "Blessed Damozels: Women in Mormon History"
1969–70	Is appointed Distinguished Lecturer for Utah by the Utah Commission for Higher Education
17 April 1970	Presents his presidential address to the Agricultural History Association, "Western Agriculture and the New Deal"
24 August 1970	As a member of the Committee of Historians, meets with N. Eldon Tanner, Counselor in the First Presidency of the LDS Church, to discuss the organization and function of the Church Historian's Office
1971	Publishes *William Spry: Man of Firmness, Governor of Utah*
6 January 1972	Meets with N. Eldon Tanner, who asks him to become Church Historian
14 January 1972	Public announcement of Leonard's appointment as Church Historian, and as the Lemuel Redd Chair of Western History at Brigham Young University and director of the Charles Redd Center for Western Studies
6 April 1972	Leonard's name as Church Historian is presented to the general conference of the LDS Church for a sustaining vote
June 1972	Moves his family to Salt Lake City, Utah
1973	Completes "Bankers Extraordinary: A History of First Security Corporation, 1928–1973," commissioned by the company but not released to the public
2 July 1973	Receives permission from the First Presidency to use the facilities of the Church Historical Department to complete a history of the Church for Alfred A. Knopf
1974	Publishes *Charles C. Rich: Mormon General and Western Frontiersman*
1974	*Brigham Young's Letters to His Sons*, edited by Dean Jessee, becomes the first publication of Leonard's historical department
1975	Publishes *David Eccles: Pioneer Western Industrialist*

1975	Joins general authorities, including President Spencer W. Kimball, for a three-week tour of the Far East
1976	*From Quaker to Latter-day Saint: Bishop Edwin D. Woolley* is published, as is *Building the City of God: Community and Cooperation Among the Mormons*, co-written with Dean May and Feramorz Y. Fox
1976	*Mormon Sisters: Women in Early Utah*, edited by Claudia L. Bushman, is published and recognizes Leonard's interest in women's history by dedicating the book "To Leonard Arrington: He takes us seriously."
July 1976	*Story of the Latter-day Saints*, a one-volume history of the LDS Church produced under the direction of the Church History Division, is published
20 September 1976	Meets with the First Presidency to account for the *Story of the Latter-day Saints*, which some general authorities regard as offensive
29 April 1977	G. Homer Durham takes over as managing director of the Historical Department, thereby becoming Leonard's "boss." Durham subsequently works to rein in the department, which he and other general authorities believe is running out of control and producing history that is not faith-promoting for Latter-day Saints
April 1979	Alfred A. Knopf releases *The Mormon Experience: A History of the Latter-day Saints*, co-authored with Davis Bitton
4 September 1979	Signs a contract with Alfred A. Knopf to produce a biography of Brigham Young
26 June 1980	Meets with G. Homer Durham and Jeffrey R. Holland, president-designate of Brigham Young University, to discuss the transfer of the Historical Department to that institution
1981	Publishes *Saints Without Halos: The Human Side of Mormon History*, co-written with David Bitton
1981–82	Serves as president of the Pacific Coast Branch of the American Historical Association
10 March 1982	Grace dies from heart disease
Summer 1982	Official transfer of the Historical Department to Brigham Young University, ending Leonard's asso-

	ciation with the Church as Church Historian. He becomes director of the Joseph Fielding Smith Institute for Church History, the new name of the Historical Department
1982–87	Continues teaching at Brigham Young University
19 November 1983	Marries Harriet Horne from Salt Lake City
1984	Publishes *Tracy-Collins Bank and Trust Company: A Record of Responsibility* and *Sunbonnet Sisters: True Stories of Mormon Women and Frontier Life*, co-written with Susan Arrington Madsen
23 April 1984	Is notified that *Brigham Young: American Moses* has won the David Evans and Beatrice Cannon Evans Biography Award in its inaugural year
24 April 1984	Successfully undergoes a sextuple heart-bypass operation performed by Dr. Russell M. Nelson
April 1985	*Brigham Young: American Moses* is released by Alfred A. Knopf
1985	Receives the Mormon History Association's Best Book Award for 1985 for *Brigham Young: American Moses* and is also nominated by the National Book Critics Circle for a "distinguished work of biography"
1986	Publishes *The Hotel, Salt Lake's Classy Lady: The Hotel Utah, 1911–1986*, co-written with Heidi Swinton
Summer 1986	Makes a two-week trip to England with Harriet to speak to stakes, wards, and general audiences on the Mormon experience in England, in preparation for the British Mission sesquicentennial in 1987
Summer 1986	Is notified that he has been elected a member of the Society of American Historians, the first Utahan and first Mormon to be so elected
1987	Publishes *Mothers of the Prophets*, co-written with Susan Arrington Madsen, and *In the Utah Tradition: A History of the Governor's Mansion*, co-written with Heidi Swinton
2 July 1987	Retires from his Brigham Young University duties
1988	Publishes *The Mormons and Their Historians*, co-written with Davis Bitton
1990	The Idaho legislature passes a measure commissioning Leonard to write a full history of the state.

1991	Publishes *From Small Beginnings: A History of Steiner Corporation, American Linen Supply Company, and Their Affiliates*
1992	Publishes *Harold F. Silver: Western Inventor, Businessman, and Civic Leader*, co-written with John R. Alley Jr. Also sees the second editions of *The Mormon Experience* and *Building the City of God* appear
1993	The second edition of *Great Basin Kingdom* is issued by the University of Utah Press
21 July 1993	Presents the Juanita Brooks Lecture at the dedication of the renovated St. George Tabernacle
1994	Publishes the two-volume *History of Idaho*
1994	Makes a two-week trip to Hawaii, accompanied by Harriet, as a guest of Brigham Young University's campus, and delivers five lectures on faith and intellect
1995	Publishes *Utah's Audacious Stockman: Charlie Redd*
7 November 1995	Presents "Faith and Intellect as Partners in Mormon History" as the first lecture given in the Leonard J. Arrington Mormon History Lecture Series sponsored by Utah State University's Special Collections and Archives
1996	Receives the Governor's Award in the Humanities
1998	Publishes *Madelyn Cannon Stewart Silver: Poet, Teacher, and Homemaker* and *Adventures of a Church Historian*
14 December 1998	Reaches an agreement with Utah State University's Special Collections & Archives to establish the Leonard J. Arrington Historical Archives to house his papers, his family's papers, and the papers of prominent scholars in Mormon history
11 February 1999	Dies in Salt Lake City from heart failure

Leonard J. Arrington Photographs

Leonard and his friend Gaines Black,
near Twin Falls, Idaho, on 13 June 1926.

Twin Falls FFA Stock Judging Team, 6 January 1933. (*left to right*) Howard Annis, Leonard Arrington, and Iro Kuykendall.

(*opposite, top left*) Leonard, age 12, exhibiting buttons won in the junior high school spelling bee. (*opposite, top right*) Leonard, age 18, newly graduated from high school. He was elected first vice president of the National Future Farmers of America. (*opposite, bottom*) Leonard in his chicken house, spring of 1934.

Taken during World War II, this is a photograph of Leonard and his parents and siblings. (*seated, left to right*) Noah, Ross, Edna, and Doris; (*standing*) LeRoy, Wayne, Donald, Kenneth, Ralph, Leonard and Marie. Wayne and Leonard were actually not present, but their pictures were inserted. Edna was a "six-star mom."

(*above*) Leonard and Grace courting in Raleigh, North Carolina, July 1942.

(*left*) Leonard (who at this time was known by the southerners as "Jimmie") and Grace in Raleigh, North Carolina, 24 April 1943—the day they were married.

(*right*) Leonard during World War II. Rome, 1944.

(*below*) Leonard and Alberto Mueller, director the United States Information Service, Genova, Italy, 26 November 1958.

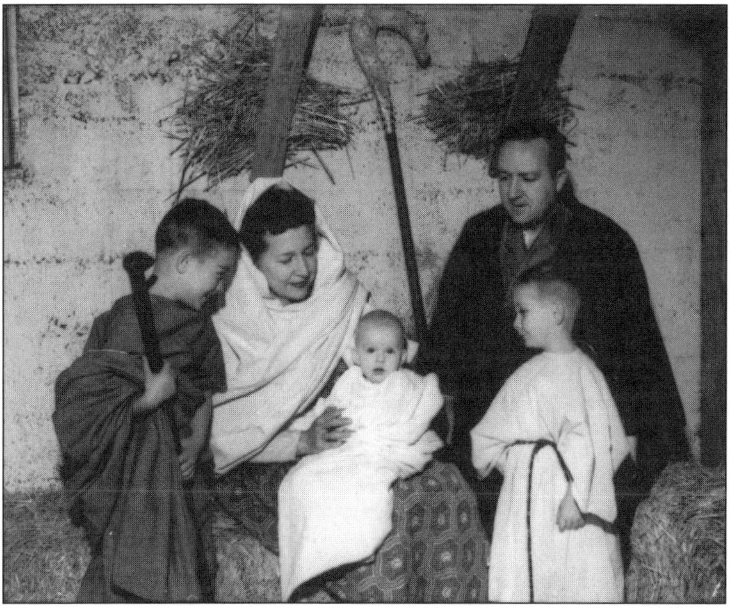

Leonard and Grace used this photograph as their family Christmas card in 1954. The photo was taken in the basement of their home at 754 North 500 East in Logan.

Grace and Leonard and their three children, (*left to right*) James, Susan, and Carl, 1959. The family had just returned from living a year in Italy.

(*top*) Leonard always said his favorite Church calling was that of a Counselor in the USU Stake, which at that time included both single and married students. Taken in 1961, this photograph shows various Church leaders on the stage of the USU Stake Center Cultural Hall, while they convened in Stake Conference. (*left to right*) President Asa Beecher of Mount Logan Stake, Leonard, Counselor in Stake Presidency, President Reed Bullen, Utah State University president Daryl Chase, Henry D. Moyle, Counselor in the First Presidency; President Wendell Rich, unidentified man, and Jack Kidd. 1961.

(*bottom*) Leonard working in the Church Historian's Office, 1972. *Used by permission, Utah State Historical Society, all rights reserved.*

New administrators of the LDS Church Historical Department, 1972. Leonard, Church Historian, flanked by two Assistant Church Historians, (*left*) James B. Allen and (*right*) Davis Bitton.

THE HISTORY DIVISION IN FRONT OF THE SALT LAKE TEMPLE, 1976.

Front row (*left to right*): Davis Bitton, Edyth Romney, Debbie Liljenquist Biggs, Nedra Yeates Pace, Jill Mulvay Derr, Maureen Beecher, and Cathy Robison. Second row (*left to right*): James Allen, Bruce Blumell, Gene Sessions, Gordon Irving, Dean Jessee, and Glen Leonard. Third row (*left to right*): Leonard Arrington, Bill Hartley, Richard Jensen, Jim Kimball, Ron Esplin, and Dean May.

(*right*) Leonard in his office in the LDS Church Office Building, 1975.

(*below*) Leonard spoke to staff members of the Church History Division on Ensign Peak, 23 June 1978.

(*above*) Leonard was awarded an Honorary Doctorate of Humanities at USU graduation exercises, 5 June 1982.

(*below*) Brigham Young (a.k.a. James Arrington) meets his biographer. Leonard won many awards and accolades for his *Brigham Young: American Moses*, published in 1985.

Leonard was a popular speaker and gave hundreds of talks
to Church groups as well as business and community gatherings.

For those who knew and loved Leonard Arrington, this is a favorite photograph that captures his joyful, happy, and optimistic personality. *Used by permission of photographer Kent Miles.*

Portrait of Leonard Arrington, painted by William Whittaker.
© Arrington Archives and Lecture Foundation at Utah State University.

PART ONE

Arrington as Historian

Chapter 1

Historian as Entrepreneur
A Personal Essay

WEDNESDAY, 5 JANUARY 1972. I was planning my lectures for the next day in my office at Utah State University when the telephone rang. "Hello, Dr. Arrington? This is President Tanner. I would like to see you; when will you next be in Salt Lake City?" I replied that I would come whenever he wished. "How about yesterday?" he asked with a chuckle. We agreed on eleven the next morning.

In recent years I had had several conversations with President N. Eldon Tanner and had been impressed with his grasp of historical perspective and gratified by his encouragement of responsible scholarship. A Canadian, he had served many years as minister of lands and mines in Alberta, and later as president of Trans-Canada Pipelines. He is a person of great personal charm who, as a counselor in the First Presidency, directs the business operations of the LDS Church. A call from him to a Mormon like me was like a call from the president of the United States to a potential cabinet appointee. Several months earlier A. William Lund had died after sixty years of service as Assistant Church Historian. As I drove that frosty morning the ninety miles to Salt Lake City, I decided President Tanner wanted to ask me the names and qualifications of persons who ought to be considered to replace Brother Lund.

Upon my arrival in the Church Office Building in Salt Lake City, I was immediately ushered into President Tanner's office and

---

First published as "Historian as Entrepreneur: A Personal Essay," *BYU Studies* 17 (winter 1977): 193–209.

seated in the big leather easy chair next to his own. He was friendly, unhurried, and gracious. "Brother Arrington, I'll come straight to the point and not waste our time," he said.

> You know that our assistant Church Historian, Brother Lund, died last February and we have not replaced him. For the past two years, as you know, Elder Howard Hunter of the Quorum of Twelve Apostles has served as Church Historian. He has been a fine administrator, but, as you know, he is not really a historian. Elder Hunter is a lawyer by profession. We would now like to reorganize the Church Historian's Office by establishing a formal Historical Department of the Church. We would like Brother Alvin Dyer [a former member of the Church First Presidency] as managing director; you, Brother Arrington, as Church Historian; and Brother Earl Olson [who has served many years as a librarian-archivist] as Church archivist. Will you accept the position of Church Historian?

Naturally, I accepted. It was a historian's dream. Since 1831 "Church Historian" had been an ecclesiastical office primarily concerned with the preservation of documents and artifacts. In more than 150 years only a handful of trusted Church leaders had had unrestricted access to the Church Archives—one of the most important depositories of Americana in the Mountain West. The new Church Historian was charged with assisting the librarian-archivist in making this preservation archive a working archive. For the first time he was to have a professionally trained staff of researchers and writers to produce articles, monographs, and books of a scholarly nature. Based on original source materials, many previously untouched, these publications were bound to have a significant impact on the understanding not only of Mormon history but also of Western American history.

That was five years ago. From that time, my career as historical administrator has been amply rewarded. Since 1972 staff members of our History Division have published fifteen books, sixty-two articles in professional journals or chapters in scholarly books, twenty-two reviews in professional journals, and seventy-one articles in Church publications. Five books and many more articles are scheduled for publication in 1977.

How did a farm boy from Idaho come to such a position? Certainly it was not from youthful inclinations, for of all subjects in high school and college, I disliked none more than history. Only by a circuitous—and fortuitous—route did I migrate from chicken farmer to agriculture major; from agriculture to economics; from regional economics to western economic history; and finally from western history to Mormon studies. In ecclesiastical affairs I evolved from branch president of a North Carolina congregation of Mormons (while working on my doctorate) to a member of the presidency of the Utah State University Stake, a student stake composed of married and single LDS students attending Utah State University.

Born 2 July 1917 in a one-room, frame house on a farm near Twin Falls, Idaho, I was the third of Noah and Edna Corn Arrington's eleven children. At Twin Falls High I participated in debate and Future Farmers of America, eventually serving as Idaho state president and national first vice president of the latter organization. At home, I contributed to the family income by raising two thousand baby chicks, caring for four hundred Rhode Island Red laying hens, and helping with the farm.

Attending the University of Idaho was an exciting experience for me. I was active in politics and debate, worked as a reporter for the school newspaper, pitched "gold dust" on the university's dairy farm, and earned the Phi Beta Kappa key when I graduated in general economics.

Actually, it was more my distaste for chemistry than my dislike for manure that induced me to switch from agriculture to economics. Perhaps my interest in economics was first piqued in 1932 when many farmers had given up harvesting their crops because of depressed prices. I was fifteen when my father was selling his No. 1 Idaho baking potatoes for ten cents per hundred pounds. That year, upon my father's encouragement, I included slips of paper in some of the sacks of potatoes. "We are getting ten cents for these potatoes," I wrote. "But we are paying $1.50 to $2.70 for them here," came several replies from California. Obviously something was wrong; evidently, not all the manure was in the barnyard. I decided that when I went to college I would study agricultural economics. But the rigid requirement that every graduate of the College of Agriculture must have two full years of chemistry caused me to switch, after one year, to the College of Social Sciences, with a major in general economics.

Graduating from the University of Idaho in 1939, I was offered a Kenan Teaching Fellowship in economics at the University of North Carolina. I was delighted to accept because the university had a good reputation for sound scholarship, and because my ancestors, for many generations, had lived in the Tarheel State. Two years later, I began teaching at North Carolina State University in Raleigh.

It was in my upper-class years at the University of Idaho and the two years at Chapel Hill that I read the writers who had the greatest influence on my life. They included novelists as well as economists, philosophers as well as ecclesiastics. I was much attracted to the southern agrarians and their regional and distributist approach to social problems (Allen Tate, John Crowe Ransom, Herbert Agar, Frank Owsley, and books like *I'll Take My Stand*[1] and *Who Owns America?*,[2] together with Douglas Jerrold, Christopher Dawson, G. K. Chesterton, and George Bernard Shaw in England). I read most everything they had written, and found myself agreeing with much they said.

When World War II came along, I volunteered for an officer's commission in the navy but was rejected as being too short—I couldn't quite reach 5 feet 6 inches even after three weeks of exercises. The air force and Marines rejected me for an asthmatic condition. So I obtained a leave of absence from North Carolina State to help in the civilian war effort, working for the North Carolina Office of Price Administration. After six months of setting prices for firewood, laundry service, and dairy products, I was finally drafted into the U.S. Army.

On my last weekend pass from Fort Bragg, North Carolina, I married Grace Fort of Raleigh. I had been courting her for some eighteen months, but she would not consent to marriage until I was about to be shipped overseas. I don't know what that tells about my attractiveness. Our platoon embarked for North Africa in July 1943.

For the first eighteen months we processed Italian prisoners of war in Morocco, Algeria, and Tunisia. I was slated to make the invasion of southern France until an order came at the last minute to send us to Italy instead. Through a fortunate circumstance, this private first class was inexplicably appointed Allied controller of the Central Institute of Statistics in Rome, known as "Il Controllore Americano." It was something approaching a sub-cabinet post in the military government—certainly the best job any army PFC could ever hope for. With a personal staff of thirty, including a personal chauffeur, an usher, secretary, errand boy, and others, I had time to survey the Italian economic scene and attend more than fifty operas. I was stationed for eight months in Rome. Assigned to the Committee for Price Control in Milan, I participated in the invasion of northern Italy, arriving in time to see Benito Mussolini and Clara Petacci hanging by their heels in front of a Milanese gas station. Finally, after thirty-three months overseas, I was ready for an honorable discharge.

On 4 January 1946, I was reunited with my weekend bride. We had exchanged more than a thousand letters during my nearly three years' absence. Somehow we felt closer because of our separation. We have had an enjoyable marriage and three children. James is a professional actor; Carl is a staff writer for the *Detroit Free Press*; Susan is a graduate of Utah State University and the wife of the conductor of the symphonic and marching bands there.

During my years in North Carolina, social scientists were rediscovering the South—surveying in depth the economy and culture and accumulating a mass of statistics that eventually went into Howard Odum's monumental *Southern Regions of the United States*.[3] An idea often repeated at that time was that all culture is local culture, all history local history; rather than begin with Greece and Rome, one ought to begin with one's own neighborhood, state, and region. The more one understood the culture in which he lived, the closer he came to understanding humanity.

I was excited about the regional approach to economic analysis. My major professor, Milton S. Heath, encouraged me in these studies, and I felt a "burning in my bones" to participate in doing for the American West what Odum, Vance, Heath, and others had done for the American South. There was no systematic, scholarly appraisal of the Mountain West—nothing equivalent to what had been done and was being done for the South.

So in the summer of 1946, having accepted an offer to teach economics at Utah State University, I went to Salt Lake City to discuss dissertation topics with various people. Dr. John A. Widtsoe, former president of Utah State University and of the University of Utah, and an apostle of the LDS Church, suggested I concentrate on Mormon country, rather than all the western states. He pointed out that there was a common cultural heritage and economic background within this broad community, and there was much that could be done. Teaching at Logan, I would have relatively close access to documents in Salt Lake City, and he thought, if I were politic, I would be given access to the abundant materials in the LDS Archives.

Church Historian Joseph Fielding Smith was somehow persuaded to give the project his blessing, and I began researching my dissertation, "Mormon Economic Policies and Their Implementation on the Western Frontier, 1847–1900."[4] The summers were spent in the Historian's Office reading and taking notes from the five or six hundred-volume Journal History and other documents in the archives. I was allowed perfect freedom in using these materials. Elder Widtsoe was right. Perhaps no other part of the world its size is as completely documented as Utah. Letters, minutes, speeches, sermons, account books, diaries—everything necessary to recreate regional history from original source materials—were available to me.

The historic Mormon community was a complete society—diversified and well-balanced. As early as 1850, for example, eighty-five occupations were being practiced in the territory. Utah's relatively well-rounded economy stood in sharp contrast with that of neighboring states and territories. Called upon to service overlanders, miners, and other westerners in a number of ways, Mormon communities were essential to the progress of non-Mormon settlement and industry in much of the Mountain West.

I sought to locate other persons interested in Mormon studies, and was very much benefited when a group of three other USU faculty members and their wives—S. George and Maria Ellsworth, Eugene E. and Beth Campbell, and Wendell O. and Pearl Rich—agreed to meet once a month with Grace and me to read original papers by each of us on Mormon culture and history. Some of these papers were subsequently published. I was particularly benefited by attending seminars by George Ellsworth on the sources and literature of history. He was my mentor in historical method.

In 1951 I began publishing some of my findings. Beginning that year some of my articles on Mormon economic programs and activities found their way into *Rural Sociology*, *Journal of Economic History*, *Economic History Review*, *Western Humanities Review*, *Pacific Historical Review*, *Business History Review*, and other historical journals, books, and encyclopedias.

Upon the advice of my thesis director, my dissertation, completed in 1952, was submitted to the Committee on Research in Economic History, a standing committee of the Economic History Association funded by the Rockefeller Foundation. Following the suggestions of the appointed readers, Arthur H. Cole of Harvard and Lewis Atherton of the University of Missouri, I began to revise the dissertation for publication. In 1956 I received a sabbatical from USU and a six-month fellowship, later extended to a full year, at the Henry E. Huntington Library and Art Gallery, in San Marino, California, where the 700-page manuscript of *Great Basin Kingdom: An Economic History of the Latter-day Saints, 1830–1900* was completed. After eleven years of research and writing, without the aid of research assistants but with the critical comments and suggestions of George Ellsworth, I finished the book.

It was published in 1958 by Harvard University Press while I was in Italy lecturing to university students as a Fulbright Professor of American Economics.[5] There, with the approval of Professor Edward C. Kirkland and his publishers, I rewrote and adapted his splendid book, *A History of American Economic Life*, to serve as a text for Italians interested in American economic history.[6]

Returning to America in 1959, I found that some of those who had read *Great Basin Kingdom* wanted to know whether I was a Mormon. A number of Mormon students wrote to congratulate me that a non-Mormon had written such a fair book. At the same time some non-Mormon readers wrote to express surprise that a Mormon could produce such an objective work. It was my intention in that book to write an impartial study of the Mormon economic system, and how Brigham Young and his associates and successors managed to preserve some of the more unique aspects of the Mormon economic way. In the preface, I presented the need for, and value of, an objective study of this religious economic system:

> The true essence of God's revealed will, if such it be, cannot be apprehended without an understanding of the conditions surrounding the prophetic vision, and the symbolism and verbiage in which it is couched. Surely God does not reveal His will except to those prepared, by intellectual and social experience and by spiritual insight and imagination, to grasp and convey it. A naturalistic discussion of "the people and the times" and of the mind and experience of Latter-day prophets is therefore a perfectly valid aspect of religious history, and, indeed, makes more plausible the truths they attempted to convey. While the discussion of naturalistic causes of revelation does not preclude its claim to be revealed or inspired of God, in practice it is difficult, if not impossible, to distinguish what is objectively "revealed" from what is subjectively "contributed" by those receiving the revelation.[7]

This still represents my point of view as to the necessity and possibility of "naturalistic" history of religion.

Great Basin Kingdom, however, was only a beginning. Much remained to be done. Established for religious purposes, dominated by religious sentiments, and long managed by religious leaders, Mormon country—Utah and parts of Arizona, New Mexico, Nevada, Idaho, and Wyoming—is an important laboratory for the study of religion and its relationship to social development. Utah's history illustrates problems connected with settlement of isolated, mountainous, and semiarid regions. Perhaps more importantly, it demonstrates the possibility and techniques of economic development without outside capital. But a perusal of twelve standard works on American history in 1959 revealed only two that mentioned the Mormons and Utah. Of the eight leading texts on American economic history, I found Mormons mentioned in only one, and that in connection with colonization. In Arnold Toynbee's monumental ten-volume history of civilization, Utah and the Mormons are mentioned three times, each time with one line—once in connection with plural marriage, once regarding the trek west from Nauvoo, and once concerning the Book of Mormon.

I felt that neglect of the Mormon heritage in the general American literature did not necessarily reflect a low opinion of their achievements; Theodore Roosevelt, Richard T. Ely, Thomas Nixon Carver, Ray Stannard Baker, William Smythe, and others had made repeated references to Mormon experiments, and eventually voluntary associations, corporations, and state and federal bureaus frankly adopted policies suggested by the Mormon experience. Moreover, that modern westerner, Walter Prescott Webb, in planning for his television series of seventy lectures on the history of American civilization, planned for two lectures on the Mormons and invited me to present these, in 1963, at the University of Texas.

It seemed clear to me that the superficial treatment of Utah and Mormon history was due to the lack of good, scholarly monographs on which general history authors might base their work. This, in turn, could be attributed to the attitude held by many Utah Mormons that their history was family history, having no significance for anyone but themselves. Or, if they were devout Latter-day Saints, they found Utah history important only insofar as it contributed to an understanding of the history of their Church.

To help improve this situation I applied in 1959 for a grant from Utah State University to fund summer work on Utah and western economic history. Each summer for thirteen years, according to the terms of the grant, I was able to employ a senior or graduate student to collaborate in researching and writing articles and monographs. This began the broadening of my career. Henceforth I would be not only an individual scholar, but a "historical entrepreneur," organizing large projects and team efforts, and often working in collaboration with graduate students and colleagues.

We began with a study of Utah's defense industry. The state had just become a leader in the missile industry, and with Jon G. Perry, I published an article on the development of "Utah's Spectacular

Missiles Industry." Then came a series of ten articles in the *Utah Historical Quarterly* on Utah's defense bases—eight in collaboration with Thomas Alexander, one with Archer L. Durham, and one with Tom Alexander and Eugene Erb. There were also articles and monographs on the economy of the Wasatch Front with George Jensen; the beginnings of commercial mining in Utah, Utah industries established by the Defense Plant Corporation during World War II with Anthony T. Cluff and Tom Alexander; the Horn silver bonanza with Wayne Hinton; and studies of several major federal irrigation projects in Utah.

One of the most significant of these early group studies resulted in the publication in 1963 of *The Changing Economic Structure of the Mountain West, 1850–1950*.[8] Under the USU grant I was able to employ two accounting majors and two other assistants for an entire summer to do a detailed analysis of the occupational census reports for each of the eight western states. These compilations were made in such a way as to compare occupational changes within each state or territory over time, and also to compare states and territories at any given stage of development. Comparisons were also made between the mountain states as a group and the United States as a whole. This analysis antedated the use of the computer and foreshadowed the kind of studies which the computer has made possible in recent years. The study has been incorporated in the Bobbs-Merrill Reprint Series in History and demonstrates the contributions which an economist can make to the study of western history.

While finishing a history of the Utah and Idaho Sugar Company, *Beet Sugar in the West*,[9] I became more involved in projects relating to the intellectual, social, and institutional history of Mormonism, as well as its economic aspects. I became acquainted with scholars at other universities and in a variety of disciplines who were interested in western, Utah, and Mormon studies. We exchanged study-group speakers and papers. At historical conventions we made it a point to look up others with similar interests. Then, at the September 1965 meeting of the Utah Academy of Sciences, Arts, and Letters, a dozen of us agreed to prepare for a formal organization of the Mormon History Association. I was designated temporary chairman, a committee was appointed to prepare a constitution and to nominate a slate of officers. At the December meeting of the American Historical Association in San Francisco approximately fifty persons attended the organizing meeting of the MHA. I was elected president, with Eugene Campbell of Brigham Young University and James L. Clayton of the University of Utah, vice presidents; Dello G. Dayton of Weber State College was secretary-treasurer, and the following were members of the council: Robert B. Flanders, Graceland College; Davis Bitton of the University of California at Santa Barbara; Alfred Bush of Princeton; and Merle Wells of the Idaho State Historical Society. (This list included a non-Mormon and a member of the Reorganized Church of Jesus Christ of Latter Day Saints as well as Latter-day Saints.) The stated purpose of the organization was the promotion of understanding, scholarship, and publication in the field of Mormon history.

For the first few years the Mormon History Association met in conjunction with the annual American Historical Association convention, and then with the Western History Association. By 1970 membership had increased to around 200 and a separate annual convention was initiated each April in Utah or at a historical Mormon location. The association now has a membership of 750, including nearly all professional LDS historians, many seminary and institute-of-religion teachers, Reorganized LDS historians, and a few persons from other faiths and fields.

We had intended in 1965 to commence publication of a journal entitled *Latter-day Saint History*, but in discussing such a publication we discovered that Eugene England, Wesley Johnson, Joseph Jeppson, and others at Stanford were about to found a new independent journal under the name *Dialogue: A Journal of Mormon Thought*. They agreed to give special attention to historical articles, and we agreed to submit manuscripts and support their publication. I became an advisory editor for *Dialogue* and organized and edited a special Mormon history issue, "Reappraisals in Mormon History," in 1966.

At that time, I was a visiting professor of history at UCLA, teaching classes in Western American history. Alfred A. Knopf contacted me there, suggesting I write a history of Utah and the Mormons for his company—a history that would, he said, "fill the biggest single gap in western history." To my knowledge this was the first time a national publisher had asked an active Mormon to write a major work on the history of his people. I regarded it as a significant opportunity to demonstrate that Mormon scholars could write responsibly and professionally about their heritage, and provide an antidote for the works of openly hostile or at least unsympathetic writers.

Such a history could not, however, be written from published accounts alone. Knowing of their desire to improve the Mormon Church's image in the nation's history books, I wrote the First Presidency of the Church requesting access to Church correspondence, diaries, minutes, and other documents heretofore restricted. They soon replied with permission for unrestricted use of materials in the Church Historian's Library and Archives. This was the first time such authorization had been given a professional historian, and paved the way for subsequent developments in the use of Church Archives. Because of my appointment as Church Historian, the Knopf book was delayed, but with the collaboration of Davis Bitton, it is now nearing completion.[10]

When I returned to Utah State in the fall of 1967, George Ellsworth suggested we approach Gaurth Hansen, the new academic vice president of USU, with the idea that USU sponsor a new *Western Historical Quarterly* under the auspices of the Western History Association. I was then vice president of the association, and since previous efforts to convert other publications (*Pacific Northwest Quarterly*, *Arizona and the West*, *Pacific Historical Review*)—into a journal suitable for general WHA circulation had failed, we drew up a proposal, which was accepted, for USU to pay for overhead and editorial work, and the association and its members to pay for printing and distribution.

The following year I was elected president of the association and editor of the quarterly, with George Ellsworth as associate editor.

Dr. Ellsworth played a leading role in basic policy decisions, format, and copy. We received some fifty manuscripts and published about sixteen the first year.

In 1971 the American Historical Association formed a committee consisting of the editors of leading historical journals in the nation to study potential cooperative activities. Representing the *Western Historical Quarterly*, I was pleased to discover the esteem this publication had acquired among editors of the *American Historical Review*, *Journal of American History*, *William and Mary Quarterly*, and *Southern Historical Review*.

In the meantime, with the continued support of the Utah State University Research Council, I still directed research on western, Utah, and Mormon history and benefited from collaboration with others. A brilliant graduate assistant of mine at UCLA, Jon Haupt, persuaded me to make an intensive study of fictional works relating to Mormons, and generously shared his own expertise in literary criticism by collaborating with me on several articles in this genre. We have other articles in our heads if we can only find time to develop them. Working with Truman Madsen of Brigham Young University, I helped develop plans for an annual Mormon history issue of *BYU Studies*. The first such issue, appearing in 1969, contained articles treating the early Joseph Smith period of Mormon history. Special issues have appeared annually on the Ohio, Missouri, and Illinois periods.

Meanwhile, under the USU grant I directed the preparation of three books: "A History of the First Security Corporation, 1928–1973," which the corporation has chosen not to publish; a biography of David Eccles, published in 1975 by Utah State University Press under the title *David Eccles: Pioneer Western Industrialist*;[11] and a biography of a Mormon apostle published in 1974 by Brigham Young University Press under the title *Charles C. Rich: Mormon General and Western Frontiersman*.[12] While I am listed as the author of each of these publications, they really represent the research and writing skills of a large number of undergraduates, graduate students, and colleagues who contributed their time and expertise in return for compensation out of project grant funds. It would not be possible to mention all of their names here, but they are credited in the prefaces of these publications. These books represent an attempt to demonstrate that bright students can get good experience and training in research and writing by working under a historian director—and they can produce a creditable product. The two books which were published have received generally favorable reviews. My most recent books are *Building the City of God: Community and Cooperation Among the Mormons*, with the collaboration of Feramorz Y. Fox, now deceased, and Dean L. May;[13] and *From Quaker to Latter-day Saint: Bishop Edwin D. Woolley*.[14]

At the time of my call to be Church Historian, President Tanner informed me that he had talked with President Dallin Oaks of Brigham Young University, and that, if I agreed, I was to serve also as Lemuel Hardison Redd Professor of Western History and the inaugural director of the Charles Redd Center for Western Studies at that university. Both positions were made possible by a generous grant from Charles Redd, who made funds available for research and publication in Western American history, lecturers' fees, research fellowships, travel, and the purchase of rare books and manuscripts. It was decided that I should divide my time between BYU and the Historical Department of the Church, with Tom Alexander assisting as associate director of the Redd Center. I asked James B. Allen of Brigham Young University and Davis Bitton of the University of Utah to serve as the two Assistant Church Historians. Both divide their time between their respective universities and the Church Historical Department.

The Historical Department as it now stands includes four divisions: the Church Library, consisting of published works about Mormon history; the Church Archives, comprising the unpublished works—letters, diaries, minute books, financial ledgers, photographs, films, and phonograph records and tapes; the Church Curator's Division, with charge of the Church's historic sites and collection of art and artifacts; and the Church History Division, under my direction, in which there are fourteen full-time historians and six secretaries and typists. Our mission is to do in-depth research and compile and write books and articles for Church publication and for professional journals. Eight of our fourteen historians have the Ph.D., while others are working toward that goal. All of us are under the general direction of Elder Joseph Anderson, formerly secretary to the First Presidency of the Church and now a member of the First Quorum of Seventy.

Our History Division staff in the Historical Department is both professionally trained and personally complementary. James Allen is a talented writer and loyal associate. With an extensive background in American history and a Ph.D. from the University of Southern California, Dr. Allen has had experience in the Church's institute system and at BYU. He is probably the best-informed student of twentieth-century Mormon history among Mormon scholars. Davis Bitton, after receiving the Ph.D. from Princeton, taught Renaissance and Reformation history at the University of Texas and at UCSB before coming to the University of Utah. In the preparation of a monumental bibliography (soon to be published), he has read or supervised the reading of every known Mormon diary of the nineteenth and early twentieth centuries, and he has a marvelous capability for critiquing historical manuscripts.[15] Our editor, Maureen Ursenbach Beecher, a Ph.D. in comparative literature from the University of Utah, served as managing editor of the *Western Humanities Review* and taught at the University of Utah before joining our staff. She is a warm, attractive personality, as well as a skillful literary critic.

The program of research and writing which attracted these professional historians and editors to the new Church Historical Department was initiated by the longtime Church Historian, Joseph Fielding Smith. Elder Smith, serving from 1910 to 1970, had been primarily concerned with the preservation of historical documents and artifacts. He sent Earl Olson, Church Archivist, to professional seminars throughout America, where he became acquainted with modern classification and security systems in anticipation of the day when the archives would be more accessible to the general public. After 1967, Brother Olson secured clearance from the First Presidency for several historians in addition to myself to have unrestricted access to the archives for scholarly work. It was when

Elder Smith became president of the Church in 1970 that Howard W. Hunter, a Church apostle, was appointed Church Historian. Under his direction the archives were prepared to become a working archive as well as a preservation depository. This was finally realized with the organization of the Historical Department in 1972.

With our own appointments in 1972, we members of the History Division sensed we were on the brink of a new era of Mormon and Western American historiography. And our expectations are being fulfilled. Within the first year of operations we:

1. Inaugurated a sixteen-volume sesquicentennial history of the Latter-day Saints, signing contracts with sixteen Mormon scholars and authors located at various universities throughout the nation.
2. Began a Mormon Heritage series of important edited documents, beginning with Brigham Young's letters to his sons.[16]
3. Discovered and catalogued more than fifty boxes of previously unknown materials containing especially valuable Brigham Young documents.
4. Assisted archivists with the preparation of registers and guides to archive collections.
5. Produced articles for several magazines and professional journals.

In the years since 1973, we have worked on biographies, community and area histories, demographic studies, monographs on special topics, and various in-house historical background reports. We have also conducted an ongoing Oral History Program and have taped more than 2,000 hours with some 800 persons thus far. Our program of work is developed by James B. Allen, Davis Bitton, and myself, in consultation with our professional staff and ecclesiastical supervisors (who have been unfailingly supportive of our efforts). We have also assisted others to do research in our archives by granting a number of $1,000 fellowships each year. We have also assigned certain book projects to professors at Brigham Young University and elsewhere and have thus involved the entire community of Mormon historians in a systematic program of exploring and publishing materials on Mormon history.

Our stewardship as historical entrepreneurs requires many decisions that scholars working alone seldom face. We must decide how to allocate our research-staff time and research monies. Should we be preparing research aids and reference works for other scholars, or should we be supplementing the works of other scholars by writing interpretive essays and monographic treatments? Should we approach the task of research by restricting our efforts to the materials in our own archives, basically those previously unused; or should we work on topics that need treating and supplement our own materials with those at other libraries and archives? Should we produce books and articles primarily for our professional colleagues and a national audience, or primarily for members of our own faith?

There are many related questions which require decisions. Assuming we think a good biography of Brigham Young is needed, should we do a highly detailed biography, which might require as many as six volumes? Or restrict ourselves to a conventional one-volume biography? Should it be directed primarily at our fellow Church members, or should it be a definitive "scholarly" biography submitted for national publication?

There is one problem which may be more characteristic of a Church research center such as ours than of many other historical archives. Under what circumstances are we justified in making confidential materials available to professional historians? There are lodged in our archives many hundreds of letters which were written on a confidential basis to the president of the Church or to other high Church officials. Some of these contain confessions of murder, adultery, fornication, burglary, or other crimes. Are we violating the deceased's right to privacy by making such material available to scholars? Other documents contain minutes of Church trials, where details of wrongdoing are spelled out. Still other minutes tell of disputes between Church officials and record statements made in the heat of passion which the officials must later have regretted.

Some scholars are anxious to get their hands on such documents and emphasize the public's right to know. Others would like to take the information in them into consideration, but feel no necessity to make public the names of the perpetrators. Still others prefer not to know or make known what was in confidential sources. Whether such material should be made available to outside scholars is one question; whether my colleagues and I should see them is another. And if we should, inadvertently or not, see such materials, to what extent are we justified in using them? These questions face us and our ecclesiastical advisers every day.

That no satisfactory "final" answer is apt to be forthcoming is suggested by the lack of agreement as to whether or not Robert Woodward and Carl Bernstein were ethically responsible in their second book on Watergate, *The Final Days*.[17] Other archives housing such records as the files of social workers and marital counselors face a similar dilemma. It requires the wisdom of a Solomon to determine the delicate balance between the individual's right to privacy and the public's right to know. Personally I have no wish to be in the position of suppressing useful and relevant information. On the other hand, it would not be proper for me—nor would I wish—to expose the Church, its leaders, and its members to unfair or sensational disclosures about their personal lives. It is inevitable that in my present position I should occasionally feel like the Grand Inquisitor in *The Brothers Karamazov*.[18] Not only are the administrative problems weighty; the ethical problems require soul-searching. Fortunately, I am able to counsel with understanding brethren.

Happily, the richness of our archives and the complex, exciting events of Mormon history assure that there are many topics of undeniable importance which are unaffected by such ethical complexities. These occupy most of our research attention. Even in areas where the source material does raise questions of privacy, I am optimistic that we are discovering ways of getting at what we need to see and of using our findings in a responsible way, often by means of a quantitative approach that will provide a good sense of what was going on while avoiding the sensationalism of individual exposure that is typical of some of the more slick popular magazines.

It is almost imperative that Arrington, Allen, Bitton, and Beecher read every article and book manuscript prepared by our own staff, and often the manuscripts of others who request our review. Handling administrative chores during office hours, I usually spend two or three hours each evening, and most of the weekends, reading manuscripts. I spend one day a week at Brigham Young University on projects associated with the Redd Center for Western Studies. Weekly speaking engagements occupy additional time. Consequently, there is not as much time available for independent research and writing as I should like—nor for football games or dinner parties, or for summer vacations. The long conversations I used to enjoy with colleagues and with our children are now replaced by frequent dictated letters.

Nevertheless, I would not change places with any historian in America; nor, as a Mormon, would I change places with any Church official with a different assignment. I am blessed to have what I regard as the most challenging assignment in the field of history, and the most pleasant and exciting assignment in my Church, and I am proud to add that all my work in the documents of the Church has increased my love for it and my faith in its divine mission.

Chapter One Notes

1. Peter Smith, ed., *I'll Take My Stand: The South and the Agrarian Tradition* (New York: Harper and Brothers, 1930).
2. Herbert Agar and Allen Tate, eds., *Who Owns America? A New Declaration of Independence* (Boston: Houghton Mifflin, 1936).
3. Howard W. Odum, *Southern Regions of the United States* (Chapel Hill: University of North Carolina Press, 1936).
4. Leonard J. Arrington, "Mormon Economic Policies and their Implementation on the Western Frontier, 1847–1900" (Ph.D. diss., University of North Carolina at Chapel Hill, 1952).
5. Leonard J. Arrington, *Great Basin Kingdom: An Economic History of the Latter-day Saints, 1830–1900* (Cambridge, Mass.: Harvard University Press, 1958).
6. Leonard J. Arrington, *Introduzione Alla Storia Economica Degli Stati Uniti* (Genova, Italy: M. Bozzi, 1959).
7. Arrington, *Great Basin Kingdom*, ix.
8. Leonard J. Arrington, *The Changing Economic Structure of the Mountain West, 1850–1950* (Logan: Utah State University Press, 1963).
9. Leonard J. Arrington, *Beet Sugar in the West: A History of the Utah-Idaho Sugar Company, 1891–1966* (Seattle: University of Washington Press, 1966).

10. Leonard J. Arrington and Davis Bitton, *The Mormon Experience: A History of the Latter-day Saints* (New York: Alfred A. Knopf, 1979).
11. Leonard J. Arrington, *David Eccles: Pioneer Western Industrialist* (Logan: Utah State University Press, 1975).
12. Leonard J. Arrington, *Charles C. Rich: Mormon General and Western Frontiersman* (Provo, Utah: Brigham Young University Press, 1974).
13. Leonard J. Arrington, Feramorz Y. Fox, and Dean L. May, *Building the City of God: Community and Cooperation Among the Mormons* (Salt Lake City: Deseret Book, 1976).
14. Leonard J. Arrington, *From Quaker to Latter-day Saint: Bishop Edwin D. Woolley* (Salt Lake City: Deseret Book, 1976).
15. Davis Bitton, *Guide to Mormon Diaries and Autobiographies* (Provo, Utah: Brigham Young University Press, 1977).
16. Dean C. Jessee, *Letters of Brigham Young to His Sons* (Salt Lake City: Deseret Book, 1974).
17. Bob Woodward and Carl Bernstein, *The Final Days* (New York: Simon and Schuster, 1976).
18. Fyodor Dostoyevsky, *The Brothers Karamazov* (New York: Modern Library, 1970).

Chapter 2

Reflections on the Founding and Purpose of the Mormon History Association

DURING THE YEARS after World War II, partly because of the assistance given returning veterans by the G. I. Bill of Rights (Public Law 346), graduate research in the field of Mormon history began to flower. Whereas only a handful of historians had written doctoral dissertations on topics connected with Mormon history before 1946, several dozen were completed in the late 1940s and early 1950s—twenty in the 1950s alone. A sizable group of scholars spent their summers working in the Church Archives in Salt Lake City and became intimately acquainted with each other and with each other's projects. We shared research findings. Perhaps more importantly, we shared strategems by which we could overcome the reluctance of A. William Lund, watchdog of the archives, to allow us access to the rich materials housed there.

In the years that followed the granting of our degrees, as we prepared books and articles for publication, we continued to visit the archives to fill in gaps in our research. We also kept in touch with each other by attending historical conventions, often staying up half the night in someone's room discussing facts and interpretations of the Latter-day Saint past. Virtually all of us were practicing, believ-

---

First published as "Reflections on the Founding and Purpose of the Mormon History Association, 1965–1983," *Journal of Mormon History* 10 (1983): 91–103.

ing members of the Church, and we shared also our experiences in our various wards and branches. We hunted up persons we had not met who had written on the Mormons; and we speculated about the trends in Church politics. We also made it a point to become acquainted with professional historians who were members of the Reorganized Church of Jesus Christ of Latter Day Saints and spent some evenings discussing our common heritage with them. Some of us talked about the founding of a journal of Mormon history, even toying with possible names for the journal, such as *Latter-day Saint Quarterly*, *LDS Historical Review*, or *Journal of Mormon History*. These discussions were temporarily ended by the founding of *BYU Studies* in 1959. Although the first editors of *Studies* were anxious to run sound historical essays, we were taken aback when an interpretive article by one of us was published in the first issue, creating such an opposition on the part of one zealous General Authority that the journal was suspended for a year.[1]

Through these activities a community of LDS historians was developed. Our interrelationships, at annual meetings of the American Historical Association, Organization of American Historians, and Pacific Coast Branch of the American Historical Association, were strengthened with the formation of the Western History Association in 1963. They were also buttressed by meetings in Utah of the Utah State Historical Society, Utah Conference on Higher Education, and Utah Academy of Sciences, Arts, and Letters. On our various campuses there were also smaller study groups of historians and social scientists engaged in Mormon studies. At Utah State University where I was teaching, for example, George Ellsworth, Eugene Campbell, Wendell Rich, and myself met once a month with our spouses to read and critique papers we had prepared on aspects of LDS history. We also shared with graduate students the excitement of seminars conducted by George Ellsworth on the sources and literature of Mormon history.

The dullest meetings Utah educators had to attend were the annual September sessions of the Utah Conference on Higher Education. At these sessions administrators from Brigham Young University, the University of Utah, Utah State University, and the various junior colleges in the state harangued us on administrative problems and policies. In anticipation of the conference to be held on 9 September 1965, at Logan, Utah, a group of us decided to hold our own "rump session" to discuss the formation of a Mormon History Association. Professors Ellsworth, Campbell, Rich, and myself arranged the meeting, to be held in the Hatch Room of the Merrill Library at Utah State University. We had strong letters of support from Davis Bitton and John Sorenson, both then at Santa Barbara, California. We, also had verbal support from several scholars around the nation, as well as from many at BYU and elsewhere in Utah. In anticipation of such a meeting some of us had acquired information about the American Catholic Historical Association and the Jewish Historical Society which might be helpful. The following agenda was provided those expected to be in attendance:

AGENDA FOR A "RUMP" SESSION
OF MORMON HISTORIANS
Hatch Room, USU Library
9 September 1965 — 1:30–5:30 P.M.

1. Should we organize formally? If so, what is an appropriate name? Organization of Mormon Historians? Mormon Historical Association? LDS History Association? Or what?
2. Do we need a constitution? If so, maybe one of you would write a draft of one. At least, we ought to have a chairman or president or secretary who can serve as a focus for communications. Nominations for such a person or persons are now open!
3. Would it be desirable to publish a newsletter each quarter? If so, how to finance it? Assess each person $1 a year? There is good precedent for this in some of the professional organizations.
4. What stand should we take with respect to the new proposed journal *Dialogue: A Journal of Mormon Thought*? Should we support it, at least temporarily, or make plans to sponsor our own journal?
5. What kind of arrangements should we make for meeting with other Mormon historians at the time of the American Historical Association meetings in San Francisco, 28–30 December? Someone should reserve a place and time for meeting and arrange for a program.

Any other business that any member would like to propose?

As the result of the meeting, the following letter went out to a wide circle of historians and social scientists interested in Mormon history.

UTAH STATE UNIVERSITY
Logan, Utah
15 September 1965

Letter No. 1
Dear Friend

In line with the suggestions of many persons, a group of Mormon historians met in the Hatch Room of the Utah State University Library the afternoon of 9 September 1965, to discuss the desirability of forming a Mormon history association. Fourteen persons were in attendance, and they included historians from Brigham Young University, Utah State University, and the L.D.S. Institute of Religion in Logan. The following actions were agreed upon.

1) To arrange to go to the annual meetings of the American Historical Association in San Francisco, 28–30 December as a group. Professor Thomas Alexander of Brigham Young University will attempt to arrange a time and place for Mormon historians to meet at the time of that convention. Professor Richard Bushman of Brigham Young University, with the assistance of James Allen, agreed to arrange for a program. Professor Stanford Cazier of Utah State University will attempt to coordinate the transportation so that all of us can obtain group air rates from Salt Lake to San Francisco for ourselves and wives.
2) To suggest to the Mormon historians gathered there the formation of an organization. The group was evenly divided between two names: Mormon History Association and Association for Mormon History.
3) Professor Eugene Campbell of Brigham Young University accepted the assignment of preparing the draft of a constitution and bylaws to present to the assembled Mormon historians in San Francisco.
4) Professor Leonard Arrington agreed to serve as a focus for intercommunication and to send out a newsletter to prospective members. If all of you will send a paragraph mentioning the research interests which you have and research projects on which you are currently working that have any connection with Mormon history, these will be included in the newsletter. For the purposes of sup-

porting financially the preparation and mailing of the newsletter, each prospective member is asked to send $1.00 to me.

5) We discussed at some length the problems connected with organizing the group. We agreed that it ought to be intended primarily for professionally trained historians interested in Mormon history. We assumed that most of the members would be Mormons, but there might be others who would want to participate. We also assumed that there would be Mormon members whose primary field of interest is something other than Mormon history, but who would want to belong because of professional kinship. We mentioned the following possible objectives:
   a. To sponsor a session at the annual meetings of the Pacific Coast Branch, Organization of American Historians, and American Historical Association. While these would be partly social, we thought it would be useful to have two or three papers on subjects connected with Mormon history.
   b. To encourage publication on Mormon history topics. After considerable discussion we agreed to recommend that Mormon historians support the new journal of Mormon thought, *Dialogue*—at least, for the time being. We are hopeful that we might induce the editors of *Dialogue* to publish frequent articles on Mormon history subjects and/or to devote at least one annual issue to Mormon history. We think Mormon historians will be among the most frequent contributors, as well as enthusiastic supporters, of *Dialogue*.

6) After this discussion the group listened to an interesting paper by Jim Allen on "The Historical Significance of Joseph Smith's First Vision."

Leonard J. Arrington

Within the next few weeks I received letters from many persons—perhaps thirty-five or forty. Most of them enclosed $1.00. This enabled me to send out the following Letter No. 2 on 10 November 1965.

MORMON HISTORY ASSOCIATION
10 November 1965

Letter No. 2

1. For those of you who just joined our mailing list, it is proposed that

as many of us as can—our wives, friends, and others interested—meet for two or more hours at San Francisco in December in connection with the annual meetings of the American Historical Association. Tom Alexander has arranged for us to meet from 7:30 to 10:00 P.M. on Tuesday, 28 December in the Monterey Room of the Sir Francis Drake Hotel, corner of Taylor and Center, San Francisco. There should be no convention conflicts. The room seats in excess of 60 persons, and should therefore hold all those interested. Jim Allen and Richard Bushman have arranged a program as follows:

Conducting: Leonard Arrington

Discussion of purposes and procedures: 10 minutes

Discussion of a proposed name and constitution: Eugene E. Campbell 20 minutes

Election of officers for the coming year: 15 minutes

Discussion of projects and programs for the Association: Richard Bushman: 30 minutes

Dialogue: A Journal of Mormon Thought—Its possible relationship to the Association: G. Wesley Johnson—30 minutes

Panel and discussion—"The Writing of Mormon History: Prospects and New Approaches." Truman Madsen, Ralph Hansen, Alfred Bush—30 minutes

2. Many of you responded to our first letter by sending $1.00 to provide money for stamps and paper, and secretarial help in connection with getting started. To this date, I have received $30.00. Of course, this will be considered your dues for the first year. Most of you also appended a note giving enthusiastic support to the idea of forming the Association. Several of you added names to our list of those interested. (The list now has 80 names.) Several of you made extended comments about purposes and procedures. (This is a very exciting thing, both intellectually and emotionally, to be in touch with all these kindred spirits.) On one point, may I respond that the original list was only a beginning, and was drawn up by thinking of those who would be most likely to attend the San Francisco meeting of AHA. No attempt was made to exclude Reorganized historians, non-Mormons, lapsed Mormons, persons who are not professional historians, or anyone else.

3. I have omitted mentioning "the doings" of some of the members in this letter because of the bulk of organizational items which must be included.

Leonard J. Arrington

The organizational meeting was held in San Francisco in connection with the annual meeting of the American Historical Association (their first meeting in the American West), in the Monterey room of the Sir Francis Drake Hotel. Minutes of this founding meeting were as follows:

MINUTES OF THE FORMATIVE MEETING OF THE MORMON HISTORY ASSOCIATION

San Francisco, California, 28 December 1965

This meeting was held in connection with the annual meeting of the American Historical Association. Leonard J. Arrington conducted, and fifty-two persons were in attendance. Among those present were representatives of the Church Historian's Office, major western universities, L.D.S. Institutes of Religion, the Idaho Historical Society, and the Reorganized Church of Jesus Christ of Latter Day Saints. At least one prominent non-Mormon historian was present.

I. Meeting commenced at 7:30 P.M.

II. Invocation by Earl E. Olson.

III. Introductory comments by Leonard J. Arrington included the following:

a. Welcome and personal introductions of all present. Each person was asked to introduce himself and indicate his interest in the Association.

b. Dr. Arrington discussed the background of the organization, indicating that for some years various people interested in Mormon history had been talking about some kind of formal organization. Last fall in Logan, Utah, a group of historians got together during the Utah Conference on Higher Education and made definite plans which resulted in this meeting. Dr. Arrington was assigned to write the newsletter and do the necessary mailing; Eugene Campbell was assigned to write a proposed constitution; Thomas G. Alexander made arrangements for the meeting place; and Richard Bushman and James B. Allen arranged the program.

c. Dr. Arrington reported that only yesterday he had met with the board of the Pacific Coast Branch of the American Historical Society. The Pacific Coast Branch agreed to allow the Mormon History Association to become affiliated with this organization and to be included in the program of its annual meetings.

The only stipulation was that the Mormon History Association remain a professional organization interested primarily in scholarly research and writing. Dr. Arrington was charged personally with keeping the Pacific Coast Branch assured that this was the case. The next meeting of the Pacific Coast Branch will be held on 30–31 August and 1 September 1966, in Portland, Oregon. This will be our first annual meeting, and we will work to make it most rewarding. Chairman of the session will be Dr. James Clayton and arrangements are under the direction of Davis Bitton. A question was raised concerning the reason for having our organization meet at the same time as the Pacific Coast Branch—why not in connection with some other meeting? It was explained by Dr. Arrington that the location of most of the members of the association made it most convenient for the largest number to attend this meeting. It is planned, however, to also have meetings in connection with other associations, but this one will be the official annual meeting.

d. It was announced that three annual awards of $25.00 each will be announced in the next meeting in August. These will go to the author of the best book on Mormon history published in the preceding twelve months; the author of the best article on Mormon history published in the preceding twelve months; and the author of the best thesis or dissertation on Mormon history approved during the preceding twelve months. Awards in all three categories will not necessarily be made every year. For the present, judges will consist of the officers of the Association. Nominations for the awards to be given in August 1966 are welcome.

e. LeRoy Hafen raised a question concerning membership in the Association—is it restricted to Mormons? Dr. Arrington explained that the original thought was that it should include all persons who are interested in Mormon history, regardless of their Church affiliation. It should also include professional historians who may not be doing actual research and writing in Mormon history, but who have a kinship of interest. It was seemingly the consensus of the group that there should be no restriction of this nature on membership.

IV. Eugene E. Campbell discussed the proposed constitution, and general discussion from the floor was held on each item. A modified version of the constitution was adopted, and accompanies these minutes. One of the most serious items raised concerned the term of office of the officers. It was suggested that a two-year term would be more meaningful than a one-year term. Dr. Campbell explained that those involved in writing the constitution agreed with this, but felt that it should not actually be written in, in case the people constituting the nominating committee saw the necessity of changing an unsatisfactory officer. It was assumed, however, that the nominating committee would work this out and would probably re-nominate the president and other officers for a second term. It was felt best, however, not to make a constitutional fiat in this respect. The group accepted this explanation. In connection with Article IV of the constitution, dues were raised from $1.00 to $2.00, and all present members were asked to pay their additional $1.00 as soon as possible.

V. Eugene Campbell, as chairman of the nominating committee, nominated the following people as officers of the Association

President:	Leonard J. Arrington, Utah State University
1st Vice President:	Eugene E. Campbell, Brigham Young University
2nd Vice President:	James L. Clayton, University of Utah
Secretary Treasurer:	Dello G. Dayton, Weber State College
Council Members:	Alfred Bush, Princeton University
	Robert Flanders, Graceland College
	Davis Bitton, University of California at Santa Barbara
	Merle Wells, Idaho State Historical Society

Dr. Campbell explained that these nominations generally reflected the names which had been mentioned most frequently on the ballots that had come in. Nominations from the floor were called for. There being no further nominations, these officers were installed by acclamation.

VI. Richard Bushman discussed the general topic: "Projects and Programs."

a. He indicated that his discussion was only to present ideas of what we might be doing, in addition to our regular meetings and research, but certainly not intended to commit the Association to any of these programs, or to call for immediate action on them.

b. Since Truman G. Madsen, who is director of the Institute of Mormon Studies at B.Y.U., could not attend because of illness, Dr. Bushman gave a brief report on some of the things the Institute might do, and which this Association might be interested in. He explained that the Institute was still involved primarily with doing special research projects of interest to Church leaders. Some of these projects, however, would involve some historical research, and money may be available to scholars who are interested in working on such projects.

c. Dr. Bushman suggested that we should be looking forward to the possibility of preparing for a new comprehensive history of the Church which could be published in connection with the 1980 sesquicentennial. The administration of B.Y.U., and the Institute of Mormon Studies are interested, and some money is available for appropriate projects. Several things might possibly be done in cooperation with the Institute.

d. It would be important to collect ideas on areas which need to be worked on—a broad survey which would include not only new ideas, but a way of collecting all the materials already being worked on. It would hopefully include a broad listing from many universities, libraries, etc. The Institute of Mormon Studies would volunteer to collect materials, and to dispense one-page summaries of items submitted. The Mormon History Association could contribute by collecting problems, materials, etc.

e. In discussion from the floor, objection was raised to the possibility of an official connection between this Association and the Institute of Mormon Studies. It was generally felt that this Association should stand alone, not being dependent upon any other group for its projects or its activities. Dr. Bushman explained that he did not intend to suggest an official connection, and agreed with the general feeling. He was merely presenting ideas about what needed to be accomplished.

VII. Wesley Johnson, one of the managing editors of *Dialogue: A Journal of Mormon Thought*, reported on the plans for this new publication, the first issue of which will appear early in 1966.

a. He indicated that it will include articles, a book review section (including essay reviews), and bibliographical essays.

b. The present thought is to put out three regular issues each year, plus a special issue on a particular topic or theme. He made an informal proposal that the Mormon History Association take over the third issue as the first of these special theme issues. Leonard Arrington was appointed guest editor for such an issue.

c. He expressed his hope that *Dialogue* would stand for the spirit of free but responsible inquiry. They have had a wide response from people in all parts of the country with a wide variety of backgrounds.

d. He indicated that *Dialogue* wanted to stimulate good writing as well as responsible scholarship. The editors invite all interested to submit good articles, and to help obtain good articles from others. Perhaps a series of annual prizes can eventually be awarded by *Dialogue*.

e. In response to a question about the relationship of the non-Mormon to *Dialogue*, he indicated that it was intended that basic control of the publication remain with Church members. Articles, however, were solicited from all sources, regardless of Church affiliation, and there would be absolutely no discrimination on the basis of Church membership. The only basis for selection would be good scholarship, good writing, and appropriateness of the material.

f. When Dr. Johnson finished, Dr. Arrington asked that all members submit to him ideas for articles to be included in the third issue which, it was generally assumed, the Mormon History Association would take over. He asked that members submit articles by June 1, 1966, and that we also inform others who have good material of this deadline, encouraging them to submit their work.

VIII. A panel discussion was held on the general topic of ideas for new approaches to Mormon history. Participants on the panel were Ralph Hansen of Stanford University and Klaus Hansen of Utah State University. James B. Allen was moderator.

a. Ralph Hansen emphasized the need for more research in primary sources. He suggested the possibility of a more concerted effort to collect more manuscripts and place them in depositories where they would be readily available for research. He decried the fact that so many valuable manuscripts were still highly restricted in their use, and suggested that the best insight into Mormon history can be obtained only when they are available.

b. Klaus Hansen suggested that many non-Mormons are now taking Mormon history very seriously and that Mormons ought therefore to take themselves a little less seriously. By this he implied that Mormons ought not to write their history with the idea of regulating the future, as some have done. An important function of the historian is that of critic. We need to clarify our criticism, and evaluate the past critically, but we should not see ourselves in the role of priest and prophet. That is, we should not assume that our history gives us all the answers. We need to explode a few myths, but we do not need to try to create a new society. We should take ourselves a little tongue-in-cheek, but we ought to consider ourselves as the memory, not the prophets of the future.

c. A brief discussion ensued.

IX. The meeting adjourned at 10:20 P.M.

James B. Allen
Secretary Pro tem

THE FOLLOWING CONSTITUTION was adopted.

MORMON HISTORY ASSOCIATION:
CONSTITUTION

Article I—In order to foster scholarly research and publication in the field of Mormon history, and to promote fellowship and communication among scholars interested in Mormon history, an international organization is hereby formed with the name: "Mormon History Association."

Article II—The officers of the Mormon History Association shall be as follows:

President
1st Vice President
2nd Vice President
Secretary-Treasurer
Council—3 year term—East: To arrange meetings in connection with the American Historical Association.
Council—2 year term—Midwest: To arrange meetings in connection with the Organization of American Historians.

Council—1 year term—Far West: To arrange meetings in connection with the Pacific Coast Branch, American Historical Association.

Council—1 year term—Far West: To arrange meetings in connection with the Western History Association.

Council—1 year term: Immediate Past President.

Article III—The officers shall be nominated by an official nominating committee consisting of the president and any two of the council members. Nominations shall be listed in the newsletters preceding the annual meeting of the Association. Suggestions for nominations may be submitted to the nominating committee by any member, and additional nominations may be made from the floor at the elections to be held at the annual meeting. The term of office of the president, vice presidents, secretary-treasurer, and past presidents shall be one year. The term of office of each council member, beginning with those elected in 1966, shall be three years. All of the officers shall comprise the Executive Council of the Association.

Article IV—Annual dues of two dollars shall be assessed all members. Such dues must be paid within a month after the annual meeting in order for a member to remain in good standing for the ensuing year.

Article V—The annual meeting shall be scheduled in conjunction with the annual convention of the Pacific Coast Branch of the American Historical Association. Other meetings shall be promoted by the officers in conjunction with the annual conventions of the American Historical Association, the Organization of American Historians, the Western History Association, and at the call of officers or at the request of members.

Article VI—Membership in the Association shall consist of charter members who have paid. dues before 1 February 1966, and others who indicate their desire to join by the payment of annual dues.

Article VII—Amendments to this constitution may be proposed from the floor at the annual meeting or by petition signed by five members and forwarded to the president. Voting on proposed amendments shall be by secret ballot sent to each member. The proposed amendment shall become part of the constitution when a majority of the members who submit their ballots before the established deadline shall vote in the affirmative.

SUBSEQUENT CORRESPONDENCE invited the submission of articles to be published in the MHA issue of *Dialogue*; informed members of planned get-togethers at meetings of the Organization of American Historians, Western History Association, American Historical Association, and Pacific Coast Branch; and announced that eighty charter members had paid their dues by 1 February 1966, of which two were Reorganized Church Historians and three were non-Mormons (Merle Wells, Jan Shipps, P. A. M. Taylor). The memberships included a liberal sprinkling of professors outside of Utah, LDS Institute instructors, and persons not affiliated with academic or archival institutions (e.g., Juanita Brooks, David L. Wilkinson, Ward Forman). Suggestive of the important role women would play in the organization, there were five women charter members of Mormon History Association. The roster of members included persons living in all sections of the United States and at least two in foreign countries. Some were professors or students specializing in Western American history. Others were in ancient, medieval, modern European, Latin American, and American history. Some were in such other fields as literature, economics, sociology, and anthropology. Others were "amateurs" who wished to deepen their understanding of Mormon history and to support the various undertakings of the association.

In the three years that followed, 1966–1969, MHA held its annual meeting in August in association with conventions of the Pacific Coast Branch. In 1970 the official meeting was in Los Angeles during the April meetings of the Organization of American Historians. In 1971 the business meeting was held in October in Santa Fe, in connection with the convention of the Western History Association. During these years meetings were also held in association with the Organization of American Historians in April, Pacific Coast Branch in August, Western History Association in October, and American Historical Association in December.

Finally, in 1972, the officers decided to hold three-day conventions in the spring in chosen settings separate from other historical groups. The flowering of scholarship was such that there was a need for dozens of persons to present papers, and also for the hundreds of interested nonprofessional historians to hear the papers. This move also coincided with the creation of the LDS Historical Department and the appointment of a group of professional historians to do sponsored research, writing, and publication in the field of Mormon history.

Since 1972 the custom has been for MHA to hold meetings one year in historic Mormon settings (Palmyra, Kirtland, Nauvoo, Independence, and Winter Quarters) and the next year in the Far West (Logan, St. George, Rexburg, Ogden, Provo, Salt Lake City). Officers have conscientiously sent out newsletters, arranged programs, and conducted other business appropriate for the association. In 1974 the organization, with almost one thousand members, felt itself strong enough to begin the annual publication of the *Journal of Mormon History*. In addition to MHA business and announcements, the *Journal* has contained papers presented in the annual meeting and other submitted articles.

If one of the purposes of MHA was to stimulate research and the exchange of ideas among historians, the organization has been remarkably successful. The number of papers presented at our meetings now runs into the hundreds, and the vast majority of these have been published in refereed journals. In addition to its third issue sponsored by the association in 1966, *Dialogue* has also published other issues specializing in historical topics. For its part, *BYU Studies* has carried a section in each issue entitled "The Historian's Corner," which carries short articles, notes, and documents of interest to historians. Each summer a special issue is devoted to articles on some historical theme. The number who attend the annual conventions now averages in excess of five hundred persons.

Some reflections on the functioning of MHA in encouraging sound scholarship seem to be warranted.[2] All who profess to be Mormon historians suffer from a certain amount of tension because of a dual loyalty. On the one hand, virtually all of us are loyal, believing, practicing Latter-day Saints. We love the Church and want to render service on behalf of it. On the other hand, we are seekers and writers of historical truth, and are therefore loyal to the best ideals of our profession. We would be ashamed if we, consciously or unconsciously, distorted events as they actually happened to fit the demands of denominational or political prejudice.

No one would suggest that our members from BYU or Graceland, or LDS Institutes or seminaries, or the Church Historical Department, or those who write for the *Ensign* or *Saints' Herald*, are any more orthodox or loyal than our members at non-Church universities, or who write for *Dialogue*, *Sunstone*, *Exponent II*, or *Courage*. Clearly, all of us have our place; all can honestly search for truth and make important contributions to our common culture. We all believe in vigorous, open-minded, and creative historical thinking and writing.

This tension between our historical training and our religious commitments manifests itself in several ways. Our testimonies tell us that God intervenes in history, and we see abundant evidence of this both in our personal lives and in our historical research. But our historical training tells us to be skeptical; we may be imagining this, or our religious beliefs may be intruding beyond their proper limits. We see evidence that God's love and power have frequently broken in upon the ordinary course of human affairs in a direct and self-evident way. But our caution in declaring this is reinforced by our justifiable disapproval of chroniclers who take the easy way out and use divine miracles as a short circuit of a causal explanation that is obviously, or at least defensibly, naturalistic.

The professional in us fights against religious naiveté—believing too much. The religionist in us fights against secular naiveté—believing too little. And if this internal warfare weren't enough, we have a similar two-front war externally—against non-Mormons who think we LDS historians believe too much, and against super-Mormons who think we believe not enough. There is no alternative to this encounter with the four kinds. If we are to succeed as Mormon historians, we must have deep within us a faith, counted to us as righteousness I trust, that a person may be a converted Latter-day Saint and a competent and honest historian. That others support us in this calling, even while criticizing some products of our labors, is suggested by the remark of President Kimball to me before his recent illness. "Our history is our history, Brother Arrington, and we don't need to tamper with it or be ashamed of it." A similar statement was made to me before his death by his predecessor, President Harold B. Lee. "The best defense of the Church," he said (in a statement similar to the one made earlier by Pope John XXIII), "is the true and impartial account of our history."

Let me suggest four principles to help guide us in our struggles to "do the right thing" in writing the history of our people. First, we should rise as far as humanly possible above all parochialism of time and place that might narrow or distort our historical vision. We must judge the people we write about by their own standards rather than by those of our own day.

Second, granted the inevitability of having to make judgments of men, women, organizations, policy-decisions, and programs, we should obtain and weigh all the relevant data before judgment is inferred. Those of us who have been in the field for many years recognize that the result of a long and honest attempt to get at all the historical evidence about any disputed event or personality is an overwhelming sense of the complexity and relativity of the issues. In trying to be fair, we tend to show mercy. To take a concrete case, any historian who writes about the Prophet Joseph Smith is sooner or later forced to take up an attitude toward him. Our ideal must be to see him as nearly as possible as the Lord saw him, in his weaknesses and his strengths, his compromises and his triumphs, his creative decisions and his forced compliances with circumstances beyond his control. In the resulting judgment justice is tempered with mercy.

Third, we should be realistic. We must deal with the competition of individuals and groups for wealth and power, the game of power politics, the cruelties which poverty forces on people, and the awful destruction of earthquakes and wars. At the same time, however, we see instances of unexpected and unexplainable triumphs in human nature. Although we must be realistic, our realism must be balanced by a certain wonder and appreciation of the potentials of goodness and greatness in human beings.

Fourth, we must be relativists; that is, understand that all policies and procedures, standards and expectations, are subject to change. But while man is immersed in history, he may also, with God's help, transcend history. In giving economic, political, and intellectual factors their due, we must also give faith and religion their due.

In a way, we LDS historians have certain advantages in writing the history of our people. We have an obligation to apply in our professional work the doctrine of consecration and stewardship. The work of historical inquiry is a way of sanctifying ourselves—a way of exercising our stewardship. This means that we have an added incentive to be diligent, hardworking, and honest, even when honesty (i.e., fidelity to the documents) forces us to speak contrary to the usual ideas on the subject. Historical research conducted with the usual rigor is for us not only a professional requisite but a spiritual adventure as well. Research into the history of the Church is not only a vocation, but capable of becoming a religious experience.

If we members of MHA do our work properly, we will come to be associated in the minds of our nonmember colleagues with a certain attitude toward history, with the quality of our concern about it, with the sense of reverence and responsibility with which we approach our assignments. To say this another way, our self-image and our public image will be influenced by the quality of our individual religious faith and life. There will be a certain reverence and respect for the documents we work with, a certain feeling for human tragedy and triumph in history. We will try to understand before we condemn, and if we condemn we will do it with the sense that we, too, being human, are involved in any judgment we may make of others. We will not use history as a storehouse from which deceptively simple moral lessons may be drawn at random. We will not know it all, and will submit our analyses as tentative and subject to refinement. We will neither sell our fellow human being short, nor overrate them. Behind the personal decisions and the vast impersonal forces of history we will also see divine purposes at work. We will look for the working of God both in the whirlwinds and in the still small voices.

One of the things that excites me about our work is the way in which it enables us to have an encounter with our fellow Saints of former years. LDS history is more than the establishment of certain objective facts—dates, places, numbers, and names. It is a history of Saints, in their mutual relationships, in their conflicts and contacts, in their social intercourse and in their solitude and estrangement, in their high aspirations and in their errors and corruptions. In fulfilling our obligations as scholars we must be responsible to the whole amplitude of human concerns—to human life in all its rich variety and diversity, in all its misery and grandeur, in all its ambiguity and contradictions.

I trust that we will all, as members of MHA, resolve that our histories will be marked by thorough research, superior writing, and the display of the true spirit of Latter-day Saintism, and that our history will give us and our readers new understandings of Mormon experiences in the past and present.

Chapter Two Notes

1. Leonard J. Arrington, "An Economic Interpretation of the 'Word of Wisdom'," *BYU Studies* 1 (winter 1959): 37–49.
2. With respect to my reflections in the last half of the article, I have profited from reading the following: C. T. McIntire, ed., *God, History, and Historians: An Anthology of Modern Christian Views of History* (New York: Oxford University Press, 1977); Frank E. Manuel, *Freedom From History, and Other Untimely Essays* (New York: New York University Press, 1971); Christopher Dawson, *Progress and Religion: An Historical Enquiry* (London: Sheed and Ward, 1929), and *The Historic Reality of Christian Culture: A Way to the Renewal of Human Life* (New York: Harper and Row, 1960); Herbert Butterfield, *Christianity and History* (New York: Charles Scribner's Sons, 1950); E. Harris Harbison, *Christianity and History: Essays* (Princeton, N.J.: Princeton University Press, 1964); Page Smith, *The Historian and History* (New York: Alfred A. Knopf, 1964); Arnold Toynbee, *An Historian's Approach to Religion: Based on Gifford Lectures Delivered in the University of Edinburgh in the Years 1952 and 1953* (New York: Oxford University Press, 1956); Robert N. Bellah, *Beyond Belief: Essays on Religion in a Post-Traditional World* (New York: Harper and Row, 1970); and George Santayana, *The Life of Reason* (New York: Charles Scribner's Sons, 1936).

   Latter-day Saint essays which deal with these problems include: Richard L. Bushman, "Faithful History," *Dialogue: A Journal of Mormon Thought* 4 (winter 1969): 11–25; Leonard Arrington, "The Search for Truth and Meaning in Mormon History," *Dialogue* 3 (summer 1968): 56–66; Richard D. Poll, "God and Man in History," *Dialogue* 7 (spring 1972): 101–9; Robert B. Flanders, "Some Reflections on the New Mormon History," *Dialogue* 9 (spring 1974): 34–41; Rodman W. Paul, "The Mormons as a Theme in Western Historical Writing," *Journal of American History* 54 (December 1967): 511–23; Louis C. Midgley, "A Critique of Mormon Historians: The Questions of Faith and History," typescript, paper delivered at the Western History Association, San Antonio, Texas, 15 October 1981; Philip L. Barlow, "Since Brodie: The

Writing of the Mormon Past, 1945–1981," 1981, typescript, copy provided the writer by the author; Davis Bitton, "Ten Years in Church History: A Personal Memoir," typescript, 1982, copy provided the writer by the author; Thomas G. Alexander, "Toward a New Mormon History: An Examination of the Literature on the Latter-day Saints in the Far West," in Michael P. Malone, ed., *Historians and the American West* (Lincoln: University of Nebraska Press, 1983), 344–68; James B. Allen and Glen M. Leonard, *The Story of the Latter-day Saints* (Salt Lake City: Deseret Book, 1976); Leonard Arrington and Davis Bitton, *The Mormon Experience* (New York: Alfred A. Knopf, 1979); Boyd K. Packer, "The Mantle is Far, Far Greater Than the Intellect," *BYU Studies* 21 (summer 1981): 259–78; LeAnn Cragun, "Mormons and History: In Control of the Past" (Ph.D. diss., University of Hawaii, 1981); and Clara Viator Dobay, "Essays in Mormon Historiography" (Ph.D. diss., University of Houston, 1980).

Chapter 3

The Founding of the LDS Church Historical Department

THE FOUNDING OF the Historical Department of the Church in 1972 may be traced to preparatory actions taken by President N. Eldon Tanner and Elder Howard W. Hunter.[1] As a counselor in the First Presidency beginning in 1963, President Tanner sought to acquaint himself with the current research in the field of Church history. He held several meetings to discuss historical literature, acquaint himself with LDS scholarship, and explore how to encourage research with Dr. Lyman Tyler, a historian who was then director of libraries at Brigham Young University. Lyman was a friend of mine; we had known each other as boys in Twin Falls, Idaho. On 28 January 1966, at Lyman's invitation, I drove to Salt Lake City from Logan, where I was a professor of economics at Utah State University, to attend one of these meetings.

President Tanner was very friendly, asked me many questions, and seemed interested in my answers. I sensed that he had an understanding of the frustrations historians felt about obtaining access to materials in the Church Historian's Library and Archives and that he sympathized with my arguments about the need for more openness. But he was a diplomat, reserved in expressing his opinions.

Paper presented at the Mormon History Association annual meeting, St. George, Utah, 15 May 1992. First published as "The Founding of the LDS Church Historical Department, 1972," *Journal of Mormon History* 18 (fall 1992): 41–56.

Since 1921 Elder Joseph Fielding Smith, a member of the Council of the Twelve, had served as official Church Historian. Elder Smith was primarily a student of the scriptures and an expounder of doctrine. His principal interest as Church Historian was archival—that is, in acquiring materials and preserving them. The Assistant Church Historians managing the library-archives were A. William Lund and Earl E. Olson. Their objectives were similar—to acquire and preserve historical documents. Building on the work of their predecessors, particularly Andrew Jenson, Elder Smith and his associates had amassed an enormous body of materials, an unbelievably large and complete archive consisting of about two thousand diaries and personal histories, almost every book published by or about the Church throughout its history, a full set of Church periodicals, and thousands of minute books, letters, and historical records. Very little of this collection was readily available to historians. I had some hope, based on President Tanner's response, that changes might be coming that would better meet the Church's historical needs.

To my surprise and delight about six months later, I received a letter from the First Presidency dated 15 June 1966, which President Tanner signed. It was a thank you-note for the helpfulness of the earlier interview but went beyond courtesies to create what amounted to a virtual calling. President Tanner wrote:

> We sincerely appreciate your willingness to take the leadership in encouraging Mormon scholars to produce positively written articles and monographic studies on Mormon social and religious institutions. . . . We realize that research is very demanding in time and effort and would suggest that you consider your participating in this program equivalent in importance to other major assignments you have held in the Church. [He knew that I had been a high councilor and a counselor in the presidency of Utah State University Stake]. If you feel that I can be of assistance I shall appreciate having you call on me. May we again commend you for your efforts and for your faithfulness.

Three months later I took my family to Pacific Palisades, California, to spend the academic year 1966–1967 as visiting professor of Western History at the University of California at Los Angeles. During the winter of that year I received several letters from

Alfred A. Knopf, the "dean" of western publishers, and from Professor Rodman Paul, a distinguished western historian at the California Institute of Technology in Pasadena, urging me to prepare a volume on the role of the Mormons in the settlement and development of the West. Such a work, wrote Knopf, agreeing with a similar pronouncement by Professor Paul, would "fill the biggest gap in Western American history." I was very interested in such a project—a natural companion volume to *Great Basin Kingdom*—but knew the book could not be written without access to primary materials in the Church Historian's Office.[2] On 11 January 1967, I wrote President Tanner, explaining the request and pointing out that this was the first time a leading national publisher had asked an active Latter-day Saint to write a major work on the history of the Mormons. I asked if the First Presidency would grant permission to use the necessary primary materials, including correspondence, the diaries of certain leaders, minutes of specific meetings, pertinent financial records, and other documents. "I regard this opportunity as a splendid chance to demonstrate that Mormon scholars can write responsibly and professionally about their faith, their Church, and their people," I wrote.

Within a week I had a reply from the First Presidency. They enclosed a copy of a record from their meeting of 17 January, which said that "President [Hugh B.] Brown and President Tanner both felt it was an opportunity for us to have a professional writer who is a devoted Church member prepare such a history. It was agreed that authorization may be given to use the materials in the Historian's Office, with the understanding that he could not take any of these materials out of the office." President Tanner's accompanying letter of 18 January stated: "With President Joseph Fielding Smith's approval I am authorized to tell you that it will be quite in order for you to arrange with Earl Olson of the Historian's Office to use material available in that office and library."

I immediately wrote to Earl Olson, who quickly confirmed the approval and promised full cooperation. Knowing the importance of this permission, I turned down an offer to remain permanently at UCLA and, on 1 July 1967, resumed my position at Utah State University where I would be able to commute to the Church

Archives. That summer I spent many days examining materials in the archives and continued this effort, when possible, in the years that followed. During this time I became well acquainted with that devoted and intelligent archivist, Dean Jessee, who introduced me to many documents that had not previously been studied by historians. I also became well acquainted with the cheerful and indefatigable Sister Edyth Jenkins Romney, who worked in the archives with her husband, Thomas Cottam Romney, and after his death continued to make typescript copies of original manuscripts. In the years that followed, unsolicited letters came from the Historian's Office to several Latter-day Saint scholars inviting them to use the facilities of the Library Archives for their research. President Tanner had taken a major step in opening the archives to earnest and established historians.

The completion of my book had to await many developments. The materials in the archives were so vast, so unbelievably complete and rich, that I could not possibly compass them in a few months. I taught a full load of economics classes at USU during this time period and, at the request of the Research Council of the university, directed several projects that brought in research grants and awards. With the Research Council's encouragement and support, I continued to do articles on western economic history and, with the help of USU students, wrote monographs on federally financed industrial plants and reclamation projects in Utah, coauthored a biography of Governor William Spry,[3] compiled a history of First Security Corporation,[4] and wrote biographies of David Eccles[5] and Charles C. Rich.[6]

Alfred Knopf, then moving through his eighties, was becoming impatient and complained that he would die before my book appeared. Actually the book was not published until 1979, and then only because of the willingness of Davis Bitton to coauthor it and of fellow staff members and friends to help out. *The Mormon Experience: A History of the Latter-day Saints* came out when Alfred Knopf was in his eighty-seventh year.[7] He was overjoyed with the publication and wrote one of the most heart-warming letters I have ever received, expressing his approbation and enthusiasm. The book was the choice of the History Book Club and was favorably reviewed in the *New York Times*. The volume also received an appreciative welcome from Presidents Kimball and Tanner and several members of the Twelve, who voiced their gratitude for a book which, as they stated, they could give to their well-placed non-Mormon friends.

Upon the death of President McKay in January 1970, Joseph Fielding Smith, then president of the Council of the Twelve, became president of the Church. The way was open for the appointment of a new Church Historian; and since the days of Willard Richards, the Church Historian had always been an apostle. Even if tradition had not been a consideration, internal promotion seemed unlikely. A. William Lund, in his eighties, was not a candidate; and Earl Olson, although a grandson of Andrew Jenson, had no college training in history. President Smith and his counselors chose Elder Howard W. Hunter as the new Church Historian.

Elder Hunter, a native of Idaho and a corporate attorney from southern California, took his appointment seriously. With the approval of President Tanner, he held several conversations with prominent LDS historians. I was one of a "Committee of Historians" called to his office on 24 August 1970, to discuss the organization and function of the Church Historian's Office. As I recall, the meeting was suggested by Davis Bitton, professor of history at the University of Utah and current president of the Mormon History Association. Also present were James B. Allen, professor of history at BYU and vice president of the Mormon History Association; LaMar Berrett, chairman of Church history and doctrine at BYU; and Reed Durham, director of the Institute of Religion at the University of Utah. I think Brother Olson may also have been present for at least part of the meeting. At the request of Elder Hunter I sent him a letter dated 31 August 1970 that summarized this committee meeting. As outlined in the letter, we historians made six suggestions, all important in the later establishment of the Historical Department of the Church:

1. That an advisory Council of LDS historians be appointed to meet quarterly with Elder Hunter. The Council would include representatives from the departments of history and Church

history at BYU, departments of history at the University of Utah and USU, the Institutes of Religion of the Church, the Utah State Historical Society, and LDS historians outside the Mountain States area.

2. That the Church appoint a professionally trained person as Assistant Church Historian who would be a coordinator and supervisor of historical research and publications. A budget should be established for a staff of five persons—a secretary, an editor, a director of research, an investigator who would serve the needs of General Authorities and other Church officials and agencies, and a traveling historian librarian who would go "into the field" to uncover documents, letters, journals, and diaries in the homes of members, and conduct oral history interviews.
3. That the Historian's Office make available "Fellowship Grants" to established historians to do work in the archives—summer fellowships to Mormon and non-Mormon historians doing work on Mormon history, and internships to promising graduate students.
4. That the Assistant Church Historian maintain close relationships with professional historical associations related to LDS history: American Historical Association, Organization of American Historians, American Society of Church History, Western History Association, and the various historical associations of the states with substantial numbers of Latter-day Saints.
5. That sequels to the seven-volume documentary *History of the Church* and Andrew Jenson's *Biographical Encyclopedia* be prepared.
6. That a multivolume sesquicentennial history of the Church be prepared for publication in 1980.

Many of these concepts were apparently on Elder Hunter's agenda as he met with the First Presidency and others in the months that followed.

Less than six months later, on 8 February 1971, A. William Lund died, age eighty-four. Earl Olson remained as the sole Assistant Church Historian, and many LDS historians fervently hoped that

Elder Hunter would now appoint a professionally trained person as an assistant to replace Brother Lund. When Elder Hunter again convened the historians' committee in Salt Lake City on 19 November 1971, he confessed that the Church Historian's Office had done almost nothing to compile Church history since B. H. Roberts's multi-volume *Comprehensive History of the Church* had been completed in 1930, although revelations had clearly required them to do so.[8] They had not published important documents, had not compiled biographies, and had not written narrative or interpretive history. Almost nothing had been done to compile material on Church history in the twentieth century. Discussing the possible appointment of a professional historian, a Ph.D., as assistant historian in charge of research and publications, Elder Hunter pointed out the limited budget for the Church Historian's Office. Our committee then suggested a dual appointment by BYU and the Church Historian's Office, with the appointee spending half-time at BYU and half-time at the Church Historian's Office. Even a part-time appointment would make possible documentary histories that would satisfy the canons of scholarship and which would open the way for writing interpretive histories that would be simultaneously friendly and intellectually respectable.

Elder Hunter seemed excited by this suggestion. During November and December, he held private conversations with various historians, especially Richard Bushman, then Boston Massachusetts Stake President, in whom he had great confidence, and reported back to President Tanner. I do not know the content of that report; but on 5 January 1972, President Tanner telephoned me in Logan, asking me to come see him at my earliest convenience. I taught my 8:00 A.M. class at Utah State the next morning, then Grace and I drove to Salt Lake City. I suspected that President Tanner might ask for my recommendation for an Assistant Church Historian. I had someone in mind and organized my arguments all the way down to "sell" my candidate.

We parked in the ZCMI Center, and I walked over to 47 East South Temple. When I entered his office, President Tanner smiled warmly and motioned me into the big leather easy chair next to his own. "Brother Arrington," he began, "I'll come straight to the point. We would like to initiate a reorganization of the Church Historian's Office as part of a general reorganization in which members of the Council of the Twelve will cease to occupy staff positions in the various organizations and programs of the Church. We would like Elder Alvin Dyer to be managing director of the Historian's Office, you, Brother Arrington, to be Church Historian, and Brother Earl Olson to be Church Archivist. Will you accept the position of Church Historian?" I was astonished but tried not to show it.

We spent most of the next hour talking about the new post. "We have done very little writing of Church history in the last forty years," President Tanner acknowledged. "We are under obligations to write our history for the benefit of the generations to come, and we want it done in a thoroughly professional way. We have confidence that you can do it. You will occupy an endowed chair at BYU that will pay half your salary, and the Church will pay the other half. You may tell your wife and President [Glenn] Taggart at USU, but otherwise keep it quiet until I contact President Oaks of BYU and we will make a joint announcement." President Tanner then telephoned Dallin H. Oaks, who suggested they make the announcement a week from that Friday, 14 January. President Tanner said he would announce the change at a meeting of the Historian's Office staff the afternoon of 14 January, which he hoped I would attend. He wanted me to start immediately, but I pointed out that I had classes at USU and would not be able to leave until the end of winter quarter, about the middle of March. He urged me to come to Salt Lake City as often as possible in the meantime to get things started. He said that Elder Hunter was not a historian and that he, Elder Hunter, would be delighted to have me take his place.

As I left the office about noon, I saw Grace waiting for me in the antechamber. President Tanner asked me to bring her in, shook hands with her, and gave her the news. She was as surprised as I had been and was both delighted and chagrined. While she was pleased for me and for the cause of Church history, she loved Logan, thoroughly enjoyed the home we had built there, and was visibly dismayed at the thought of moving to Salt Lake City. However, her instinctive supportiveness caused her to say, "Yes," when President Tanner asked if she approved.

President Tanner set another meeting for the afternoon, after he talked with Elder Dyer and Earl Olson. In our afternoon meeting, President Tanner said that Elder Dyer had agreed to serve as my liaison during the organizational phase to ensure that I received the cooperation and help of the apostles and First Presidency. Elder Dyer, a former counselor in the First Presidency and at that time an assistant to the Council of Twelve, was in a good position to arrange coordinating meetings for Earl Olson and me with key personnel and to obtain clearances for appointments and programs.

I cannot praise highly enough Elder Dyer's subsequent support. From our first meeting a few days later until his service was curtailed by a stroke on 21 April 1972 (and to a limited extent thereafter until December, when Elder Joseph Anderson was appointed to serve in his stead), Elder Dyer firmly reiterated his desire to give the new historical team "the wheels to run on." And he did so with enthusiasm and eagerness. He arranged for Earl and me to attend a meeting with the Twelve in the upper room of the temple and to meet several times with the First Presidency. He presented me to Church magazine editors for interviews that were later published.[9] Elder Dyer asked over and over what he could do for us that would help the work along.

The weeks between 6 January and the end of the quarter at USU on 15 March were crammed. I was teaching history of economic thought and government regulation of business, and supervising several research projects. My department head, B. Delworth Gardner, was understanding in permitting my frequent absences from the campus, and I was able to travel to Salt Lake City two days a week. We put our Logan house up for sale and purchased a Salt Lake home on 22 February. I stayed in it part of the week and returned to Logan to administer research projects the rest of the week. We made the final move to our Salt Lake City home when school was out in June. A lot of media attention was given to my appointment, and my children and colleagues felt that a great honor had come to me. There were many calls and letters of congratulations. I was fifty-four years old, had published several books and monographs, had contributed many articles to professional journals and Church magazines, and had served as president of the Mormon History Association, Western History Association, and Agricultural History Society. I was now entering upon a new work during which I would have to shift my emphasis from teaching and research to administration and historical entrepreneurship.

Elder Dyer, Earl Olson, and I held our first meeting on 20 January 1972; and at the time, we discussed a possible change in the name and organization of the Church Historian's Office to take account of the fact that it now included more than a Church Historian. In a follow-up meeting on 25 January, we agreed to change the name of the CHO to the Historical Department of the Church of Jesus Christ of Latter-day Saints, with an Archives Division headed by Earl Olson, a Library Division to be directed by a trained librarian (Donald T. Schmidt, librarian at BYU, was appointed to this post on 10 March), and a History Division that I would supervise. Later, in 1974, the department created the Arts and Sites Division with Florence S. Jacobsen as Church Curator. Florence had previously served as a consultant to Elder Mark E. Petersen's committee on museums and visitors' centers. Under her leadership, Arts and Sites collected art and artifacts and planned the magnificent Museum of Church History and Art that opened in 1980.

Also in the 25 January meeting, I requested the appointment of two Assistant Church Historians, James B. Allen and Davis Bitton, each to remain at his university and serve half-time with me. Both had been close personal friends and professional associates for many years. They were in their early forties. I prepared a page on each of the two, and Elder Dyer held conversations with his advisors from the Twelve and First Presidency, Elders Howard W. Hunter and Spencer W. Kimball. The Twelve endorsed the appointments at a meeting in the upper room of the temple on 24 February, to which Elder Dyer, Earl, and I were invited. In this meeting, the First Presidency and Twelve approved the new name for the department and heard oral reports from Earl and me. It was a solemn, even sacred, moment as we watched them raise their hands to sustain us and our plans.

After this meeting, Elder Hunter invited me to his office where he candidly discussed the condition and function of the Historical Department during the two years he had been Church Historian and Recorder. He was very relaxed and friendly. He said that my own appointment had come about because of the strong feeling of some of the brethren that the Church needed a professionally trained historian and that the professionally trained historians they had consulted had recommended me. According to my diary entry, he further said that he felt the Church was mature enough that our history should be honest. He did not believe in suppressing information, hiding documents, or concealing or withholding minutes for possible censorial scrutiny. He thought we should publish the documents of our history. Why should we withhold things that are a part of our history? he asked. He thought it in our best interest to encourage scholars—to help them and cooperate with them in doing honest research.

Shortly after these meetings, Elder Dyer had to leave for conference appointments in Central America and so was unable to make the formal calls to Jim Allen and Davis Bitton until 10 March. I drove down from Logan on that Friday to be present for this important event. Upon learning that all had turned out well, something for which I had fasted and prayed, I called Dean Jessee into the office; and Dean, Jim, Davis, and I knelt in prayer to express our thanks and to ask blessings upon our endeavors as we were now entering into our work.

In the weeks that followed, I asked for additional historians to do research and writing of benefit to the Church. Among the first of these historical associates whom Elder Dyer interviewed and cleared were Dean Jessee (already a cataloguer in the Church Archives), Michael Quinn, Richard Jensen, Bill Hartley, Gordon Irving, and Maureen Ursenbach (Beecher). Added later were Glen Leonard, Dean May, Rebecca Cornwall (Bartholomew), Gene Sessions, Bruce Blumell, Jill Mulvay (Derr), Ron Esplin, Ronald Walker, and Carol Cornwall Madsen.

Until November 1972 when we moved into the east wing of the recently completed high-rise Church Office Building on North Temple Street, we were housed on the third floor of the Church Administration Building at 47 East South Temple. I was placed in the office previously occupied by A. William Lund, the office occupied for many years by Susa Young Gates, sometimes called the Thirteenth Apostle. Our staff was located along the east end of the third floor in a series of desks that faced toward my office. The library-archives occupied the west end of the third floor and much of the basement.

After the February endorsement by the First Presidency and Twelve, Jim Allen, Davis Bitton, and the staff joined me in mapping out a detailed program for the History Division that was presented to the First Presidency on 8 August and approved, according to a letter they sent us on 13 September, in which they also commended me and my associates "for the excellent way in which you have been fulfilling the assignments given to you." The program included the following:

1. The preparation of a series of articles for the *Ensign* and *New Era*.
2. The commencement of books for a "Heritage Series" to be published by Deseret Book. These would be edited documents like the diaries of Joseph Smith, letters of Brigham Young to his sons, letters of Brigham Young to Indian chiefs, selections from the letters and diaries of women, and so on.
3. The preparation of a sixteen-volume sesquicentennial history of the Church. Although this program was dropped in 1980, each author was paid for his work and urged to publish a volume on his own auspices. Seven of the books have been published to this date.
4. The preparation of two one-volume histories of the Church, one to be published by Deseret Book, intended primarily for members of the Church, the other, to be published by Alfred Knopf, intended to reach nonmembers. These were later published as *The Story of the Latter-day Saints* by Allen and Leonard and *The Mormon Experience* by Arrington and Bitton.[10]
5. The preparation of biographies of Brigham Young, Eliza R. Snow, and other Church leaders.
6. The inauguration of a program of oral history.

7. The awarding of summer research fellowships.
8. The assignment of various trained associates to work on specific topics: Jill Mulvay (later replaced by Susan Staker Oman) and Carol Madsen on a history of the Primary, Bill Hartley on priesthood quorums, Richard Jensen on immigration, Jill Mulvay on women in Church history, Bruce Blumell on the Church Welfare Plan, Dean Jessee on the Prophet Joseph Smith, and others.

During the ten years the History Division remained a part of the Historical Department of the Church, we had reason to believe that we enjoyed the confidence of the presidents of the Church. President Harold B. Lee, who became president upon the death of Joseph Fielding Smith on 2 July 1972, talked with me several times about the work of the division. He told me that he thought *Great Basin Kingdom* was the finest book on the history of the Church since Roberts's *Comprehensive History* appeared in 1930 and favored our doing a similar general history directed at members of the Church. This is the volume that eventually came out in 1976 as *Story of the Latter-day Saints*. President Lee said he thought our history should be written by professionally trained persons and that he supported the programs that we had reported to him. "The best thing that could happen to us," he said, "is to have a history that is so honestly written that it would be equally acceptable to members of the Church and the outside world." Joined by President Marion G. Romney and Elder Hunter, he pronounced a personal blessing on my head, which, among other things, declared: "Brother Arrington . . . the Lord will bless you and enlarge you and will open new doors to you to enable you to amass material and write histories and prepare necessary documentation for the benefit of generations yet unborn so that [all] will know what has gone on before."

After President Lee's premature and unexpected death in December 1973, President Spencer W. Kimball assumed office. He was also very supportive. He asked me to spend an afternoon in his office reading his diary in order to acquaint myself with its nature and to give him suggestions on how to make it more effective. On two different occasions he told me that he was fully aware two or three of the brethren were not entirely pleased with our publications but that he himself had confidence in us and that, more importantly, the Lord was blessing us in our work. He encouraged Davis Bitton and me as we wrote *The Mormon Experience* and was especially pleased that, as a Knopf publication, it would find ready acceptance in most libraries throughout the country. President Kimball later asked me to prepare a biography of Brigham Young that would join *The Mormon Experience* on the shelves of these same libraries and give a clear picture of this prophet and his contribution to Church leadership and the settlement of the American West.

On 24 July 1978, while he was still in good health, President Kimball and I spoke by invitation at the Days of '47 Banquet in Hotel Utah's Lafayette Ballroom. Honored guests on that occasion were Bruce Babbitt, governor of Arizona; John Evans, governor of Idaho; Mike O'Callaghan, governor of Nevada; and Scott Matheson, governor of Utah. My talk was a review of Mormon colonization in the West. President Kimball followed with an address on the "spirit" of the pioneers. At the conclusion of the meeting, President Kimball came over to where I was seated. As I rose to greet him and congratulate him on his talk, he put his arms around me, kissed me on the cheek, and said movingly, "I want you to know that I love you very much and that the Lord is pleased that you are the historian of his Church." How I have cherished that loving blessing!

Two years later, in 1980 during the sesquicentennial year, the First Presidency and Twelve transferred the History Division to Brigham Young University to serve as the Joseph Fielding Smith Institute for Church History. Under the direction of Gordon B. Hinckley of the First Presidency and G. Homer Durham, who had been managing director of the Historical Department since 1977, nine members of the History Division were transferred, with an agreement that their offices would remain in the Church Office Building in Salt Lake City until 31 August 1982, when they would be relocated in the Knight-Mangum Building at BYU. "This is a forward step," said President Kimball in a news release dated 1 July 1980. "The stature, objectivity, and effectiveness of our fine professional historians will be enhanced by association with the Church's university, where they can perform their scholarly tasks in a university atmosphere with increased interchange with professional colleagues and the teaching process." President Kimball sincerely believed he was protecting us and giving professional recognition to our work by moving us to Brigham Young University where we could continue to do research under academic rather than ecclesiastical supervision. I feel sure that this kind, loving, but straight-shooting man of integrity would be pleased with the efforts of present Church Historian Loren Dunn and his advisors to allow responsible historians greater freedom in making use of materials that, for a period at least, were under restriction.

During the ten years our History Division was affiliated with the Historical Department of the Church, 1972–82, we dedicated ourselves to writing important, interesting, and well-prepared papers on many aspects of Church history. In addition to hundreds of talks in sacrament meetings, firesides, historical occasions, professional societies, and study groups, members of the staff published 20 books; completed 8 book length manuscripts, most of which have since been published; submitted 364 articles for publication in Church magazines, professional journals, and other periodicals; and wrote about 300 other papers, most of which were later published. No one questions that this was a prodigious output of scholarly work. The prizes awarded for some of these publications indicate the high quality of the work. Surely, President Tanner's commission that we research and write our history in a professional way was met during this era.

In addition, our History Division did something else of which we all are proud. We made contributions to a nonprofit entity administered by us called the Mormon History Trust Fund. When Sister Edyth Romney was retired from the Historical Department because of age, we arranged, with a salary financed by the Mormon History Trust Fund, for her to continue her work of transcribing precious documents in the archives until we left the

Historical Department in 1982. She transcribed thousands of letters signed by Brigham Young and the diaries of Willard Richards and other Church officials. In short, she produced one of the most remarkable legacies of our stay in the Historical Department—thousands and thousands of pages of typed transcripts. She is still consecrating her time and energy for the benefit of Church history to this day.

Officers of the Mormon History Association have asked me to evaluate our experience in working those ten years in the Historical Department and to freely employ the well-known historical device of hindsight.

First, I can plainly see that, after the death of Elder Dyer in 1973, we would have done well to have published a regular newsletter or circular letter to inform General Authorities of the work we were doing. This would have given them more information about our efforts and provided a sound basis for decisions about our activities in the years that followed.

Second, in all fairness, the move to BYU had some real benefits. For one thing, the Church was embarrassed about the salaries we were being paid. Even though we received less than we would have earned as university professors, we were, in fact, among the highest-paid employees of the Church. This did not bother President Tanner, who believed in paying people what they were worth, but it was a concern to some who believed that the Church should pay modestly—less-than-competitive wages and salaries. I personally never urged the issue of satisfactory pay; but for some of my associates who were buying their homes and raising young families, the issue was an important one. From this standpoint it was logical for the Church to transfer us to BYU where, I might add, administrators immediately raised our salaries. This, of course, pleased the wives and husbands of the research professors in the Joseph Fielding Smith Institute.

Third, our experience demonstrated conclusively that the enormous mass of material in the Church Archives was constructive and faith-promoting, revealing positive and inspiring glimpses of the Church and its officers. As to the few items in the archives that have been viewed as damaging to the Church, copies were made by unfriendly people long before we began our work; the appearance of these documents is not traceable to our policy of openness but to theft or permissions wrongly given well before our own researches. Although some urged us to spend our time answering the unfavorable accounts that appeared, we were counseled by our advisors to proceed with our own task of telling the Church's history, and this is what we did.

Through the Joseph Fielding Smith Institute, splendid books, articles, and papers will continue to be produced; and I have faith that this work will continue to have the blessing of the Lord. As I continue to research and write and enjoy the companionship of my precious wife, Harriet, I appreciate and benefit from the blessings pronounced on my head by Presidents Lee and Kimball and by my stake president, later a member of the Second Quorum of Seventy, George I. Cannon. On this twentieth anniversary of the establishment of the History Division and the Historical Department, I congratulate those who have been and are associated with it, and I offer my solemn testimony that the Lord will continue to look upon this work with the approval that has been so evident in the past.

Chapter Three Notes

1. The best published account of our stewardship in the Historical Department of the Church is Davis Bitton, "Ten Years in Camelot: A Personal Memoir," *Dialogue: A Journal of Mormon Thought* 16 (autumn 1983): 9–33. My own contemporary account is in "Historian as Entrepreneur: A Personal Essay," *BYU Studies* 17 (winter 1977): 193–209. [The essay is reprinted in chapter one of this volume.] The present account is based on a perusal of my personal diaries and letters. I have written brief accounts of Presidents Tanner, Smith, and Kimball in "N. Eldon Tanner, Man of Integrity;" *Dialogue* 15 (winter 1982): 8–10; "Joseph Fielding Smith: Faithful Historian," *Dialogue* 7 (spring 1972): 21–24; and "Spencer W. Kimball, Apostle of Love," *Dialogue* 18 (winter 1985): 10–13. I am grateful for the suggestions of Heidi Swinton and Davis Bitton.
2. Leonard J. Arrington, *Great Basin Kingdom: An Economic History of the Latter-day Saints, 1830–1900* (Cambridge, Mass.: Harvard University Press, 1958).
3. William L. Roper and Leonard J. Arrington, *William Spry: Man of Firmness, Governor of Utah* (Salt Lake City: Utah State Historical Society and the University of Utah Press, 1971).

4. Leonard J. Arrington, *Bankers Extraordinary: A History of First Security Corporation, 1928–1973*. Submitted to First Security Corporation, 1973. It has not been released to the public.
5. Leonard J. Arrington, *David Eccles: Pioneer Western Industrialist* (Logan: Utah State University Press, 1975).
6. Leonard J. Arrington, *Charles C. Rich: Mormon General and Veteran Frontiersman* (Provo, Utah: Brigham Young University Press, 1974).
7. Leonard J. Arrington and Davis Bitton, *The Mormon Experience: A History of the Latter-day Saints* (New York: Alfred A. Knopf, 1979).
8. Joseph Smith Jr., *The History of the Church of Jesus Christ of Latter-day Saints*, ed. B. H. Roberts, 7 vols. (Salt Lake City: Deseret Book, 1930).
9. "History Is Then and Now: A Conversation with Leonard J. Arrington, Church Historian," *Ensign* 5 (July 1975): 8–13 and Leonard J. Arrington, "Learning About Ourselves through Church History," *Ensign* 9 (September 1979): 6–8.
10. James B. Allen and Glen M. Leonard, *The Story of the Latter-day Saints* (Salt Lake City: Deseret Book, 1976) and Leonard J. Arrington and Davis Bitton, *The Mormon Experience: A History of the Latter-day Saints* (New York: Alfred A. Knopf, 1979).

Chapter 4

Myth, Symbol, and Truth

MY PATH OF COMMITMENT to and belief in the Church of Jesus Christ of Latter-day Saints developed around four basic religious questions I encountered as I grew up. First, is there a living God? Second, was Jesus a teacher worthy to be worshipped? Third, was Joseph Smith a prophet deserving of allegiance? And fourth, is our Latter-day Saint culture meritorious—worth defending and working for?

As these questions may reveal, I believed the intellect to be enormously important—more important than the heart, more important than tradition. If my mind could not confirm the truth of my religion, I felt I would be unsettled and apprehensive. Nevertheless, I felt very comfortable with poetry, music, art, drama, testimony, ritual, ceremony, and other expressions of religious feeling and thought. I was also comfortable with people who contended that religion was a matter of spirit, not mind, and that testimonies could come only through the assurance of the Holy Ghost.

My struggle with the first question began when I was a freshman at the University of Idaho and continued until the third year of graduate school. I acted as a believer, willing to assume there was a loving and powerful Creator. But I was not satisfied until I had studied the matter through and came to a conviction that my intellect could defend. My first satisfying experience was with Low-

---

Paper presented at the Sunstone Symposium, Salt Lake City, Utah, 26 August 1983. First published as "Why I Am a Believer," *Sunstone* 10 (January 1985): 36–38. Reprinted in *A Thoughtful Faith: Essays on Belief by Mormon Scholars,* ed. Philip L. Barlow (Centerville, Utah: Canon Press, 1986), 225–33; and as "Myth, Symbol and Truth," in *Faithful History: Essays on the Writing of Mormon History*, ed. George D. Smith (Salt Lake City: Signature Books, 1992, 303–10.

ell Bennion's *What about Religion?*[1] This manual, used in the Church's Mutual Improvement Association for the youth, taught a crucial truth, namely that the restored gospel represents truth and enlightenment, not superstition and ignorance. Scholarship and education are part of the gospel; Mormonism undertakes to foster the discovery and spread of truth; God has commanded that we study and learn and become acquainted with all good books; the glory of God is intelligence; and it is impossible for a man or woman to be saved in ignorance (D&C 90:15; 93:36; 88:118; 131:6). The manual also quoted with approval Brigham Young's statements in the *Journal of Discourses* that we accept truth no matter where it comes from, that Mormonism comprises all truth, and that there is an indissoluble relationship between religion and learning.[2] These became articles of my religious faith and continue to remain so.

When I went to the university, my roommate, anxious to test my mettle, provoked me into reading *Why We Behave Like Human Beings*, by George A. Dorsey.[3] This widely read treatise by a noted anthropologist and behavioral scientist gave a rather mechanistic interpretation of the ultimate questions and was not intended to inculcate faith in religion. Men and women were little more than complete biophysical machines. The book did not make me cynical, as it apparently had done to my roommate, but it did help to keep alive within me a quest for certainty. I vividly remember one phrase from it. Dorsey quoted Dr. John B. Watson, the famous behaviorist, as saying that thinking was no more than "laryngeal itch." That stimulated me to read several books on organic evolution, including *On the Origin of Species and The Descent of Man*, by Charles Darwin.[4]

Dissatisfied with the superficial and uninformed views that were being conveyed in certain publications to which I was referred, I concentrated on the works of philosophers. First I read *The Story of Philosophy*, by Will Durrant, which introduced me to the names of the most prominent persons who had pondered the great issues.[5] For the same purpose I read C. E. M. Joad's *Guide to Philosophy*[6] and Wilhelm Windelband's brilliant but tedious *History of Philosophy*.[7] I then systematically read some of the great thinkers—Plato, Aristotle, Thomas Aquinas, Spinoza, Immanuel Kant, Josiah

Royce, and William James. I read some philosophical novels: Somerset Maugham's *Of Human Bondage*[8] and George Santayana's *The Last Puritan*.[9] I read Robert Shafer's *Christianity and Naturalism*[10] and George Santayana's *Reason in Religion*.[11] I read the autobiographies of St. Augustine, John Henry Newman, and John Stuart Mill. I read several books that reviewed what the great thinkers had said about God, humanity, and the universe, and had personal experiences that confirmed their views in an intimate way. By the time I began my third year of graduate work, I had satisfied myself about the existence of God. And my religious experiences in my mature years have merely served to corroborate what I had then come to believe. While philosophers have not always argued that the existence of God is demonstrable, they have presented arguments that have been persuasive to me. My experience suggests that Francis Bacon was correct when he contended, "a little philosophy inclineth man's mind to atheism; but depth in philosophy bringeth men's minds about to religion."

My conceptions of Jesus emerged when I was still in high school. I must confess that I read the Bible through when I was thirteen but, country boy that I was, I was turned off by the King James Version, which was to me a strange and unfamiliar idiom. When I went to the university, George Tanner, my LDS Institute of Religion instructor, gave direction to my search for Jesus as a person, as a leader. He introduced me to new translations of the Bible, and I read through the New Testament version of James Moffatt and Edgar Goodspeed, and Richard G. Moulton's *Modern Reader's Bible*. These were very helpful and I still often use them. At his suggestion I also read Shirley Jackson Case's *Jesus: A New Biography*,[12] Ernest Renan's *The Life of Jesus*,[13] Albert Schweitzer's *The Quest of the Historical Jesus*,[14] and James E. Talmage's *Jesus the Christ*.[15] All of these persuaded me that Jesus was, indeed, a historical figure, that the values he taught were superior to anything humanity had ever devised, that Jesus was indeed a divine person, and that his life provided a model worth imitating in meeting today's difficult problems.

As to Joseph Smith, I am grateful that I was not introduced to some of the views of his philosophy and theology that are being advocated today—views of his life and thought that clash with impressions I have acquired and confirmed in my years of research in the Church Historian's Office. I was very fortunate in having been given, as a teenager, John Henry Evans's book *Joseph Smith: An American Prophet.*[16] I read the book while still in high school and was very impressed with the prophet. I remember giving some two-and-one-half minute talks that were based on the book. Unquestionably Joseph had a marvelous intellect and also acute spiritual sensitivity. He honestly sought to resolve the many intellectual, spiritual, social, and personal problems that arose in his lifetime. He was an imaginative thinker and leader. He accepted truth from many sources. And he had good values; people were more important than money, and the law of eternal progression pointed us all in the right direction.

What about the prophet's accounts of his own experiences: the first vision? the visit of the angel Moroni to tell him about the golden plates of the Book of Mormon? the return of John the Baptist to confer the Aaronic Priesthood, and of Peter, James, and John to confer the Melchizedek? Can one accept all of the miraculous events that surrounded the restoration of the gospel? I was fortunate to have read Santayana's *Reason in Religion* before confronting these historical problems. I do not say that I fully understood it or that I agreed with his basic premise, but the book gave me a concept that has been helpful ever since—that truth may be expressed not only through science and abstract reason but also through stories, testimonies, and narratives of personal experience; not only through erudite scholarship but also through poetry, drama, and historical novels. Santayana used the term "myth"—a term well understood in recent religious literature—to refer to the expression of religious and moral truths in symbolic language.

The worth "myth" has some pejorative connotations in modern English. It can mean a story of belief asserted to be true but without any basis in fact. It can be an invented explanation of some natural or historical phenomenon or a wholly fictitious supposition or belief. However, this is not what Santayana had in mind. What he called myth was a traditional account of events and happenings that have religious significance. To say that something is a myth is not to say that it was deliberately fabricated but to identify it as an account that may or may not have a determinable basis of fact or natural explanation. The truth of a myth is beyond empirical or historical accessibility. Examples are the Christian story of the Resurrection, the Virgin Birth, and the creation of the world as described in the book of Genesis. These are ways of explaining events or truths having religious significance that may be either symbolical or historical.

To go one step further, even in the Shakespearean tragedy where, unlike episodes of Mormon and Christian history, the characters and events are wholly fictional, one can find philosophical and religious truth. Examples of novels disclosing religious truths that I had read during the formative stages of my religious beliefs include: Pearl Buck's *The Good Earth*,[17] Knut Hamsun's *Growth of the Soil*,[18] William Henry Hudson's *Green Mansions*,[19] Fyodor Dostoyevsky's *Brothers Karamazov* and *Crime and Punishment*,[20] and Leo Tolstoy's *Anna Karenina* and *War and Peace*.[21] And, for that matter, the philosophical drama in the Old Testament's book of Job.

Because of my introduction to the concept of symbolism as a means of expressing religious truth, I was never preoccupied with the question of the historicity of Joseph Smith's first vision—though I find the evidence overwhelming that it did occur—or of the many reported epiphanies in Mormon, Christian, or Hebrew history. I am prepared to accept them as historical or as metaphorical, as symbolical, or as precisely what happened. That they convey religious truth is the essential issue, and of this I have never had any doubt. Ineffable experiences, messages, and value affirmations do not always lend themselves to scientific, literal, or precise articulation. It does not bother me at all that, in describing a religious experience that transcends his or her ability to express it, a narrator, a testimony-giver, often resorts to traditional phrases in presenting it. Indeed, I do it myself, as those who have heard me speak in testimony meetings can vouch. The Italians have a useful expression for this sort of thing: "Se non e vero, e ben trovato," which means, roughly, "Whether it is literally true or not, it is still true."

This brings me to my fourth basic question: Are Mormon values, policies, practices, and leadership sufficiently superior to justify a lifetime of devotion? Can one work as effectively in furthering the work of God through Mormonism as through other causes? I came to the conclusion that Mormonism was indeed a positive influence worth contributing to and perpetuating.

In 1985 Alfred Knopf published *Brigham Young: American Moses*.[22] In preparing that biography I learned that Brigham saw and read the Book of Mormon in 1830, when he was twenty-nine. Why then did he wait almost two years before joining the infant Church of Christ, as it was then called? When asked to explain this, he replied that he wanted time to observe the character of those who were leading the movement. "I watched," he said, "to see whether good common sense was manifest."[23] After twenty-two months of observation and investigation, he decided that the movement did indeed manifest "good sense." He joined in 1832 and spent the rest of his life laboring on its behalf.

My examination of Mormon cultural institutions did not begin until 1941, when I was twenty-three and in my second year of graduate work. This study was the result of my surprising discovery at that time that there was a historically based Mormon culture. I had grown up on a farm in a non-Mormon community in southwestern Idaho, the son of parents who had grown up in North Carolina, Tennessee, southern Indiana, and Oklahoma. Neither parent had had any experience with the Mormon way of life. There were no Mormon schoolteachers or administrators in our local school system, and none of our close neighbors was Mormon.

Then I went to the University of Idaho, where there were few Mormons in attendance. (At that time, most Idaho Mormons went to Brigham Young University or to Utah State University in Logan.) After four years in Moscow, Idaho, I went to the University of North Carolina at Chapel Hill where I was the only Latter-day Saint in the university and the community. So all these years I was outside the Mormon cultural community.

My major at the University of North Carolina was economic theory. While doing some teaching at North Carolina State University in Raleigh, I took a minor in agricultural economics and rural sociology. One day, as I was perusing some books for a class, I happened to come across a description of the Mormon village in a new book on *The Sociology of Rural Life*, by the young sociologist T. Lynn Smith.[24] I did not know at the time that T. Lynn was a Latter-day Saint and a graduate of BYU, but I was absolutely fascinated with his pages on the Mormon village—something I had never heard of before. I hunted for discussions on the subject in other texts and was delighted to find that Mormon rural life was of great interest to sociologists.

About the same time, partly as the result of the curiosity aroused by discovery that there was a recognized Mormon rural life pattern, I ran across an article by Bernard DeVoto in *Harper's Magazine* that was about his grandfather, a Mormon farmer who had lived at Uinta, southeast of Ogden; and also two articles by Juanita Brooks, whom I had not heard of before, that were also in *Harper's*: "The Water's In" and "A Close-Up of Polygamy."[25] These introduced me to the literature on Mormon culture—something I had not been aware of because I had not grown up in Utah or in a Mormon village. Basically, I have spent the rest of my life trying to keep abreast of this literature and trying to make some contributions myself to that body of writing.

My study of this literature very quickly told me that Mormon culture was praiseworthy—that my people did indeed believe in education and were willing to sacrifice to put their children through college; that Mormon educators were remarkably loyal to the Church, were well respected, and sought to preserve the best values of the culture; that the people were not provincial but, partly because of missionary contacts, had an interest in the peoples of the world; and among the influential leaders of the faith were a number of impressive intellectuals. I came to believe this was a great church. It perpetuated fine ideals of home, school, and community life; its approach and philosophy enabled its members to reconcile religion with science and higher learning; its strong social tradition taught its members to be caring and compassionate; and its strong organizational capability empowered its people to build better communities. As Brigham Young said, a central doctrine of Mormonism is that God's primary work is through people, and so our principal concern was with the here and now.

In short, it was a religion and a church worth working for. I went into the American armed services soon after reaching these conclusions, and upon my return at the end of World War II, I expected to live in a Mormon village to rear my children and to perform my life's labor.

After three years overseas in North Africa and Italy, I did return, obtained a professorship at Utah State University in the Mormon village of Logan, and remained there to rear our family in what Grace and I always regarded as sacred space, because in Logan we actually experienced the way of life we had read and dreamed about. Except for three sabbaticals, we did not leave our beloved Cache Valley until I was called to be Church Historian in 1972. With my appointment, as well as the appointments of others to the historical department, we inaugurated a number of books on aspects of Latter-day Saint history; began a series of important edited documents, beginning with Brigham Young's letters to his sons; discovered and catalogued previously unknown historical materials; assisted archivists with the preparation of registers and guides to archive collections; gave papers on LDS history at historical conventions; and produced articles for Church magazines, professional journals, and encyclopedias. In my capacity as Church Historian I was able to examine the most intimate records of the Church—records that are replete with faith-promoting incidents that served to strengthen my belief in the divinity of the latter-day work. Particularly meaningful to me was my private knowledge of the divine circumstances that led up to the announcement in 1978 by the First Presidency that the priesthood might be conferred on all worthy males without regard to race or color.

Although now released from the position of Church Historian, I am still devoted to carrying out responsibilities that I trust continue to help build the Kingdom of God on earth. Many satisfying spiritual experiences, as well as my continued study of the Saints and their leaders throughout our history, have intellectually and emotionally validated my decision to serve the faith that I committed myself to many years ago, and that I believe to be based on true principles. "Blessed is he who has found his work," wrote Thomas Carlyle; "he need to ask no other blessedness."

Chapter Four Notes

1. Lowell L. Bennion, *What about Religion?* (Salt Lake City: General Boards of the Mutual Improvement Association, 1934).
2. Brigham Young, *Journal of Discourses*, 26 vols. (Liverpool: F. D. Richards, 1855–86), 1:334; 11:375; 15:160.
3. George A. Dorsey, *Why We Behave Like Human Beings* (New York: Harper and Brothers, 1925).
4. Charles Darwin, *The Origin of Species by Means of Natural Selection, or, The Preservation of Favoured Races in the Struggle for Life and The Descent of Man and Selection in Relation to Sex* (New York: Modern Library, 1948).
5. Will Durant, *The Story of Philosophy* (New York: Garden City, 1933).
6. C. E. M. Joad, *Guide to Philosophy* (New York: Random House, 1936).
7. W. Windelband, *A History of Philosophy* (New York: Harper and Row, 1958).
8. W. Somerset Maugham, *Of Human Bondage* (Garden City, N.Y.: Doubleday, Doran and Company, 1936).
9. George Santayana, *The Last Puritan: A Memoir in the Form of a Novel* (New York: Scribner's Sons, 1936).
10. Robert Shafer, *Christianity and Naturalism: Essays in Criticism* (New Haven, Conn.: Yale University Press, 1926).
11. George Santayana, *The Life of Reason* (New York: Scribner's Sons, 1936).
12. Shirley Jackson Case, *Jesus: A New Biography* (Chicago: University of Chicago Press, 1928).
13. Ernest Renan, *Life of Jesus* (New York: Grosset and Dunlap, 1895).
14. Albert Schweitzer, *The Quest of the Historical Jesus* (New York: Macmillan, 1948).
15. James E. Talmage, *Jesus the Christ: A Study of the Messiah and His Mission According to Holy Scriptures both Ancient and Modern* (Salt Lake City: Deseret News, 1915).
16. John Henry Evans, *Joseph Smith: An American Prophet* (New York: Macmillan, 1933).
17. Pearl S. Buck, *The Good Earth* (New York: Grosset and Dunlap, 1931).
18. Knut Hamsun, *Growth of the Soil* (New York: Alfred A. Knopf, 1921).
19. W. H. Hudson, *Green Mansions: A Romance of the Tropical Forest* (London: Duckworth, 1904).
20. Fyodor Dostoyevsky, *The Brothers Karamazov* (New York: Modern Library, 1970) and *Crime and Punishment* (Cleveland, Ohio: Fine Editions Press, 1947).
21. Leo Tolstoy, *Anna Karenina* (Garden City, N.Y.: Doubleday, 1944) and *War and Peace* (New York: Simon and Schuster, 1942).
22. Leonard J. Arrington, *Brigham Young: American Moses* (New York: Alfred A. Knopf, 1985).
23. Brigham Young, *Journal of Discourses*, 8:38.
24. T. Lynn Smith, *The Sociology of Rural Life* (New York: Harper and Brothers, 1940).
25. Bernard DeVoto, occasional articles in "The Easy Chair" in *Harper's Magazine*; Juanita Brooks, "The Water's In!" *Harper's Magazine* 175 (1941): 608–13, and "A Close-up of Polygamy," *Harper's Magazine* 168 (1934): 299–307.

PART TWO

Reflections on Mormon History

Chapter 5

The Search for Truth and Meaning in Mormon History

THE PHILOSOPHER PLATO, to whom dialogue was the highest expression of intellectuality, defined thought as "the dialogue of the soul with itself." It is thus altogether fitting that the editors of *Dialogue* should encourage Mormon scholars to conduct periodic soul-searchings in regard to the relevance of their studies to the Gospel. I am grateful for this opportunity of reappraising Mormon history and of relating historical studies to the Church and its historic mission of building the Kingdom of God on earth.

I.

FROM ITS VERY INCEPTION the Church of Jesus Christ of Latter-day Saints sought to leave an accurate and complete record of its history. On 6 April 1830, the date of the organization of the Church, a revelation was given to Joseph Smith that began, "Behold, there shall be a record kept among you." (D&C 21:1) To accomplish this purpose the Second Elder of the Church, Oliver Cowdery, was selected to serve as Church Recorder. When Elder

---

First published as "The Search for Truth and Meaning in Mormon History," *Dialogue* 3 (summer 1968): 56–66. This article was awarded the Mormon History Association Prize as best article on Mormon history published during the year 1967–68. Reprinted in *Personal Voices: A Celebration of Dialogue*, ed. Mary Lithgoe Bradford (Salt Lake City: Signature Books, 1987), 63–79; and in *The New Mormon History: Revisionist Essays on the Past*, ed. D. Michael Quinn (Salt Lake City: Signature Books, 1992), 1–11.

Cowdery was transferred to other work a year later, John Whitmer was appointed, by revelation, to "write and keep a regular history" (D&C 47:1). Whitmer served in this capacity until 1835 and wrote a brief manuscript narrative, which is now in the possession of the Reorganized Church of Jesus Christ of Latter-day Saints.[1]

Thus, from the earliest years the Church designated an official to record its story and preserve its records. Twenty-five men have been sustained during the years 1830 to 1968 as Church Historians and recorders. In addition to the records kept by these men, each of the organizations of the Church has kept minutes of its meetings and other documents, individuals have kept diaries and journals, and newspapers and magazines have published items of contemporary and earlier history. Thus, a surprisingly complete record of the Church and its instrumentalities, from 1830 to the present, can be found in the Church Historian's Library and Archives, in Salt Lake City. The records in the Church Archives appear to be "honest," in the sense of presenting the facts as nearly as the designated historians could determine them, and there does not appear to have been any destruction of or tampering with the records or the evidence.

The second phase of official Church historiography began in 1838 when Joseph Smith and his associates began the preparation of a documentary record entitled "History of Joseph Smith." This detailed chronology, written as an official diary of the Prophet, appeared in serial form in the *Times and Seasons* (Nauvoo, Illinois), beginning in 1842. When that publication was discontinued in 1846, the remainder of the "History" was published in issues of the *Latter-day Saints' Millennial Star* (Liverpool), during the years 1853–1863. A follow-up "History of Brigham Young" and other Church officials covered the years to 1844, and was published in *The Deseret News* (Salt Lake City) and *Millennial Star*, 1863–1865. In subsequent years Church Historians and Assistant Church Historians worked through these manuscripts, corrected errors, added corroborative material, and "improved" the narrative. The result was the seven-volume *History of the Church*, edited and annotated by B. H. Roberts, which is still the standard "documentary history" of the Church.[2]

A third stage of the recording of the history of the Church was initiated by Andrew Jenson at the turn of the century, when he commenced three important projects: (1) the preparation and accumulation of biographies of the founders and subsequent officers of the Church, many of which eventually found an outlet in the *L.D.S. Biographical Encyclopedia*.[3] Unfortunately, subsequent volumes have not been issued with information on Church officials of the past thirty years. (2) The preparation of an encyclopedia of Church history, subsequently published as *Encyclopedic History of the Church*.[4] (3) The preparation of a massive multi-volume scrapbook record of the day-to-day activities of the Church, with excerpts from available sources, both published and unpublished. This "Journal History of the Church" now comprises more than 1,300 legal-size scrapbooks, from three to five inches thick; it is being extended daily by the addition of clippings from Salt Lake City and other newspapers. Happily there is an index to this mammoth collection so that one is able to trace references to individuals and organizations with considerable ease.

A fourth stage in the setting down of Mormon history was the preparation of synthesis histories. Overlooking the fragmentary histories of Elders Cowdery, Whitmer, and Corrill,[5] and the publication of various missionary tracts with historical sections, the first attempt of Mormon historians to set down a synthesis history was that of Edward Tullidge, who was granted access to materials in the Church Archives for the preparation of his *Life of Brigham Young*, *History of Salt Lake City*, and *History of Northern Utah and Southern Idaho*.[6] Hubert Howe Bancroft also received extensive materials from the Historian's Office, and had the personal help of Orson Pratt, Franklin D. Richards, John Taylor, and Wilford Woodruff in the preparation of his *History of Utah*, which might be said to contain the first "professional" history of the Mormons.[7] Bancroft's one-volume history was followed by Orson F. Whitney's four-volume *History of Utah*, which was written almost exclusively from Mormon sources.[8] The next history was B. H. Roberts's "History of the Mormon Church," which appeared in serialized form in *Americana* (New York), 1909–1915. With some additions and changes it reappeared in *A Comprehensive History of the Church: Century I.*[9] A one-volume synthesis history, originally prepared as a manual for priesthood classes and since reissued many times with additional material, is Joseph Fielding Smith's *Essentials of Church History.*[10]

With the exception of the Bancroft volume and some sections of Roberts's *Comprehensive History*, most of our Latter-day Saint histories and the monographs that have been written from them, represent what might be called "documentary histories." They attempt to give an account of the important events of the past without critical analysis or interpretation. They depend, essentially, on the statements of participants and observers, whose testimonies have been excerpted and combined, with due regard for their trustworthiness, and "compiled" into a narrative. Some of the histories have been written to prove a theological thesis, such as that the Lord looked after the Saints, punished them when disobedient, and frustrated their enemies. They have dealt primarily with the externals of the events which transpired, and have not concerned themselves with the internals—the underlying motives or thoughts of those who made the actions happen. Above all, our historians were perhaps unduly respectful of certain authorities, placing credence in accounts that should have been subjected to critical analysis.

This tradition of unquestioning "compiled external history" presented not only an authoritative narration of the succession of events, but also set the tone for a large proportion of the subsequent studies in Mormon history. These have dealt primarily with changes in the institutional structure of the Church—with the development of its doctrine, program, and organization. Particularly popular objects of study have been histories of the missions, wards, and stakes, auxiliaries, educational and cultural institutions and programs, and economic enterprises. One reason for the popularity of such studies is the survival and availability of the records of the organizations and programs. Personal records were hardly available to anyone outside of given families, and these were widely scattered. There was always a problem about family records because every family organization had at least *one* person who did not want anyone to know that grandpa once shared a bottle of wine with his battalion buddies, or that Aunt Jane once served tea to an officer of the Relief Society. Thus, using organizational records rather than family records, scholars tended to describe the "outside" of the events.

There is, of course, another kind of history—the type which the British historian and philosopher R. G. Collingwood has called the history of the inside of the event. This history seeks to determine and expose the thoughts in the minds of the persons "by whose agency the events came about."[11] The historian does this by creatively re-thinking the thoughts of the participants in the context of his knowledge, analyzing them and forming his own judgment of the validity of their explanations. He invests the narrative with meaning by consciously selecting from the sources what he thinks important, by interpolating in the reports of the participants and observers things which they do not explicitly say, and by rejecting or amending what he regards as due to misinformation or mendacity. Above all, he puts his sources in the witness-box, and by cross-examination extorts from them information which in their original statements they withheld, either because they did not wish to give it or because they did not realize they possessed it. In other words, the Mormon historian, like other historians, must read contemporary accounts with a question in his mind, and seek to find out, by inference and otherwise, what he wants to find out from them. Every step in his research depends on asking a question—not so much whether the statement is true or false, but what the statement means. Obviously, since his informants, by and large, are dead, the historian must put the questions to himself.[12] The historian, as with scholars in other disciplines, must engage in the continuous Socratic questioning that Plato described so well (in the quotation used at the beginning of the article) as "a dialogue of the soul with itself."

This kind of history, which we may call Socratic or interpretive history, must by its very nature be a private and not a Church venture. Although this history is intended to imbue the written record with meaning and significance, the Church cannot afford to place its official stamp of approval on any "private" interpretation of its past. Interpretations are influenced by styles and ideas of the times, not to say the personalities and experiences of historians, and the Church itself ought not to be burdened with the responsibility of weighing the worth of one interpretation as against another. Contrariwise, the historian ought to be free to suggest interpretations without placing his faith and loyalty on the line.

Fortunately, the Church Historian's Library and Archives is now admirably arranged to permit responsible historians to get at the "inside" of the events in our history.[13] Materials are filed in three separate sections, each of which has its own card catalogues and indexes:

1. Library Section. This includes a nearly complete library of books, pamphlets, tracts, and periodicals published by and about the Church, including "Anti-Mormon" works. There are also newspapers and maps, films and filmstrips.
2. Manuscript Section. In addition to the "Journal History of the Church" initiated by Andrew Jenson, there are similar journal or manuscript histories of each of the wards, stakes, and missions; Name Files of several thousand Church officials and members (and some non-members as well); and the diaries and journals of several hundred persons.
3. Written Records Section. This section features tens of thousands of minute books and other records of wards, stakes, priesthood quorums, auxiliary organizations, and missions, as well as emigration records.

The alphabetically arranged Name Files in the Manuscript Section, which are now in the process of being indexed, are of particular value in the rewriting of our history. Typically, they include autobiographical sketches, newspaper clippings, letters to and from the person, and other personal records and documents. Thus, these files permit us to look at the record from the standpoint of many individual participants. These records must be examined with care, and because of the intimate family information which they contain can often be made available only to professional historians who are accustomed to handling confidential data.

After working through several hundred of these Name Files, I do not see any major revisions of our history—that is, revisions of conclusions to which sophisticated historians have come in years past. Indeed, on some of the conclusions reached long ago by our historians but doubted by some recent historians, there is a wealth of material, heretofore unused, which corroborates the "official" point of view. For this reason, it is fortunate that this material is now more generally available. The records contain numerous accounts and evidences of individual greatness, heroism, and sacrifice. My own impression is that an intensive study of Church history, while it will dispel certain myths or half-myths sometimes perpetuated in Sunday school (and other) classes, will *build* testimonies rather than weaken them.

II.

THE MORE ONE WORKS with the materials of Mormon history the more one becomes aware of certain built-in biases that have influenced our impressions of Church history. Let me suggest five of these:

1. THE THEOLOGICAL MARIONETTE BIAS. One gets the impression from some of our literature and sermons that the Prophets and their associates in the First Presidency and Quorum of the Twelve were pious personages who responded somewhat mechanically, as if by conditioned reflex, to explicit instructions from On High, and that God manipulated the leaders much as marionettes in a puppet show—that Church leaders themselves were not significant as agents of history. While this may very well have been the case in some instances, all developments did not come about "naturally" or even "supernaturally," nor can we describe innovations naively as "expedients necessitated by the times." The introduction of theological and organizational changes is done by people—by learned scripturists, talented organizers, and energetic innovators. They may have operated individually or in groups; they may have been motivated by ambition, prestige, or the good of the Church. In any event, they introduced new programs and organizational instrumentalities, and assumed the responsibility for the adjustment to external circumstances without which the programs would not work. To study the mentality,

personality, and character of our leaders is to study the activators of history. Biographical and psychological studies are an indispensable but little-used vehicle for the study and comprehension of our history.

2. THE MALE BIAS. This is the notion that men hold all the important policy-making positions, therefore they are the ones who determine the course of events. The priesthood holds the key leadership offices, we reason, so the priesthood is responsible for everything that happens. We are inclined toward a male interpretation of Mormon history. A few years ago, the Gospel Doctrine classes studied a manual prepared by Dr. Thomas C. Romney entitled *The Gospel in Action*.[14] Each week we studied the life of one historic Latter-day Saint—and we discussed some truly interesting and inspiring lives. Forty-five biographies were given in the manual; and while half of the persons attending Gospel Doctrine classes were presumably women, forty-two of the biographies were of men, and only three were of women. We studied the life of Angus M. Cannon, who was a long-time president of Salt Lake Stake; but we did not study his fascinating wife, Martha Hughes Cannon, who was the first woman state senator in the United States. (As a matter of fact, when the Republican Party nominated her husband for the state senate, the Democratic Party had no one who thought it worthwhile to run against him—that is, until some party member conceived the idea of running Sister Cannon. She won against her husband, served two terms, and proved a brilliant and resourceful senator.) We studied Orson Spencer, the president of the University of Nauvoo; but we did not study his equally intelligent and fascinating daughter, Aurelia Spencer Rogers, the founder of the Primary Association of the Church. This pattern of assumed male dominance is characteristic of all our histories. Edward Tullidge gave biographies of thirty persons in his *Life of Brigham Young*; all of the thirty were men. The fourth volume of Orson F. Whitney's monumental *History of Utah* contains the biographies of 351 persons, only 29 of which were women. One section entitled "First Immigrants," presents biographies of 30 persons, in only two of which was any attempt made to recognize the fact that

women also came to Utah. (As a matter of fact, 83 women had arrived in the Salt Lake Valley by the end of July 1847, 3 from the original "pioneer" company, 60 from the Mormon Battalion, and 20 with the "Mississippi Saints.")

Another category in the Whitney biographies is entitled "Farmers and Stockraisers." Sixty-two biographies are presented, but in only two instances does the biography make any attempt to identify and describe the history of the wife or wives, along with that of the husband. This, despite the fact that the men were away on missions so often that in many cases the women were the effective farmers of the family. This was even more true in the case of polygamous households where the husband could not possibly manage on a day-to-day basis the farms of his various families. It may well be true, as some historians have asserted, that the Mormons were the best farmers in the West, but very often Mormon farms were managed by women, not men.

In any event, anyone who spends a substantial amount of time going through the materials in the Church Archives must gain a new appreciation of the important and indispensable role of women in the history of the Church—not to mention new insights into Church history resulting from viewing it through the eyes of women.[15]

3. THE SOLID ACHIEVEMENT BIAS, with emphasis on the word "solid." We have tended to remember the tangible, the material, the visible, simply because these have had greater survival value. We have tended to measure the accomplishments of the pioneers by such *durable* achievements as the construction of canals and dams, temples and meetinghouses, houses and cooperative stores. We have forgotten that the pioneers also made contributions in thought, in human relations, in education. From the evidence of pioneer life still surviving, we are led to conclude that the Mormons were good farmers and engineers, but poor poets and philosophers. By thus giving emphasis to the achievements of the more active members of the community, we have overlooked the quiet and immeasurable achievements of the reflective and contemplative. An extended experience among the Name Files has

convinced this historian that the role of the writer and the intellectual was greater than we have ever acknowledged. These contributions are more subtle—more difficult to discover and to trace—but they are nevertheless there.

4. THE CENTRIFUGAL BIAS—the notion that the important influences and forces in Mormon history originated in the center and moved outward from there. This bias, which results partly from the greater survival value of materials collected and protected by the central Church, has had a discernible effect on our attitudes. Some Latter-day Saints have seemed to think that their primary task is to sit down and wait for instructions from 47 E. South Temple Street, Salt Lake City. This was clearly not the attitude of earlier generations, who were told by revelation that they were personally invested with the responsibility of contributing toward the building of the Kingdom and did not wait on anybody to tell them when to start.

> For behold, it is not meet that I should command in all things; for he that is compelled in all things, the same is a slothful and not a wise servant; wherefore he receiveth no reward.
>
> Verily I say, men should be anxiously engaged in a good cause, and do many things of their own free will, and bring to pass much righteousness;
>
> For the power is in them, wherein they are agents unto themselves. And inasmuch as men do good they shall in nowise lose their reward.
>
> But he that doeth not anything until he is commanded . . . , the same is damned (D&C 58:26–29).

Clearly that revelation had an impact, for a large share of the creativity in thought and practice in the Church came from what might be called the "private sector," or from the geographical and organizational periphery, and moved centripetally toward the center and universal adoption. To give some examples, the Relief Society originated as a voluntary ladies' aid society in Nauvoo, and was quickly reconstituted by the Prophet Joseph Smith as an official organization. The *Woman's Exponent*, first magazine for women west of the Mississippi (with one fly-by-night exception) originated as a semi-private venture in which the leading part was played by a twenty-two-year-old girl journalist from Smithfield, Utah. After many years of splendid service, it came to be recognized as the official organ of the relief societies. The *Contributor* and the *Young Woman's Journal*, the two periodicals which later formed *The Improvement Era*, were both initiated by the altruistic desire on the part of young men and young women writers to make a literary contribution to the Church. The United Order, as established by the Church in 1874, was modeled along the lines of cooperative general stores established in Brigham City, Utah, in 1864, and in Lehi, Utah, in 1868. The welfare plan, as introduced in 1936, was built on experiences in St. George Stake, in southern Utah, and Liberty Stake, in Salt Lake City. All missionaries know of "good ideas" which were tried in one mission and quickly spread to others. All of this is quite "natural," and, upon reflection, is what we would expect; an examination of the archives helps to demonstrate its validity. Brigham Young used to say that more testimonies were obtained on the feet than on the knees. What he obviously meant was that we must all be "about our Father's business."

5. THE UNANIMITY BIAS. This is the notion that Mormon society has, from the earliest years, been characterized by concert in thought and behavior—by cooperation, concord, and consensus. In this respect, our historians have been so charmed with the unity of the Saints after they have decided on a course of action, that they have neglected to inquire into the process by which they made up their minds what to do. As with other peoples, the Saints have had their controversies, conflicts, and questionings. The substantial disagreement on doctrine, practice, and collective policy becomes evident when one leaves the "official" sources to focus on the minds and careers of individuals. While the records of the Church emphasize the triumphs of union and accord, individual diaries often dwell on the difficulties of resolving differences. When one intensively studies certain controversies—whether they be doctrinal, economic, or political—one occasionally uncovers widely disparate positions, both among general authorities and among the "lay" members of the Church. The Saints were not without opportunities for criticism and the free expression of opinion—in general priesthood meetings, in quorum meetings, and in other encounters; and sometimes opinions were articulated with considerable vigor and determination. Then, just as the divisiveness was threatening the unity

of the Saints, the Prophet spoke, conflicts were resolved, and the Saints closed ranks to get the job done. There was apparently such debate over proper policy preceding the exodus from Nauvoo, before the coming of the railroad to Utah, and during the anti-polygamy "raid" of the 1880s and the Depression of the 1930s. In each instance, there were a few "die-hards" who could not reconcile themselves to the "final" solution and left the Church.

III.

It is with respect to the last bias, perhaps, that the historian can make his greatest contribution to the Church today. There is now, as in early epochs, a certain amount of dissent. Some of it has to do with the Church's role in politics, some with the Church's business operations, and some with the emphasis on certain doctrines and practices such as "the Negro question" and the Word of Wisdom. We cannot deny the uneasiness that these strains and conflicts produce. But anxiety seems so much easier to bear when we understand the magnitude of the tensions and challenges of earlier generations. Indeed, one might make out a very good case for the fact that the Church has grown and prospered precisely *because* of the dissent and discord, the obstacles and difficulties. Just as the Book of Mormon peoples seemed closest to God when they were meeting the greatest trials, the Saints of the latter-day also felt His presence most intimately when their individual and collective problems seemed so insurmountable that they were forced to call upon Him for help. For our pioneer ancestors, worship was not a running away or withdrawal from the battles of the world; neither was it an ostrich-like refusal to look problems in the face. They could not, even if they had wished, gloss over their many obstacles, physical and human, external and internal.

In his autobiographical recollections and reflections, *Little Did I Know*, the great Jewish novelist and Zionist Maurice Samuel asserts that the "authentic Jew" is "the one who understands and is faithful to his own personal and social identity. One who, in short, accepts his history."[16] May we not make an analogous definition of the Latter-day Saint? Are we authentic Latter-day Saints (i.e., real Mormons) unless we receive messages from our collective past? And who but the historian is prepared to relay authentic messages from the past? Our individual and collective authenticity as Latter-day Saints depends on the historians telling the truth, the whole truth, and nothing but the truth about our past. This includes the failures as well as the achievements, the weaknesses as well as the strengths, the individual derelictions as well as the heroism and self-sacrifice.

History can give meaning and purpose to life; it can help to formulate attitudes and policies for the future. As we prepare to celebrate the sesquicentennial anniversary of the Church in 1980, we must intensify our historical inquiries. May the images conveyed by our historians help us to continue the restoration of the Gospel of the Master, and may they assist us in building the Kingdom of God on earth.

Chapter Five Notes

1. *John Whitmer's History* (Salt Lake City, 1966), 24. A similar history, overlapping the Whitmer account, is the "Far West Record," in the LDS Church Historian's Library and Archives, Salt Lake City. Parts of it have been published in B. H. Roberts, *A Comprehensive History of The Church of Jesus Christ of Latter-day Saints, Century One*, 6 vols. (Provo, Utah: Corporation of the President, The Church of Jesus Christ of Latter-day Saints, 1965). It was published in its entirety by Donald Q. Cannon and Lyndon W. Cook, eds., *Far West Record: Minutes of The Church of Jesus Christ of Latter-day Saints, 1830–1844* (Salt Lake City: Deseret Book, 1983).
2. Joseph Smith Jr., *History of The Church of Jesus Christ of Latter-day Saints*, ed. B. H. Roberts, 7 vols. (Salt Lake City: Deseret Book, 1930).
3. Andrew Jenson, *Latter-day Saint Biographical Encyclopedia: A Compilation of Biographical Sketches of Prominent Men and Women in The Church of Jesus Christ of Latter-day Saints*, 4 vols. (Salt Lake City: Andrew Jenson History, 1901–36).
4. *Encyclopedic History of The Church of Jesus Christ of Latter-day Saints* (Salt Lake City: Deseret News, 1941).
5. A series of letters by Oliver Cowdery and W. W. Phelps in the *Latter-day Saints' Messenger and Advocate* (Kirtland, Ohio, 1834–1837) contain much history. John Corrill published *A Brief History of the Church* (St. Louis, 1839).
6. Edward W. Tullidge, *Life of Brigham Young; or, Utah and her Founders* (New York: 1876); Edward W. Tullidge, *The History of Salt Lake City and its Founders* (Salt Lake City: Edward W. Tullidge, Publisher and Proprietor, 1886); and Edward W. Tullidge, *Tullidge's Histories. Volume II: Containing the history of all the northern, eastern and western counties of Utah, also the counties of southern Idaho* (Salt Lake City: Press of the Juvenile Instructor, 1889).

7. H. H. Bancroft, *History of Utah, 1540–1886* (San Francisco: The History Company, 1889).
8. Orson F. Whitney, *History of Utah: Comprising preliminary chapters on the previous history of her founders, accounts of early Spanish and American explorations in the Rocky Mountain region, the advent of the Mormon pioneers, the establishment and dissolution of the provisional government of the State of Deseret, and the subsequent creation and development of the territory* (Salt Lake City: G. Q. Cannon and Sons Company, 1892–1904).
9. B. H. Roberts, *A Comprehensive History of The Church of Jesus Christ of Latter-day Saints: Century I*, 6 vols. (Salt Lake City: Deseret Book, 1930).
10. Joseph Fielding Smith, *Essentials in Church History: A History of the Church from the Birth of Joseph Smith to the Present Time (1922), with Introductory Chapters on the Antiquity of the Gospel and the "Falling Away"* (Salt Lake City: Deseret News Press, 1922).
11. R. G. Collingwood, *The Idea of History* (New York: Oxford University Press, 1956), 215. The first English edition was 1946.
12. Compare Collingwood, 237–55, 269, 273–275. This paragraph is very close to a paraphrase of Collingwood.
13. Certain materials are not in the Church Historian's Library and Archives; for example, minutes of meetings of the First Presidency, certain diaries of members of the First Presidency, certain financial records, etc., are in the vault of the First Presidency.
14. Thomas Cottam Romney, *The Gospel in Action* (Salt Lake City: Deseret Sunday School Union Board, 1949).
15. A good example of the "new look" at the inside of Church history by viewing it through the life of a woman is K. K. Thurston, *The Winds of Doctrine: The Story of the Life of Mary Lochwood Komp in Mormon Utah During the Last Half of the Nineteenth Century* (New York: Exposition Press, 1952). An interesting recent essay emphasizing the role of women is Kenneth Godfrey, "Feminine-flavored Church History," *Improvement Era* (January 1968): 52.
16. Maurice Samuel, *Little did I Know: Recollections and Reflections* (New York: Alfred A. Knopf, 1963). See Daniel Stern, Review of Maurice Samuel, *Little Did I Know* in *Saturday Review* (25 January 1964): 35.

Chapter 6

Clothe These Bones
The Reconciliation of Faith and History

IN ASSIGNING THIS PART on the program of the retreat, the committee asked me to give—not a historical discourse, not a faith-promoting talk, not an autobiographical reminiscence, but a sermon.[1] Recognizing that the audience for the sermon would consist of some of the best intellects in the Church—and I really mean that—I could think only of the Oxford sermons of John Henry Newman—or perhaps those of Jack Adamson or Lowell Bennion—models which I am manifestly incapable of imitating. So this has been a formidable challenge—all the more so because I knew I would have to do it alone—it would be plainly improper for me to involve any of you in its preparation. So I have prepared something that is really pretty sober—some random reflections on our callings as Church Historians. Nedra Yeates Pace and I have entitled it "Clothe These Bones: The Reconciliation of Faith and History." Pretty pretentious; but then any sermon is pretentious.

I begin with an anecdote related by Lord Acton in his inaugural lecture on "The Study of History." A theologian who had written an eloquent history of the Reformation met the historian Ranke in Berlin and embraced him effusively as one would an admired friend. "Ah please," said the father of modern scientific history, drawing himself away. "There is a great difference between us: you are first of all a Christian, and I am first of all a historian." This story dramatizes vividly the nineteenth-century belief that history

Previously unpublished address delivered at a retreat of the History Division, The Church of Jesus Christ of Latter-day Saints, Ensign Peak, Salt Lake City, Utah, 23 June 1978.

is a "science," and that science is knowledge of an utterly different order from religion. A difference still exists in the academic mind between one who would call himself "first of all a Christian" and one who would call himself "first of all a historian." I think one would find some agreement that there is a similar tension within the community of Mormon historians between those who would proudly acknowledge that they are first of all Latter-day Saints and those who would contend just as strongly that they are first of all seekers and writers of historical truth. An example of this was the tension between Joseph Fielding Smith and B. H. Roberts. "You are trying to be a historian after the manner of the world," Joseph Fielding might have said. "My way is more sure. I start with what the Lord has said and then proceed from there."

That this is a complex matter—not at all simple—is the knowledge that Ranke himself was a deeply religious person, just as was the theologian who embraced him an accomplished historian. Both would have striven against the conscious or unconscious distortion of events as they actually happened to fit the demands of denominational or political prejudice. The cause of Christian truth, if we may use that term, did not suffer through the writing of either. It is too simple to say that Ranke represented something called history and the theologian something called Christianity. Each in a different sense was a Christian historian. In our own tradition, it would be difficult to assert, as between Joseph Fielding Smith and B. H. Roberts, which was the more orthodox Latter-day Saint. Or to be still more current, a lively debate could be conducted on the question as to which serves best the cause of Latter-day Saint history, a writer attached to the History Division or one attached to a secular university. Clearly, both have their place, both can honestly search for truth, and both can make important contributions.

All of us were trained to be competent historians, and deep at the heart of the academic world where we trained was the belief that a real "scholar" cannot tolerate any qualifying adjective like Christian or Latter-day Saint. Once a man allows himself to be anything before he is scholar, so the argument runs, truth flies out the window and prejudice fills our historical narratives and analyses. The word Communist historian conjures up certain images, as do Catholic historian, black historian, and even, at least in some circles, woman historian. Historians know very well what happens to the historical profession and the historical record in the hands of totalitarian governments, which inevitably attack the disinterested pursuit of truth for its own sake as not only dangerous but fundamentally immoral. The jealous fear of coupling any adjective implying zealous faith with "scholar" is not altogether unjustified.

Trained as we were in a university setting, we cannot but have admiration for the intellectual honesty of the so-called scientific historians. There is a refusal to be taken in, an ascetic renunciation of wishful thinking. What is not admirable is the tendency of many of them to go farther and conclude that history ultimately has no meaning: it just happens; historical experience is simply a meaningless chaos. The incessant doubters cannot bring themselves to seriously consider our intimations of divine patterns and moral "lessons." For that matter, they are skeptical of any patterns or lessons or designs in history. It is hard to nourish vigorous, open-minded, and creative historical thinking on the thin gruel of thorough-going skepticism.

Curiously, the last twenty or thirty years have seen a watering-down or dilution of the goal of objective history—especially in Europe, but to an increasing extent in the United States as well. When I was in Italy during World War II, I observed that educators who had lived under Fascist thought-control learned to use objectivity as an escape from publicly committing themselves to the dominant philosophy. But when I returned as a Fulbright lecturer, I noted that Italian students had begun to have contempt for the tendency of their professors to avoid commitment. They warmed to teachers who believed something. To many students, objectivity was either a hypocritical dodge designed to cover up unspoken assumptions, or an immoral escape from the necessity of taking a stand on the vital issues of the day. Most younger scholars there today, I'm told, deny the possibility of objectivity. The only attainable objectivity is a frank and detailed confession in the prefaces of one's books of all his subjective prejudices. To some extent this conscious recognition of subjective values has spread to America. The majority of older American scholars—those over fifty, let us say—continue to take pride in disinterested inquiry. They still have faith in the possibility of objective knowledge. But many of our younger colleagues view impartiality as a pose adopted by fearful academicians with desensitized social consciences and dried-up emotions. Some now assert that Ranke was not necessarily any more objective than his theological friend. The knower, they would say, is intimately and indelibly involved in the process of knowing.

Our move into LDS history in the 1970s has occurred during a period when the national and international trend has been away from so-called scientific history. We write in an environment that does not ridicule attempts to integrate or synthesize religious beliefs and historical philosophy and methodology. But this does not mean that the integration we seek is easy or smooth. Each of us senses, I'm sure, a never-ending tension between our historical training and our religious commitments. On the one hand our testimonies tell us that God intervenes in history, and we see abundant evidence of this. But our historical training tells us to be skeptical; we may be imagining this, or our religious belief may be intruding beyond its proper limits. On the one hand, there is moral meaning and spiritual significance in historical events. On the other hand, the divine concealment is such that none of us can be completely confident that any particular judgment or meaning or significance is unambiguously clear. It would seem that the actual course of history cannot be positively identified with God's will. But neither can it be wholly divorced from His will. Those who have unquestioning assurance of a particular interpretation of events may be guilty of too much pride. Those who are over-diffident may be guilty of sloth and temerity. We see evidence that God's love and power have frequently broken in upon the ordinary course of human affairs in a direct and self-evident way. But our caution in declaring this is reinforced by our justifiable disapproval of chroniclers who take the easy way out and use divine miracles as a short circuit of a causal explanation which is obviously, or at least defensibly, naturalistic.

A professing LDS historian, in short, is in a constant struggle with himself—the professional in him fights against religious naiveté—believing too much. The religionist in him fights against secular naiveté—believing too little. And if this internal warfare weren't enough, we have a similar two-front war externally—against non-Mormons who think we LDS historians believe too much, and against super-Mormons who think we believe not enough. There is no alternative to this encounter with the four kinds. There is no wall for us to put our backs to, and the consciousness that the confrontation is inevitable may be the ultimate mark of our calling. If we are to succeed as Church Historians, we must have deep within us a faith, counted to us as righteousness. I trust, that in spite of the expressed conviction of Ranke, a person may be first of all a converted Latter-day Saint *and* a competent and honest historian. That others support us in this calling, even while criticizing some products of our labors, is suggested by the remark of Elder Bruce McConkie to Ron Walker: "Our history is our history, bishop, and we don't need to tamper with it or be ashamed of it." A similar statement was made by President Lee to me: "The best defense of the Church," he said, "is the true and impartial history of its life."

We are probably closer to our secular colleagues than either they or we would be glad to admit. We and they share many qualities and attitudes. Let me mention four.

The first is a cosmopolitan outlook. The best historians of whatever hue cannot be satisfied until by a rigorous intellectual asceticism they have risen as far as humanly possible above all parochialism of both time and place which narrows or distorts their historical vision. Both professional historians and Latter-day Saints want to judge people by their own standards rather than by those of our own day.

The second agreement is on the inevitability of judgment. Historians of every type find themselves, explicitly or implicitly, making judgments of men, organizations, and movements. Even monographs that simply "give the facts" betray underlying judgments in the very choice and arrangement of these facts. Judgment is implicit in the conscious choice of materials presented in papers—and even in the unplanned and half-conscious tone of voice or facial expression that betrays us as we give lectures and direct seminars. Granted the inevitability of making judgments, the real question is on what basis they are to be made. Surely, we must obtain and weigh all the relevant data before judgment is inferred. Most historians of any experience will acknowledge that the result of a long and honest attempt to get at all the historical evidence about any disputed event or personality is an overwhelming sense of the complexity and relativity of the issues, a sense, as Davis might say, of *tout comprendre, c'est tout pardonner*. The desire to be just, in other words, often ends in the desire to extend mercy. And this is as true of purely secular historians as it is of consciously religious historians. To take a concrete case, any historian who writes about Joseph Smith is sooner or later forced to take up an attitude toward him. A Protestant evangelist may vent his righteous indignation upon this self-proclaimed prophet; a pious LDS may make a spotless leader of him; a Marxian may point out that Joseph was a mere puppet in the grip of irresistible economic forces. The best ideal for all of us, secularists and religionists alike, is to see Joseph Smith as nearly as possible as the Lord saw him, in his weaknesses and his strengths, his compromises and his triumphs, his creative decisions and his forced compliances with circumstances beyond his control. In the resulting judgment justice is tempered with mercy.

Our third shared attitude is that of realism. Humanist historians are often shocked by the realities of human nature as they are encountered in history. The historian and the social scientist habitually deal with human nature at its lowest level, the level at which, to use a favorite Niebuhr expression, moral man is absorbed in immoral society. They are concerned with such things as the competition of groups for wealth and power, the game of power politics, the cruelties which poverty forces on people, and the awful destruction of revolution and war. Neither the humanist historian nor the religious historian can be a Pollyanna. Both have learned that one cannot have excessive faith in human nature. But tough-mindedness must be balanced by open-mindedness. One must be open to unforeseen possibilities in human nature and history. Even the most cynical historian, if he is honest, will acknowledge instances of unexpected and unexplainable triumphs in human nature—and movements which turn out better than their sordid origins would lead one to expect. While good events in history may produce unlovely results, good results may just as frequently arise out of selfish conflicts. So all historians must cultivate open-mindedness to the infinite possibilities in human nature. There must be realism, but the realism must be balanced by a certain wonder and appreciation of the potentials of kindliness in human beings.

Fourth, both secular and religious historians must be relativists; that is, cultivate the feeling that all standards are subject to change and moral codes are relative to time and place. This does not mean that man is immersed in history; for man may also transcend history. Believing in relativism also implies that the good historian must give religion its due, just as he gives other factors—economic, political, and intellectual—their due. There appears to be a tendency to ignore or minimize the role of religion in history as the story gets closer to the present. The average college text in European history, I am told, devotes 30 percent of its allocated space on the Middle Ages to religious developments, but only 2 percent to religion after 1800. No one doubts that specifically religious ideas, religious images, religious institutions, and religious influences were not as dominant in the Europe of 1800 as in 1500, but surely 2 percent is too little. This economic historian would suggest that the economic and political philosophies of modern times—and I have in mind Naziism, Fascism, and Communism—to the extent to which they have moved people—have utilized a religious dynamic. They have appealed to religious emotions, organized themselves along lines strikingly similar to the medieval church, and made demands upon their followers that are best described as religious. Not only is religion still a major force in the world, but one could justifiably argue that, given these powerful pseudo-religions, we live in a more religious age than even the Middle Ages.

In addition to the four qualities and attitudes he shares with his secular colleagues, the LDS historian has certain distinctive qualities or advantages in writing the history of his people. He is obliged to know something about doctrine, and thus has an appreciation of the historical importance of doctrinal questions. Second, he is obliged to recognize the value of the individual man and woman as objects of historical investigation and to admit the possibility that individual wills, passions, and perceptions of the divine, can be active agents in the historical process. And third, he has an obligation to apply in his professional work the doctrine of consecration and stewardship. He must regard the work of historical inquiry as a way of sanctifying himself, as a way of exercising his stewardship. And this means that he has an added incentive to be diligent, hardworking, and honest—even when honesty (i.e., fidelity to the documents) forces him to speak contrary to the usual ideas on the subject. Historical research conducted with scientific rigor is for him not only a professional requisite but a spiritual adventure as well. Research into the history of the Church is not only a vocation, but a religious experience.

If we in the History Division do our work properly, we will come to be associated in the minds of our colleagues, whether at BYU, in the institutes, at the universities, or in the Church departments, with a certain attitude toward history, with the quality of our concern about it, with the sense of reverence and responsibility with which we approach our assignments. To say this another way, our self-image and our public image will be influenced by the quality of our individual religious faith and life. Indeed, our attitude toward the past will be like our attitudes toward our contemporary fellow beings. There will be a certain reverence and respect for the documents we work with, a certain feeling for human tragedy and triumph in history. We will try to understand before we condemn, and if we condemn we will do it with the sense that we, too, being human, are involved in any judgment we may make of others. We will also not use history as a storehouse from which deceptively simple moral lessons may be drawn at random. We will not know it all. We will neither sell our fellow human beings short, nor overrate them. Behind the personal decisions and the vast impersonal forces of history we will also see divine purposes at work. We will look for the working of God both in the whirlwinds and in the still small voices.

There is another thing that excites me about our work. The ultimate purpose of our inquiries is not in the establishment of certain objective facts, such as dates, places, numbers, and names—important as these are—but in the encounter with human beings. LDS history is the history of Latter-day Saints, in their mutual relationships, in their conflicts and contacts, in their social intercourse and in their solitude and estrangement, in their high aspirations, and in their depravity. Only persons live in history—live and move and struggle and create and destroy. So if we are to fulfill our obligations, we must be responsive to the whole amplitude of human concerns—to human life in all its rich variety and diversity, in all its misery and grandeur, in all its ambiguity and contradictions.

There is one other aspect of our responsibility that concerns me deeply. I certainly don't know the answer, the solution, but I would like to have you join me in thinking about it for a moment. I suppose it has impressed itself on my mind because of the events that have surrounded the announcement of and reactions to the revelation of 9 June [1978] on the priesthood. Early Christian history consisted of stories, of testimonies, of narratives of personal experience. For example:

> In those days Jesus of Nazareth gathered tax collectors and sinners around him and told them a story. "Once upon a time," he began, "there lived a man who had a hundred sheep. One day one of the sheep was lost. The man left the flock on its own and went off to look for the lost sheep. After a long time and much trouble he found it, happily put it on his shoulders and brought it back to the flock." (Luke 15; cf. Ezek. 34:5–6)
>
> Now among the audience was a young woman who was carrying a purse with money in it. While Jesus was telling his story a coin fell out of her purse and rolled away. She immediately jumped up and ran after the coin until she caught it. The rest of the audience looked very severe and said to Jesus, "Master, tell this woman not to distract us while we're listening."
>
> Jesus smiled and told them another story. "Many years ago there lived a woman who had ten drachmas. One day she lost one drachma. She searched through the whole house and shone a light into every corner until at last she found the coin she had lost. Full of joy, she called all her friend and neighbors together and told them the good news of how she had found the drachma."

Obviously Jesus spent a good part of his public life telling stories, but these were not all personal experience stories. He borrowed the story of the lost sheep, for example, from another storyteller, the prophet Ezekiel, and maybe Ezekiel retold it from someone else. If we compare the stories in Ezekiel and Luke, we discover that they do not agree word for word. Retelling doesn't necessarily require literal repetition; it includes altering the text. Immediately after this story in Luke we find the story of the lost coin, implying that this story is also connected in tradition with the story of the lost sheep. It may well be a retelling, for it transposes the story of the lost sheep from its setting in a pre-monetary economic system into a literary form appropriate to a monetary economy. Is it legitimate to modernize metaphors in order to make a traditional story more meaningful? The Italians would give a resounding affirmative. In fact, they have a saying: "Se non e vero, e ben trovato," which means, roughly, "Even if it isn't true, it's a good idea." George Santayana probably said it better: "Sometimes we have to change the truth in order to remember it."

Early Christian history transmitted itself in a chain of retellings of stories—of testimonies. This was the vehicle of proselyting and conversion; it also built the experience of life and fostered the salvation of the disciples. But in Greek culture storytelling (or what came to be called myth) was subordinate to argument or logos. Mythmakers' stories were subjected to the arguments of the philosophers, who tended to denigrate testimony into a second place. And ultimately, there was a tendency to drive narrative and testimony out of Christian literature through demythologization. Another influence tended to discourage the creative retelling of stories, and that was the concept of the closed canon. The core of God's message to humankind ended with the Old and New Testaments. There was to be no retelling or further telling of stories in accordance with the contemporary situation. Endless repetition of scripture replaced creative adaptation of the gospel spirit in stories and metaphors, appropriate to the contemporary scene.

What a glorious thing when the Prophet Joseph reopened the canon of scripture, reintroduced testimony, and revived the practice of storytelling or what the scholars call myth-telling. We have got to convey, in some way, the importance of this part of the Restoration to the readers of Latter-day Saint history.

Ernst Cassirer suggests that language is not only man's instrument of reason, but reflects his mythmaking or storytelling tendency as well. Language, he said, exhibits two entirely different modes of thought: it expresses itself in discursive logic (i.e., common sense and science), and also in creative imagination (i.e., in the development of explanatory narratives or myths). Reason and mythmaking are both avenues to truth and beauty and goodness. Man requires and benefits from both reason and poetry, both reason and imagination, both reason and religion. If reason helps man to think objectively, myth enables him to utilize and exhibit the power of subjective feeling of the poetic aspect of life.

In trying to keep abreast of developments in the field of religion I have become fascinated with the effective influence in Jewish tradition of Hassidism. Among these people the narrative tradition is alive and prospering. There are marvelous collections of Hassidic tales. One of the most exciting I have read recently is *Souls on Fire: Portraits and Legends of Hasidic Masters.*[2] Through the stories in this collection the narrator communicates an experience in such a way that the narrator and the listener cannot avoid becoming closely involved in the experience. Our people came close to something of the same nature in the Faith-Promoting Series of the 1880s and 1890s. The purpose of the stories is moral instruction; that is, doing something with the reader. Stories based on historical experiences are transformed into the experiences of those who read. The stories told in our testimony meetings and in our temple services perpetuate this tradition. The narratives I am speaking about are more than reflections—the sacred experiences to which they bear witness continue to live in them. The wonder that is narrated becomes marvelous and the listener has a sacred experience that he will then relate to his family and friends and ward. We've heard some of this as a sequel to the revelation of June 9.

Listen to this from Martin Buber:

> A rabbi, whose grandfather had been a pupil of Baal Shem Tov, was once asked to tell a story. "A story ought to be told," he said, "so that it is itself a help," and his story was this. "My grandfather was paralyzed. Once he

> was asked to tell a story about his teacher, and so he told how the holy Baal Shem Tov used to jump and dance when he was praying. My grandfather stood up while he was telling the story and the story carried him away so much that he had to jump and dance to show how the master had done it. From that moment, he was healed. This is how stories ought to be told."

Somehow, we must recognize and keep alive the storytelling, or myth-forming part of our culture. We are an argumentative and reasoning community, but we are also a storytelling community, and we receive spiritual uplift and enjoyment from the exchange of experiences of faith. There is a time for critical history and argument; there is also a time for testimony. This is partly what President Kimball meant, I suppose, when he told the students and faculty of BYU, in his "Second-Century Address," that they must be "bilingual." "As LDS scholars," he said, "you must speak with authority and excellence to your professional colleagues in the language of scholarship; and you must also be literate in the language of spiritual things."[3]

Mind you, I am not suggesting that we convey untrue history. The stories of our history must be proved by the recognized methods of history to be true; they must be tested and subjected to the same critical examination that we give to all our research. But a factual basis is not the only condition for a story to say something to us or move us. Simple retold stories can produce an effect on the hearers that causes them to go and do likewise. I am told that not long ago Elder Howard Hunter introduced President Kimball to a group of Jewish visitors. Our beloved Prophet's intuitive response was: "Gentlemen, our people are the descendants of your brother, Joseph." That was a reminder of the story of our mutual heritage, and recreated, in that way, a very old storytelling community.

Let me close with a final story, this one also from Ezekiel:

> The hand of the LORD was upon me; and the Lord carried me out by the spirit, and set me down in the midst of a valley which was full of bones. He led me all round them, and lo! there were very many of them on the surface of the valley, and they were very dry. Then he said to me,
>
> "O mortal man, can these bones live?"

> And I answered,
> "O Lord GOD, thou knowest."
> Then he said to me,
> "Prophesy over these bones, and say to them, 'O dry bones, hear the word of the LORD! Behold, I am causing breath to enter you, and you shall live. I will put sinews upon you, and will clothe you with flesh and cover you with skin; then I will put breath into you, and you shall live; and you shall know that I am the LORD.'"
> So I prophesied as I had been commanded; and as I prophesied, there was a sound; and lo! there followed a rustling; and the bones came together, bone to its bone. And as I looked, lo! there were sinews upon them, and flesh came up and skin covered them over; but there was no breath in them.
> Then he said to me, "Prophesy to the breath; prophesy, O mortal man, and say, to the breath, 'Thus says the Lord GOD: Come from the four winds, O breath, and breathe into these slain men, that they may live!'"
> So I prophesied as he had commanded me; and the breath came into them, and they lived, and stood upon their feet—an exceedingly great host. (Ezek. 37:1–11)

May we, as the Lord's historians, Ezekiel-like, enter into the valley of the dead and make the dry bones of the past live again. This is my challenge and my prayer, in Jesus' name, Amen.

Chapter Six Notes

1. Since this was prepared for oral delivery only, I have taken liberties with quotations from the scriptures, working from the Edgar J. Goodspeed and J. M. Powis Smith translations of Luke and Ezekiel, and I have not made any attempt to give specific credit to articles and books from which I have borrowed ideas and phrases.

   Some of the ideas and perhaps some of the phrasing in this paper have come from C. T. McIntire, *God, History, and Historians: An Anthology of Modern Christian Views of History* (New York: Oxford University Press, 1977). Essays in that volume that I particularly profited from reading were: Wolfhart Pannenberg, "Revelation as History," 113–32; E. Harris Harbison, "The Marks of a Christian Historian," 331–56; Herbert Butterfield, "Historical Scholarship and Its Relation to Life," 358–72; Georges Florovsky, "The Predicament of the Christian Historian," 407–42; and Eric Cochrane, "What Is Catholic Historiography?" 444–65. The last section of the talk benefits from my reading Harald Weinrich, "Narrative Theology;" Johann Baptist Metz, "A Short Apology of Narrative" in Johann Baptist Metz and Jean-Pierre Jossua, eds., *The Crisis of Religious Language* (New York: Herder and Herder, 1973), 46–96; and also Frank E. Manuel, *Freedom From History and other Untimely Essays* (New York: New York University Press, 1971), 3–21.

I have also profited from reading: Christopher Dawson, *Progress and Religion: An Historical Enquiry* (London: Sheed and Ward, 1937); and *The Historic Reality of Christian Culture: A Way to the Renewal of Human Life* (Westport, Conn.: Greenwood Press, 1979); Herbert Butterfield, *Christianity and History* (New York: Scribner, 1950); E. Harris Harbison, *Christianity and History: Essays* (Princeton, N.J.: Princeton University Press, 1964); Page Smith, *The Historian and History* (New York: A. A. Knopf, 1964); Arnold Toynbee, *An Historian's Approach to Religion* (New York: Oxford University Press, 1956); Ernst Cassirer, *Language and Myth* (New York: Dover Publications, 1946); Robert N. Bellah, *Beyond Belief: Essays on Religion in a Post-Traditional World* (New York: Harper and Row, 1970); and George Santayana, *The Life of Reason: Or the Phases of Human Progress* (New York: Scribner's Sons, 1914).

2. Eliezer Wiesel, *Souls on Fire: Portraits and Legends of Hasidic Masters* (New York: Random House, 1972).
3. Spencer W. Kimball, "Second-Century Address," BYU *Studies* 16 (summer 1976): 446.

Chapter 7

Personal Reflections on Mormon History

I HAVE DECIDED TO PRESENT a few observations that have come to me as I have had the pleasure of reading in diaries and letters, books and manuscripts, of some of the early Saints.

The first observation is that becoming a Mormon was a "freeing experience" for those who joined the Church during the first thirty or forty years of its history. Most of those who heard the gospel message in the early nineteenth century were very serious about religion—and their parents were equally serious. To most of them, living a proper and God-fearing life involved the repression of desires and instincts that today seem perfectly healthy and wholesome. One could not dance, listen to a violin, go for a nature walk on Sunday, read a novel, or attend a comedy at the theater. Many of these early converts had a strong sense of guilt and they expressed that guilt in a sanctimonious demeanor and grave countenance. They gave every appearance of looking on the serious side of things that, in reality, had no serious side—regarding humor as incompatible with religion. It was said that Brigham Young's brother, Joseph, had never been seen to smile during the six years before he became a Mormon.

Happily, the teachings of Joseph Smith "released" converts from such strict beliefs. Under his influence, the early Saints were encouraged to shed the artificially solemn mantle that contempo-

---

Paper presented at the Mormon History Association annual meeting, Omaha, Nebraska, 6 May 1983. First published as "Personal Reflections on Mormon History," *Sunstone* 8 (July–August 1983): 41–45.

rary religion seemed to insist upon. By following his example, they could be both serious and playful; pious, but not inhibited. There was spontaneity, joviality, and a combination of good humor and seriousness of purpose that made the Church attractive to many. Humor and religion were finally reconcilable. Mormonism taught that men and women are that they might have joy, and that they might have it more abundantly. Mormons were happy because the restored gospel permitted them to develop all facets of their personalities, allowing them to participate in recreational and cultural activities and to enjoy a positive attitude towards sexuality. Whatever their trials, whatever the obstacles they had to overcome as members of the Church, they enjoyed a fuller and more joyful life than they would have lived in the culture in which they were brought up. Partly with this in mind, Brigham Young once declared, "I feel like shouting hallelujah all the time when I think that I ever knew Joseph Smith, the Prophet."[1]

This brings me to a second observation, namely, that a sense of humor played an important role in sustaining the Saints under difficult circumstances. There was, for them, no conflict between piety and moderate levity. The interspersing of spiritual communion with boisterous activity shocked many other so-called Christians, but it prepared the Saints for the arduous and exacting life that faced them. Their diaries suggest that their lives could be exhilarating and exciting even when there was hardship and want. Mormonism loosened the Saints up, as it were, offering some relief from the tense and humorless pursuit of immediate goals. It gave them balance, helped them enjoy the pick-and-shovel aspect of life and helped them overcome sorrow and frustration. There was hope and buoyancy, optimism and faith. Acceptance of the new and everlasting covenant served to expand their souls. Humor helped them dispose of contradictions, conflicts, and frustrations in a socially healthy manner. What modern missionary could not sympathize with Parley P. Pratt who, upon returning to his digs one cold, wet, disappointing night is said to have disrobed, bounced onto one knee with a quick, "Dear Lord, bless Parley, Amen," and then scrambled into bed before his startled companion could even get the door closed?

I especially like the diary of a sister who reports the neighborhood gossip. One neighbor woman who apparently "wore the pants" in her family is reported to have become angry, grabbed a broom, and pursued her husband through the house, finally cornering him under the bed with a rain of blows. "Come out," she cried, "come out." "No," he retorted. "I'm staying right here. I'll show you who holds the priesthood in this house!"

Or, here is Wilford Woodruff's account of a missionary breakfast:

> In those days it was the custom of the Missourians to ask you to eat even though they were hostile to you; so he asked us to take breakfast. . . . He knew we were Mormons; and as soon as we began to eat, he began to swear about the Mormons. He had a large platter of bacon and eggs, and plenty of bread on the table, and his swearing did not hinder our eating, for the harder he swore the harder we ate, until we got our stomachs full; then we arose from the table, took our hats, and thanked him for our breakfast. The last we heard of him he was still swearing. I trust the Lord will reward him for our breakfast.[2]

Dining with a cursing mobster hardly sounds inviting, but Wilford Woodruff's sweetly reasonable tone and his skill in bringing out the incongruity of the situation suggest that the early Saints enjoyed the comic reenactment of experiences shared during the rough days in Missouri.

Pioneer humor, as found in letters, diary entries, missionary stories, occasional pranks, and the bestowal of nicknames, was a means of attacking pretension, hypocrisy, vanity, and excessive pride. I like the way the younger intelligentsia of 1870 parodied the pompous hyperbole used in speeches of certain leaders as they commemorated the settling of the Salt Lake Valley in 1847. "Twenty-three years ago," wrote one youthful editor, "at six o'clock in the morning, this whole territory was one vast, howling wilderness. The red Indian scoured the plain where now our plain women scour the floors, while the sagebrush and greasewood, towering in majesty over it, lent a grateful shade to the bloodthirsty cricket and the carnivorous grasshopper. The modest mouse and timid bedbug went forth, hand in hand, peacefully, over this broad land, with none to molest or make them afraid. . . . Everything was dull, dark and torpid; the world needed waking up."[3]

The Saints' sense of humor did not undermine their loyalty to the Church, but instead gave them a strong sense of group identity and illustrated the weaknesses and strengths of their own movement. More generally, it helped them develop the cultural pride that one would expect of God's chosen people.

A third observation has to do with the nature of our apostate literature and of the people who have written it. Sooner or later, every Mormon historian has to come to grips with this literature—the writing of Philastus Hurlbut, John C. Bennett, John Hyde Jr., Fanny and T. B. H. Stenhouse, Hans Freece, and others. By and large, the writers of these books were persons of talent and sensitivity who had once made a total commitment to Mormonism, must have felt a sense of guilt about leaving the faith, and sought to purge that guilt by writing about it. They felt a compulsion to explain to the group—and perhaps to themselves—why they had left. Because the Saints were persecuted throughout much of the nineteenth century, their sense of guilt must have been especially acute. And because these people had strongly identified with Mormonism for many years, in seeking to create a new role for themselves "in the world," they simply kept talking and writing about it, now taking a negative instead of a positive tack. Torn between love and hate, uneasy about laughing at a religion they had once immersed themselves in so ardently and one that was regarded so dearly by people they loved, they poured out their vitriol in self justification. Angry about punctured dreams, broken promises, and human weaknesses, they justified their decision to break from their moorings by turning around and attacking the culture, values, beliefs, and standards that once guided their lives.

One wishes that, instead of the shallow diatribes and bitter epithets, they had written more about how they felt when they joined the movement. What was it in Mormonism that attracted them and obtained their allegiance? Through what stages did they go in their subsequent disillusionment? Wouldn't it have been helpful to future Saints if they had provided a description of the struggles of conscience they went through before they made the final agonizing withdrawal from the Church? Was the creative part of their "expose" not, in reality, a merciless interrogation of their own motives and character? Why did the most virulent apostasy often occur among people who were once the most confiding, the most obedient? And is there not a lesson here for all of us—that a healthy discipleship is not sycophancy, that it is not healthy to be either fanatically for or against? Is there not danger in becoming such hysterical, uncompromising advocates that we may reverse ground and begin to focus too heavily on the shortcomings?

Psychologists talk about the law of reversed effect, a principle that states that our efforts to keep from having wrong ideas can be so determined and make us so tense that our chances of accepting those very ideas are actually magnified. I saw this principle in action in Italy at the end of World War II when, frequently, those who had been the most fanatical Fascists became fanatical Communists. In religion, our difficult struggles with conscience require a certain relaxation and surrender. This is true not only in our personal lives but also in the study of Church history. We should give the Lord and the Holy Ghost a chance to help us see things in perspective—the failures along with the triumphs, the achievements along with the deficiencies and imperfections. We must have neither exaggerated expectations nor cynical doubts about what our history can demonstrate.

This brings me to the fourth observation, namely, that our prophets and other leaders were great men and women, but they were also human beings. I know that it sounds silly to say that, but so much of our literature suggests that our leaders were above human weakness and foible that it is necessary to keep reminding ourselves that they were also capable of human error, that they were something short of divine. What Lorenzo Snow said of Joseph Smith is worth repeating:

> I saw Joseph Smith the Prophet do things which I did not approve of; and yet . . . I thanked God that He would put upon a man who had these imperfections the power and authority which He placed upon him . . . for I knew I myself had weakness and I thought there was a chance for me. These same weaknesses . . . I knew were in Heber C. Kimball, but my knowing this did not impair them in my estimation. I thanked God I saw these imperfections.[4]

Even Brigham Young, who loved Joseph Smith with a constancy that bordered on idolatry, admitted that he sometimes thought that Joseph was not always right in his management of affairs. "It gave me sorrow of heart to see this," he said, but "I clearly saw and understood that if I was to harbor a thought in my heart that Joseph could be wrong in anything, I would begin to lose confidence in him and that feeling would grow until at last I would have the same lack of confidence in his being the mouthpiece for the Almighty." So Brigham decided to let the Lord deal with Joseph's failings. "Though I admitted in my feelings and knew all the time that Joseph was a human being and subject to err, it was none of my business to look after his faults. He was called of God; and if God had a mind to leave him to himself and let him commit an error, that was no business of mine. . . . Though he had his weaknesses," Brigham continued, "he was all that any people could require a true prophet to be."[5]

Unfortunately, Joseph Smith's contemporaries did not leave a record of just what faults the founding prophet had. Was he sometimes arrogant in his treatment of others? Was he a little too physical for contemporary dispositions? Did he occasionally lack good judgment in his choice of assistants and advisors? Did his decisions on political matters seem to smack of expediency? Although he maintained complete confidence in his calling and in the validity of his revelations, the Prophet's personal diary shows that he was fully aware of his own weaknesses and found it a struggle to live worthily in every respect. The diary also reveals an abundance of desirable and wholesome human traits. He prayed often—to be forgiven, for help in overcoming his weaknesses, for his personal salvation. He loved people: he loved Emma, he loved his children, he loved his parents, he loved his brothers and sisters, he loved old people, he loved tiny children, he loved boys, he loved girls, he loved to have people around him. Clearly a warm and engaging personality, he kissed babies, took children for rides in the country, put cranky children on his lap to be lulled to sleep, played horsy with his children, played ball with the boys, and pulled sticks with the junior Nauvoo Legion. He was extremely generous and far more interested in helping people than in making a profit—a fact that helps to explain why his businesses failed. He loved learning; he took classes and encouraged others to do so, enjoyed lectures, and always sought to know more. He believed that the world was a wonderful place, and he wanted to enjoy and understand it—a healthy attitude for an imperfect human being striving to improve himself.

Many of you know I have spent several years studying Brigham Young. Did he also have imperfections? Clearly, he did. He could be harsh in his censure. He occasionally showed contempt for intellectuality. He was inclined to stretch the truth in his use of hyperbole. He could be very stubborn. And he sometimes called upon people to make sacrifices that most would describe as unconscionable.

But because he was human in these respects, he was also human in ways that caused thousands to love him, admire him, imitate him, and seek his advice. He cried when he saw the suffering of helpless people. His compassion for orphans caused him to invite dozens into his household. He was hard on men who neglected their wives or treated widows unfairly; he was patient with violators of Church standards; he was a good listener, had a sense of humor, and could be very spiritual. In short, as is the case with most of us, his humanness had a positive side that overshadowed the negative. Is it possible that the Lord chose Joseph to be the leader in the restoration of the gospel because his human qualities were an indispensable accompaniment to his revelatory qualities? Is it also possible the Lord chose Brigham Young to lead the Church during the late Nauvoo, Winter Quarters, and early Great Basin periods precisely because of his human qualities, both those which we assess today as being positive and those we might regard as negative?

Brigham was a short-legged man with powerful shoulders and a massive chest whose forceful voice urged a whole generation of Saints to build the Kingdom of God in a desolate and inhospitable region. He gave the appearance of being a hard man—one who did not hesitate to call a spade a spade, one whose tongue cut down hypocrites, betrayers, and malingerers. Upon his departure from Missouri, according to a diary entry made by one who heard him give an address to friends, he cursed the Missourians:

> Bro. Brigham arose and [made] some pointed and appropriate remarks. He called upon the Lord to bless this place for the good of the Saints, and curse every Gentile who should attempt to settle here with sickness, rottenness, and death. Also to curse the land of Missouri, that it might cease to bring forth grain or fruit of any kind to its inhabitants, and that they might be cursed [with] sickness, rottenness and death, that their flesh might consume away on their bones, and their blood be turned into maggots and that their torments never cease.

In his sermons he sometimes used strong metaphors: he would whip out his bowie knife to fight evil, he would scatter the enemy across lots, he would drive the sword of righteousness to its plummet.

But perhaps these violent expressions were only a cover for Brigham's basically non-violent feelings. (For he was basically non-violent.) Perhaps his verbal ferocity masked a tender, softhearted person who was ashamed to admit his compassion because he was afraid people would think him feminine and cowardly. It is possible that his sarcastic criticism of others was an external indication of discontentment with his own ambivalence.

Perhaps his essential nature is more clearly indicated by his statement, made just a few years after cursing the Missourians, about a horde of hungry grasshoppers who almost devoured his fields of grain:

> Last season when the grasshoppers came on my crops, I said, "Nibble away, I may as well feed you as to have my neighbors do it; I have sown plenty, and you have not raised any yourselves." And when the harvest came, [he said] you would not have known that there had been a grasshopper there. . . . Pay attention to what the Lord requires of you and let the balance go.[6]

And so his solution to the grasshopper problem was simply to plant as much as possible in the good years and store the surplus to take care of the years of drought and grasshopper incursions.

Which was the real Brigham and which was the facade? Was he a kindly, benevolent, tender-hearted father-figure or the sarcastic, hate-spouting chief of the Danites? As he systematically dressed down some people, even close associates, was he really chastising them, or was he, by chance, talking to himself? Was his criticism of Orson Pratt the result of a considered judgment that Orson's doctrines were wrong? Or was it, instead, an argument with his reasonably certain self that his own doctrinal insight, untutored as it was, was nevertheless a more accurate reflection of the divine nature than the systematically thought-out speculations of the educated scholar? Should he be considered a generous man because he put dozens of children not his own through school, or a skinflint because he adamantly refused to raise the wages of some young men he had employed to survey for the transcontinental railroad? Should he be thought of as a financial wizard because he was one of the most successful businessmen in western America, or as a failure because so many of his enterprises—the manufacture of iron, the manufacture of sugar, the colonization of southern Nevada, and the Deseret Alphabet—were unsuccessful?

I want to make one final observation. My reading of pioneer diaries, letters, and other available documents has impressed me with the nobleness of the lives of many individual Latter-day Saint men and women—persons who, despite suffering and anguish, remained faithful to their highest ideals. These included converts from abroad who joined the Church and were disclaimed by their parents, brothers, and sisters; women who remained with the Church though they had to give up the security that would have been provided by their unfaithful husbands; people who courageously stood up for righteous principles despite society's opposition; persons such as Oliver Cowdery, B. H. Roberts, and Andrew Jenson who had similar difficulties with stubborn personalities or unwise bureaucrats inside the Church; Florence Jacobsen, who kept fighting for what she knew was good for the Church; Sterling McMurrin, who remained sweet and supportive despite certain authorities' objections to some of the beliefs that he expressed and knew to be unwelcome.

The pioneers' capacity for being courageous in the face of disaster, smiling in the face of disappointment, persisting in the face of failure, and standing up for right and principle are worthy of our remembrance. I think of Robert Gardner, who heard his name called from the stand to go on a colonizing mission to southern Utah to raise cotton. He was to start "right away." He reported in his personal history, "I looked and spat, took off my hat, scratched my head, thought, and said, 'All right.'" He goes on:

> The next day I went to the City and saw George A. Smith in the Historian's office. He laughed when I went in, and said, "Don't blame anyone but me. The President [Brigham Young] told me to get a list of names suitable for that mission, so I thought of you for one, and thought you would be willing to go if called, so I put your name down. If you don't want to go, step to the President's office and ask him to take your name off the list and he will do it."
>
> I said, "I expect he would, but I shan't try him. I have come to find what kind of an outfit is wanted and when to go."
>
> He said, "This is the kind of men we want." So he advised me, if I could sell out to good advantage, to take one of my families and go down and make a start. So I came home and worked to that end. I left a hired man and my son William, a boy fifteen years old, to gather the crops. I traded for a span of mules, and started on my mission the 12th of November 1861.[7]

Whatever his personal shortcomings, and he certainly had some, Robert Gardner was a Latter-day Saint worth remembering.

I think of Sariah Louisa Chamberlain Redd, the grandmother of President Marion G. Romney. Sariah was the daughter of Solomon Chamberlain, who had been one of the very first persons to read the Book of Mormon and join the Church, and had been an 1847 pioneer to the Salt Lake Valley. Sariah, from the age of nine, had to look after her aged father during his last years, once rescuing him from a flood. After his death she supported herself by going from house to house to do spinning and weaving. Ultimately she joined a household as a plural wife and gave birth to fourteen children and reared them to be industrious citizens and faithful Latter-day Saints.

I think of Mary Rollins Lightner, who, as a girl of fifteen, risked her life to save the printer's signature sheets of the Book of Commandments; of Drusilla Dorris Hendricks, whose husband was gravely injured by the Missouri mob and who, despite her personal revulsion, allowed her son to join the Mormon Battalion. I think of Ephraim Hanks, who discovered too late that a company had gone from Salt Lake City to rescue the Willie and Martin handcart companies of 1856 and who, despite the danger of freezing to death alone in the heavy snow, took off alone to help out in some way in that valiant rescue effort. I think of Jacob Hamblin, who placed himself in front of the gun of his captain to save the life of a poor and helpless Indian. I think of Helmut Huebner, an idealistic young German who knowingly endangered and ultimately lost his life in a struggle against a force he recognized to be evil. There are many examples of such heroism. They help to assuage one's own disenchantment, disappointment, and frustrations. They help one forget the blindness of certain self-important people in our history and keep in mind instead the many humble and valiant disciples who have practiced the pure love of Christ.

Life is inevitably complex. People are not always predictable, and organizations, even the Lord's church, are not always benign. The reporting of our history, if readers are to have confidence in it, must reflect these ambiguities and complexities. Just as important, we must demonstrate our true love for those who have questions, who are perplexed by certain aspects of our history, who are disturbed about a few personalities and policies. While being true to our own sense of integrity we must help others be true to theirs, without becoming bitter against those with punctured illusions who seem to enjoy the bad truths more than the good truths. We must practice warmth in our personal relationships with people of varying degrees of faith, belief, and practice.

I believe, with Brigham Young, in doing the best we can and leaving the balance to God. We must not become cynical; we must not become morbidly preoccupied with some of the unsavory elements in our peoples' history. If our history furnishes examples of man's inhumanity, it also furnishes examples of man's humanity. We should not hesitate to mention both. Both ancient and modern scriptures make clear that God is fully aware that he has to depend upon imperfect human instruments in accomplishing his divine purposes.

Let me repeat an observation made by the renowned Roman Catholic theologian, Hans Kung: "The neglect of truthfulness leads to hypocrisy, but the exaggeration of truthfulness leads to destructive fanaticism." We must guard against both. Let us here resolve that our histories will be marked by thorough research, superior writing, and the display of the true spirit of Latter-day Saint-ism. Just as drama effected catharsis of the soul for the ancient Greek audience, may our history give us and our readers another experience, another soul, new understanding to guide us as we attempt to learn more from the Mormon experience of the past.

Chapter Seven Notes

1. Brigham Young, *Discourses of Brigham Young*, compiled by John A. Widtsoe (Salt Lake City: Deseret Book, 1978), 458.
2. Matthias F. Cowley, *Wilford Woodruff: Fourth President of The Church of Jesus Christ of Latter-day Saints—History of his Life and Labors as Recorded in His Daily Journals* (Salt Lake City: Deseret News, 1909), 50.
3. *Keep-A-Pitchin in* (1 August 1870): 42.
4. As quoted in Stanley B. Kimball, *Heber C. Kimball: Mormon Patriarch and Pioneer* (Urbana: University of Illinois Press, 1981), xv.
5. Brigham Young, *Journal of Discourses*, 26 vols. (Liverpool: F. D. Richards, 1855–86), 4:297.
6. Brigham Young, *Journal of Discourses*, 3:159.
7. Robert Gardner, "History of Robert Gardner, Jr.: Written by himself at St. George, Utah, 1884 Jan. 7," photocopy of typescript, page 38, L. Tom Perry Special Collections, Harold B. Lee Library, Brigham Young University, Provo, Utah.

Chapter 8

The Questing Spirit in Mormon History, 1880–1933

"THE GLORY OF GOD is intelligence, or, in other words, light and truth," the Lord told Joseph Smith (D&C 93:36). And Mormons have remained committed to the truth. As Brigham Young put it: "Our religion embraces all truth and every fact in existence, no matter whether in heaven, earth, or hell. A fact is a fact [and] all truth issues forth from the Fountain of truth."[1] But from its inception, Mormonism also saw itself as a "practical religion." Its theology was "practical" and so was its education. Brigham Young declared that "The religion of Jesus Christ is a matter-of-fact religion, and taketh hold of the every-day duties and realities of this life."[2] "Practical religion" was a popular theme in Church magazines, manuals, and books, and there was some mistrust of the theoretical, speculative "philosophies of men." That there existed a certain tension between "practical" religion and "intellectualized" religion is not surprising. Latter-day Saint prophets did not wish to "put down" either.

Education was a good thing, and knowledge highly desirable, but the pride that often accompanied higher learning was to be carefully guarded against: "O the vainness, and frailties, and the foolishness of men!" cried the Book of Mormon prophet. "When they are learned they think they are wise, and they hearken not

---

Previously unpublished paper presented at the Sunstone Symposium, Washington, D.C., 28 April 1995.

unto the counsel of God, for they set it aside, supposing they know of themselves, wherefore, their wisdom is foolishness and it profiteth them not. And they shall perish. But to be learned is good if they hearken unto the counsels of God" (2 Nephi 9:28–29).

The University of Deseret, founded in 1850 and accelerated in 1869, offered advanced training for Latter-day Saint men and women. As the number of young people grew, Brigham Young established the Brigham Young Academy (1875) in Provo, Utah, and the Brigham Young College in Logan (1877) and laid plans for a Young University in Salt Lake City.[3] A few years later (1888) Wilford Woodruff organized a Church Board of Education, founded the Latter-day Saint College (also variously known as the Salt Lake Stake Academy and the Latter-day Saint University), and initiated an ambitious program under which each stake was instructed to establish its own academy. These academies were essentially high schools, although from the beginning the Brigham Young Academy in Provo and Brigham Young College in Logan also had a "normal" program for training teachers and eventually became universities or part of universities. Other academies developed into junior colleges and some later became universities.[4] A number of promising students were given grants and loans to pursue degrees in the Midwest and East with the understanding that they would return to teach in the Church education system.

Mormon Students Go East

A substantial exodus of Mormon students began in the 1880s and 1890s when several bright young Latter-day Saint men and women matriculated at eastern and midwestern universities to study law, physics, engineering, architecture, home economics, and other subjects. Most of them retained a strong allegiance to Mormonism through their university experience and returned to Utah full of new ideas and anxious to share them with their fellow Latter-day Saints. For some of them, it was Mormonism's first confrontation with serious, persistent intellectual challenges.[5]

One of the forerunners of this movement was James E. Talmage.[6] Talmage was born in 1862 in Hungerford, Berkshire, England, the first son and second child of eight. He attended local Berkshire and Wiltshire schools and was the Oxford diocesan prize scholar when he was twelve. In 1873 the family was converted to Mormonism, and in 1876, when James was thirteen, they emigrated to the United States and settled in Provo, Utah, where James enrolled at Brigham Young Academy. After five years he graduated first in his class with majors in English and science and a teaching certificate. He was at once engaged to teach at the academy.

Eager to pursue a higher education in science, Talmage attended Lehigh and Johns Hopkins universities (1882–84) and returned to teach at the academy, serving as professor of chemistry and geology. While in Provo he became an American citizen, Provo city councilman, alderman, justice of the peace, High Councilor, and stake superintendent of schools. He married Merry May Booth and the couple had eight children. In 1888, he became principal of the Brigham Young Academy but was quickly called by the Church to serve as first president of the new Latter-day Saint College in Salt Lake City (1888–93).

Impressed with his academic achievements and religious orthodoxy, the First Presidency commissioned Talmage to prepare a text in theology for use in Church schools and religion classes. The book, *The Articles of Faith*, was based on Sunday lectures delivered in 1893 and 1894 in the Assembly Hall in Salt Lake City. The first lecture was attended by more than five hundred; the last, six months later, by nearly thirteen hundred. After review by a committee of General Authorities and Board of Education members, *The Articles of Faith* was published in 1899 and has served as a standard Mormon reference to the present time.[7] The work is important as the first extensive statement of Mormon doctrine and practice since the Woodruff Manifesto of 1890. A moderate, carefully reasoned work with scriptural support, *The Articles of Faith* continues to be a good introduction to basic Mormon beliefs.

Meanwhile, Talmage was president of the University of Utah, 1894–97, from which he resigned in 1897 to devote full time to the Deseret Chair of Geology, which he held until his resignation in 1907 to serve as a consulting mining geologist and engineer. He was awarded a Ph.D. in 1896 by Illinois Wesleyan University for non-resident work. He became a fellow of numerous scientific societies in Great Britain and the United States, including the Royal Microscopical Society of London, the Royal Society of Edinburgh, Royal Scottish Geographical Society, Geological Society of London (and of America), the Philosophical Society of Great Britain, and the American Association for the Advancement of Science. In 1911 he was ordained an apostle and became a member of the Council of Twelve. His scientific books included *First Book of Nature*, *Domestic Science*, *Tables for Blowpipe Determination of Minerals*, and *The Great Salt Lake, Present and Past*.[8] His religious books, in addition to *The Articles of Faith*, included *The Story of "Mormonism," The Great Apostasy*, *The House of the Lord*, *Jesus the Christ*, and *The Vitality of "Mormonism."*[9] He had an unusual ability in expository writing and speaking. His connections with learned societies gave him a prestige among Latter-day Saints that was seldom equaled by any other LDS leader of thought. His talks were based on reason, and he defended science from irrational dogma. He died in 1933. The epitaph on his tombstone expresses his scholarly and religious perspective: "Within the Gospel of Jesus Christ There is Room and Place for Every Truth Thus Far Learned by Man or Yet to be Made Known."[10]

Buoyed by Talmage's success, other students and teachers began to flock to out-of-state universities. Joseph M. Tanner, a Brigham Young Academy student named principal of the Brigham Young College in Logan in 1888, left that position in 1891 to study law at Harvard and later became superintendent of LDS Church schools. Tanner took some of his most promising students with him to Harvard, several of whom returned to teach at the Brigham Young College. Among them was John A. Widtsoe, who graduated with highest honors in biochemistry and completed a Ph.D. at the University of Gottingen in Germany. His *Joseph Smith as Scientist* (1908) supported the widely held view of the time that Joseph Smith was a prophet of science as well as of religion, anticipating the "modern" understanding of the nature of matter and even evolution.[11] Widtsoe, as we shall see, became president of Utah State Agricultural College in 1907, president of the University of Utah in 1917, and an apostle in 1921.

What was the relationship, if any, between Mormonism and scientific-technological progress? It was common for Mormons to say, with B. H. Roberts, that since the Restoration "there has come into the world, almost imperceptibly, a more generally diffused and brighter spirit of intelligence than was known before [by which] men have been led to those great discoveries in the arts and sciences and in mechanics, which make our age so wonderful as an age of progress and enlightenment."[12]

Many Latter-day Saints desired to become leaders in the world's advancement. By the outbreak of World War I, many Latter-day Saint leaders had received advanced degrees from large universities. These included two who were later members of the First Presidency (J. Reuben Clark Jr. and Stephen L. Richards); five apostles (James E. Talmage, Stephen L. Richards, Richard R. Lyman, John A. Widtsoe, and Joseph F. Merrill); three members of the First Council of Seventy (Charles H. Hart, Levi Edgar Young, and Oscar A. Kirkham); and five superintendents of Church schools and commissioners of education (Horace H. Cummings, Adam S. Bennion, Joseph F. Merrill, John A. Widtsoe, and Franklin L. West). And, of course, the Latter-day Saint presidents of the University of Utah, Brigham Young University, and Utah State Agricultural College.

Michigan became a popular law school for Latter-day Saints, beginning with James H. Moyle and George Sutherland in 1881. Sutherland had studied law in Utah and obtained his Michigan degree in six months. He later became a U.S. senator and associate justice of the United States Supreme Court. Moyle, who received his degree in 1885, was the first Mormon to have high office in the national government, serving as assistant secretary of the treasury in the cabinet of Woodrow Wilson. Moyle was also a loyal churchman and helped demonstrate that education at an eastern (as opposed to western) university would not necessarily lessen the Mormon student's loyalty to his Church. Sutherland and Moyle were followed at Michigan by Charles H. Hart (1887), who helped prepare Utah's constitution and became a member of the First Council of Seventy. The president of Michigan's class of 1895 was Richard R. Lyman, an engineering student who went on to obtain a Ph.D. from Cornell and who was called to the apostleship in 1918.

His wife, Amy Brown Lyman, who studied at the University of Chicago and did volunteer work with Jane Addams at Hull House, later became general president of the Relief Society. Benjamin Cluff Jr. also graduated from Michigan (1886) and upon completing his master's degree there was named president of Brigham Young University. Don B. Colton, congressman from Utah (1920–32), and William H. King, Utah's senator from 1917 to 1941, were two other Latter-day Saints to obtain their LLBs from Michigan.

Equaling Michigan in popularity among Latter-day Saint students was the University of Chicago. Amy Brown Lyman estimated that there were thirty Utah students with her in 1902, including Alice Louise Reynolds, who had graduated from Brigham Young Academy in 1890, then studied at Michigan, Chicago, California, Columbia, Paris, and Queens College (London) between teaching assignments in English at BYU. Henry D. Moyle and Stephen L. Richards, later members of the Church's First Presidency, and Apostle Albert E. Bowen obtained their law degrees at Chicago. In addition, there were Franklin L. West, who had studied at Stanford before completing a Ph.D. at Chicago in physics and later became Church commissioner of education; Horace H. Cummings, who studied at Chicago and Columbia before serving thirteen years as general superintendent of Church schools (1906–19); Harvey Fletcher, father of stereophonic sound; Ephraim E. Ericksen, professor of philosophy and dean at the University of Utah; and his colleague on the Young Men's Mutual Improvement Association General Board, Arthur L. Beeley, dean of social work at the University of Utah.

At Columbia, Levi Edgar Young of the First Council of Seventy obtained a master's degree in history. Apostle Adam S. Bennion completed a master's degree there in 1912 and a Ph.D. at the University of California, Berkeley, in 1923. Frederick J. Pack, who taught geology at the University of Utah and wrote a defense of evolution for Mormons (*Science and Belief in God*), obtained his Ph.D. in 1906.[13] Lyman L. Daines, dean of the School of Medicine at the University of Utah, completed his Ph.D. at UCB and his M.D. at Rush Medical College. Apostle Joseph F. Merrill studied at Michigan (1889–93), Cornell (1892), and Chicago (1894) and completed a

Ph.D. in physics in 1899 at Johns Hopkins. Franklin S. Harris, president of Brigham Young University, finished his Ph.D. at Cornell.

As these men and women completed their university studies and returned to Utah to begin their careers, often as teachers in the Church system, many were called to positions on Church general boards—Education, Young Men's and Young Women's MIA, Primary, Relief Society, and Sunday School. They wrote articles for Church magazines and manuals for the Sunday School, MIA, and Relief Society. Gradually, higher education was enriching the intellectual atmosphere of Mormon society.

"Liberal" Spokesmen

Of all the advocates of higher education among the Mormons, none was more enthusiastic or optimistic than the popular B. H. Roberts.[14] Born in 1857 into a poor family in Warrington, Lancashire, England, Roberts was named for Brigham Young by his mother, who had just become a converted Mormon. Wife of an alcoholic, she took two of her children and went to Salt Lake City, leaving five-year-old Brigham and his older sister behind. Brigham was not well cared for and wandered the streets as a poverty-stricken, unshepherded Dickensian ragamuffin for four years until, at age nine, he was able to cross the ocean and walk, barefoot, across the plains to Utah.

Settling with his mother in a one-room cabin in Centerville, north of Salt Lake City, Roberts began life as a humble farmhand, then a construction worker. At age fourteen he joined mining camps in western Utah, where he spent evenings gambling and learning to drink, swear, and carouse. Warned that he was on his way to hell, he returned to Centerville, apprenticed himself to a blacksmith (his father's trade), and although poorly educated, attended the University of Deseret, walking twelve miles daily. An avid learner, within three years he graduated at the top of his Normal School class and gave the valedictory address. He married, taught school, and plied his trade as blacksmith until 1880, when he was sent on a proselytizing mission to the southern states.

Roberts became president of the mission in 1883, when he was only twenty-six. He was then sent as a missionary to England, where he served two years as editor of the *Millennial Star*. After his return, he became a journalist, serving briefly as editor of the Salt Lake *Herald*. In 1888, at age of thirty-one, he was sustained to the Council of Seventy, eventually becoming the senior president. He was an effective and vigorous missionary. Having developed his speaking ability in the South, he was one of the Church's greatest orators. Preston Nibley, who watched him preach many times, described his style:

> How often have we seen him arise and face an audience, beginning at first to talk in a modulated tone, so low that he could scarcely be heard, increasing gradually in volume, making a point here and there, and then upon reaching his climax with a perfect Niagara of words, that left us almost breathless, and ending finally in a voice that was scarcely audible. There is power in oratory, and nature never lavished this gift more freely than she did on B. H. Roberts.[15]

Another observer wrote, "When repelling an attack launched against his faith or his people he wields the rapier of defense 'as though the strength of twenty men were in his arm.' He is truly a formidable champion."[16]

Roberts seemed to have a promising political career ahead of him when he was elected by a large majority to the U.S. House of Representatives in 1898. But there was a bitter national outcry because he was a polygamist, and the House refused to seat him. He was appointed Assistant Church Historian in 1902 and held that position until his death in 1933. During World War I, at age sixty, Roberts volunteered for service as a chaplain with the 145th Field Artillery in France.

During most of his adult life, Roberts published extensively: *The Gospel*, *Life of John Taylor*, *Outlines of Ecclesiastical History*, *A New Witness for God*, *The Missouri Persecutions*, *The Rise and Fall of Nauvoo*, *Mormon Doctrine of Deity*, *Defense of the Faith and the Saints*, and *The Mormon Battalion*.[17] He also edited the seven-volume *History of the Church* by Joseph Smith and wrote the six-volume *Comprehensive History of the Church*, most of which had appeared in serial form in the *American* magazine from July 1909 to July 1915 under the title "History of the Mormon Church."

Roberts was a voracious reader, devouring great quantities of history, science, philosophy, and religion. Perhaps no other Mormon leader before or since has mastered such a range of scholarly works, discussing them intelligently and relating them to Latter-day Saint beliefs. Roberts's belief in the divine origins and destiny of Mormonism was unquestioned, but he frequently took a broader view of its place in the heavenly scheme of things than did some of his colleagues. In 1902 Roberts told the Saints that "while the Church of Jesus Christ of Latter-day Saints is given a prominent part in this great drama of the last days, it is not the only force nor the only means that the Lord has employed to bring to pass those things of which His prophets in ancient times have testified."[18] In the scientific and artistic advance of civilization, Roberts saw the hand of God. Mormonism, he said, is "one of the great world-movements for the accomplishment of the mighty purposes of God. It is connected with all the other great world movements that are bringing to pass the revolutions now going on in the earth." Through science, "physical conditions are being brought into existence that will co-ordinate with those spiritual and moral conditions which 'Mormonism' will yet establish, and will bring to pass, the realization of the world's hope for that reign of peace and righteousness called the millennium." Roberts was anxious for Latter-day Saints to take full advantage of educational opportunities in order to advance the cause of God.[19]

Roberts, an independent thinker who believed in human reason aided by divine revelation, left an indelible mark on the scholarly tradition of the Church with his famous manual series, *The Seventy's Course in Theology*, in which he wrote in the last volume:

> It requires striving—intellectual and spiritual—to comprehend the things of God—even the revealed things of God. . . . "Simple faith"—which is so often ignorant and simpering acquiescence, and not faith at all—but simple faith taken at its highest value, which is faith without understanding of the thing believed, is not equal to intelligent faith, the faith that is the gift of God, supplemented by earnest endeavor to find through prayerful thought and research a rational ground for faith—for acceptance of truth; and hence the duty of striving for a rational faith in which the intellect as well as the heart—the feeling—has a place and is a factor. . . . Whatever position other churches and their religious teachers may take, the

> Church of Jesus Christ in the New Dispensation can do no other than to stand for mental activity, and earnest effort to come to a knowledge of truth up to the very limit of man's capacity to find it.[20]

The spirit of learning and intellectual tolerance fostered by Roberts in his prominent Church position was furthered by several Mormon educators of the early twentieth century, foremost of whom was William H. Chamberlin.[21]

Personally, Roberts and Chamberlin were quite different. Roberts was outspoken, obstinate, always ready to interject himself into the fray. Chamberlin was quiet and unassuming. Both men had an insatiable appetite for knowledge, but Roberts was largely self-educated. Chamberlin graduated from the University of Utah (1896), served a three-year mission to Tahiti, studied ancient languages and higher criticism at the University of Chicago (summers of 1901 and 1902), completed a master of arts degree in philosophy from the University of California at Berkeley under George Howison (1906), studied psychology at the University of Chicago (summer 1907), and studied philosophy under Josiah Royce at Harvard (1907–8).

Chamberlin published very little; Roberts, prodigiously. Although Roberts authored numerous doctrinal and historical works, as mentioned earlier, his magnum opus, "The Truth, the Way, and the Life," the theological equivalent of his *Comprehensive History*, remained unpublished until 1994, when two editions were issued, one by BYU *Studies*, edited by John W. Welch, and one by the Roberts family, edited by Stan Larson.[22] Both carry introductory essays by noted scholars, and in both volumes Roberts's text is accompanied by notes of clarification and explanation.

Roberts's intention in "The Truth, the Way, and the Life"—a three-volume typescript—was monumentally ambitious: "a search for *The Truth*, as it relates to the Universe and to man; a consideration of *The Way*, as it relates to the attainment of those ends which may be learned as to the purpose of man's earth-existence; and the contemplation of *The Life*—that will result from the knowledge of the Truth and the Way."[23] The title was chosen, as Truman G. Madsen has observed, "because through a lifetime of reflection he saw that the great system of 'truth' that 'gives unity to all history and proper relationship to all existing things; that fills life with a real meaning, and makes existence desirable,' centers in and is embodied in Jesus the Christ."[24]

Roberts's theology was bold and audacious, for it "combined elements of traditional fundamentalism with the modern liberal doctrine of man and the optimism of the nineteenth century, and it required a bold, rebellious, and specious mind to grasp its full implication." Roberts "not only shaped the outlines of a systematic theology but developed, as well, the perspectives which placed the Church as an institution within the framework of history and provided the Mormon people with the instrument of rationalizing and defending their beliefs and practices."[25]

Self-education, however rigorous and comprehensive, carries inevitable limitations. In nearly every discipline Roberts, though possessing one of the finest minds Mormonism has produced, showed himself a wide-ranging explorer rather than, like Chamberlin, the resident at home in his field. Without the benefit of association with other scholars, Roberts on occasion failed to discriminate between original thinkers and their popular imitators, between faddish trends and enduring movements. Such limitations notwithstanding, Roberts's numerous writings introduced Mormons to some of the most advanced thinkers of the age as no other Church authority could have done.

Though he published little, Chamberlin's contribution to the life of the mind in Mormonism was, like Roberts's, substantial. Chamberlin's influence was in the classroom, where he taught many persons who later served as professors, department heads, and deans in universities attended by Latter-day Saint students. He taught in public schools (1889–91); science and mathematics at the LDS College (1891–97); geology and mathematics, then theology at Brigham Young College (1900–1, 1903–4); philosophy and ancient languages at Brigham Young University (1909–16); philosophy at the University of Utah (1917–20) and the Utah State Agricultural College (1920–21). (Becoming an expert in so many fields would be impossible in modern academia; Chamberlin's competence in so many fields is a reflection of Utah education in the 1890s and early years of the twentieth century.) Fourteen years younger than Roberts, Chamberlin died twelve years earlier, at the age of fifty.

When William H. Chamberlin went to Brigham Young University in 1909, he joined on the faculty his brother Ralph and Henry and Joseph Peterson. Ralph had completed his Ph.D. in biology at Cornell in 1905, the year the Peterson brothers graduated from the University of Chicago. Henry Peterson went on to a master's in psychology at Harvard (1906) and Joseph to a Ph.D. in literature from Chicago (1907). Brigham Young University had recently been confirmed as the Church university (over LDS University in Salt Lake City and Brigham Young College in Logan), and the four new faculty members had high hopes of helping to lift the quality of education at the school to the level of a major university. The four worked energetically—and successfully—to stimulate interest in intellectual pursuits. They spoke to Church groups and student audiences on higher criticism and evolution, and both subjects became popular topics for debate and discussion on campus. Though other Latter-day Saints had advocated evolution as God's means of creation before the Chamberlins and the Petersons, none had attracted so much attention.[26] Ralph Chamberlin spoke at a memorial service commemorating the birth of Darwin and Lincoln and described Darwin as one of the greatest scientific minds of the age. In the school paper he published "The Early Hebrew Conception of the Universe" and "Early Hebrew Legends," drawing upon higher criticism to point out the "constant evolution" of Hebraic thought and "the progressive unfolding of the divine Will" revealed in the Bible.

William Chamberlin published a monograph titled "The Theory of Evolution as an Aid to Faith in God and Belief in the Resurrection" in which the philosophy of "personal idealism" played an important role. Stressing divine immanence in the processes of nature, Chamberlin found in the theory of evolution evidence for faith in the Resurrection. He also spoke of the parabolic and mythical elements of Old Testament writings, which, when properly understood as literary and didactic elements, effectively disarmed petty critics of the Bible who objected to stories such as Jonah and the whale.

Though the modernist ideas of the Chamberlins and the Petersons seem to have met with the enthusiastic approval of many faculty and students, Superintendent of Church Education Horace H. Cummings reported that more than a dozen stake presidents had complained of heresies being taught at BYU by the new faculty members. Opposed to both higher criticism and evolution, Cummings was motivated by concern for the spiritual and religious welfare of the students rather than by scientific concerns. After a brief investigation, he reported the teachers were "applying the evolutionary theory and other philosophical hypotheses to principles of the gospel and to the teachings of the Church in such a way as to disturb, if not destroy, the faith of the pupils."[27] The Petersons and Ralph Chamberlin were named as chief offenders. The Church Board of Education informed the three they would have to alter their teachings or face dismissal.

A storm of controversy was raised in the Salt Lake City and Provo presses, heightened by the publication of a petition reportedly signed by 90 percent of the student body protesting the board's action. Nevertheless, the decision remained, and the Petersons and Ralph Chamberlin left the university for teaching careers outside the Church Educational System. William Chamberlin remained five more years, prepared his lectures with care, and enjoyed the privilege of teaching among his people.[28]

Mormonism had had its first brush with modernism. In a sense, it was mild and successfully contained. There were no books banned, no excommunications or schisms.[29] No official Church position was taken with regard to evolution or higher criticism. In *The Juvenile Instructor* President Joseph F. Smith wrote that the decision had only been not to discuss evolution in Church schools. He described it as "a question of propriety [without] undertaking to say how much of evolution is true and how much false."[30]

By deciding not to decide the evolution question, President Smith avoided a head-on confrontation between the newly educated Saints who found in it support for Mormon doctrine and those of a more traditional persuasion who perceived the seeds of apostasy. By removing such controversial issues from the classroom, authorities hoped to avert a doctrinal crisis. The popularity of the professors' innovative interpretations threatened to undermine the authority of the apostles and prophets as sole adjudicators of Church doctrine.[31]

In the action against the professors, the prerogatives of the priesthood were affirmed but not without adverse repercussions. BYU gained an anti-intellectual reputation that persisted for several years. To many Saints much of the academic world became suspect; professions in the life sciences, religious studies, and philosophy were highly dubious.[32]

Spokesmen for "Moderation"

THE THEOLOGICAL APPROACH of B. H. Roberts was bold and creative, but none of his doctrinal books became standard reference works in the same sense as did two by James E. Talmage. In addition to *The Articles of Faith*, discussed earlier, Talmage's *Jesus the Christ* (1915) is found in nearly every Mormon home. Permeated with Talmage's deep personal piety and stately style, *Jesus the Christ* is a blend of Mormon scripture and conservative biblical scholarship. Whereas Roberts's approach was often to consider alternate points of view broadly before settling on a Mormon position, as in his *Seventies Course in Theology*, Talmage seemed concerned only to present Mormon doctrine with careful precision, buttressed by evidence and argument from non-Mormon sources when available. Talmage's distinguished bearing and orderly presentations made him a popular lecturer. The call of this prominent geologist to the apostleship in 1911 helped allay suspicions after the BYU controversy that the Church was anti-scientific. With a long list of honorary degrees and appointments to international scientific societies, Apostle Talmage was an important figure in the mainstream of Mormon thought and an effective emissary to the non-Mormon world.

Talmage's successor as moderate doctrinal spokesman with a scientific background was John A. Widtsoe.[33] Having served as president of the Utah State Agricultural College (now Utah State University) and University of Utah, Widtsoe was ordained an apostle in 1921. Returning from six years presiding over the European missions, Apostle Widtsoe became the active editor of *The Improvement Era* in 1935. Three years later he began a monthly column in the magazine, entitled "Evidences and Reconciliations," which, continuing to his death in 1952, answered such questions as: How does God have constant knowledge of the whole universe? Was the Fall inevitable? Why are we called a covenant people? The first column responded to the question, What is the attitude of the Church toward science? "Every scientific discovery," said Widtsoe, "may be incorporated into the Gospel, and . . . therefore, there can be no conflict between true religion and correct science. The Church teaches that the laws of nature are but the immutable laws of the Creator of the universe."[34] One must be careful that the facts are accurately observed and that the interpretation of fact be labeled as inference and not be confused with fact, but there is no inherent conflict between science and religion, he stated.

Through *The Improvement Era*, numerous books—*Joseph Smith as Scientist*, *A Rational Theology*, *Priesthood and Church Government*, *An Understandable Religion*, *In Search of Truth*—and many study course manuals and articles, Widtsoe greatly influenced the common understanding of Mormon doctrine.[35] The titles of his column and books are indicative of his approach. He was a systematizer and simplifier who sought to reconcile the fundamentals of Mormonism with the modern world. "Rational" and "understandable" were favorite words in the Widtsoe lexicon. Rather than become engaged in acrimonious controversy, Widtsoe downplayed differences and emphasized similarities. His scientific background enabled him to allay the fears of those who considered science a threat to revealed religion and those who suspected an anti-intellectual bias on the part of some Church leaders. Viewing evolution as only a theory that could be revised by new data, for instance, he maintained an openness to scientific advance without jeopardizing theological orthodoxy.[36] Mormon theology was a rational system of universal, fundamental truths; knowledge of truth was man's highest possession; and true secular (scientific) knowledge and true spiritual (religious) knowledge agree, for truth is one harmonious whole. Revelation and reason were the ways of learning truth. One must have complete freedom to pursue truth.[37]

By training and profession, the dean and chief critic of Mormon social philosophy after William H. Chamberlin was E. E. Ericksen.[38] A son of immigrant Danish farmers, Ericksen attended the Brigham Young College in Logan, where he studied psychology, philosophy, and biblical scholarship under Mosiah Hall and William H. Chamberlin. At the University of Chicago he studied philosophy under James H. Tufts, George H. Mead, and Edward S. Ames. After four years as principal of the Church's Murdock Academy of Beaver, Utah, Ericksen was hired to teach philosophy at the University of Utah (1915–43), where he became, in turn, professor, department head, and dean.

In 1922 the University of Chicago published Ericksen's doctoral dissertation, *The Psychological and Ethical Aspects of Mormon Group Life*, an analysis of three periods of "maladjustment" in Mormon history: Mormons and Gentiles (the Joseph Smith period); Mormons and Nature (territorial period); New Thought and Old Institutions (early twentieth century).[39] Ericksen admired Joseph Smith's sensitivity to the spiritual needs of his people, and he praised Brigham Young's pragmatic genius in conquering a hostile environment, but he was critical of those twentieth-century students and speakers who, he said, had failed to come to grips with the religious challenges of their age. Critical of the Church's conservative posture in a progressive era, Ericksen concluded: "What Mormonism needs today is the vitalization of its institutions, which need to be put into use rather than merely contemplated. . . . When Mormonism finds more glory in working out new social ideals than in contemplating past achievements or the beauty of its own theological system, it will begin to feel its old-time strength."[40]

The year his short book was published, Ericksen was called to serve on the general board of one Church institution most concerned with social programs, the Young Men's Mutual Improvement Association, where, with great energy, he served thirteen years. He was influential in the development of the Church's extensive recreation program, as well as the course of instruction.[41] After Ericksen's release from the board in 1935, he continued to lecture and to write as a social critic decrying the rise of what he called the priestly mentality at the expense of the prophetic.[42] But he remained loyal to his Mormon heritage and optimistic for its future. "In both thought and attitude," wrote Sterling McMurrin in the 1976 reprint of *Mormon Group Life*, Ericksen "was a religious liberal in the best sense of that term, not seeking the destruction of faith, belief, or worship, but demanding that the Church and its religion come to terms with reason, science, and the dictate of the moral conscience. He was the first . . . generation of authentic Mormon liberals, and he was their foremost philosophical spokesman."[43]

While Ericksen and his colleagues had been formulating innovative social thought and action in the MIA, their counterparts in the Church Educational System were introducing recent historical research and biblical scholarship into Church seminaries and institutes. Sidney B. Sperry was the first Latter-day Saint to earn a Ph.D. at a divinity school.[44] In 1925 he began studies in the Old Testament languages and literature at the Chicago Divinity School, completing a master's degree in 1926 with a thesis on "The Text of Isaiah in the Book of Mormon." The following year he became director of the Church's first Institute of Religion at the University of Idaho, and after one year he joined the religion faculty at Brigham Young University. He later received the Ph.D. degree from the University of Chicago and was professor of Old Testament languages and literature at Brigham Young University. Meanwhile, Heber C. Snell, a teacher of education and psychology at Snow College in Ephraim, Utah, began his Old Testament studies at Berkeley's Pacific School of Religion. He was a student of William H. Chamberlin and E. E. Ericksen and was editor of the student paper at the time of the 1911 BYU controversy. In 1928, at the BYU summer session for seminary teachers, Snell offered a course in Old Testament literature, and the following year Sperry taught, inspiring several teachers to follow his steps to Chicago Divinity School.

Joseph F. Merrill, who had resigned as dean of mines and engineering at the University of Utah in 1928 to become commissioner of Church education, was a strong advocate of higher education for seminary and institute teachers. At Sperry's suggestion, he persuaded Church President Heber J. Grant to approve the invitation of New Testament scholar Edgar J. Goodspeed and three other faculty members from Chicago Divinity School to conduct six-week courses in biblical scholarship at the 1930 summer session at BYU for seminary teachers. Merrill also arranged to pay Daryl Chase, George S. Tanner, and Russel B. Swensen, three seminary teachers, half-salary as they began their advanced education at Chicago in the fall. By the end of the decade, seven more students arrived, most of whom completed Ph.D.'s in biblical studies or Church history and returned to teach in the Church system.[45]

Not all in Zion were pleased with the liberal and increasingly intellectual spirit beginning to manifest itself in the seminary and institute system. Some Church authorities cautioned teachers that they must stick to the revealed Gospel, using as sources and authorities the standard works of the Church and words of the prophets. World War II and the Church's official concern over unauthorized teachings infiltrating its educational system deterred Latter-day Saints from attending divinity schools (but not other graduate schools) for a number of years. Nevertheless, the Chicago Divinity School group of the 1930s continued in Church service. Nearly all had long careers in Church education, including Russel Swensen, who completed his degree in New Testament and taught many years at BYU. He authored three Sunday School manuals: *The Synoptic Gospels*, *The Gospel of John*, and *New Testament: The Acts and the Epistles*, which demonstrated a positive attitude toward modern biblical scholarship while remaining well within doctrinal orthodoxy.[46]

The Questing Spirit

MORMON THOUGHT, with its strong individualism, has been too rich and challenging to be frozen in time or to be compressed between the covers of a single book. Every year new books and lesson manuals appear, adding gradually to the linear feet on library shelves taken up by Mormon doctrinal works. While in a certain sense Mormons are not, and may never be, in the forefront of theological dialogue with their fellow Christians, due to the different premises from which they proceed including the absence of "academic" theological training of Mormon General Authorities, there continues to be in Mormonism the vital process that has always generated theology in historical religions: reconciling statements within the canon and additional pronouncements by later prophets with respect to the canon and to modern conditions—what the Mormon calls "continuous revelation." There has been and continues to be at least some awareness of developments in scriptural scholarship and of developments in other traditions where parallels might prove illuminating. Each year hundreds of young Mormons continue pursuing graduate degrees—a few in theology or religious studies, more in history and the social sciences, still more in psychology, medicine, and the natural sciences. There is little or no effort to insulate them from the ideas around them. Rather, home and church reinforce the religious life. As in all religious groups there are some losses to the faith, but Mormonism has proved extraordinarily strong in retaining the interest, loyalty, and involvement of its young people, including its intellectuals. In the traditional centers of Utah, in university cities and towns across the United States, and increasingly in Europe, Latin America, and Asia, intelligent, educated Mormons seek fulfillment and expression in their Church meetings and assignments but also in private study groups, private correspondence, and private periodicals not under the same constraints as those published officially by the Church.

Such a situation may not be encouraging to those who like their Mormons to fit a common, simple mold. This was never so. But generally the Church has drawn from its own traditions in allowing multiple kinds of expression and some latitude of belief and behavior. Perhaps the most careful expression of this point of view was that given in 1967 to the students and faculty of Brigham Young University by President Hugh B. Brown:

> We are very grateful in the Church and in this great university that freedom, dignity and integrity of the individual is church doctrine as well as in democracy. Here we are free to think and express our opinions. Fear will not stifle thought, as in the case of some areas which have not yet emerged from the dark ages. God himself refuses to trammel man's free agency even though its exercise sometimes teaches painful lessons. Both

creative science and revealed religion find their fullest and truest expression in the climate of freedom. . . .

I hope that you will develop *the questing spirit*. Be unafraid of new ideas for they are the stepping stones of progress. You will, of course, respect the opinions of others but be unafraid to dissent—if you are informed.

Now I have mentioned freedom to express your thought, but I caution you that your thoughts and expressions must meet competition in the market place of thought, and in that competition truth will emerge triumphant. Only error needs to fear freedom of expression. Seek truth in all fields and in that search you will need at least three virtues: courage, zest, and modesty. The ancients put that thought in the form of a prayer. They said, "From the cowardice that shrinks from new truth, from the laziness that is content with half truth, from the arrogance that thinks it has all the truth—oh God of truth deliver us."[47]

Chapter Eight Notes

1. Brigham Young, *Journal of Discourses*, 26 vols. (Liverpool: F. D. Richards, 1855–86), 14:117.
2. Brigham Young, *Journal of Discourses*, 11:133.
3. Property intended for Young University by Brigham Young was acquired from his heirs, a building was constructed and furnished, and James E. Talmage, president of the LDS College, was engaged to head the new institution, but the panic of 1893 abruptly cut off all appropriations for Church schools from the general fund. University of Utah officials approached the First Presidency, suggesting the Church throw its support to the state institution rather than try to establish a competing school in the same city. The presidency of the university was offered to James E. Talmage as assurance that it would not fall into the hands of the anti-Mormons. With the encouragement of the First Presidency, Talmage accepted the position and an endowed chair-professorship of geology. He served as president from 1894 to 1907 and as professor geology until his call to the apostleship in 1921. See D. Michael Quinn, "The Brief Career of Young University at Salt Lake City," *Utah Historical Quarterly* 41 (winter 1973): 69–89.
4. On the history of Latter-day Saint education, see Ernest L. Wilkinson, ed., *Brigham Young University: The First One Hundred Years*, 4 vols. (Provo, Utah: Brigham Young University Press, 1975–76), 1:3–50; Leonard J. Arrington, "The Latter-day Saints and Public Education," *Southwestern Journal of Social Education* 7 (spring–summer 1977): 9–25; and M. Lynn Bennion, *Mormonism and Education* (Salt Lake City: Department of Education of the Church, 1939).
5. I have made good use of a paper prepared by Davis Bitton and myself entitled "Twentieth-Century Mormon Thought." I am grateful to Dr. Bitton, who generously gave me permission to use material from that paper in connection with this chapter. Some of Dr. Bitton's thinking may have changed since the paper was written, so I take full responsibility for what is said here.

6. John R. Talmage, *The Talmage Story* (Salt Lake City: Bookcraft, 1972); excellent shorter biographies include those in Orson F. Whitney, *History of Utah*, 4 vols. (Salt Lake City: George Q. Cannon and Sons, 1892–1904), 4:357–60; Andrew Jenson, *Latter-day Saint Biographical Encyclopedia: A Compilation of Biographical Sketches of Prominent Men and Women in The Church of Jesus Christ of Latter-day Saints*, 4 vols. (Salt Lake City: Andrew Jenson History, 1901–36), 3:787–89; Lowry Nelson in *Dictionary of American Biography*; and Richard S. Van Wagoner and Steven C. Walker, *A Book of Mormons* (Salt Lake City: Signature Books, 1982), 343–47. See also Dennis Rowley, "Fishing on the Kennet: The Victorian Boyhood of James E. Talmage, 1862–1876," *BYU Studies* 33 (fall 1993): 480–520.
7. James E. Talmage, *The Articles of Faith: A Series of Lectures on the Principal Doctrines of the Church of Jesus Christ of Latter-day Saints* (Salt Lake City: Deseret News, 1899). The main topics of the book are the thirteen short "Articles of Faith" written by Joseph Smith and others in 1842 from a pamphlet published earlier by Orson Pratt.
8. James E. Talmage, *First Book of Nature* (Salt Lake City: Contributor Company, 1888); James E. Talmage, *Domestic Science* (Salt Lake City: Juvenile Instructor Office, 1891); James E. Talmage, *The Great Salt Lake: Present and Past* (Salt Lake City: Deseret News, 1900).
9. James E. Talmage, *The Story of "Mormonism"* (Liverpool: Millennial Star Office, 1907); James E. Talmage, *The Great Apostasy: Considered in the Light of Scriptural and Secular History* (Salt Lake City: Deseret News, 1909); James E. Talmage, *The House of the Lord: A Study of Holy Sanctuaries, Ancient and Modern* (Salt Lake City: Deseret News, 1912); James E. Talmage, *Jesus the Christ: A Study of the Messiah and His Mission According to Holy Scriptures both Ancient and Modern* (Salt Lake City: Deseret News, 1915); and James E. Talmage, *The Vitality of "Mormonism": Brief Essays on Distinctive Doctrines of the Church of Jesus Christ of Latter-day Saints* (Boston: R. G. Badger, 1919).
10. Van Wagoner and Walker, *A Book of Mormons*, 347.
11. John A. Widtsoe, *Joseph Smith as Scientist: A Contribution to Mormon Philosophy* (Salt Lake City: Young Men's Mutual Improvement Association, 1908). Widtsoe's book was preceded by an eleven-part series on the subject in the Improvement Era in 1903–4, including one on "The Law of Evolution." In 1904 BYA professor of composition Nets L. Nelson published *Scientific Aspects of Mormonism; or, Religion in Terms of Life* (New York: G. P. Putnam's Sons, 1904). The First Presidency loaned Nelson $800 to pay an eastern publishing house to put the book out, then circulated a letter throughout the Church praising it. Like many other Mormons of the period, Nelson linked secular ideas of evolution with Joseph Smith's doctrine of eternal progress. Turn-of-the century Mormons found much scientific support for their religious beliefs, inducing many students to take up studies in the physical sciences.
12. B. H. Roberts, in *74th Semi-Annual Conference of The Church of Jesus Christ of Latter-day Saints* (Salt Lake City: The Church of Jesus Christ of Latter-day Saints, 1903), 72.
13. Frederick J. Pack, *Science and Belief in God: A Discussion of Certain Phases of Science and their Bearing upon Belief in the Supreme Being* (Salt Lake City: Deseret News, 1924).
14. The standard references are Truman G. Madsen, *Defender of the Faith: The B. H. Roberts Story* (Salt Lake City: Bookcraft, 1980); and B. H. Roberts, *The Autobiogra-*

phy of B. H. Roberts, ed. Gary Bergera (Salt Lake City: Signature Books, 1990). See also Brigham H. Roberts, "The Life of B. H. Roberts," typescript, Church Archives; Robert H. Malan, *B. H. Roberts: A Biography* (Logan: Utah State University Press, 1963); Davis Bitton, "B. H. Roberts as an Historian," *Dialogue* 3 (winter 1968): 25–44; Leonard J. Arrington, "The Intellectual Tradition of Mormon Utah," *Proceedings of the Utah Academy of Sciences, Arts and Letters* 45 (1968): 1–20.

15. Quoted in Van Wagoner and Walker, *A Book of Mormons*, 245.
16. T. Pauly, "Brigham H. Roberts—A Tribute," *Improvement Era* 36 (November 1933): 783.
17. B. H. Roberts, *The Gospel: An Exposition of its First Principles* (Salt Lake City: Contributory Company, 1888); B. H. Roberts, *The Life of John Taylor, Third President of the Church of Jesus Christ of Latter-day Saints* (Salt Lake City: George Q. Cannon and Sons, 1892); B. H. Roberts, *Outlines of Ecclesiastical History* (Salt Lake City: George Q. Cannon and Sons, 1893); B. H. Roberts, *A New Witness for God* (Salt Lake City: George Q. Cannon and Sons, 1895); B. H. Roberts, *The Missouri Persecutions* (Salt Lake City: George Q. Cannon and Sons, 1900); B. H. Roberts, *The Rise and Fall of Nauvoo* (Salt Lake City: Deseret News, 1900); B. H. Roberts, *The Mormon Doctrine of Deity* (Salt Lake City: Deseret News, 1903); B. H. Roberts, *Defense of the Faith and the Saints*, 2 vols. (Salt Lake City: Deseret News, 1907–12); B. H. Roberts, *The Mormon Battalion and its Monument* (Salt Lake City: State of Utah Mormon Battalion Committee, 1916).
18. B. H. Roberts, in *73rd Annual Conference of The Church of Jesus Christ of Latter-day Saints* (Salt Lake City: The Church of Jesus Christ of Latter-day Saints, 1902), 14–16.
19. Ibid.
20. B. H. Roberts, *The Seventy's Course in Theology, Fifth Year: Divine Immanence and the Holy Ghost* (Salt Lake City: Deseret News, 1912), 4–6.
21. Ralph V. Chamberlin, *Life and Philosophy of William H. Chamberlin* (Salt Lake City: Deseret News Press, 1926); and Ephraim E. Ericksen, "William H. Chamberlin: Pioneer Mormon Philosopher," *Western Humanities Review* 8 (autumn 1954): 275–85.
22. B. H. Roberts, *The Truth, The Way, The Life: An Elementary Treatise on Theology*, John W. Welch, ed. (Provo, Utah: BYU Studies, 1994) and B. H. Roberts, *The Truth, The Way, The Life: An Elementary Treatise on Theology*, edited by Stan Larson (San Francisco, Smith Research Associates, 1994).
23. B. H. Roberts, *The Truth, The Way, The Life*, 5. (Stan Larson edition)
24. Truman G. Madsen, "The Meaning of Christ—The Truth, The Way, The Life: An Analysis of B. H. Roberts' Unpublished Masterwork," *BYU Studies* 15 (spring 1975): 261.
25. B. H. Roberts, *Joseph Smith the Prophet-Teacher, with an Introduction by Sterling M. McMurrin* (Princeton: The Deseret Club of Princeton University, 1967), introduction unpaged. Although Roberts was not in any sense a scientist, as a prolific writer and an influential exponent of science, he had a strong impact on Mormon thought. See especially Erich Robert Paul, *Science, Religion, and Mormon Cosmology* (Urbana: University of Illinois Press, 1992).
26. The 1911 BYU controversy is discussed and documented in Wilkinson, *Brigham Young University* 1:409–37; Richard Sherlock, "The Evolution Controversy," unpublished paper in possession of the writer; and Duane E. Jeffrey, "Seers, Savants, and Evolution: The Uncomfortable Interface," *Dialogue* 8 (1973): 41–75.

27. Horace Cummings's report, as quoted in Wilkinson, *Brigham Young University* 1:419.
28. Although attendance at Chamberlin's religion and philosophy classes remained high, the administration denied permission for him to teach any religion classes in 1913, his name and courses were omitted from the 1914–15 catalogue, and in 1916 he was informed that he was being transferred to the department of education. Chamberlin resigned, spent a year of study at Harvard, then taught philosophy through the University of Utah Extension (1917–20) and Utah State University Extension (1920–21). Ralph V. Chamberlin, *Life and Philosophy of W. H. Chamberlin* (Salt Lake City: Deseret News Press, 1926), 209, 211, 217–18, 270, 272.
29. For a review of the modernist-fundamentalist controversy, see Sydney E. Ahlstrom, *A Religious History of the American People* (New Haven, Conn.: Yale University Press, 1972), 763–824, 839–41, plus bibliography.
30. Joseph F. Smith, "Philosophy and the Church Schools," *Juvenile Instructor* 46 (April 1911): 209.
31. The institutionalization of prophecy has been a key factor in the strength and unity of Mormonism. Antinomian tendencies in Joseph Smith's day were minimized by allowing that every member was entitled to revelation, but only pertaining to his or her own sphere of responsibility. Thus, the Prophet-President was the only one authorized by God to receive revelation or to declare doctrine for the entire Church.
32. See Davis Bitton, "Anti-intellectualism in Mormon History," *Dialogue* 1 (autumn 1966): 111–34, with an accompanying reply by James B. Allen, 134–40. Shortly after the BYU affair, E. E. Ericksen, a Ph.D. student in philosophy at the University of Chicago, was visited by Superintendent Cummings and told that "the philosophy I was being taught at the University of Chicago was not the kind that was wanted by my Church" and "that should I be given a position in the Church school system I would be in for trouble as were the BYU professors." Ericksen transferred to economics but later passed his exams in both philosophy and economics. Scott G. Kenney, "The Religious Life and Thought of E. E. Ericksen," an unpublished paper in my possession, p. 10. Also Scott G. Kenney, ed., *Memories and Reflections: The Autobiography of E. E. Ericksen* (Salt Lake City: Signature Books, 1987).
33. John A. Widtsoe, *In a Sunlit Land: The Autobiography of John A. Widtsoe* (Salt Lake City: Deseret Book, 1954). Especially helpful is Dale C. Le Cheminant, "John A. Widtsoe: Rational Apologist" (Ph.D. diss., University of Utah, 1977).
34. John A. Widtsoe, "Evidences and Reconciliations," *Improvement Era* 41 (October 1936): 586.
35. John A. Widtsoe, *Joseph Smith as Scientist: A Contribution to Mormon Philosophy* (Salt Lake City: Young Men's Mutual Improvement Association, 1908); John A. Widtsoe, *Rational Theology* (Salt Lake City: Deseret News, 1915); John A. Widtsoe, *Priesthood and Church Government* (Salt Lake City: Deseret Book, 1939); John A. Widtsoe, *An Understandable Religion* (Salt Lake City: The Church of Jesus Christ of Latter-day Saints, 1944); John A. Widtsoe, *In Search of Truth: Comments on the Gospel and Modern Thought* (Salt Lake City: Deseret Book, 1930).
36. John A. Widtsoe, "How Old Is the Earth?" *Improvement Era* 41 (December 1938), 713, 755; also, John A. Widtsoe, "How Did the Earth Come Into Being?" 42 (February 1939): 73, 124; John A. Widtsoe, "What is the Origin of Life on Earth?" 42 (March 1939): 136–37; John A. Widtsoe, "To What Extent Should the Doctrine of Evolution Be Accepted?" 42 (July 1939): 417, 444.

37. See Le Cheminant, "John A. Widtsoe: Rational Apologist," passim. An excellent volume by a scholar competent in Mormon intellectual history and the history of modern science, with extensive treatment of Orson Pratt, B. H. Roberts, James E. Talmage, John A.Widtsoe, and others is Erich Robert Paul, *Science, Religion, and Mormon Cosmology* (Urbana: University of Illinois Press, 1992). See also Gene A. Sessions and Craig J. Obert, eds., *The Search for Harmony: Essays on Mormonism and Science* (Salt Lake City: Signature Books, 1993).
38. The best source on Ericksen is the Scott Kenney paper mentioned above.
39. E. E. Ericksen, *The Psychological and Ethical Aspects of Mormon Group Life* (Chicago: University of Chicago, 1922).
40. Ericksen, *The Psychological and Ethical Aspects of Mormon Group Life*, 99.
41. In the early thirties, Ericksen and James E. Talmage's daughter, Elsie T. Brandley, wrote two MIA manuals on *Challenging Problems of the Twentieth Century* (Salt Lake City: General Boards of the YMMIA and YLMIA, 1932), presenting the view of non-Mormon scholars and social scientists on the economic, political, social, and religious problems current in the years of the Great Depression. Though popular with the Church's young adults, some Church officials regarded it as too secular. See Kenney, "Ephraim Ericksen," 34, et. seq.
42. "Priesthood and Philosophy," *Utah Academy of Arts, Sciences and Letters Proceedings* 34 (1957): 13–22.
43. "Introduction" to E. E. Ericksen, *The Psychological and Ethical Aspects of Mormon Group Life* (reprint; Salt Lake City, 1975), x.
44. Russel B. Swensen, "Mormons at the University of Chicago Divinity School: A Personal Reminiscence," *Dialogue* 7 (summer 1972): 37–47.
45. Swensen mentions Sperry, who also studied at the American School of Oriental Research and the Hebrew University in Jerusalem and taught at BYU from 1952 to 1970; Heber Snell; T. Edgar Lyon, who went into institute work and became director of Nauvoo Restoration, Inc.; Daryl Chase, in Church education in 1932, dean of students at Utah State University, and president of USU (1954–68); George S. Tanner, director of University of Idaho Institute, then at the USU Institute and director of the Hawaiian Temple Bureau of Information; Russel B. Swensen, BYU professor and author of Church articles and manuals; Vernon Larsen; Wesley P. Lloyd, dean of students, dean of graduate school at BYU, and graduate dean of the U.S. International University; and Anthony S. Cannon, institute teacher, FBI agent, and professor of sociology at the University of Utah (1947–66).
46. Russel B. Swensen, *The Synoptic Gospels* (Salt Lake City: Deseret Sunday School Union Board, 1944); Russel B. Swensen, *The Gospel of John* (Salt Lake City: Deseret Sunday School Union Board, 1945); and Russel B. Swensen, *The New Testament: The Acts and the Epistles* (Salt Lake City: Deseret Sunday School Union Board, 1944).
47. Hugh B. Brown, address at Brigham Young University, 25 March 1958, as published in *Dialogue* 2 (spring 1967): 136. Italics supplied.

Chapter 9

Faith and Intellect as Partners in Mormon History

THROUGHOUT ITS HISTORY the Church of Jesus Christ of Latter-day Saints, through its leaders and apologists, has declared that faith and intellect have a mutually supportive relationship.[1] Faith opens the way to knowledge, and knowledge, in turn, often reaches up to reverence. Spiritual understanding comes with faith and is supported by intellect. Church President Spencer W. Kimball told Brigham Young University students in his "Second-Century Address" in 1976: "As LDS scholars you must speak with authority and excellence to your professional colleagues in the language of scholarship, and you must also be literate in the language of spiritual things."[2]

The theme of faith *and* intellect, not faith *versus* intellect, was established in the early days of the Restoration. Joseph Smith taught that "it is impossible for a man to be saved in ignorance" (D&C 131:6), and that "a man is saved no faster than he gets knowledge."[3] "If a person gains more knowledge and intelligence in this life through his diligence and obedience than another, he will have so much the advantage in the world to come" (D&C 130:19). "Seek

---

Paper presented as the inaugural Leonard J. Arrington Lecture, Merrill Library, Utah State University, Logan, Utah, 7 November 1995. First published as *Faith and Intellect as Partners in Mormon History*, vol. 1 in the Leonard J. Arrington Mormon History Lecture Series (Logan, Utah: Utah State University Press, 1996). Reprinted in *The Collected Leonard J. Arrington Mormon History Lectures* (Logan: Special Collections and Archives, University Libraries, Utah State University Press, 2005), 1–29, 243–47.

ye out of the best books words of wisdom, seek learning even by study and by faith" for "the glory of God is intelligence, or, in other words, light and truth" (D&C 109:7; 93:36). In a revelation that came to Joseph Smith in 1829, Oliver Cowdery was instructed that spiritual insight is not a product of the "heart" only. The use of the intellect could not be ignored in seeking the revealed word of God (D&C 8 and 9).[4] Indeed the visions and revelations of the founding prophet initiated, as the *Encyclopedia of Mormonism* declared, "a dynamic interplay between mind and spirit."[5]

Intellectual activity has been the means of developing and enriching life and faith among the Latter-day Saints and furthering the growth and betterment of the kingdom of God.[6] Mormon theology, based, as it is, upon the scriptures and modern revelation, reaches a balance between rationalistic explanation and faith in heavenly experiences.

This belief that intellectual activity was clearly an aspect of worship was built upon the teaching of Jesus, who inferred the harmony of faith and intellect: "Thou shalt love the Lord thy God with all thy heart, and with all thy soul, and with all thy mind" (Matt. 22:37). There is a similar statement in section 4 of the Doctrine and Covenants: "See that ye serve him [God] with all your heart, might, mind and strength" (D&C 4:2). Under these divine instructions Latter-day Saints sought knowledge out of the best books (D&C 88:118) and established schools for instruction in both sacred and secular matters. These began with the Schools of the Prophets in Kirtland and Missouri and continued on the western frontier with the establishment of ward schools, stake academies, and colleges and universities in many settlements and stakes.

Speaking as a Latter-day Saint, I believe faith means trust in God and the Restored Gospel—a confidence that the world is God's and that when the gospel dwells among us and we teach and instruct one another with the wisdom in the best books we shall have the spirit of Christ (Col. 3:16). Far from being the antithesis of faith, intellect helps us express our profound wonderment and eager enthusiasm in creative and meaningful ways—ways that may awaken a sense of gratitude and awe.[7]

Mormon leaders in every decade of the Church's history have been persons of high intellect—and at the same time persons of undoubted faith. In each period of the Church's history, persons in leadership positions, with God's blessing, established a partnership of faith and intellect. There may have been occasional confrontations of faith and intellect, as with all religious leaders, but such tensions were resolved with the accommodations of mind to the spirit and spirit to the mind.[8]

Although the question of the relationship between faith and reason has a long history and is not limited to any one faith community, I have chosen five Latter-day Saint leaders of thought to discuss this evening: three men and two women. I begin with Joseph Smith and then follow with four who knew the founding prophet personally: Eliza R. Snow, Brigham Young, Emmeline B. Wells, and George Q. Cannon.[9] Unlike many leaders of religious thought, they did not experience a period of wrestling with the problem of being pulled in two directions, as had been true of the Apostle Paul, St. Augustine, Erasmus, Ralph Waldo Emerson, and John Henry Newman.[10] They seem to have readily accepted the desirability and necessity of maintaining a healthy balance between faith and reason, regarding the two as complements, not competitors. When Jesus said, "Ye shall know the truth and the truth shall make you free" (John 8:32), they seem to have assumed that He meant both reasoned truth and spiritual truth. All five of those I shall discuss were human beings, with observable imperfections, but they exhibited astonishing intellectual vitality, spiritual power, and moral courage, and appealed to "the better angels of our nature." As Latter-day Saints believe, the divine spirit shone brilliantly through their writings and acts. For each of them, faith and intellect were partners.[11]

Joseph Smith

Our founding prophet was a man of both intellect and personal charm; he is remembered for his divine revelations, sociability, and warm personality.[12] A visionary, city-planner, candidate for president of the United States, and father of eleven (of whom two were adopted), he was also an imaginative organizer, friend of the helpless, brilliant debater, and intense student of the scriptures. In an era when religious revivalism was characterized by intense enthusiasm, preachers pounding the pulpit demanding fealty and fear of God, he spoke of ideas and images, expanded perspectives of a largely uneducated people, and respected the commentary of others. He was at home discussing complex religious philosophies or playing a game of ball with a group of boys and young men. He walked the streets of Nauvoo, played with children, chatted with neighbors, and opened his home to every kind of visitor. His followers thought he was precisely the kind of person the Lord would choose to restore his church.

Although not schooled or well read by traditional standards, Joseph Smith was a person with both intellectual powers and charisma. Dr. John M. Bernhisel, graduate of the Philadelphia Medical School and Utah's first (and four-term) delegate to Congress, a new convert who was a physician for the Saints in Nauvoo, Illinois, lived for most of a year in the household of Joseph and Emma Smith. Just before the prophet's death in June 1844, Dr. Bernhisel gave this appraisal of his friend:

> Joseph Smith is naturally a man of strong mental powers, and is possessed of much energy and decision of character, great penetration, and a profound knowledge of human nature—He is a man of calm judgment, enlarged views, and is eminently distinguished by his love of justice. He is kind and obliging, generous and benevolent, sociable and cheerful, and is possessed of a mind of a contemplative and reflective character; he is honest, frank, fearless, and independent, and as free from dissimulation as any man to be found. But it is in the gentle charities of domestic life, as the tender and affectionate husband & parent, the warm and sympathizing friend, that the prominent traits of his character are revealed.[13]

Here is a similar appraisal by Emmeline B. Wells who, as a bright and well-educated girl of fourteen, left Massachusetts and joined the Saints in Nauvoo in the spring of 1844: "In the Prophet Joseph Smith, I believed I recognized the great spiritual power that brought joy and comfort to the Saints; and withal he had that strong comradeship that made such a bond of brotherliness with those who were his companions in civil and military life, and in which he reached men's souls, and appealed most forcibly to their friendship and loyalty. He possessed too the innate refinement that one finds in the born poet, or in the most highly cultivated intellectual and poetical nature."[14]

Not a systematic theologian, Joseph Smith was a revelator; that is, he made known divine truths that had been revealed to him by heavenly voices and angels in dreams and visions. He communicated these to his followers in books of scripture, in articles in Church periodicals, and in frequent sermons. In addition to the Book of Mormon and the book of Abraham, translated from ancient documents, and the book of Moses, an explication and emendation of the text of the Old and New Testaments, the products of his mental and revelatory powers included many revelations published in the Book of Commandments and in the Doctrine and Covenants, doctrinal instructions recently published in *The Words of Joseph Smith*,[15] and comments about such previously neglected texts as the Apocrypha and Pseudepigrapha. Above all, with his introduction of new scriptures and revelations, he demonstrated the limitations of Bible literalism which circumscribed the religious doctrines and practices of the Protestants of his day.[16] His thoughts and expressions challenged many widely held doctrines. Yet he was convincing as a pulpit orator and presenter of ideas well conceived and expounded.

Joseph Smith became concerned about religion when he was twelve; he read the scriptures carefully, prayed frequently, had religious discussions with his father and mother, attended a variety of religious services, and joined a debating society. In his 1832 description of his early conversion experience, Joseph Smith reveals that he had been torn between the universalism and rationalism of his father's beliefs and his mother's emphasis on the spiritual quality of religion. Here was the conflict between faith and intellect that Joseph prayed about and which heavenly revelations helped him to resolve. Thus, through his father, Joseph inherited the rationalism of the Enlightenment and the philosophical movement of the seventeenth and eighteenth centuries that stressed the power of human reason and worked for improvements in politics, religion, and education. From his mother he inherited the enthusiasm and religious excitement and warmth, zeal, and ardor of contemporary New England.[17] One gets true religion "by study and by faith," "through the mind and through the heart;" you "must study it out in your mind" (D&C 9:8). "I will tell you in your mind and in your heart" (D&C 8:2). On the one hand, he did not fear intellectual inquiry; on the other hand, he welcomed "gifts of the spirit," such as faith healing, speaking in tongues, and shouts of "hosanna" at the dedication of temples.[18]

Joseph Smith was no Thomas Aquinas, the thirteenth-century Italian Catholic philosopher whose *Summa Theologica* gave a carefully organized and precise analysis of God, his attributes, and his relation to the universe, and who systemized Catholic theology and the moral and political sciences in a superb monument of the medieval intellect. Nevertheless, Joseph's teachings provided satisfying answers to the major questions of human existence; he was a prophet to his people, a conveyor of the will of deity. His sermons, according to those who heard them, were intellectually and spiritually uplifting and satisfying. Joseph's King Follett discourse, given before several thousand Saints in Nauvoo in April 1844, is still regarded by Latter-day Saints as one of the great sermons in human history. In this last general-conference address, delivered less than three months before he was martyred, the Prophet discussed the character of God, the origin and destiny of man, the unpardonable sin, the resurrection of children, the creation, the tie between the living and their progenitors, and the Prophet's love for all men.[19]

In short, the Prophet's mind and heart were alive and alert. Faith and intellect were partners in achieving both spiritual and temporal goals. The works he published, whatever his own contribution to their substance and wording, were sophisticated, had significant intellectual content, and are worthy of the attention of students of American intellectual history.[20] The Prophet exercised leadership in relating individual members and the group to the universe and to society at large, he legitimated Church authority and defined its responsibilities, and he interpreted the Church's historical role.

Eliza R. Snow

One person on whom the prophet had enormous influence was Eliza R. Snow. She was present at the 28 April 1842 meeting of the Female Relief Society of Nauvoo at which the Prophet told the assembled sisters: "I now turn the key to you in the name of God, and this Society shall rejoice, and knowledge and intelligence shall flow down from this time. This is the beginning of better days for this Society."[21] Eliza knew that an essential part of the Restoration was restoring to women the status they enjoyed in early Christian communities. Eliza and the other women present at this meeting believed this to be a revelation on their behalf, and as they saw a gradual improvement in the position of women—in the Church and in civilized society—they were quick to attribute this to God, to divine influences for good. Eliza was a leader in this activity.[22]

Born in Massachusetts and reared in Ohio, Eliza R. Snow, who had lived as a governess in the household of Joseph and Emma Smith, was baptized in 1835.[23] She wrote: "As I was reflecting on the wonderful events transpiring around me, I felt an indescribable, tangible sensation . . . commencing at my head and enveloping my person and passing off at my feet, producing inexpressible happiness. Immediately following, I saw a beautiful candle with an unusual long, bright blaze directly over my feet. I sought to know the interpretation, and received the following, 'The lamp of intelligence shall be lighted over your path.'"[24]

Eliza R. Snow organized and directed schools in Nauvoo. She herself taught the children of the prophet and Emma. And, since she had an original poem for every occasion, she was known as "Zion's poetess." She was the first secretary of the Nauvoo Relief Society, for which she drafted the constitution.

With the assurance that came from the prophet's inspiration, in Salt Lake City she directed the woman's section of the Endowment House on Temple Square and gave instruction on prayers and administrations to midwives who were appointed to care for women who were about to give birth. Eliza and several female associates often administered to sick women and children, a practice that had the support of Church authorities.

In 1854, with the help of her brother Lorenzo, Eliza organized the Polysophical Society, a group that met bi-weekly at Lorenzo Snow's home or the Seventies Hall. Eliza referred to the meetings as a "magnificent moral, intellectual and spiritual picnic." There were original speeches, songs, readings, and recitations, as well as instrumental music on guitar, organ, piano, and bagpipe. In a time of general male domination, the women were there with their husbands and brothers as equals, performing as well as listening, and Eliza contributed often—poetry, essays, and inspirational thoughts.[25]

A charismatic, highly visible person, Eliza was instrumental in the formation of Relief Societies in the 1850s and 1860s. As the number of Relief Societies grew, particularly after 1867, Eliza was set apart as president of the sisterhood of the entire Church, in which position she served until her death in 1887. She became, in effect, a counselor to Brigham Young on matters pertaining to women and was often introduced as "presidentess." Eliza also formed in each ward and settlement the Young Ladies' Mutual Improvement Associations (YLMIA) for young women from ages twelve to twenty-five and the Primary Associations for boys and girls from three to twelve.

On 13 January 1870, Eliza presided at a mass meeting in the Old Tabernacle in Salt Lake City (where the Assembly Hall now stands), where some six thousand women came to protest the passage by the U.S. Congress of the Cullom Bill, a bill that removed authority from local courts and juries, deprived wives of immunity as witnesses against their husbands, and authorized the use of the U.S. military to enforce these and other federal anti-Mormon regulations. Eliza's address was strong and eloquent, as were those of other LDS women leaders. The meeting was given good national coverage, and from that time Mormon women were no longer regarded by national commentators as submissive and degraded. A month later the women of Utah agitated for and were granted suffrage, the first women in the nation to exercise this privilege. Now, as Eliza observed, "no woman in Zion need mourn because her sphere is too narrow."[26]

Eliza exerted another influence when she encouraged Utah women to go east to study medicine. Under her direction and with the financial support of the relief societies, Utah quite possibly had, around the turn of the century, the largest colony of trained women doctors of any region in the nation.[27]

In 1876–77 Eliza directed the preparation of a manuscript which, with the assistance of Edward W. Tullidge, was published under the title *The Women of Mormondom*. This 552-page book, containing the personal histories and important talks of twenty-six LDS women and shorter sketches of fifty-six additional women, was remarkable for the 1870s when women were just emerging as a visible force in Mormon society and culture. The final paragraphs testify to the influence of Joseph Smith:

> Paul, in the egotism of man's apostleship, commanded, "let the woman be silent in the church," . . . and the Prophet Joseph corrected Paul, and made woman a voice in the church, and endowed her with an apostolic ministry. . . . First, woman in her ever blessed office of motherhood; next, in her divine ministry. . . . Woman shall leaven the earth with her own nature. She shall leaven it in her great office of maternity, and in her apostolic mission. . . . This is the woman's age. . . . Woman must, therefore, lay the cornerstone of the new civilization.[28]

In the late 1870s and early 1880s, Eliza continued to organize and supervise relief societies, Young Ladies' Mutuals, and primaries in local wards and settlements; taught them the proper forms of washing and anointing women who were ill or about to give birth; made a special effort to work on behalf of American Indian women; published a hymnal;[29] prepared a book of *Bible Questions and Answers for Children*;[30] assisted in establishing the Deseret Hospital, of which she was president; published a *First and Second Speaker* or book of recitations for the Children's Primary Association (1882); and completed her *Biography and Family Record of Lorenzo Snow*.[31]

While one seldom finds any intellectual issues addressed by Eliza in her books and letters, her poems do reflect in veiled ways the seeds of such confrontations and struggles over plural marriage, the rights of women, Brigham Young's penchant for giving advice to girls and women, and such doctrinal issues as the nature of the resurrection and the existence of the Heavenly Mother. Eliza accepted authority, but she sometimes challenged policies and procedures and, particularly on issues relating to women, was not timid in exerting her own authority.

Until her death in 1887, at the age of eighty-three, Eliza was an intellectual center around whom women clustered for mental stimulation. A born leader, an efficient organizer, her firmly established convictions of the principles of the Gospel, which had been personally taught her by the prophet, "gave her the confidence and assurance to act independently in places, and at times, when other women would have faltered or hesitated to undertake such heroic efforts."[32]

Brigham Young

Just as Joseph Smith had been the dominant figure in the early days of the Mormon Church, Brigham Young was the most prominent person in pioneer Mormon country. He was the first governor of Utah Territory, the first superintendent of Indian Affairs, the founder of many industries and enterprises, the leading colonizer, and president of the Church from 1844 until his death thirty-three years later. Like Joseph Smith, Brigham Young came close to being all things to all Latter-day Saints. He supervised the construction of houses, canals, roads, and the erection of fences. He counseled settlers on farm operations; household management; relationships with wives, husbands, and children; and on the careful husbanding of cash. A superb organizer, Brigham formed wards and stakes, established courts and community offices, helped obtain machinery and equipment for the erection and operation of mills and factories, and fostered friendly relations with the native Americans in the region.[33] Brigham Young was a disciplinarian on the trail west, a hard-headed businessman, a practical politician, and a visionary prophet; but he was also a kind and helpful human being—tender, understanding, and compassionate, and with a lively sense of humor.

Living on the frontier of western New York as a child and young man, Brigham Young had only eleven days of formal schooling.

His invalid mother, who suffered from tuberculosis, helped Brigham, who sometimes carried her from bed to table and back to bed, by schooling him in the basics of reading, writing, and arithmetic. He read the Bible daily, kept informed of current events by reading the newspaper, and listened carefully to visiting preachers and other educated persons. As the ninth child in a family of eleven, he learned to cook, keep house, clear fields of timber and brush, plant and tend crops, trap animals and birds. Occasionally, he attended religious meetings. He was bright, inquisitive, and interested in everything.

Brigham had seen a copy of the Book of Mormon when it first appeared in 1830, and he was convinced of its authenticity. But he postponed baptism until he had determined that the members and officers of the Mormon Church manifested "right good sense." After meeting with Joseph Smith in 1832, he was baptized, undertook his first mission, and strove to learn all he could from the prophet. He was with him on Zion's Camp; he directed the Saints' migration from Missouri when the prophet was in jail; and he served as one of Joseph's most trusted advisors.

Brigham Young became an apostle in 1835, led a group of apostles in a massive missionary effort in Great Britain in 1839–1841, served as a business manager of the Church until Joseph Smith's death in 1844, and from his position as senior president of the Quorum of Twelve Apostles succeeded Joseph Smith as leader of the Saints in 1844. He was formally sustained as president of the Church in 1847, the year he led the advance company of pioneers to the Salt Lake Valley.

As Joseph Smith had been, Brigham Young was a persuasive speaker. He believed that most Christian sermons were too formal and other-worldly. Instead, he spoke earnestly about everyday and practical concerns. In a spirited manner he castigated the malfeasant politicians in Washington, warned his people to expect more of the same kind of treatment unless they repented and united, and pled with them to obey their leaders. Let the idle find employment, he said—the discouraged seek to obtain the Spirit of God. He often closed with a ringing affirmation of his testimony of Joseph Smith and the eventual victory of the Restoration.

Between such items he delivered nuggets of doctrinal wisdom. He sometimes used stern images and folksy humor and conducted impatient chastenings, but his primary focus was to maintain the unity of the Latter-day Saints in the face of political, legal, social, and military pressure.[34]

Brigham Young was no more a formal theologian than Joseph Smith. He considered himself an eminently practical man whose religion was centered in earthly concerns and pragmatic admonitions. When his more educated colleagues voiced their speculative instincts, he curbed and corrected their effulgences in the light of hardy New England common sense. He believed in the simple Gospel. Once, in 1857, after listening to one of Orson Pratt's long, involved, abstractly reasoned arguments, he declared: "[It] makes me think, 'O dear, granny, what a long tail our puss has got!'"[35] Young's scattered and unsystematized theological pronouncements were generally directed to the here-and-now. His great overriding vision was the literal establishment of the Kingdom of God in the valleys of the mountains. The Mormon village was a covenant community, based on the concept of gathering for those who had been converted in the East and foreign lands.

There was in Brigham's theology something of the medieval ideal of community. For him the injunction "the earth is the Lord's and the fullness thereof" was not simply a poetical metaphor. God ruled. Brigham and his fellow Saints were human stewards erecting at long last the divine commonwealth. Its citizens must yield personal desires to the whole. Temporal and spiritual unity and equality were emphasized.[36]

Although Brigham realized that environment and events limited human agency, still enough individual freedom remained to allow mankind to choose good or evil. Correct choices, in turn, were rewarded by unending personal growth and the opportunity for eternal procreation. His eschatology for the righteous climaxed with the promise of a harmonious social order based upon enduring family relationships. Conversely, evil acts would bring upon the offenders diminution of self, the loss of increase, and inferior social organization.

While he frequently urged, cajoled, and reproved his congregations, Brigham never preached depravity nor damnation. He believed that men and women were good, perfectible, and possessed of the divine. To realize their potential they must be liberated from erroneous tradition. They were, in fact, Gods in embryo, men and women seeking a heavenly partnership. Such a lofty, optimistic opinion of mankind, when joined with his view that men should never seek gifts from God which sweat and sinew could independently achieve, proved enormously energizing. It was a theology of empire building.

At every turn Brigham pulled his theology and metaphysics earthward. Having a keen understanding of human nature, he believed that self-discovery brought a knowledge of God, and he accordingly molded this theology around daily human experience. Thus his laws of freedom, reward, growth, procreation, and organization were earthly as well as heavenly. They could be validated by experience. When asked why God's determining hand did not more often intercede for the Saints, Young replied: "Man is destined to be a God, has to act as an independent being, and is left [by God] to see what he will do, to practice depending on his own resources, to be righteous in the dark, to do the best he can when left to himself to show his capacity."[37] The mission and responsibility of men and women, their destiny and privilege, Brigham said, was to build society—to plant trees, gardens, and vineyards; to build houses, shops, and meetinghouses; to dig ditches and dugways; to organize schools, concerts, and study classes. The whole face of the earth must be beautiful until it shall become like the Garden of Eden.[38] A prime imperative is to keep learning—to grow, to develop, and to have joy.

Empiricism undergirded all this thought; he was eminently practical. Both he and Joseph Smith believed that if the realm of God was to have any applicability to humankind, it must be explicable in terms men and women could understand and employ in their daily lives. If, on the other hand, the heavens operated on principles fundamentally different from the earth, he could see little hope or relevancy in discussing them. Brigham believed that revelations came frequently and that they were based on natural principles—not always (perhaps seldom) conveyed by ineffable experiences. Yet he did have an interior life of rich spirituality. He prayed—in private, in his family circle, and in council meetings and congregations. And he was a devoted participant in sacred ceremonies. There Brigham, removed from the ordinary routine of life, experienced an approach to God. A daring and courageous leader who dealt with a wide variety of practical matters, he was also responsive to the chords of celestial music as mediated through the liturgical experiences of the Salt Lake Endowment House and the Nauvoo and St. George temples. In most respects Brigham's theology was simple, literalistic, and conservative in the Mormon context.

Although Brigham was not an intellectual in any narrow definition of the term, he was unquestionably a person of intellectual power and mental alertness and had enormous influence on his generation of Saints—influence on doctrine, on "practical" thought, on the images and metaphors that have become part of the Gospel. He founded Brigham Young Academy, now Brigham Young University; Brigham Young College in Logan, which educated many early Utah teachers before closing in 1926; and the University of Deseret, which educated undoubted intellectuals like B. H. Roberts, James E. Talmage, John A. Widtsoe, William H. Chamberlin, Ephraim E. Ericksen, and other Mormon intellectual giants, and later evolved into the University of Utah.

All truth—scientific and philosophical as well as doctrinal—was a part of Mormonism. "'Mormonism,'" Brigham said, "embraces all truth that is revealed and that is unrevealed, whether religious, political, scientific, or philosophical."[39] Such a pronouncement encouraged his followers not only to develop moral excellence and purity but also to grow in knowledge and intelligence. The arts and sciences came from God and were designed for the good of the Lord's children. Since God operated on the basis of natural principles, learning more about the geology, chemistry, and other aspects of the order of nature was expected: "Every art and science known and studied by the children of men is comprised within the gospel. Where did the knowledge come from which has enabled men [and women] to accomplish such great achievements in science and mechanism [engineering] within the last few years? We know that knowledge is from God."[40] This approach encouraged young Mormons of the second generation to seek higher education in colleges and universities where they could make the best of their abilities.

Under Brigham Young's leadership, the hierarchical structure of the Church continued. The theophanous works of Joseph Smith were canonized, and the doctrine and organizational structure of the Church were firmly fixed. An accelerated educational program resulted in the founding of several colleges and universities and many academies and high schools in the various settlements.

George Q. Cannon

Brigham Young's appreciation for intellect is manifested by his calling George Q. Cannon, a bright young immigrant from Great Britain, to serve as a counselor in the First Presidency, a position he held from 1873 to 1901.[41] He was in Nauvoo as a teenager and became well acquainted with Prophet Joseph Smith.

Born in 1827 in Liverpool, England, the eldest of seven children of a family living on the Isle of Man, his family was converted to the Mormon Church in 1840 by his uncle, John Taylor, then an apostle. In 1842 they moved to Liverpool, then to Nauvoo. His mother died on the ocean voyage from Liverpool; his father died in Nauvoo. A young orphan, he was taken into the John Taylor home, where he worked with his uncle on the *Times and Seasons* and the *Nauvoo Neighbor* as both a writer and printer. He was adopted by John Taylor in 1846 in the Nauvoo Temple and moved west with the Taylor family in 1847, when he was twenty.

In the fall of 1849 Cannon and two or three dozen other young men were called to California to mine gold for the benefit of the Church and some of its aging but faithful early members. They worked for almost a year but their mining was not particularly successful. In the fall of 1850 he and nine others were called to preaching missions in the Sandwich Islands (Hawaii). Although five of the elders returned to Utah when they met with little success with the White settlers in the Islands, young Cannon remained, mastered the language, and worked with Hawaiian natives. He acquired the language rapidly. The natives loved and revered him. Within four years four thousand native Hawaiians had joined the Church, and Cannon began translating the Book of Mormon into Hawaiian. In 1854 he returned to Salt Lake City to marry Elizabeth Hoagland. The two moved to San Francisco to publish the Hawaiian Book of Mormon and the Church's *Western Standard* magazine.

When the U.S. Army's Utah Expedition invaded in the spring of 1858, the *Deseret News* press was moved to Fillmore, Utah, and Cannon was appointed managing editor. He held this position and that of editor until 1880, when Charles W. Penrose became editor-in-chief. Later in 1858 Cannon was sent to preside over the Eastern States Mission with instructions to influence eastern editors who were pressured by anti-Mormon sentiments.

In 1860 Cannon returned to Utah and was ordained an apostle; he was only twenty-seven. Sent to England with Apostles Charles C. Rich and Amasa M. Lyman to preside over the European Mission, he edited and published the *Millennial Star*, remaining four years with the exception of part of 1862 when he was called back to Washington, D.C., to lobby for Utah statehood. Back in Salt Lake City from 1864 to 1867, he worked as private secretary and assistant president to Brigham Young. He was named general superintendent of the Church's Sunday schools in 1867 and held this position until his death in 1901. He founded the semi-monthly (after 1880 a monthly) *Juvenile Instructor* for the Sunday schools beginning in 1866. Profusely illustrated with clever and faith-promoting drawings and art work, the magazine continued in expanded form as the organ of the Sunday school until 1970.

Through the George Q. Cannon and Sons Publishing Company, he printed the "Faith Promoting Series" of journals, biographies, and personal histories. Above all, he promoted education: "Latter-day Saints are ardent friends of learning, true seekers after knowledge. They recognize in a good education the best of fortunes, it broadens the mind, creates liberal and noble sentiments, and fits the possessor for a more successful struggle with the obstacles of life. . . . The possession of knowledge is of itself the highest pleasure."[42]

With his publications aimed primarily at the youth, Cannon was an important bridge between the first generation of Church leaders and the late nineteenth-century Church membership. He served as an assistant president and then in the First Presidency from 1873 to 1901 as a counselor to four Church presidents. He was intelligent, articulate, and well informed and had a wide circle of friends, both Mormon and non-Mormon. Next to Orson Pratt he was probably the pioneer who was recognized most widely for his faith and intellect.

Cannon was a careful, thoughtful observer, a constant reader, and a student of men and policies. He was a "natural" diplomat, ready conversationalist, and popular speaker. He served in the legislature, was often called to Washington, D.C., to lobby for the Church, undertook several short-term religious missions, and, as mentioned earlier, supervised the *Deseret News.* "More than any of the Mormon leaders," as Orson F. Whitney wrote, "he was prepared to meet men of the world."[43]

Cannon was a counselor to Brigham Young, 1873–1877, to John Taylor, 1877–1887, to Wilford Woodruff, 1887–1898, and to Lorenzo Snow, 1898–1901. He was Utah's elected delegate to Congress in 1872 and served nine years. With his affable and engaging manner, his knowledge of departments and functions of government, and his wide acquaintance with people, he was a human book of ready reference. He was one of the ablest speakers in the House and had wide influence. He was known as "smooth-bore Cannon." As Brigham's secretary and confidant, he was one of the three executors of Brigham Young's estate after Brigham died in 1877. As delegate to Congress he welcomed two presidents to Utah: Ulysses S. Grant in 1875 and Rutherford B. Hayes in 1880. As an active member of the First Presidency, he helped promote the electric industry, mining, beet sugar, salt, Saltair Resort, railroads, and many other enterprises.

President Cannon's writings include *My First Mission*, *The Life of Nephi*, *The Latter-day Prophet*, *The Life of Joseph Smith, The Prophet*, and *The First Book of the Faith Promoting Series*.[44] He produced about three hundred recorded sermons or discourses and thousands of editorials and magazine and newspaper articles. He died in 1901 in California at the age of seventy-four.

None of Cannon's books or articles suggests that he experienced tension between his faith and intellect at any stage of his life. Those who believe this was inevitable may find evidence in his personal diary, which, since his death, has been in the vault of the First Presidency, and selections from which are currently being prepared for publication by his family. He was too bright not to have been aware of conflicting viewpoints. Orson F. Whitney, himself a distinguished Mormon intellectual, wrote of Cannon: "Possessed of an unusual mentality, he absorbed knowledge as a sponge takes in water, and what his quick and wide apprehension encompassed, his marvelous memory ever after retained."[45]

Cannon was among the finest orators in the Mormon Church's history, one of the finest writers, one of the brightest intellects—eloquent and magnetic—and certainly one of the most faithful.

Emmeline B. Wells

Emmeline Blanche Woodward, a woman of brilliant intellect, talented writing and editorial skills, determination, and perseverance, was born in Petersham, Worcester County, Massachusetts, in 1828, the seventh of nine children of descendants of early Puritan settlers.[46]

Her grandfather fought in the Revolutionary War and her father, who died when Emmeline was four, was in the War of 1812. A precocious child, Emmeline attended local schools and then was sent off to a select boarding school in New Salem. During her absence, her mother joined the Mormon Church. When Emmeline returned from school in 1842, she accepted the Gospel and was baptized in an ice-covered pool on their farm on her fourteenth birthday. She taught school for a year in Orange, Massachusetts, and then at the urging of her mother, who worried that she might succumb to the pressure of her friends and superiors to give up Mormonism, she married James Harris, the son of the local branch president. They moved to Nauvoo, Illinois, arriving aboard a Mississippi River steamboat in March 1844. She met Joseph Smith, was electrified by his presence, and forever after bore testimony that he was a prophet of God.[47]

"Emmie," as she was called at the time, taught grade school and Sunday school in Nauvoo. She gave birth to a son who died within a month. Shortly after, her husband, perhaps intending to earn quick income, left her, never to return. Emmeline was befriended by Elizabeth Ann Whitney, wife of Presiding Bishop Newel K. Whitney and a counselor to Emma Smith in the first Relief Society. Emmeline married Whitney as a plural wife in 1845. After the exodus from Nauvoo, Emmeline taught school and Sunday school in Winter Quarters, Nebraska, and arrived with the Whitneys in the Salt Lake Valley in October 1848. She resumed teaching in a small log schoolhouse in Salt Lake City's Twelfth Ward.

After the death of Bishop Whitney, by whom she had two daughters, Emmeline married Daniel H. Wells as a plural wife and had three daughters by him. A prominent Salt Lake City businessman, superintendent of public works for the Church, and later a counselor to Brigham Young in the First Presidency, Wells was able to provide Emmie with a home and some income. He paid for the education of her five daughters and allowed her to concentrate on her reading, writing, and public speaking. Through him, she also gained a prominent place in the community.

Emmeline was a small woman, barely five feet tall and weighing about one hundred pounds, but she had a strong will. Having suffered, with other women, from discriminatory actions, such as low pay, she vowed, in her words, "to do all in my power to help elevate the condition of my people, especially women . . . to do those things that would advance women in moral and spiritual, as well as educational work and tend to the rolling on of the work of the Lord upon the earth."[48]

Beginning in 1869, under Eliza Snow's presidency, she began to serve as secretary of the Young Ladies' Retrenchment Association of the Church. Impressed with the importance of providing cultural development for young people along literary and musical lines, she joined with others in 1874 to organize the Wasatch Literary Association. The thirty young Salt Lake City men and women, all active Latter-day Saints, met weekly to present original essays, poems, orations, plays, and dramatic readings, as well as vocal and instrumental musical renditions. Two of the group later became apostles, one was Utah's first elected governor, one became head of the Christian Science Church in Boston, one became Utah's first general in the U.S. Army, one became president of the LDS Church, and several were stake presidents. One became senior president of the First Quorum of Seventy, and one served twenty-four years as president of the Primary Association of the Church.[49] Others became members of the YWMIA general board. With Emmeline's assistance and encouragement, these high-spirited future leaders fostered as much culture as their theocracy and pioneer economy would permit.

As an educated product of Massachusetts schools, Emmeline read national newspapers and magazines, and as she reared her children, she watched with mounting interest the formation of a female reform movement aimed at social, educational, economic, and political equality with men. She was well aware of the efforts of Massachusetts women, particularly Abigail Adams, who agitated for women's rights in the federal constitution, and she had read Margaret Fuller's American feminist statement *Woman in the Nineteenth Century*.[50] Emmeline also read of the first women's rights convention in Seneca Falls, New York, which Elizabeth Cady Stanton organized in 1848 and which launched the woman suffrage movement.[51] In 1874 Emmeline became vice president for Utah of the National Woman Suffrage Association.

Emmeline knew there were good reasons for these movements. Women could not vote, hold office, sit on juries, or, if married, own property unless by special dispensation. Women were not expected to hold high positions in Church, go to college, practice law, or speak in public.[52] Emmeline rejoiced when Utah women were given the vote in 1870 and she began immediately, eagerly, to exercise her prerogatives. She became a member of the Central Committee of the People's Party, the Church's political party; she was a member of several constitutional conventions when Utah was attempting to become a state; and she was nominated for the territorial legislature but was forced to withdraw when it was not clear from the constitution whether women could hold elective office. In 1879 she experienced first-hand discrimination when she was denied the office of Salt Lake City treasurer because she was a woman.

In 1872, when the *Woman's Exponent* was founded by Louisa Lula Greene, under the careful tutelage and protection of Eliza R. Snow and Brigham Young, Emmeline submitted material for it, often using the pen name "Blanche Beechwood." Many of her articles dealt with women's issues—equal pay for equal work and equal treatment in athletic programs. Emmeline became assistant editor of the *Exponent*, then editor in 1877, a position she held for thirty-seven years. Under her editorship the *Exponent* recorded the national story of women's suffrage, the silk industry, the activities of the Relief Societies, literary and other club functions, and welfare organizations and educational institutions. She commented on slavery, polygamy, European diplomacy, congressional reform, and presidential elections. If it happened to women, whether locally, nationally, or overseas, Emmeline reported it in the *Exponent*, believing that Mormon women "should be the best-informed of any women on the face of the earth, not only upon our own principles and doctrines but on all general subjects."[53] For more than twenty years, the masthead carried the motto "For the Rights of Women of Zion and All Nations."

In strong editorials Emmeline campaigned against the "Cult of True Womanhood" of the period:

> [Ladies] must be preserved from the slightest blast of trouble, petted, caressed, dressed to attract attention, taught accomplishments that minister to man's gratification; in other words, she must be treated as a glittering and fragile toy, a thing without brains or soul, placed on a tinselled and unsubstantial pedestal by man, as her worshipper.[54]

> Is there nothing then worth living for, but to be petted, humored and caressed, by a man? . . . That man is the only thing in existence worth living for I fail to see. All honor and reverence to good men; but they and their attentions are not the only sources of happiness on the earth, and

> need not fill up every thought of woman. And when men see that women exist without their being constantly at hand, that they can learn to be self-reliant or depend upon each other for more or less happiness, it will perhaps take a little of the conceit out of some of them.[55]

A woman ought to be "a joint-partner in the domestic firm." To Emmeline, a satisfying marriage was one in which both partners supported and uplifted the other.[56]

Indeed, through the pages of the *Exponent*, Emmeline called for women to be given the same educational opportunities as men:

> [We] should learn that there is a better part for women than to be man's dupe, or slave, or drudge. . . . The training of daughters as well as sons should be such as to develop powers that will strengthen character, attributes that will prepare them to put into practical execution the finest talents they may possess, so that they may learn how to live without leaning wholly on, or trusting blindly to another. . . .
>
> In the name of justice, reason, and common sense, let woman be fortified and strengthened by every possible advantage, that she may be adequately and thoroughly fitted not only to grace the drawing room, and manage every department of her household, but to perform with skill and wisdom the arduous and elaborate work of molding and fashioning the fabrics of which society is to be woven.[57]

If women were given the same opportunities for work and for education as men, Emmeline insisted, they would demonstrate that they were as smart as men, as able as men to exercise leadership in social, religious, and business activities. The desirable goal was for men and women to work and learn together, to be united, to share both responsibilities and ideas.[58]

Emmeline was not contending that women should neglect their children in seeking to do "public work." She had a close relationship with her own daughters—Belle, Mellie, Emmie, Annie, and Louie—mentioning them almost daily in her diary. But she insisted that women should also be free to assume responsibilities outside the home—in church, in the community, and in the world of business.[59]

Emmeline found herself juggling family and personal challenges with her work with the *Woman's Exponent*, the woman suffrage movement, and the Relief Society.[60]

Several specific assignments given to Emmeline in the 1870s evolved into life-time responsibilities. In 1870 Church leaders encouraged Emmeline and Zina Young Williams to attend the meeting of the National Woman Suffrage Association in Washington, D.C.; Relief Society leaders continued to take an active role in that association until the ratification of the Nineteenth Amendment to the Constitution granting suffrage to women in 1920. Utah women already had the right to vote, which was what the national suffrage leaders were fighting for; and national leaders believed that legislation should not be enacted to limit women's rights, which Congress sought to do in the passage of anti-Mormon legislation. So here was a partnership; national leaders respected and admired Mormon women leaders, and the high regard was reciprocated. Emmeline wore a gold ring Susan B. Anthony gave to her, declaring, "It is a symbol of the sympathy of two great women for one great cause."[61] On Miss Anthony's eightieth birthday Emmeline presented her with a black brocaded dress made from Utah silk. Emmeline formed close friendships with other national women leaders: Frances E. Willard, Elizabeth Cady Stanton, Anna Howard Shaw, Sarah Andrews Spencer, Lucy Stone, Julia Ward Howe, May Wright Sewall, Clara Barton, Matilda Joslyn Gage, Elizabeth Stuart Phelps Ward, and others.

In 1891 Emmeline went to Washington, D.C., with Jane S. Richards to attend the first session of the National Council of Women. At that time the council accepted the Relief Society as a charter member of the feminist organization.

At the World's Congress of Women, held in Chicago at the Columbian Exposition in 1893, Emmeline was a prominent figure and presided at one of the important council meetings. May Wright Sewall, national chairman of the Congress of Women, recognized the importance of the Relief Society and Young Ladies' Mutual Improvement Association and used her influence to arrange department meetings for them in connection with the congress. At the Relief Society session, Emmeline gave papers entitled "Western Women in Journalism" and "The Storage of Grain." Emmeline also edited two books exhibited in the Utah Pavilion:

Charities and Philanthropies: Woman's Work in Utah and *Songs and Flowers of the Wasatch*, both published in 1893 by George Q. Cannon and Sons.[62]

In the years that followed, Emmeline attended suffrage conventions and women's congresses in Washington, D.C., Omaha, New Orleans, Des Moines, Atlanta, Detroit, Chicago, Indianapolis, and London and addressed several of them. At the Atlanta convention, held in 1895, she delivered an address dealing with Utah and the Mormon people. So well was her talk received that, at its conclusion, the auditorium resounded with tumultuous applause and Susan B. Anthony came forward on the rostrum and embraced her.

In June 1899, as an officer of the National Council of Women (she was recording secretary from 1899 to 1902), Emmeline attended and was a speaker at the International Council and Congress of Women held in London. She presented her address in Convocation Hall, Church House, Deanery of Westminster Abbey, London. She visited historic places while in England, Scotland, and France and spent evenings with prominent literary figures. She formed friendships with many leading European women.[63]

Emmeline also advanced in responsibility on the church scene. In 1888 she became general secretary and a member of the general board of the Relief Society and assisted in the organization of the Young Ladies' Mutual Improvement Association and the Primary Association.

On 3 October 1910, after twenty-two years of service on the general level of the Relief Society, Emmeline, now eighty-two years old, was called to be the fifth general president of the organization, succeeding her long-time friend Bathsheba B. Smith. She continued as president until 1921, when she was ninety-two. Under her dynamic leadership, belying her age, she standardized and systematized the work of the Relief Society, instituted the *Relief Society Magazine*, began the first uniform course of study, and adopted the slogan "Charity Never Faileth." Welfare work became more methodical, and she coordinated Relief Society work with those of civic and county agencies. In 1919 a social services department was organized under the direction of Amy Brown Lyman. Under Emmeline's leadership the Relief Society also established courses in theology, genealogy, art, and literature, while courses on obstetrics, nursing, "home science," and home arts were continued. Each ward and stake, however, was encouraged to work out its own program.

Emmeline also founded the Utah Woman's Press Club and the Reapers' Club and in 1895 published a book of her poetry entitled *Musings and Memories*.[64]

In recognition of her many efforts and achievements in literature, Brigham Young University, in 1912, on her eighty-fourth birthday, conferred upon Emmeline the honorary degree of doctor of letters. She was the second person to receive the honor and the first woman to do so. BYU would wait forty-four years before honoring another woman in this way.[65]

When Emmeline turned ninety, a party was given for her at the Hotel Utah. In honor of the occasion, a moving picture was made of her and other pioneers who had been living in Nauvoo during the time Joseph Smith, the prophet, was alive. On her ninety-second birthday, more than a thousand people attended her birthday party in the Hotel Utah.[66]

Shortly after her release from the presidency of the Relief Society, Emmeline died at age ninety-three, and her funeral was in the Tabernacle in Salt Lake City, the second funeral ever held in that Temple Square facility for a woman. (The first was for Bathsheba Smith, who was Emmeline's predecessor as general president of the Relief Society.)

On what would have been her hundredth birthday, seven years after her death, the women of Utah placed a bust of Emmeline in the rotunda of the Utah State Capitol building. The brief inscription reads: "A fine soul who served us."

Conclusion

We might close with the analogy of Socrates in Plato's *Phaedrus*. The human soul, like a charioteer, must drive two horses as it progresses toward heaven. The horses must work together or the chariot will just go round and round.[67] To St. Augustine the horses might be spirit and flesh, to Shakespeare passion and reason, to Joseph Smith and his successors, faith and intellect. It would be unfortunate if either should outstretch the other. Over-emphasizing intellect to the neglect of spirituality, and over-emphasizing faith without the application of reason are both unworthy of practicing Latter-day Saints. We cannot achieve spiritual excellence without intellectual rigor, and intellectual excellence is hollow without active spirituality. We need to have the spirit as we learn, and we need to have learning as we build faith. Working together, faith and intellect help us achieve the Latter-day Saint goal of eternal progression.

Chapter Nine Notes

1. I am grateful for the suggestions of Davis Bitton on this lecture and on some of the sources on which it is based.
2. Spencer W. Kimball, "Second-Century Address," *BYU Studies* 16 (summer 1976): 466.
3. Joseph Fielding Smith, ed., *Teachings of the Prophet Joseph Smith* (Salt Lake City: Deseret Book, 1976), 217.
4. See also Mark R. Grandstaff, "Having More Learning Than Sense: William E. McLellin and the Book of Commandments Revisited," *Dialogue: A Journal of Mormon Thought* 26 (winter 1993): 41.
5. Richard F. Haglund Jr. and David J. Whittaker, "Intellectual History," in *Encyclopedia of Mormonism*, ed. Daniel H. Ludlow, 4 vols. (New York: Macmillan, 1992), 2:687.
6. Ibid., 685. There may, of course, have been instances in which intellectual activity has had an opposite effect.
7. Van Austin Harvey, *The Historian and the Believer: The Morality of Historical Knowledge and Christian Belief* (New York: Macmillan, 1966), 264.
8. Penetrating essays that discuss Mormonism and intellectuals are Ephraim E. Ericksen, "William H. Chamberlin, Pioneer Mormon Philosopher," *Western Humanities Review* 8 (autumn 1954): 275–85; R. Kent Fielding, "Historical Perspectives for a Liberal Mormonism," *Western Humanities Review* 14 (winter 1960): 69–82; Davis Bitton, "Anti-Intellectualism in Mormon History," *Dialogue* 1 (autumn 1966): 111–34. See also James B. Allen, "Comment," *Dialogue* 1 (autumn 1966): 134–40; and Thomas F. O'Dea, "Sources of Strain and Conflict," in *The Mormons* (Chicago: University of Chicago Press, 1957), 222–57; Leonard J. Arrington, "The Latter-day Saint Intellectual Tradition," *Dialogue* 4 (spring 1969): 11–26; Robert L. Millet, ed., *"To Be Learned Is Good If . . ."* (Salt Lake City: Bookcraft, 1987); and Clara V. Dobay, "Intellect and Faith: The Controversy over Revisionist Mormon History," *Dialogue* 27 (spring 1994): 91–105.
9. There are, of course, others who could be mentioned: Sidney Rigdon, Orson Pratt, B. H. Roberts, James E. Talmage, John A. Widtsoe, William H. Chamberlin, Amy Brown Lyman, J. Reuben Clark Jr., Belle Smith Spafford, Henry Eyring, Hugh Nibley, and Lowell L. Bennion, to mention a few.

10. See *The Confessions of St. Augustine*, trans. F. J. Sheed (New York: Sheed and Ward, 1943); Robert Richardson, *Emerson: The Mind on Fire* (Berkeley: University of California Press, 1995); John Henry Newman, *Apologia Pro Vita Sua* (New York: Longmans Green, 1902); John Henry Newman, *An Essay in Aid of a Grammar of Assent* (New York: Longmans Green, 1902); Robert Shafer, *Christianity and Naturalism* (New Haven, Conn.: Yale University Press, 1926); Roland H. Bainton, *Erasmus of Christendom* (New York: Charles Scribner's Sons, 1969); R. G. Collingwood, *Faith and Reason*, ed. Lionel Rubinoff (Chicago: Quadrangle Books, 1968); Nels F. Ferré, *Reason in Religion* (London and Edinburgh: Thomas Nelson and Sons, 1963); George Santayana, *Reason in Religion* (New York: Charles Scribner's Sons, 1936).
11. The Arrington lectureship at Utah State University permits, but does not insist upon, a "friendly" treatment of Mormon history by the invited scholar-lecturer.
12. The best biography of Joseph Smith is Donna Hill, *Joseph Smith: The First Mormon* (Garden City, N.Y.: Doubleday, 1977). See also Leonard J. Arrington, "Joseph Smith," in *The Presidents of the Church: Biographical Essays*, ed. Leonard J. Arrington (Salt Lake City: Deseret Book, 1986), 340; Richard Bushman, *Joseph Smith and the Beginnings of Mormonism* (Urbana: University of Illinois Press, 1984); John Henry Evans, *Joseph Smith: An American Prophet* (New York: Macmillan, 1933); Preston Nibley, *Joseph Smith, the Prophet* (Salt Lake City: Deseret News Press, 1944); Truman G. Madsen, *Joseph Smith the Prophet* (Salt Lake City: Bookcraft, 1989); and Larry C. Porter and Susan Easton Black, eds., *The Prophet Joseph: Essays on the Life and Mission of Joseph Smith* (Salt Lake City: Deseret Book, 1988).
13. John M. Bernhisel to Thomas Ford, 14 June 1844, Bernhisel Collection, Church Archives, The Church of Jesus Christ of Latter-day Saints, Salt Lake City.
14. Emmeline B. Wells's statement can be found in "Joseph Smith, the Prophet," *Young Woman's Journal* 16 (December 1905): 556.
15. Andrew F. Ehat and Lyndon W. Cook, eds., *The Words of Joseph Smith: The Contemporary Accounts of the Nauvoo Discourses of the Prophet Joseph* (Provo, Utah: Religious Studies Center, Brigham Young University, 1980).
16. Joseph Smith's thought is contained in Smith, *Teachings of the Prophet Joseph Smith*; Alma Burton, comp., *Discourses of the Prophet Joseph Smith* (Salt Lake City: Deseret Book, 1956); B. H. Roberts, *Joseph Smith: The Prophet Teacher* (Salt Lake City: Deseret Book, 1908); John A. Widtsoe, *Joseph Smith: Seeker after Truth* (Salt Lake City: Bookcraft, 1957); and Garland E. Tickemyer, "The Philosophy of Joseph Smith and Its Educational Implications" (Ph.D. diss., University of Texas, 1963). See also Truman G. Madsen, "Teachings of Joseph Smith," in *Encyclopedia of Mormonism*, 3:1339–43.
17. Haglund and Whittaker, "Intellectual History," in *Encyclopedia of Mormonism*, 2:687. See also Bushman, *Joseph Smith and the Beginnings of Mormonism*, 9–42.
18. A stimulating article is the above mentioned Grandstaff, "Having More Learning Than Sense," 23–48.
19. Donald Q. Cannon, "The King Follett Discourse: Joseph Smith's Greatest Sermon in Historical Perspective," *BYU Studies* 18 (winter 1978): 179–92. In the same issue of *BYU Studies* are Van Hale, "The Doctrinal Impact of the King Follett Discourse," 209–25, and Stanley Larson, "The King Follett Discourse: A Newly Amalgamated Text," 193–208.
20. See O'Dea, *The Mormons*, 22–40.

21. Minutes, Nauvoo Female Relief Society, March 1842 to 16 March 1844, 37–40, Church Archives, The Church of Jesus Christ of Latter-day Saints, Salt Lake City.
22. Joseph Smith's attitudes toward women are discussed in Carol Cornwall Madsen, "Mormon Women and the Temple: Toward a New Understanding," in *Sisters in Spirit: Mormon Women in Historical and Cultural Perspective*, eds. Maureen Ursenbach Beecher and Lavina Fielding Anderson (Urbana: University of Illinois Press, 1987), 80–110; Linda King Newell, "Gifts of the Spirit: Women's Share," in *Sisters in Spirit*, 111–50; Jill Mulvay Derr, "'Strength in Our Union': The Making of Mormon Sisterhood," in *Sisters in Spirit*, 153–207; Leonard J. Arrington and Davis Bitton, *The Mormon Experience: A History of the Latter-day Saints* (New York: Alfred A. Knopf, 1979), 220–42; Leonard J. Arrington, "Persons for All Seasons: Women in Mormon History," *BYU Studies* 20 (fall 1979): 39–58; and Carol Cornwall Madsen, "Mormon Women and the Struggle for Definition: The Nineteenth-Century Church," *Sunstone* 6 (November–December 1981): 7–11.
23. Sources on the life of Eliza Roxey Snow Smith include Augusta Joyce Crocheron, "Eliza R. Snow Smith," in *Representative Women of Deseret* (Salt Lake City: J. C. Graham and Company, 1884), 1–9; Andrew Jenson, "Snow, Eliza Roxey," in *Latter-day Saint Biographical Encyclopedia: A Compilation of Biographical Sketches of Prominent Men and Women in The Church of Jesus Christ of Latter-day Saints*, 4 vols. (Salt Lake City: Andrew Jenson History, 1901–36), 1:693–97; Maureen Ursenbach Beecher, "Eliza R. Snow's Nauvoo Journal," *BYU Studies* 15 (summer 1975): 391–416; Maureen Ursenbach Beecher, "The Eliza Enigma: The Life and Legend of Eliza R. Snow," in *Sister Saints*, ed. Vicky Burgess-Olson (Provo, Utah: Brigham Young University Press, 1978); Maureen Ursenbach Beecher, "Eliza R Snow," in *Mormon Sisters: Women in Early Utah*, ed. Claudia L. Bushman (Cambridge, Mass.: Emmeline Press, 1976), 24–41; Janet Peterson and LaRene Gaunt, "Eliza R. Snow," in *Elect Ladies* (Salt Lake City: Deseret Book, 1990), 23–40; Maureen Ursenbach Beecher, ed., *The Personal Writings of Eliza Roxey Snow* (Salt Lake City: University of Utah Press, 1995).

    Many of Eliza's writings have been compiled and published as a separate volume: Bryant S. Hinckley, LeRoi Snow, and Arthur M. Richardson, comps., *Eliza R. Snow, an Immortal: Selected Writings of Eliza R. Snow* (Salt Lake City: Nicholas G. Morgan Sr. Foundation, 1957); *Life and Labors of Eliza R. Snow Smith* (Salt Lake City: Juvenile Instructor Office, 1888). See also Leonard J. Arrington, "The Legacy of Latter-day Saint Women," *John Whitmer Historical Association Journal* 10 (1990): 3–17; Maureen Ursenbach Beecher, *Eliza and Her Sisters* (Salt Lake City: Aspen Books, 1991); Maureen Ursenbach Beecher, "The 'Leading Sisters': A Female Hierarchy in Nineteenth Century Mormon Society," *Journal of Mormon History* 9 (1982): 25–39; Maureen Ursenbach Beecher, "The Eliza Enigma," *Dialogue* 11 (spring 1978): 30–43.
24. Hinckley, Snow, and Richardson, *Eliza R. Snow*, 6.
25. Eliza R Snow Smith, *Biography and Family Record of Lorenzo Snow* (Salt Lake City: Deseret News, 1884), 252–53. See also Maureen Ursenbach, "Three Women and the Life of the Mind," *Utah Historical Quarterly* 43 (winter 1975): 26–40. Eliza published her first book of poems in under the title *Poems, Religious, Historical and Political* (Liverpool: F. D. Richards, 1856). A second volume was published in 1877. Both were ambitious projects; the first was 270 pages, the second 284 pages.
26. "An Address by Miss Eliza R. Snow . . . August 14, 1872," *Millennial Star* 36 (13 January 1874): 21.

27. See Arrington, "Blessed Damozels: Women in Mormon History," *Dialogue* 6 (summer 1971): 22–31; Maureen Ursenbach Beecher, "A Decade of Mormon Women—the 1870s," *New Era* 8 (April 1978): 35–36.
28. Edward R. Tullidge, *The Women of Mormondom* (New York: Tullidge and Crandall, 1877), 541–51.
29. Eliza R. Snow, *Hymns and Songs* (Salt Lake City: Deseret News, 1880).
30. Eliza R. Snow, *Bible Questions and Answers for Children* (Salt Lake City: Juvenile Instructor Office, 1881).
31. Eliza R Snow Smith, *Biography and Family Record of Lorenzo Snow* (Salt Lake City: Deseret News, 1884).
32. Beecher, "Three Women and the Life of the Mind," 35–40; Emmeline B. Wells, "L.D.S. Women of the Past: Personal Impressions," *Woman's Exponent* 36 (February 1908): 49–50.
33. Biographies of Brigham Young include Leonard J. Arrington, *Brigham Young: American Moses* (New York: Alfred A. Knopf, 1985); Newell G. Bringhurst, *Brigham Young and the Expanding American Frontier* (Boston: Little, Brown, 1986); Eugene England, *Brother Brigham* (Salt Lake City: Bookcraft, 1980); Francis M. Gibbons, *Brigham Young: Modern Moses, Prophet of God* (Salt Lake City: Deseret Book, 1981); M. R. Werner, *Brigham Young* (New York: Harcourt, Brace, 1925); and Susa Young Gates, in collaboration with Leah D. Widtsoe, *The Life Story of Brigham Young* (New York: Macmillan, 1930).
34. On Brigham Young's thought: John A. Widtsoe, ed., *Discourses of Brigham Young* (Salt Lake City: Deseret Book, 1941); Carl J. Furr, "The Religious Philosophy of Brigham Young" (Ph.D. diss., University of Chicago, 1937); H. Carleton Marlow, "Brigham Young's Philosophy of History" (Master's thesis, Brigham Young University, 1959); Arrington, *Brigham Young*, chapters 12 and 17.
35. Brigham Young, *Journal of Discourses*, 26 vols. (Liverpool: F. D. Richards, 1855–86), 4:267.
36. Leonard J. Arrington, Feramorz Y. Fox, and Dean L. May, *Building the City of God: Community and Cooperation Among the Mormons* (Salt Lake City: Deseret Book, 1976).
37. Brigham Young Secretary Journal, 28 January 1857, 6, typescript, Church Archives, The Church of Jesus Christ of Latter-day Saints, Salt Lake City.
38. Brigham Young, *Journal of Discourses*, 1:254.
39. Brigham Young, *Journal of Discourses*, 9:149.
40. Widtsoe, *Discourses of Brigham Young*, 246.
41. Beatrice Cannon Evans and Janath Russell Cannon, eds., *Cannon Family Historical Treasure* (Salt Lake City: George Q. Cannon Family Association, 1967), 85–140; Joseph J. Cannon, "George Q Cannon," *Instructor*, January 1944 through November 1945, a serialized biography; Orson F. Whitney, "George Quayle Cannon," *History of Utah* (Salt Lake City, 1892–1904), 4:659–63; and George Q. Cannon, "Twenty Years Ago: A Trip to California," *Juvenile Instructor* 4 (January–June 1869): intermittently in 12 issues, 6–92.
42. George Q. Cannon, "Education and Educators," *Juvenile Instructor* 27 (15 March 1892): 210.
43. Whitney, "George Quayle Cannon," 661.
44. George Q. Cannon, *My First Mission* (Salt Lake City: Juvenile Instructor Office, 1879); George Q. Cannon, *The Life of Nephi* (Salt Lake City: Juvenile Instructor

Office, 1879); George Q. Cannon, *The Latter-day Prophet: Young People's History of Joseph Smith* (Salt Lake City: Deseret News, 1900); George Q. Cannon, *The Life of Joseph Smith, the Prophet* (Salt Lake City: Juvenile Instructor Office, 1888); and George Q. Cannon, *Faith Promoting Series* (Salt Lake City: Juvenile Instructor Office, 1882).

45. Whitney, "George Quayle Cannon," 659–63.

46. The standard biography is Carol Cornwall Madsen, "A Mormon Woman in Victorian America" (Ph.D. diss., University of Utah, 1985). Excellent short biographies include Carol Cornwall Madsen, "Emmeline B. Wells: Romantic Rebel," in *Supporting Saints: Life Stories of Nineteenth-Century Mormons*, ed. Donald Q. Cannon and David J. Whittaker (Provo, Utah: Brigham Young University, 1985), 305–41; Janet Peterson and LaRene Gaunt, "Emmeline B. Wells," *Elect Ladies* (Salt Lake City: Deseret Book, 1990), 79–94; Patricia Rasmussen Eaton-Gadsby and Judith Rasmussen Dushku, "Emmeline B. Wells," in *Sister Saints*, 457–78; Augusta Joyce Crocheron, "Emmeline B. Wells," in *Representative Women of Deseret* (Salt Lake City: J. C. Graham and Company, 1884), 62–71; Jenson, "Wells, Emmeline Blanche Woodward," in *Latter-day Saints Biographical Encyclopedia*, 2:731–34, 4:199–200; Orson F. Whitney, "Emmeline B. Woodward Wells," *History of Utah*, 4:586–90; Susa Young Gates, "Emmeline B. Wells," *History of the Young Ladies' Mutual Improvement Association*, rev. ed. (Salt Lake City: General Board of the YLMIA, 1911), 45–53. See also Rebecca Anderson, "Emmeline B. Wells: Her Life and Thought" (Master's thesis, Utah State University, 1975).

47. "Emmeline Blanche Wells," *Young Woman's Journal* 16 (December 1905): 554–56.

48. Emmeline B. Wells, Diary, 4 January 1878, 207. L. Tom Perry Special Collections, Harold B. Lee Library, Brigham Young University, Provo, Utah.

49. Ronald W. Walker, "Growing up in Early Utah: The Wasatch Literary Association, 1874–1878," *Sunstone* 6 (November–December 1981): 44–51.

50. Margaret Fuller, *Women in the Nineteenth Century* (London: Clarke, 1845).

51. Madsen, "A Mormon Woman in Victorian America," 148. See also Eleanor Flexner, *A Century of Struggle: The Woman's Rights Movement in America* (1959; rev. ed., Cambridge, Mass.: Belknap Press of Harvard University, 1975).

52. Anne Firor Scott, "Mormon Women, Other Women: Paradoxes and Challenges," *Journal of Mormon History* 13 (1986/87): 4.

53. Emmeline B. Wells to Mary Elizabeth Lightner, 7 April 1882, Wells Papers, Church Archives, The Church of Jesus Christ of Latter-day Saints, Salt Lake City.

54. Quoted in the article on Emmeline in Richard S. Van Wagoner and Steven C. Walker, *A Book of Mormons* (Salt Lake City: Signature Books, 1982), 384. The most complete description of the meaning of the objectionable phrase is Barbara Welter, "The Cult of True Womanhood: 1800–1860," *American Quarterly* 18 (1966): 151–74.

55. "Why, Ah! Why," *Woman's Exponent* 3 (1 October 1874): 67. I have made good use of Carol Cornwall Madsen, "Emmeline B. Wells: Romantic Rebel," in which many Wells quotations are found.

56. "Real Women," *Woman's Exponent* 2 (1 January 1874): 118.

57. "After Long Years," *Woman's Exponent* 6 (15 November 1877): 89; *Woman's Exponent* 4 (15 May 1876): 191.

58. See also Orson F. Whitney, "Woman's Work and Mormonism," *Young Woman's Journal* 17 (July 1906): 295–96.

59. "Life Lessons, by Blanche Beechwood," *Woman's Exponent* 4 (1 October 1875): 70.

60. Peterson and Gaunt, "Eliza R. Snow," 85, where the preceding quotations also appear.
61. Anderson, "Emmeline B. Wells: Her Life and Thought," 33.
62. Emmeline B. Wells, ed., *Charities and Philanthropies: Woman's Work in Utah* (Salt Lake City: George Q. Cannon and Sons, 1893) and Emmeline B. Wells, ed., *Songs and Flowers of the Wasatch* (Salt Lake City: George Q. Cannon and Sons, 1893).
63. Carol Cornwall Madsen, "'The Power of Combination': Emmeline B. Wells and the National and International Councils of Women," *BYU Studies* 33 (fall 1993): 646–73.
64. Emmeline B. Wells, *Musings and Memories: Poems* (Salt Lake City: George Q. Cannon and Sons, 1896).
65. About this time Susa Young Gates wrote of her: "Emmeline's mind is keen, her intellect sure, and her powers unending. She possesses a rarely beautiful spirit, and is affectionate, confiding and exquisitely pure. . . . She is an eloquent speaker, a beautiful writer, a true friend, and a wise counsellor." Susa Young Gates, "President Emmeline B. Wells," in *Album Book: Daughters of the Utah Pioneers and Their Mothers*, ed. Joseph T. Jakeman (Salt Lake City: Daughters of Utah Pioneers, 1911), 54.
66. Peterson and Gaunt, "Eliza R. Snow," 90.
67. See B. Jowett, *The Works of Plato*, 4 vols. in one (New York: Dial Press, 1938), 3: "Phaedrus," 361–449; and Neal W. Kramer, "The Intellect and the Spirit," *New Perspectives* 9 (December 1992): 14–20.

PART THREE

Mormon Historical Writing

Chapter 10

Scholarly Studies of Mormonism in the Twentieth Century

ALTHOUGH REARED IN A MORMON HOME in Idaho and although my family members were devout members of the Mormon faith, I was first introduced to Mormon studies as a graduate student in economics at the University of North Carolina. In fulfillment of an assignment in a graduate sociology course, I happened to read a book on *The Sociology of Rural Life* by T. Lynn Smith (I did not know at the time that he also had been reared a Mormon) and came to a section in which he discussed the land-settlement patterns of the Mormons.[1] Until that moment it had not occurred to me that there was more to Mormonism than "the Church," the theology, and the goal of personal righteousness. Fascinated, I immediately canvassed other works on rural sociology and found several additional references to the Mormons. I hunted through monographs concerning American history, politics, and economics and discovered to my surprise and delight that a whole literature on the "secular" aspects of Mormon culture was in the process of creation.[2]

Actually, the systematic study of Mormon institutions and history is a relatively recent phenomenon. Writings about the Mormons during the first seventy-five years after the Church was

---

First published as "Scholarly Studies of Mormonism in the Twentieth Century," *Dialogue* 1 (spring 1966): 15–28. The essay included a chronological listing of Ph.D. dissertations on Mormon history.

organized in 1830 consisted essentially of three kinds of works: (1) pietistic, missionary, and apologetic literature by Church authorities, devout writers, and missionaries of the Church;[3] (2) scathing attacks on the Church and its leaders by schismatic, disaffected, or excommunicated Mormons, and by wrathful Gentile opponents;[4] and (3) the "curiosa" literature of writers who were impressed with the peculiar characteristics of the Mormons and their religion and who wrote about the Mormons and their settlements as other journalists and travelers wrote about the Hottentots, the hairy Ainu, and the wild men of Borneo.[5]

While no historian could wish to denigrate or detract from the enormous significance of the histories by Edward Tullidge and Hubert Howe Bancroft,[6] it may be fairly said that "objective," "scholarly," and "systematic" treatises on the Mormons and their culture began in this century as a product of work toward the Ph.D. in history and the social sciences.[7] The first of more than a hundred doctoral dissertations on the Mormons was presented by Edgar Wilson at the University of Berlin in 1906.[8] It is no accident that this early study was written and published under the direction of Professor Gustav Schmoller. As the founder and leader of the Younger German Historical School of Economics, Schmoller believed that the best approach to economics and other social phenomena was through history. Taking sharp issue with "classical" and "neo-classical" economics, he contended that economics had gotten off on the wrong foot by emphasis on deductive theorizing. Generalizations of temporal phenomena, he asserted, must be built up from a wealth of detailed, factual, and historical studies and monographs.[9]

Among the hundreds of dissertations on as many subjects that were sponsored by Schmoller and his colleagues was Wilson's "Cooperative Economy and Forms of Enterprise in the Mormon Commonwealth."[10] Based upon "years of residence and study" in Utah, the dissertation discussed the nature and goals of the Mormon Church, the "communistic" phase of its history, the "cooperative company" phase, irrigation companies, business cooperatives, the "capitalistic phase," and had a concluding section on "achievements and expectations." A midwestern Lutheran, Wilson took as his text a phrase from Seneca: "For I am accustomed also to go over into alien camps, not so much as a fugitive, but as an explorer."

No one would contend that Wilson's study was objective in the modern sense; it reflected the author's personal feelings and opinions, as well as the available literature and prejudices of the time. But it is significant that Wilson sought to study Mormonism as a phenomenon in the same sense that other students of the German historicists had studied the tax system of ancient Greece, the legal contributions of the Romans, and the origins of German statecraft.[11]

Since this pioneer effort, the hundred or more dissertations on the Mormons and their culture fall into one of three categories: "analytical" social science studies, historical studies of one or more aspects of "the Mormon epic," and what might be called "quasi-official" or "institutional" studies.[12] It is not entirely a coincidence that the earliest *American* doctoral dissertations on the Mormons were completed the same year (1918), that both were written by young Mormons who had taught in the Church educational system (Ephraim Ericksen and Andrew Love Neff), and that both exemplify and suggest themes for the first two types of studies suggested above.

The first of the analytical studies, and somewhat resembling the Wilson dissertation, was "The Psychological and Ethical Aspects of Mormon Group Life" by Ephraim Ericksen.[13] Although Ericksen does not cite Wilson and does not even list a bibliography (at least in the work's published form), among his professors and advisors was Dr. J. Laurence Laughlin, a personal friend of Schmoller, who had given a series of lectures at the University of Berlin in 1906–07.[14] These, it will be remembered, were the same years that Wilson's dissertation was written and published. Ericksen's study, which was highly critical of Mormon leadership, initiated and influenced a rather substantial number of penetrating social and economic studies by persons reared as Mormons. Among these early "analytical" studies were those by Joseph Geddes, Lowry Nelson, and Feramorz Y. Fox. It is significant, and perhaps to be expected, that most of these dissertations have been written by persons who received part or all of their training in a discipline other than history—psychology, sociology, economics, or political science. It is also significant that these studies have centered on the more unusual elements of Mormon culture, giving emphasis to the differences between the Mormons and other groups of Westerners and Americans.

The second of these early dissertations, and the earliest of the "Mormon epic" studies, was "The Mormon Migration to Utah" by Andrew Love Neff. While not completed until 1918, this study was actually conceived by Neff as early as 1903 while he was a student at Stanford. Perhaps unconsciously, it reflected the influence of Frederick Jackson Turner. "To my mind," wrote Neff in 1906, "the greatest fact in American history is the spread of settlement from the Atlantic seaboard to the Pacific Ocean. And I hope to ascertain the relative part of Mormons in blazing the trail and opening up of the continent to settlement."[15] Neff's goal of a three-volume "epic" history was never fully realized because of an untimely death, but we can be grateful to L. H. Creer and others for the posthumous publication in 1940 of his intended first volume, which covers the history of Utah and the Mormons to 1869.[16] Early works built upon this "frontier" tradition include the dissertations by L. H. Creer, Dean McBrien, Joel Ricks, and Milton Hunter. These and the "Turnerian" works that followed have emphasized the "American" character of the Mormon movement and have sought to demonstrate the elements in common between the Mormons and other Westerners and Americans.

There is a third kind of monograph that has flowered in recent years with the establishment and growth of graduate studies in the College of Religious Instruction at Brigham Young University. These theses and dissertations might be regarded as "quasi-official" because, in a broad sense, they are encouraged by, or sponsored by, the Church. Directly or indirectly, consciously or unconsciously, they adduce evidence in support of the Church, its history and program. Written under the influence of what Samuel W. Taylor recently called the "positive thinking" philosophy, they serve to "build testimonies" (i.e., increase conviction) by showing the wisdom of past and present Church policies and programs.[17] Many of them consist of Ed.D. theses written by instructors in the Church's seminaries, institutes of religion, and colleges.[18]

It was the prediction of Ephraim Ericksen that these "quasi-official" monographs would increasingly characterize Mormon studies in the years after his dissertation was completed. The Church, he asserted, had gone through three stages: an early stage of conflict with neighbors in New York State, Missouri, Ohio, and Illinois—a conflict produced by the Mormons' peculiar religious ceremonies, peculiar marriage institution, distinct economic order, and the unique lay priesthood hagiography; a second stage of conflict with nature, as the pioneers in the Mountain West sought to make the desert blossom as the rose in a region hostile to human settlement; and a third stage of accommodation and adjustment to the dominant scientific and democratic culture of the nation.

It was the third stage, which Ericksen contended, would present the most difficult problems for the Church. In the earlier stages, he said, there was very slight distinction between the spiritual and temporal affairs of the Church:

> They [the Mormons] all belonged to the Kingdom of God and the church claimed the right to exercise its authority in any direction. But when sufficient private capital had accumulated and the individuals began to feel their own strength and could undertake business enterprises without the aid of the church its influence in economic matters began to decline. The state began to assume greater responsibility and was becoming stronger in all lines of general community interest. The individuals were beginning to assert themselves through the institutions of the state. The church was forced to confine its activities to that sphere in which the older group sentiments still hold sway. Its sphere was becoming less temporal and more spiritual. Its attention was being turned to its traditions, and its function was becoming more and more that of conserving its institutions and group sentiments.[19]

As secularization set in, said Ericksen, Church history would become more defensive, doctrinaire, and theological.[20] As the last refuge of their early faith, a "Mormon scholasticism" would develop which would have as its purpose the "justifying" of Mormon dogmas. "The old institutions and traditions are thus fortified on the one hand by sentiment and on the other by a well-developed system of theology."[21] But this would lead to a form of group introspection, which would prove to be essentially sterile.

> With a social group as with an individual, it [a group] tends to lose its vigor as soon as it becomes self-conscious. Its spirit weakens as soon as it begins to think about itself. . . . When Mormonism finds more glory in working out new social ideals than in the contemplating of past achievements or the beauty of its own theological system, it will begin to feel its old-time strength.[22]

Nevertheless, while Ericksen predicted the emergence of a substantial body of quasi-official studies, he failed to foresee the outpouring of scholarly secular studies by Mormon Ph.D. candidates in non-Church universities and in departments outside the College of Religious Instruction at Brigham Young University itself.

The English historian R. G. Collingwood once wrote that the historian investigating any historical event or phenomenon must make a distinction between the "outside" and the "inside" of the event.[23] In an analogous way some writers have looked at Mormon culture from the "outside" and others from the "inside." For example, one of the finest studies of Mormonism in recent years is the dissertation by Thomas F. O'Dea for Harvard entitled "Mormon Values: The Significance of a Religious Outlook for Social Action." Reared in an Irish Catholic household in Boston, O'Dea, after discharge from the Armed Forces at the end of World War II, did an honors thesis on a "fundamentalist" Catholic sect led by Father Feeney called the "Benedictines." Because of the brilliance of his work, O'Dea was invited to participate in the Comparative Study of Values in Five Cultures Project of the Laboratory of Social Relations at Harvard, under the direction of Professor Clyde Kluckhohn. It was the laboratory's plan to study the impact of religion on five different cultures located in one geographic area of northern New Mexico: Zuni, Navajo, Roman Catholic, Protestant, and Mormon. Since scholars had already been assigned to work on the first four groups, O'Dea, who knew virtually nothing about Mormonism prior to that time, was assigned the Mormon community. He devoured the literature, wrote an insightful preliminary analysis, conducted interviews with scholars and Church authorities, and reached a sympathetic understanding by residing for six months in a "frontier" New Mexico Mormon agricultural settlement. He concluded with a summer teaching assignment at a predominantly Mormon state university (Utah State University). His resulting dissertation, and the articles and books published from his research, offer unquestionably the best "outside" view of Mormon thought and practice now available.[24]

The prime example of a scholar and writer beginning from the "inside" is Juanita Brooks. Reared in a polygamous family in a Mormon settlement in southern Nevada, her brilliant, sensitive, and imaginative mind was saturated from childhood in Mormon lore—the Mountain Meadows Massacre, John D. Lee, stories of the Three Nephites, the inspirations and foibles of pioneer leaders, and the emotional and practical impact of Mormon doctrine. Her writings have illustrated the remarkable insights into Mormonism that can be obtained by a study of the lives of individual adherents, particularly in emotionally charged episodes.[25]

It is not possible to say whether Mormon studies are best done by practicing members, by "Jack Mormons" (i.e., lapsed or non-practicing members or excommunicants), or by complete "outsiders."[26] A. L. Neff felt that those reared as Mormons had an advantage. Born of pioneer parentage, Neff had been educated at the Brigham Young Academy, and later served as a principal of three "Mormon" high schools. Sensitive to the beliefs and feelings of his own people, Neff refused to accept either adverse or favorable generalizations until all the evidence was in. "I don't pretend to be very religious," he wrote, "but I have a passion for the truth in this field of American history." "In my projected historical labors," he wrote, "I intend to make allowance for inspiration. . . . I realize that if I were guided by the canons of historical criticism alone, I would make no real contribution to the already many works on the subject. But by combining the two I feel that I shall have an advantage over previous writers."[27] By adhering to this goal and by resourcefulness and circumspection in the use of sources, Neff set a high standard of integrity for others to follow.

Despite the substantial number of scholarly studies of Mormonism undertaken since the turn of the century, and of course there are significant works in addition to the dissertations listed,[28] much still remains for present and future researchers. The struggle of scholars not specializing in Mormon studies to find accounts and interpretations that would be useful and reliable for reference purposes points to serious deficiencies. At the same time, recent studies suggest new interpretations and opportunities.

With regard to the deficiencies, there is, first of all, not even a satisfactory general history of the Mormons. This appalling fact is evident from the large number of national and regional historians who still base their accounts on such "anti" works as Linn's *Story of the Mormons*, which is not only out of date but was not a reliable treatise to begin with.[29] On the other hand, the most widely used "official" history is theologically oriented, its focus is primarily on the recurring conflict between the Church and its "enemies," and it makes no attempt to relate Mormon history to contemporary national developments.[30] We continue to await the multi-volume history by Dale Morgan,[31] but many monographic studies would be helpful to a future synthesizer.[32] Particularly neglected are the "churches of the dispersion"—the dissident sects and groups that split off from the "mainstream" group headquartered in Salt Lake City.

Second, there are only a few Mormon biographies, and not all of those few are historically sound. The biography most often referred to by most scholars is Fawn Brodie's life of Joseph Smith, but earnest critics have found many inaccuracies in both fact and interpretation.[33] Despite the evidence of prodigious research, despite the charming imagery of its style and its stirring chronicle of an enigmatic career, the book has two methodological weaknesses. First, it is evident that Mrs. Brodie, who is a lapsed Mormon, not only has little patience with the pretensions of Mormonism, but little appreciation of religious phenomena generally. She refuses to accord integrity to the many men of undoubted intellect and character who associated with the Mormon prophet and believed him to be an inspired leader. Second, Mrs. Brodie was concerned, or at least it would seem, with painting a pen portrait rather than with writing a work of history. The work reads as though she began by studying the historical background sufficiently to formulate what she regarded as a reasonable and believable approach to Joseph Smith and then proceeded to mobilize the evidence to illustrate and support her interpretation. To be sure, these indictments may be overdrawn, but Mrs. Brodie's colorful adjectives and sometimes damning inferences imply a finality of judgment that is not warranted by the contradictory character of the evidence she examined.[34]

The need for a good biography of Joseph Smith must be emphasized because he was unquestionably a theological and social innovator of major significance. There are those who have deprecated Joseph Smith as a bumbling knave, far inferior to that great practical statesman, Brigham Young.[35] But, as Robert Flanders and Jan Shipps have shown in two recent doctoral dissertations, Joseph Smith was neither a charlatan nor a lunatic, but a personality of undoubted stature—a leader of imagination and energy and the person most responsible for the formulation of Mormon doctrine and practice. One can hardly obtain an understanding of Mormonism without coming to grips with his life, intellect, and character.

Just as Mrs. Brodie's biography, and certain others, are usually regarded (by the Mormons, at least) as "anti-Mormon,"[36] most of the "pro" biographies are undeviating pictures of sweetness and light. These err even more on the side of incredibility than the blacker portraits of the anti's.[37] Indeed, the only Mormon biography that appears to have withstood historical criticism in either direction is Juanita Brooks's *John Doyle Lee*. This is indeed embarrassing, considering that there have been, by now, several million Mormons. It is unfortunate for the cause of Mormon history that the Church Historian's Library, which is in the possession of virtually all of the diaries of leading Mormons, has not seen fit to publish these diaries or to permit qualified historians to use them without restriction. One result has been that "Mormons" have become known essentially through the lives and characters of some of their most notorious adherents—i.e., Porter Rockwell, John D.

Lee, and Hosea Stout[38]—rather than through such "mainstream" leaders as Brigham Young, John Taylor, Wilford Woodruff, George Q. Cannon, Joseph F. Smith, and David O. McKay. Even Brigham Young, recognized universally as one of America's great colonizers, has no satisfactory biography.[39]

There is also a need for studies of those who have contributed to the literature on Mormonism: Linn, Roberts, Ericksen, Neff, Werner, Beardsley, Anderson, Brodie, and others. How did they become interested in writing as they did about the Mormons? What familial, intellectual, and other influences colored their opinions and analyses? Here are topics for many master's theses and journal articles.[40]

The third great deficiency is the lack of studies of the period since 1877. It was right and proper that the first studies should reconstruct the great migration and the settlement of the Mormon West and analyze the social and cultural setting. Inasmuch as the great principle of history is continuity, increasing emphasis should be given to the period after Brigham Young's death—and, even more, to Mormon history in this century.[41] Of the 136 years that have elapsed since The Church of Jesus Christ of Latter-day Saints was founded in 1830, 70, or more than half, have occurred since Utah became a state in 1896. Yet virtually none of the studies of Mormondom has paid more than token attention to the "modern" half of Mormon history.

In this connection, the gradual but sure transition of Mormon country[42] from the exclusively Mormon commonwealth to a region in the American (in the broader sense) commonwealth deserves particular attention. Since completing my own study of nineteenth-century Mormon economics several years ago, I have done some research, in association with Professor Thomas Alexander and others, on the economic history of Utah and the Mountain West since 1900; the conclusion is inescapable that the economic and social history of Mormon country in this century is fully as significant, fully as regional, as that of the nineteenth century.[43] The unifying theme of the nineteenth-century Mormon economy was the Church, which promoted economic growth, regulated economic activity, and was the focus of community action. In a desert oasis like Utah and surrounding regions, strong organizational backing was required for economic success, and the Mormons were uniquely prepared to meet this challenge by virtue of their ideology and institutions. The cohesion of the Mormon settlers, their willingness to sacrifice for a great cause, and the concentration of capital in the hands of a church interested in promoting economic growth all contributed toward successful colonization.

When the activities of the Church were seriously curtailed by federal action during the latter part of the nineteenth century and the early part of the twentieth, the only remaining source of organizational strength to overcome the problems connected with the development of the region was the federal government. Happily, the nation was in the course of developing governmental organizational facilities that made that feasible. By means of reclamation, road construction, conservation and recreation activities, the construction of defense plants and installations, and other forms of federal assistance, the region has demonstrated healthy growth. The unifying theme and key to the Mormon economy in the twentieth century is the role of the federal government—its programs, aids, and consequences. That the Mountain West (i.e., the setting of "Mormon country") was unique in its heavy dependence upon federal programs for its development can be attributed to the fact that much of the region was settled and developed during years when the federal government was able and willing to assist. Without the many federal programs, the growth would unquestionably have been far less. And yet there are few who would question that the federal investment has paid off handsomely. The economic and social contributions of Mormon country to the nation have been numerous and substantial.

This obviously incomplete review should not conclude without mention of two exciting responses, quite independent of the Church itself, by young Mormon intellectuals to the need for competent professional history and commentary. The first is the founding of *Dialogue: A Journal of Mormon Thought*; the second is the formation in San Francisco, on December 28, 1965, of the Mormon History Association. Most of those who have promoted both the association and *Dialogue* are practicing Latter-day Saints; they share basic agreement that the Mormon religion and its history are subject to discussion, if not Mormon life is fair game for detached examination and clarification. They believe that the details of Mormon history and culture can be studied in human or naturalistic terms—indeed, must be so studied—and without thus rejecting the divinity of the Church's origin and work.[44]

Thus, while Mormon history has been "secularized" as the result of its study in secular graduate schools, a positive attempt is being made to promote research and writing which will give the Mormon heritage a fuller and more sympathetic hearing. Perhaps eventually a Mormon Yearbook can be published that will contribute to the elevation of Mormon studies, much as Schmoller's *Jahrbuch* contributed toward the edification and cultural advancement of central Europe.

Chapter Ten Notes

1. T. Lynn Smith, *The Sociology of Rural Life* (New York: Harper and Brothers, 1940).
2. Among the first works which I stumbled upon were: Lowry Nelson, *The Mormon Village: A Study in Social Origins* (Provo, Utah: Brigham Young University Press, 1930); Juanita Brooks, "A Close-up of Polygamy," *Harper's Magazine* 168 (1934): 299–307, and "The Water's In!" *Harper's Magazine* 175 (1941): 608–13; and Bernard DeVoto, "The Centennial of Mormonism," in *Forays and Rebuttals* (Boston: Little, Brown and Company, 1936), 77–137, and occasional articles in "The Easy Chair" in *Harper's Magazine.*
3. The basic source for early "pro" accounts was Orson Pratt, *An Interesting Account of Several Remarkable Visions* (Edinburgh: Ballantyne and Hughes, 1840). There followed the "History of Joseph Smith" first published in *Times and Seasons* (Nauvoo, Illinois), March 1842, and *Latter-day Saints' Millennial Star*, 3–5, 14–25 (Liverpool, 1842–44, 1852–64). This was later edited by B. H. Roberts and published as Joseph Smith, Jr., *History of the Church of Jesus Christ, Period I,* 6 vols. (Salt Lake City, 1902–12). One of the earliest semi-objective accounts is John Corrill, *A Brief History of the Church of Christ of Latter Day Saints, (commonly called Mormons): Including an Account of their Doctrine and Discipline; with the Reasons of the Author for Leaving the Church* (St. Louis, Ill.: Printed for the Author, 1839).
4. Among the early "anti" works were: E. D. Howe, *Mormonism Unvailed, or, A Faithful Account of that Singular Imposition and Delusion: From its Rise to the Present Time: With Sketches of the Characters of its Propagators* (Painesville, Ohio: Printed and Published by the Author, 1834), J. B. Turner, *Mormonism in All Ages: Or, the Rise, Progress,*

and Causes of Mormonism; with the Biography of its Author and Founder, Joseph Smith, Junior (New York: Published by Platt and Peters, Office of American Biblical Repository and American Eclectic, Brick Church Chapel, 1842); and John C. Bennett, *The History of the Saints, or, An Exposé of Joe Smith and Mormonism* (Boston: Leland and Whiting, 1842). The latter was the first such work to achieve a national audience and set a style followed by many subsequent works of exposé. Other widely read "anti" works in the nineteenth century were: J. H. Beadle, *Life in Utah, or, The Mysteries and Crimes of Mormonism: Being an Exposé of the Secret Rites and Ceremonies of the Latter-day Saints, with a Full and Authentic History of Polygamy and the Mormon Sect from its Origin to the Present Time* (Philadelphia: National Publishing, 1870); T. B. H. Stenhouse, *The Rocky Mountain Saints: A Full and Complete History of the Mormons, from the First Vision of Joseph Smith to the Last Courtship of Brigham Young* (New York: D. Appleton and Company, 1873); and Ann Eliza Young, *Wife no. 19, or, The Story of a Life in Bondage: Being a Complete Expose of Mormonism, and Revealing the Sorrows, Sacrifices and Sufferings of Women in Polygamy* (Hartford, Conn.: Dustin, Gilman and Company, 1875).

5. The better travel accounts include Jules Rémy and Julius Brenchley, *A Journey to Great-Salt-Lake City; With a Sketch of the History, Religion, and Customs of the Mormons, and an Introduction on the Religious Movement in the United States*, 2 vols. (London: W. Jeffs, 1861); Richard F. Burton, *The City of the Saints: And Across the Rocky Mountains to California* (New York: Harper and Brothers, 1862); Samuel Bowles, *Across the Continent: A Summer's Journey to the Rocky Mountains, the Mormons, and the Pacific States, with Speaker Colfax* (Springfield, Mass.: Samuel Bowles and Company, 1865); and Phil Robinson, *Sinners and Saints: A Tour Across the States, and Round Them; With Three Months Among the Mormons* (Boston: Roberts Brothers, 1883).
6. There were at least three reasonably impartial histories of the Mormons in the nineteenth century: Charles Mackay, *The Mormons or Latter-day Saints: With Memoirs of the Life and Death of Joseph Smith, the "American Mahomet"* (London: Office of the National Illustrated Library, 1851); Edward W. Tullidge, *History of Salt Lake City and its Founders* (Salt Lake City: Edward W. Tullidge, Publisher and Proprietor, 1886), the only one of the three by a Mormon—and at this stage he was somewhat disaffected; and H. H. Bancroft, *History of Utah, 1540–1886* (San Francisco: The History Company, 1889). Despite their excellence, one would hardly have found the first two in a typical library. As for the Bancroft, it left many readers confused by the favorable account of the Mormons in the text and the equally unfavorable account in the footnotes.
7. As will be seen, many of these dissertations and other works by their authors were subsequently influential as published works.
8. This was preceded by "Economic Aspects of Mormonism," by Richard T. Ely, who had been trained in the German Historical School, in *Harper's Magazine* 106 (1903): 667–78. The earliest Ph.D. dissertation on a Mormon subject is Woodbridge Riley's psychological interpretation of Joseph Smith, but it cannot be classed as a dissertation on the Latter-day Saints and their culture.
9. This mention of Schmoller and his somewhat marginal connection with Mormon studies at the beginning of the century should not obscure the dominating influence of Leopold von Ranke on general German and American historiography. Another

leading European historian, Eduard Meyer, wrote one of the early "scientific" studies of Mormonism, which, however, suffers from the shortcomings of Riley, Linn, and other writers on whom it was based: *Ursprung und geschichte der Mormonen, mit exkursen uber die anfange des islams und des christentums* (Halle: Niemeyer, 1912).

10. English translation. The original was published under the title "Gemeinwirtschaft und Unternehmungsformen im Mormonenstaat," *Jahrbuch für Gesetzgebung, Verwaltung und Volkswirtschaft im Deutschern Reich* (39 vols.; Leipzig, 1877–1915), 21 (1907), 1003–1056. The writer has an unpublished translation into English by Dr. Philip Flammer, of the United States Air Force Academy, which was completed several years ago while Dr. Flammer was a student at Utah State University.
11. In 1904–5, just prior to Wilson's dissertation, the famous social philosopher and economic historian, Max Weber, had published in a German review *The Protestant Ethic and the Spirit of Capitalism*, which contained an interesting footnote reference to the Mormons (London, 1930), 264 n25. This may or may not have excited the interest of Schmoller and Wilson, but it was unquestionably one of the factors which induced Lowell L. Bennion, a (Mormon) sociology student at the Universities of Vienna and Strasbourg in the early 1930s, to write a little-known Weber-type analysis of Mormonism in his doctoral dissertation entitled *Max Weber's Methodology* (Paris: Impr. Les Presses Modernes, 1933), esp. 128–35. Shortly thereafter (1934), a French student of Vilfredo Pareto, G. H. Bousquet, spent several weeks in Utah and later published a similar analysis under the title "A Theocratic Economy: The Mormon Church," in the *Revue d'économie politique* in 1936. ("Une théocratie économique: l'Eglise Mormone," *Revue d'Economie Politique* (January 1936): 106–450.) In addition to other works, Bousquet is also author of *Les Mormons: Histoire et Institutions* (Paris: Presses Universitaires de France, 1949), one of the "Que sais-je?" series of the "Presses Universitaires de France," which has been widely distributed and read in France. An authority on Arab sociology attached to the University of Algiers, Bousquet became interested in Joseph Smith and Mormon history because of supposed similarities to Mohammed and the history of Islam.
12. Obviously, the three categories are not mutually exclusive. Some of the "quasi-official" studies belong, topically, in the analytical or "Mormon epic" categories. They are classified separately because of the need to distinguish studies which tend to be basically "faith-promoting" from those done in "secular" graduate schools which insist upon naturalistic or humanistic description and analysis.
13. A year earlier Hamilton Gardner, a student at Harvard, had published "Cooperation Among the Mormons," *Quarterly Journal of Economics* 31 (1917): 461–99. He later published "Communism Among the Mormons," *Quarterly Journal of Economics* 37 (1922): 134–74. But his projected work, "Economic Activities Among the Mormons," completed in 1925, was never published. It is available on microfilm at the Utah State University Library.
14. See Laughlin, *Industrial America Berlin Lectures of 1906* (New York: C. Scribner's Sons, 1906).
15. A. L. Neff to G. H. Brimhall, 1 April 1906, manuscript, Brimhall Papers, L. Tom Perry Special Collections, Harold B. Lee Library, Brigham Young University, Provo, Utah.
16. Andrew Love Neff, *History of Utah, 1847 to 1869*, Leland Hargrave Creer, ed. (Salt Lake City: Deseret News Press, 1940).
17. Taylor decried the baneful influence of the "positive thinkers" in an address to the

Conference on "Utah and The West" at the University of Utah, 22 June 1965. It should be emphasized that religious history is not synonymous with non-objective history, and "secular" history is not always honest and impartial. Theistic history is quite capable of becoming "great" history.

18. Since only the dissertations written under Ph.D. programs are included on the appended list, many of these studies are omitted. Examples of fine Ed.D. dissertations by Mormon educators on Mormon subjects are: Wendell O. Rich, "Certain Basic Concepts in the Educational Philosophy of The Church of Jesus Christ of Latter-day Saints, 1830–1930" (Ed.D diss., Utah State University, 1954); and James R. Clark, "Church and State Relations in Education in Utah, 1847–1957" (Ed.D. diss., Utah State University, 1958).
19. Ephraim Edward Ericksen, *The Psychological and Ethical Aspects of Mormon Group Life* (Chicago: University of Chicago Press, 1922), 91.
20. Ericksen did not use the term secularization—a term that is common among sociologists of religion and others, particularly Catholics. Secularization "has usually referred to the developments of the past century or so during which what might be termed a kind of naturalistic humanism has gradually displaced life orientations of a theistic character with those focusing on the rational empirical mastery of the human condition in the here and now." John T. Flint, "The Secularization of Norwegian Society," *Comparative Studies in Society and History* 6 (April 1964): 325. The term is not ordinarily used by Latter-day Saints because of the unique association in Mormon theology of earthly life with eternal salvation. However, there is increasing justification for the use of some such term to refer to the gradual replacement of the Church as the central focus of all aspects of life—and the Church leader as the authority on all aspects of life—with a more naturalistic or "secular" humanism which accords to religion, the Church, and the Church leader a more limited role.
21. Ericksen, *The Psychological and Ethical Aspects of Mormon Group Life*, 98.
22. Ericksen, *The Psychological and Ethical Aspects of Mormon Group Life*, 99.
23. Cited in Frederic C. Lane and Jelle C. Riemersma, *Enterprise and Secular Change: Readings in Economic History* (Homewood, Ill.: Irwin, 1953), 438.
24. See Thomas O'Dea, *The Mormons* (Chicago: University of Chicago Press, 1957). His "Mormon" essays in sociological journals are as profound as they are influential; e.g.: "Mormonism and the Avoidance of Sectarian Stagnation: A Study of Church, Sect, and Incipient Nationality," *American Journal of Sociology* 60 (November 1954): 285–93; and "A Comparative Study of the Role of Values in Social Action in Two Southwestern Communities," *American Sociological Review* 18 (December 1953): 645–54 (with Evon Z. Vogt).
25. Strictly speaking, Mrs. Brooks's parents were both reared in polygamous households. In addition to many articles, her books include: *Dudley Leavitt: Pioneer to Southern Utah* (St. George, Utah: J. Brooks, 1942); *The Mountain Meadows Massacre* (Stanford, Calif.: Stanford University Press, 1950), and *John Doyle Lee: Zealot—Pioneer Builder—Scapegoat* (Glendale, Calif.: The Arthur H. Clark Company, 1961).
26. The curious may want to know how the writer classes himself. My family were Latter-day Saint converts from the South—not an established or pioneer family with "a heritage." I grew up in a town (Twin Falls, Idaho) that was at the time almost completely non-Mormon; I went to non-Mormon universities (University of Idaho and University of North Carolina); I married a non-Mormon girl (now a converted Mor-

mon) and went off to war in North Africa and Europe, where I had no Mormon associates. I did not settle down in a Mormon environment until I came to Utah State University in 1946 at the age of twenty-nine. Whatever their worth, *Great Basin Kingdom: An Economic History of the Latter-day Saints, 1830–1900* (Cambridge, Mass., Harvard University Press, 1958) and other essays and monographs thus represent attempts to see the Mormon economy and culture from the perspective of a sympathetic "outsider."

27. Neff to Brimhall, 1 April 1906, manuscript. I am grateful to Dr. Klaus Hansen, of Utah State University, who called the Neff correspondence to my attention and furnished me a copy of the letter cited here.
28. Perhaps the most significant works on Mormonism which did not originate as doctoral dissertations are: B. H. Roberts, "History of the Mormon Church," *Americana*, 1909 to July 1915, later revised, brought up-to-date, and published as *A Comprehensive History of The Church of Jesus Christ of Latter-day Saints: Century I* (6 vols.: Salt Lake City: Deseret Book, 1930); Andrew Jenson, *Encyclopedic History of the Church of Jesus Christ of Latter-day Saints* (Salt Lake City: Deseret News Publishing Company, 1941); Nels Anderson, *Desert Saints: The Mormon Frontier in Utah* (Chicago: University of Chicago Press, 1942); and Fawn M. Brodie, *No Man Knows My History: The Life of Joseph Smith, the Mormon Prophet* (New York: Alfred A. Knopf, 1945).
29. William Alexander Linn, *The Story of the Mormons: From the Date of Their Origin to the Year 1901* (New York: Macmillan Company, 1902). An example of the use of Linn as the basic reference by a scholar who ought to know better is Alice Felt Tyler, *Freedom's Ferment: Phases of American Social History to 1860* (Minneapolis: University of Minnesota Press, 1944).
30. Joseph Fielding Smith, *Essentials in Church History: A History of the Church from the Birth of Joseph Smith to the Present Time (1922), with Introductory Chapters on the Antiquity of the Gospel and the "Falling Away"* (Salt Lake City: Deseret News Press, 1922).
31. Reared as a Mormon, and a University of Utah graduate of 1937, Dale L. Morgan did extensive research on Mormon history while associated with the Historical Records Survey and Federal Writers' Project in Utah and the Office of Price Administration in Washington, D.C., and in connection with the books under his own name which began to appear in 1943. The quality of his work is evidenced in *Utah: A Guide to the State* (New York: Hastings House, 1941) and *The Great Salt Lake* (Indianapolis, Ill.: Bobbs-Merrill, 1947). A specialist in the Bancroft Library since 1954, he has become heavily involved in other historical projects and his Mormon history has been in a state of suspension.
32. At this date, the most satisfactory short narrative history of the Mormons for a non-Mormon, despite many inaccuracies and omissions, is Ray B. West Jr., *Kingdom of the Saints: The Story of Brigham Young and the Mormons* (New York: Viking Press, 1957). The best "analytic" study is O'Dea's *The Mormons*. Roberts's *Comprehensive History*, which is almost never used by non-Mormons, is surprisingly complete and objective; it is the best single reference.
33. Examples of errors in the book are given in a lengthy review in *The Deseret News* (11 May 1946), and in Hugh Nibley, *No Ma'am, That's Not History: A Brief Review of Mrs. Brodie's Reluctant Vindication of a Prophet She Seeks to Expose* (Salt Lake City: Bookcraft, 1946). Many of the factual errors in *No Man Knows My History* have been eliminated in recent printings.

34. One reader of this paper writes that it ill behooves Latter-day Saints to complain so frenetically about Mrs. Brodie when they have thus far failed to produce a scholarly study which could even hope to compete with hers as a life of Joseph Smith.
35. "Mormons," *Encyclopedia Britannica* (11th ed.; New York, 1910); DeVoto, "The Centennial of Mormonism"; and elsewhere.
36. The "anti" biographies include: Harry M. Beardsley, *Joseph Smith and His Mormon Empire* (Boston: Houghton Mifflin, 1931); and Hoffman Birney, *Zealots of Zion* (Philadelphia: Penn Publishing Company, 1931).
37. Among the better Mormon biographies are John Henry Evans, *Charles Coulson Rich: Pioneer Builder of the West* (New York: Macmillan, 1936); Clair Noall, *Intimate Disciple: A Portrait of Willard Richards, Apostle to Joseph Smith—Cousin of Brigham Young* (Salt Lake City: University of Utah Press, 1957). Several biographies by Bryant S. Hinckley are of the "sugary" kind; e.g., Bryant S. Hinckley, *Daniel Hanmer Wells and Events of His Time* (Salt Lake City: Deseret News Press, 1942) and *Sermons and Missionary Services of Melvin Joseph Ballard* (Salt Lake City: Deseret Book, 1949).
38. Charles Kelly and Hoffman Birney, *Holy Murder: The Story of Porter Rockwell* (New York: Minton, Balch and Company, 1934); John D. Lee, *A Mormon Chronicle: The Diaries of John D. Lee, 1848–1876*, Robert Glass Cleland and Juanita Brooks, 2 vols. (San Marino, Calif., Huntington Library, 1955); Hosea Stout, *On the Mormon Frontier: The Diary of Hosea Stout*, Juanita Brooks, ed., 2 vols. (Salt Lake City: University of Utah Press, 1964).
39. An excellent and sprightly-written assessment of Young is a fifty-page chapter in Jonathan Hughes, *The Vital Few: American Economic Progress and Its Protagonists* (Boston: Houghton Mifflin, 1966). Biographies include: M. R. Werner, *Brigham Young* (New York: Harcourt, Brace and Company, 1925), a researched account which is good but essentially pokes fun; and Preston Nibley, *Brigham Young: The Man and His Work* (Salt Lake City: Deseret News Press, 1936), which manages to present a life of Young without once mentioning polygamy.
40. Pieces which show what can be done are: George Ellsworth, "Hubert Howe Bancroft and the History of Utah," *Utah Historical Quarterly* 22 (April 1954): 99–124; and William F. Lye, "Edward Wheelock Tullidge, 'The Mormons' Rebel Historian,'" *Utah Historical Quarterly* 28 (January 1960): 56–75.
41. The only historical study that treats exclusively the last sixty-five years is the rather brief and topical text by James B. Allen and Richard O. Cowan, *Mormonism in the Twentieth Century* (Provo, Utah: Brigham Young University, Extension Publications, 1964). An excellent sociological study of Mormons in the 20th century is John L. Sorenson, "Industrialization and Social Change: A Controlled Comparison of Two Utah Communities" (Ph.D. diss., University of California at Los Angeles, 1962).
42. An excellent definition and description of Mormon Country is found in D. W. Meinig, "The Mormon Culture Region: Strategies and Patterns in the Geography of The American West, 1847–1964," *Annals of the Association of American Geographers* 55 (June 1965): 191–220. A delightful introduction to the folkways is found in Wallace Stegner, *Mormon Country* (New York: Duell, Sloan and Pearce, 1942).
43. Two brief essays are: Leonard J. Arrington, *From Wilderness to Empire: The Role of Utah in Western Economic History* (Salt Lake City: Institute of American Studies, University of Utah, 1961); and Leonard J. Arrington, *The Changing Economic Structure of the Mountain West, 1850–1950* (Logan: Utah State University Press, 1963).

44. The above also expresses my own conviction, it is a subject which warrants a full essay. As one reader of this paper has asked, is it really possible to humanize all phases of Mormon history without destroying Church doctrines regarding historical events? Can doctrine be examined and explained without losing its very qualities of "doctrine?" Doesn't such understanding preclude "doctrine" by definition? Aren't these the considerations that motivate Church authorities to hesitate making public the documents relating to doctrinal phases of Church history? Finally, is it a valid historical approach to begin with the assumption that the Church itself is not subject to argument?

Chapter 11

The Intellectual Tradition of the Latter-Day Saints

IN ONE OF THE EARLIEST BOOKS of imaginative literature about the American West (published in 1826), novelist-editor-missionary-biographer Timothy Flint reveals a common impression of the time that "in travelling towards the frontier, the decreasing scale of civilization and improvement exhibits an accurate illustration of inverted history." Flint's better-known contemporary, James Fenimore Cooper, although an admirer of the West, acknowledged that "refinement and gentility were conceivable only in members of an upper class with enough wealth to guarantee its leisure, and a sufficiently secure social status to give it poise and assurance." Still another contemporary, Ralph Waldo Emerson, stated, "The pioneers are commonly the off-scourings of civilized society."

Eastern intellectuals were almost unanimous in describing western settlers as uncouth, unpolished, and culturally degraded. The natural landscape of the West, in which most of the eastern romantics included the Indians, was often regarded as sublime, but the adjustment to wilderness life encouraged the squatters to slip backward in the scale of civilization. Out of the West, in the opinion of Arthur Moore, came "rank anti-intellectualism."

The reversion-to-barbarism theme was applied with special per-

---

Paper presented to the Utah Academy of Sciences, Arts and Letters, St. George, Utah, 13 September 1968, upon receiving the Charles H. Redd Award. First published with full documentation as "The Intellectual Tradition of Mormon Utah," *Proceedings of the Utah Academy of Sciences, Arts and Letters* 45, part 2 (1968): 346–65. Adapted and reprinted as "The Intellectual Tradition of the Latter-day Saints," *Dialogue* 4 (spring 1969): 13–26.

sistence to the early settlers of Utah, but here it was attributed to the religion rather than to the natural environment. Thus, while the remainder of the West at least had the hope of becoming re-civilized as soon as the physical constraints were removed and the amenities restored, this was not true of Mormon country, where the dominant religion, by virtue of its supposed inherent decivilizing character, condemned the territory and its residents to more or less perpetual savagery.[1] Nearly all of the fifty or more nineteenth-century novels that described life in Utah portrayed the Mormons as incurably ignorant, lecherous, and depraved.[2] But the most damning indictment of all was penned as recently as 1926 by Bernard DeVoto—one of Utah's own sons and probably its most brilliant literary personality. "Civilized life does not exist in Utah," DeVoto wrote. "It never has existed there. It never will exist there." "No poets lingered there, no musicians, philosophers, or scholars." Utah's settlers, he wrote, came "from localities where civilization had never penetrated," and their "only distinguishing characteristics were their servility to their leaders and their beliefs in a low-comedy God." There was "rigorous suppression of individuality, impracticability, scepticism, and all the other qualities of intelligence." As a result, Utah was poor "in everything that makes for civilization." "Who ever heard," he asked, "of a Utah painter, a Utah sculptor, a Utah novelist, or poet, or critic, or educator, or editor, or publicist—who ever heard of a Utahn?"[3]

Believing that Utah's non-Mormon residents were "less fanatical" and "less ignorant" than the Mormons, DeVoto lodged the responsibility for the poverty of Utah's culture on the narrow and unthinking character of its religious heritage. Indeed, in "A Revaluation," written some twenty years after the *American Mercury* outburst, DeVoto admitted that, while his earlier article had been "dishonest" and "irresponsible," he still believed "that Utah, and especially Mormon culture" was more provincial than most of the nation, that it was "extremely sensitive and intolerant to criticism and even to difference of opinion in which there is no criticism whatever," and that "the orthodox Mormon mind cannot tolerate any objective treatment of Mormon history whatever."[4]

An intellectual, according to *Webster's New International Dictionary*, is a person of superior intelligence; a person devoted to matters of the mind and especially to the arts and letters; a person given to study, reflection, and speculation, especially concerning large, profound, or abstract issues; a person engaged in activity requiring preeminently the use of the intellect. He is usually viewed as a person who is capable of commenting upon society and its problems "with greater detachment than those more directly caught up in the practical business of production and power."[5]

Were there persons with these qualities among our Latter-day Saint forebears? Did the Mormon community have intellectuals—and are there such persons in our community today?

There is a special problem involved in seeking to denote intellectuals in a religious group as fully committed as the Latter-day Saints. A "real intellectual," it is said, will not subordinate rationalism to other ways of knowing, such as authoritarianism or mysticism.[6] But "good Mormons" will do so, for that is a part of their being good Mormons. So-called Mormon intellectuals, it is said, will rationalize that revelation is superior to reason. Should one water down the word "intellectual" by including the bright and industrious Mormon scholars who have failed the acid test of standing outside their own culture and evaluating it all the way on the basis of the best "thinking of men"?[7] Such a high standard for the classification "real intellectuals" would reduce substantially the number of "real Mormons" who could qualify.[8] Actually, dictionary and encyclopedia definitions of "intellectual" permit the inclusion of persons with religious faith. There is no definition that would disqualify a St. Augustine, an Aquinas, a Thomas More, or a Cardinal Newman.

The primary question is the extent to which one's emotional attachment to certain "final truths" informs his intellectual activity; whether his soul-ties prevent his thought on key issues from being freely detachable from his own cultural traditions. Bertrand Russell suggests that in studying a given philosopher or line of thought "the right attitude is neither reverence nor contempt, but first a kind of hypothetical sympathy." One should cultivate the enlargement of the scope of his mind beyond his own "cherished prejudices" by exercising his historical and psychological imagination.[9] There would seem to be no inherent reason why our more sophisticated thinkers could not thus project their minds as have highly committed persons in other religions and cultures.

Richard Hofstadter posits two qualities in the intellectual's attitude toward ideas—playfulness and piety. Playfulness, he writes, is openness to the potential of ideas—"sheer delight in intellectual activity."

> Truth captured loses its glamor; truths long known and widely believed have a way of turning false with time; easy truths are a bore, and too many of them become half-truths. Whatever the intellectual is too certain of, if he is healthily playful, he begins to find unsatisfactory. The meaning of his intellectual life lies not in the possession of truth but in the quest for new uncertainties.

The other quality is piety, for the intellectual recognizes that values underlie every question that is posed; the life of the mind has a "kind of primary moral significance. . . . The intellectual is *engagé*—he is pledged, committed, enlisted. What everyone else is willing to admit, namely that ideas and abstractions are of signal importance in human life, he imperatively feels."[10]

How open and pious have Latter-day Saint scholars been in searching for truth? How creative and playful have they been in developing new interpretations and hypotheses?[11]

One might distinguish four stages in the growth of Mormon intellectuality: the formative stage, the stage of elaboration, the purification stage, and the stage of creative adaptation.[12]

The *formative stage* covers the period from the organization of the infant Church of Christ in western New York State in 1830 to the assassination of Joseph Smith in Illinois in 1844. Four persons were paramount in the introduction of new concepts and policies: Joseph Smith, Sidney Rigdon, Parley Pratt, and Orson Pratt. The historian's problem in assessing the intellectuality of Joseph Smith is magnified by the fact that the most sophisticated of his works (Book of Mormon, Pearl of Great Price, Doctrine and Covenants) are theophanous—that is, the ultimate author, translator, or inspirer of the works was represented to be Deity. But whatever the precise relative contributions of Joseph Smith, ancient theologians, and God, the words and ideas contained in these works passed through the Prophet's mind, and thus we are permitted to apply to them the same literary and philosophical criticism that we apply to other works. The noted Catholic sociologist Thomas O'Dea undertook to study the Book of Mormon from this point of view and concluded that the book did indeed have significant intellectual content and was worthy of the attention of students of American intellectual history. "The intellectuality of the *Book of Mormon*," he wrote, "is to be seen in its recognition of currents of thought other than and antagonistic to its own point of view, and especially in its awareness of current skepticism and rationalism."[13] The book also provided "a reasonable answer to problems of existence and salvation." While there is no comparable study of the content of the Pearl of Great Price and Doctrine and Covenants by a scholar of national stature, the writings and sermons of Joseph Smith have attracted and motivated several generations of Latter-day Saints. The Prophet exercised leadership in relating individual members and the group to the universe and to society at large, legitimated authority and defined its responsibilities, and interpreted the Church's historical role.[14]

With respect to the other three early leaders, Sydney Rigdon contributed most of the "Lectures on Faith" and many sermons that relate to such early principles and ordinances as faith, repentance, baptism, spiritual gifts, the millennium, and communitarianism. Parley Pratt wrote *Voice of Warning*, *Key to Theology*, *The Autobiography of Parley Parker Pratt*, and founded the *Latter-day Saints' Millennial Star* in Liverpool.[15] Parley's brother, Orson, often regarded as the foremost Mormon intellectual of the nineteenth century, wrote a series of pamphlets for distribution in England that gave philosophical meaning and depth to many of the theological teachings. Many of these were important enough to be reviewed in the foremost literary and philosophical journals in Europe.[16]

That there was intellectual ferment in early Mormonism is clear; the *History of the Church* as dictated by Joseph Smith or written by his secretaries reports many instances of interchange of ideas and dissent from authoritatively held interpretations. The dispersion, which occurred after his death in 1844, is evidence that Joseph Smith held together persons of a wide variety of opinions and beliefs. Although not always, Joseph Smith often opposed the dogmatists within the Church who, once they got hold of a "truth," sought to discourage the creative thought of others who continued to experiment with even newer "truths." For this reason, early Mormonism took on the coloration of a fellowship of believers in "Restored Christianity" rather than a sect with inflexible ideology.[17] On one occasion Pelatiah Brown, an older member of the Church, expressed in convincing language some of his own ideas with respect to "the beast full of eyes before and behind" in the Revelation of St. John. Certain members of the community disagreed with his interpretations and "hauled him up for trial before the High Council." Joseph Smith remonstrated with them for doing so, and in the next public meeting devoted the first part of his sermon to a plea for freedom of religious thought:

> I [do] not like the old man being called up for erring in doctrine. It looks too much like the Methodists, and not like the Latter-day Saints. Methodists have creeds which a man must believe or be kicked out of their church. I want the liberty of thinking and believing as I please. It feels so good not to be trammelled. It does not prove that a man is not a good man because he errs in doctrine.[18]

The *elaboration stage* (the second stage) may be said to begin with the murder of Joseph Smith in 1844 and continue to the organization of the School of the Prophets in 1867. Brigham Young, as Joseph Smith's successor (so far as the "Utah Mormons" are concerned), did not envision himself as an innovator, either in theology or in social affairs. The conditions under which Brigham Young and the Twelve Apostles assumed leadership assured a hierarchical structure designed along authoritarian lines. The theophanous works of Joseph Smith were canonized into doctrine, and the doctrine and organizational structure of the Church became more dogmatic and inflexible. Brigham's task was to preach the doctrines, carry out the policies, and administer the programs of the founding Prophet. A man of enormous determination and energy, and able to command the loyalty of men of unquestioned endowments, Brigham Young's intellect did not express itself as freely as did that of his predecessor in the creation of new ideas and symbols.[19]

Thus, the intellectual elaboration and development of the potentialities inherent in the doctrines and policies formulated during the Joseph Smith era focused around three groups in early Utah.

First are the private secretaries and advisors of Brigham Young, including John Jaques, George D. Watt, Thomas Bullock, David McKenzie, and George A. Smith. The work of these men finds expression in the letters signed by Brigham Young and directed to government officials, apostles, mission presidents, and, most importantly, to Colonel Thomas L. Kane. Having studied these documents in some detail, the writer offers his word that they are often of high quality, with substantial intellectual content.

Second are the editors of and writers for *The Deseret News*, *Latter-day Saints' Millennial Star*, *The Seer*, *The Frontier Guardian*, *The Mormon*, and other publications of the Church. These included Willard Richards, Orson Pratt, Orson Hyde, Franklin D. Richards, and John Taylor. All of these were men of intellectual substance and productivity.

Third are the educators and independent writers, including James Linforth and Frederick Piercy, who prepared the 1855 edition of *Route from Liverpool,* which was recently republished by Harvard University Press;[20] Edward W. Tullidge and E. L. T. Harrison, the editors of *Peep O'Day*, an independent weekly magazine of literature, science, and art; and Sarah Carmichael, whose poetry attracted the attention of national figures, including William Cullen Bryant, who placed one of her poems in his book of "best American poetry."

The third stage, the *stage of purification*, may be said to begin with the inauguration of the "Protective Movement" in 1867 and end with the achievement of statehood in 1896. The establishment of protection, it should be explained, is related to the approach of the transcontinental railroad. Many observers, both within and outside of Utah, recognized certain threats posed by the imminent completion of the Pacific Railroad. Eastern and midwestern enterprisers and laborers would flock in to exploit new mines and markets, thus threatening the continuance of theocratic control of the region. Increased commercial intercourse would threaten the economic autonomy of the Mormon community. Brigham Young and his associates saw this as a time for the Saints to band together to preserve their unique way of life.

A number of economic programs formed the core of Mormon protectionism: branch railroads were built by the Mormons themselves to connect LDS settlements with the main line; trade was centered in a parent wholesale store (ZCMI) and in cooperative retail outlets in the wards and settlements; new manufacturing and financial enterprises were launched; and various devices were instituted for preserving group loyalties and strengthening community institutions. The group was directed by a community planning council called the School of the Prophets, with a central body in Salt Lake City and branch schools in each of the principal settlements. At the same time, a coordinated program was established to assure the participation of the women of the Church with the organization of centrally directed auxiliary, the Female Relief Society. This group also had local organizations in each settlement, as did the Young Ladies' Retrenchment Society (later the Young Women's Mutual Improvement Association), which was formed at this time to supervise activities of the young women. (A little later, the Young Men's Mutual Improvement Association was organized for young men.) Unifying devices included the *Woman's Exponent*, which was founded in 1870 as an independent magazine for women, and the *Contributor*, commenced in 1879 as an independent magazine for young men. A central Sunday school organization likewise was established at this time to teach the gospel to young people, and a magazine was inaugurated for their use called the *Juvenile Instructor*.

Unquestionably, this movement of indoctrination for purposes of protecting the Mormon way of life involved a certain surrendering of free thought—or, at least, of the freedom to propagate heretical and hostile thought. Shortly after the protective movement was launched, a group of "liberal" Mormons—comprising several members of the Utah intellectual community— founded a "liberal" journal called the *Utah Magazine*. Boldly, they advocated accommodation to dominant forces at work in the nation. They opposed an "exclusive" social and economic policy, contended that the priesthood was not infallible, and raised questions about the influence of Church leadership on economics, politics, and education. The leaders of this group, William S. Godbe, E. L. T. Harrison, Edward W. Tullidge, Henry W. Lawrence, and others, were brought before a Church tribunal and excommunicated. Several other "liberals" left the Church in sympathy.

Intellectual leaders during the purification stage included, once again, Orson Pratt, whose *Key to the Universe*, published in Liverpool in 1873, was an early attempt to stretch the Gospel beyond a simple theological pattern, thus introducing a wider philosophical meaning to Church thought;[21] George Q. Cannon, who edited the *Juvenile Instructor*, wrote several books for young people, kept a diary which one who has read it states to be magnificent, and as congressional delegate supervised the campaign for statehood; Edward W. Tullidge, whose contributions to LDS literature included several articles for magazines of national circulation, the publication of *Tullidge's Quarterlies*, and the authorship of such books as *Life of Joseph the Prophet*, *Life of Brigham Young*, *History of Salt Lake City*, and *History of Northern Utah and Southern Idaho*;[22] and Emmeline B. Wells, who edited the *Woman's Exponent* during most of this period; and Susa Young Gates who wrote dozens of books, both fictional and non-fictional, and edited the *Young Woman's Journal*.

The purification period witnessed an accelerated educational program aimed at countering the inroads of denominational academies established in several localities in the territory. Although a vehicle of intellectual isolation, perpetuating to some extent the insularity of the period that preceded it, this renewed interest in education prompted the founding of the Brigham Young Academy in Provo (now Brigham Young University), the Brigham Young

College in Logan, and the Latter-day Saints College in Salt Lake City. In addition, the University of Deseret was revitalized and converted into the University of Utah; and many academies or high schools were established in the various settlements.

The fourth stage, which might be called the *stage of creative adaptation*, seems to have commenced about the time of statehood and has continued to the present. This stage has involved the adaptation of secular learning to the needs of the Mormons—or, to put it the other way around, the adaptation of the doctrines and practices of the Mormons to the secular world in which they live.[23]

Several events of intellectual importance have taken place during these seventy-two years. First, a number of graduates of the University of Deseret, LDS University, Brigham Young College, and Brigham Young Academy began to go east to study at secular institutions. Faced with the problem of reconciling their own teachings with those of "the outside world," they ultimately created philosophies, theories, and explanations that enriched the intellectual content of Mormon doctrine. Second, the growth and expansion of Utah institutions of higher learning, and particularly those where the students were entirely or predominantly of Mormon origin, forced the adaptation of courses of study to bridge the gap between opposing cultures and values. The writing of textbooks, in the sciences and humanities as well as in religion, fostered experimentation with creative philosophies. One of the most important developments during this period was the initiation of "religion classes," which attempted to provide training in religion on a level equivalent to that in secular classes. These were ultimately divided into seminary instruction for high school students and institutes of religion classes for those in colleges and universities. Third, the intellectual growth and intellectual changes in the nation generally emboldened Mormon educators and students to study the theory of evolution, higher criticism, behaviorism, communism, and other crosscurrents.

The adaptation of a fiercely held faith—a faith that could motivate and propel the successful settlement of a region as arid as most of Utah—was bound to produce a tension. Out of this tension many causes célèbres arose: the resignations in 1911 of three prominent staff members of the Brigham Young University who were warned about their advanced views on evolution and higher criticism; the 1915 resignations of a number of staff members at the University of Utah who protested controls and interferences by representatives of the dominant culture; and a number of excommunications, releases, displacements, and demotions within the memories of members of the academy here today. These cases were often more complex than the general public realized, and some of the official decisions were undoubtedly justified as necessary to achieving the basic objectives of the institution or the community, but it is clear that an atmosphere of isolation and fear and an emphasis on indoctrination have at times discouraged free expression and discussion. It is also clear, fortunately, that discussion and criticism, dissent if you will, continued to be heard.

The view of the Church during this "modern" stage thus has varied, as one might expect, from cautious acceptance of the "new learning" to warnings that the "word of God as expressed by the Brethren" is a more safe position than pinning one's faith on the uncertain foundations of a secular learning which holds that there is no final truth. Perhaps the Church's most careful expression of its point of view was that given ten years ago to the students and faculty of Brigham Young University by President Hugh B. Brown:

> We are very grateful in the Church and in this great university that the freedom, dignity, and integrity of the individual is basic in church doctrine as well as in democracy. Here we are free to think and express our opinions. Fear will not stifle thought, as is the case in some areas which have not yet emerged from the dark ages. God himself refuses to trammel man's free agency even though its exercise sometimes teaches painful lessons. Both creative science and revealed religion find their fullest and truest expression in the climate of freedom. . . .
>
> I hope that you will develop the questing spirit. Be unafraid of new ideas for they are as stepping stones to progress. You will of course, respect the opinions of others but be unafraid to dissent—*if you are informed.*
>
> Now that I have mentioned freedom to express your thoughts, I caution you that your thoughts and expressions must meet competition in the market place of thought, and in that competition truth will emerge triumphant. Only error needs to fear freedom of expression. Seek truth in

> all fields; and in that search you will need at least three virtues: courage, zest, and modesty. The ancients put that thought in the form of a prayer. They said, "From the cowardice that shrinks from new truth, from the laziness that is content with half truth, from the arrogance that thinks it has all the truth—Oh, God of Truth, deliver us."[24]

In preparation for this paper, the writer sent out a questionnaire to some fifty prominent LDS intellectuals—all of them, I think, with Ph.D. degrees or the equivalent. I asked them to list the five most eminent intellectuals in Mormon history.[25] Thirty-eight persons responded. Leading the list of those most frequently nominated was B. H. Roberts. Orson Pratt ranked second, Joseph Smith third, Sterling McMurrin fourth, and James E. Talmage fifth. Others mentioned by at least three persons, in the order of their ranking, were John A. Widtsoe, Lowell Bennion, Hugh Nibley, Parley P. Pratt, Ephraim Ericksen, W. H. Chamberlin, and J. Reuben Clark Jr. Of the twelve persons who were named on the lists of at least three respondents, three (Joseph Smith and the two Pratts) wrote during the first period while the remaining nine studied and wrote during the "modern" period of creative adaptation.[26]

All of the persons named seem impressive, particularly if judged by the quantity of their writings.[27] Roberts published eight books of theology and nine of history, including the monumental six-volume *Comprehensive History of the Church*.[28] Though in origin a polemical work, the *Comprehensive History* comes nearer to history than many works done subsequently that professed historicity. Roberts also wrote two volumes of biography, three of sermons and commentaries, and one novel. A leading Democrat, successful missionary, soldier's chaplain, and high Church authority, Roberts seems fully justified in being regarded—to use Davis Bitton's phrase—as the pioneer Utah equivalent of Renaissance Man.[29] A less flamboyant contemporary, James Talmage, was also a British immigrant; wrote texts on natural and domestic science for LDS high school students; authored two books on aspects of chemical and mineral geology; published seven books on religion, including the *Articles of Faith* and *Jesus, the Christ*, which are still used as standard texts;[30] and prepared hundreds of articles which were syndicated for nationwide newspaper circulation. Widtsoe, a Norwegian immigrant who grew up in secluded Cache Valley, graduated *summa cum laude* in chemistry from Harvard, studied advanced biochemistry at Göttingen, and became president of Utah State Agricultural College and, later, of the University of Utah. He wrote thirty books, seven of which were in his professional field of agriculture and the remainder on aspects of Mormonism. His pamphlets, study courses, literary articles, and editorials run to an estimated 800 titles.

Three persons still in the mid-course of their contributions to Utah and Mormon intellectuality are on the list: Sterling McMurrin, Lowell Bennion, and Hugh Nibley. McMurrin's listing rests primarily on his erudition and careful reasoning in three works which serve to place Mormon theology and philosophy in perspective: *The Patterns of Our Religious Faiths*, *The Philosophical Foundations of Mormon Theology*, and *The Theological Foundations of the Mormon Religion*.[31] Lowell Bennion, a graduate of the University of Vienna with a dissertation on the methodology of Max Weber, has specialized in writing manuals for use in the seminaries, institutes of religion, and Sunday schools. His *Religion and the Pursuit of Truth*, as with all his works, is marked by a warm humanity and humble absence of provinciality.[32] Hugh Nibley, a brilliant graduate in classical languages and history from the University of California, has written a large sheaf of articles for professional journals and Mormon periodicals, and has published five books. Perhaps the one that Mormon intellectuals regard as his most distinguished work is *The World and the Prophets*.[33] "With the passing of B. H. Roberts," writes one of his admirers, "Nibley more than anyone else has assumed the role of defender of the Faith and the Saints."[34] One might sum up these three current leading Mormon intellectuals in the following manner: McMurrin is concerned with ideas, Bennion with people, and Nibley with the faith.

It is interesting to note that the top three persons—Roberts, Pratt, and Smith—were essentially self-taught. This should give the modern generation of Mormon scholars ample cause for humility. Considering our enormous advantages, we ought to be making far greater contributions than we are. It is humbling to realize that B. H. Roberts, the top person on virtually everybody's list, was the son of poor English converts, that he crossed the ocean and walked across the plains to Utah when he was only nine years of age, and that he worked on farms and in mines with virtually no time or opportunity for schooling. He apprenticed himself to a blacksmith, achieved some local notoriety as the "village blacksmith orator," and was called to a mission among country people in the Southeast. Eventually, he became a general authority of the Church, was elected to Congress, and produced a respectable shelf of books on varying subjects. Who would have guessed that out of such a background would have come the man whom thirty-five learned LDS scholars would select as the most distinguished intellectual in the Church's history!

Intellectuals such as those listed in the survey perform three functions for the societies in which they live. They provide symbolic and other expressions of the relationship of man to the universe, to God, and to the world of men; they initiate and maintain a flow of helpful suggestions for modification and improvement; and they seek to safeguard their societies' standards of excellence by criticizing low performance. Intensely patriotic in the broadest sense, and often ethical purists, they sometimes find their society failing to come up to its expressed ideals, and thus become disenchanted. Their "apostasy" in such instances is merely an inverted manifestation of their loyalty to the ideals.[35] Honest and frank—perhaps excessively so—they may advocate changes which society's leaders have reasons to oppose; they may point out weaknesses when it is not politic to do so; and they may insist upon standards that society and its leaders (including intellectual leaders) are not able to meet. However much we deplore their occasional lack of tact and humility, we must grant, with Daniel Bell, that, "One can be a critic of one's country [or church] without being an enemy of its promise."[36] Since there is substantial agreement that the history of societies which lack social criticism is "in the main a record of stagnation and decline," the nurturing of independent intellectuals is society's way of assuring its future.[37]

All of us who are members of the academy are favored to be associated with bright and spirited young intellectuals, the most honest of whom sometimes express a fear of "joining the Establishment."[38] They do not want to glide over shortcomings or settle for less than they and society are capable of achieving. They imagine a dilemma to be facing them. On the one hand, if the Establishment rejects them it is guilty of philistinism. On the other hand, if it gives them an honored place it is buying them off.[39]

Surely many sensitive souls in every generation have imagined themselves to be impaled on the horns of this dilemma. By and large, as they mature they learn that close identification with the so-called Establishment (be it church, state, or commercial) does not, of itself, involve or necessitate a sellout to the principles of integrity and creativity.[40] "The intellectual who has relinquished all thought of association with power understands well—almost too well—that his state of powerlessness is conducive to certain illuminations. What he is prone to forget is that an access to power and an involvement with its problems may provide other illuminations."[41]

I hope that the members of this academy share with me an impression of the growing number of "participating intellectuals" within the Mormon culture. Personally, I have been delighted with the increasing number and improved quality of bright young Mormon intellectuals who are strongly committed to their Church and society, and who are equally committed to sound scholarship in the humanities and sciences. On the one hand, they are determined to work within the best traditions of their culture; on the other hand, they insist upon the highest standards of integrity in their chosen fields. In recognition of their influence and needs the Church has established semi-autonomous university wards, stakes, and institutes of religion where LDS students are able to attain spiritual, social, and intellectual maturity under the most favorable conditions. In responding to the challenge of adapting their faith and its practices to the university setting around them, they remind one of the early converts to Mormonism who, nearly all in their twenties and early thirties, restored a faith and founded a community in the wilderness. A most significant development is the founding of *Dialogue*, whose stated aim is "to express Mormon culture and examine the relevance of religion to secular life." Edited by young Latter-day Saints who wish to "bring their faith into dialogue with human experience as a whole and to foster artistic and scholarly achievement based on their cultural heritage," the journal encourages a variety of approaches and viewpoints.

In no field has the growing maturity of LDS scholarship been more welcome than in history. An important article by Moses Rischin in a recent issue of *The Journal of American History* describes scholarly developments in Mormon history as "most exciting." The Mormon story is explored, he states, "with a new depth and perspicacity." Recent books and essays represent "a breakthrough in appreciation and understanding of this strategic historic group," and "reflect an intellectual poise, sophistication, and candor that augur a new secularization of the Mormon posture."[42]

No one will deny that our pioneer forebears were worthy builders—that they were adventurous frontiersmen, devoted farmers, and ingenious engineers. But those who redeemed the wilderness and made the desert blossom also included poets, artists, teachers, and scholars. Not only did they perfect society with their well-articulated criticisms, but they created symbols and images of lasting value. May our studies establish the relevance of our intellectual heritage for the present, help us in stating more explicitly our aspirations for the future, and propel us to higher levels of achievement in all our endeavors.

Chapter Eleven Notes

1. Two recent works that emphasize the positive cultural and intellectual contributions of frontier religious groups and institutions hitherto disparaged are: T. Scott Miyakawa, *Protestants and Pioneers: Individualism and Conformity on the American Frontier* (Chicago: University of Chicago Press, 1964); and Charles A. Johnson, *The Frontier Camp Meeting: Religion's Harvest Time* (Dallas: Southern Methodist University Press, 1955).
2. Jon Haupt and I have discussed this in "Intolerable Zion: The Image of Mormonism in Nineteenth Century American Literature," *Western Humanities Review* 22 (summer 1968): 243–60, and "The Missouri and Illinois Mormons in Ante-bellum Fiction," in *The Mormons in Early Illinois*, Stanley B. Kimball, ed. (Edwardsville, Ill.: Lovejoy Library of Southern Illinois University, 1970), 37–50.
3. Bernard DeVoto, "Utah," *American Mercury* 7 (March 1926): 319–22.
4. Bernard DeVoto, "A Revaluation," *Rocky Mountain Review* 10 (autumn 1945): 7–10. An earlier westerner, Bret Harte, complained that the best brains of California—meaning especially his own—were unappreciated. Accepting such statements at face

value, some literary critics have alleged that sensitive writers were scorned by their home towns. Psychoanalysis might see a relationship between such derogatory outbursts and the personal frustrations of western writers. See, e.g., Franklin Walker, *San Francisco's Literary Frontier* (New York: Alfred A. Knopf, 1939), 266–68.

5. Christopher Lasch, *The New Radicalism in America, 1889–1963: The Intellectual as a Social Type* (New York: Alfred A. Knopf, 1965), ix.
6. The word "authoritarian" refers to subjection to authority—an undesirable state; "authoritative" means sanctioned by authority and is usually regarded as something desirable. Lowell Bennion cautions that Mormonism is authoritative but not authoritarian. Lowell L. Bennion, *Religion and the Pursuit of Truth* (Salt Lake City: Deseret Book, 1959), 24–29.
7. One reader suggests that some dedicated Mormon scholars fail this acid test because of cowardice, others because of intellectual and/or psychological incapability, and still others because they are unable to make up their minds whether their first loyalty is to objective scholarship or to revered churchmen.
8. One respondent to the questionnaire described below states that in one sense there have been no Mormon intellectuals because Mormons fled from the strife and contentions of religious and intellectual debate and sought authoritarian ("authoritative"?) answers to intellectual questions. Another opined that anyone who passed the test of evaluating Mormon culture on the basis of the best "thinking of men would" necessarily be persona non grata, and thus those Mormons who became intellectuals were, by definition, apostates.
9. Bertrand Russell, *A History of Western Philosophy* (New York: Simon and Schuster, 1945), 39.
10. Richard Hofstadter, *Anti-Intellectualism in American Life* (New York: Alfred A. Knopf, 1963), 27–30.
11. A prominent non-Mormon historian, who in his capacity as head of his department at a large university has interviewed many young Mormons, tells me that he thinks young Mormon scholars are too tense—too serious—as if they were uneasy in an environment which must play with hypotheses, even with cherished ones. My own experience is that young Mormon intellectuals are quite free in playing around with new ideas and concepts when they are with "kindred souls," and that they become more guarded—and "tense"—when among non-Mormons or highly dogmatic Mormons. As they grow older, they tend to become more relaxed and secure about their faith and commitment.
12. Four penetrating essays which discuss Mormonism and intellectuals are: Ephraim E. Ericksen, "William H. Chamberlin, Pioneer Mormon Philosopher," *Western Humanities Review* 8 (autumn 1954): 275–85; R. Kent Fielding, "Historical Perspectives for a Liberal Mormonism," *Western Humanities Review* 14 (winter 1960): 69–82; Davis Bitton "Anti-Intellectualism in Mormon History," *Dialogue* 1 (autumn 1966): 111–34. See also the "Comment" of James B. Allen, *Dialogue* 1 (autumn 1966): 134–40; and Thomas F. O'Dea, "Sources of Strain and Conflict," in *The Mormons* (Chicago: University of Chicago Press, 1957), 222–57.
13. O'Dea, *The Mormons*, 30–31.
14. Among the most admired and respected works of Joseph Smith, in addition to the three mentioned, are his "Inspired Translation" of the Bible, the King Follett Sermon, his letters from Liberty Jail, and his dictated history of the Church.

15. P. P. Pratt, *A Voice of Warning and Instruction to all People* (New York: W. Standford, 1837); Parley P. Pratt, *Key to the Science of Theology* (Liverpool: F. D. Richards, 1855); and Parley P. Pratt, *The Autobiography of Parley Parker Pratt*, Parley Parker Pratt, ed. (New York: Russell Brothers, 1874).
16. See F. Mark McKiernan, "The Voice of One Crying in the Wilderness: Sidney Rigdon, Religious Reformer, 1793–1876" (Ph.D. diss., University of Kansas, 1968); Reva Stanley, *A Biography of Parley P Pratt: The Archer of Paradise* (Caldwell, Idaho: Caxton Printers, 1937); T. Edgar Lyon, "Orson Pratt—Early Mormon Leader" (Master's thesis, University of Chicago, 1932).
17. Dogmatic theology regarding the traditional questions of soteriology, ecclesiology, and the like, were far less important to Mormons than their eschatology. The announcement of the fact of the Restoration, the call to gather, the expected coming of Christ—these were the central elements. These ideas, and the specific programs for which they provided the rationale, were flexible.
18. "History of Joseph Smith," *Millennial Star* 20 (4 December 1858): 774. See also B. H. Roberts, *A Comprehensive History of The Church of Jesus Christ of Latter-day Saints, Century One*, 6 vols. (Provo, Utah: Corporation of the President, The Church of Jesus Christ of Latter-day Saints, 1965), 5:340.
19. In a letter to the writer, Davis Bitton argues that I have overdone the contrast between Joseph Smith and Brigham Young, leaving the impression that there was more fluidity under the former and more hardening under the latter than actually was the case. He cites evidence that Brigham was not really a dogmatist when it came to doctrine.
20. Frederick Hawkins Piercy, *Route from Liverpool to Great Salt Lake Valley*, Fawn M. Brodie, ed. (Cambridge, Mass.: Belknap Press of Harvard University Press, 1962).
21. Orson Pratt, *Key to the Universe* (1873: 2nd edition, Salt Lake City: Published by the author, and for sale at the Historian's Office, 1879).
22. Edward W. Tullidge, *Life of Joseph the Prophet* (New York: Tullidge and Crandall); Edward W. Tullidge, *Life of Brigham Young; or, Utah and her Founders* (New York: 1876); Edward W. Tullidge, *The History of Salt Lake City and its Founders* (Salt Lake City: Edward W. Tullidge, Publisher and Proprietor, 1886); and Edward W. Tullidge, *Tullidge's Histories. Volume II: Containing the history of all the northern, eastern and western counties of Utah, also the counties of southern Idaho* (Salt Lake City: Press of the Juvenile Instructor, 1889).
23. Although creative, the period has also been frustrating. Some Mormon intellectuals have not remained to enrich the intellectual content of Mormon doctrine but abandoned both the region and the Church. The problems and negative aspects of this fourth period have been well described by Bitton, Fielding, and Ericksen in the essays previously cited. I am simply recognizing here that there have also been positive achievements during the period.
24. Hugh B. Brown, "What Is Man and What He May Become," in *BYU Speeches of the Year, 1957–58* (Provo, Utah: Brigham Young University, 1998), 141–48.
25. My definition of "intellectual" was framed in such a way that it seemed to exclude natural scientists. This is unfortunate, since a major contribution to Mormon intellectuality has been made by our natural scientists.
26. The listings, with number of placings on the responses were: B. H. Roberts, 35; Orson Pratt, 30; Joseph Smith, 19; Sterling McMurrin, 18; James E. Talmage, 17; John A. Widtsoe, 14; Lowell Bennion, 11; Hugh Nibley, 10; Parley P. Pratt, 5; E. E. Erick-

sen, 4; W. H. Chamberlin, 4; J. Reuben Clark Jr., 3. It is significant that no woman received as many as three listings, and that no apostates were listed by that number. The former is probably due to the failure of historians to call attention to the contributions of women in Mormon history; the latter is perhaps due to the manner in which I worded the questionnaire, asking: "Excluding yourself (and myself), who are the five leading Mormon intellectuals in the Church's history?" I should have thought that Eliza R. Snow, Susa Young Gates, and Emmeline B. Wells might have received more listings, and also Sidney Rigdon, Edward W. Tullidge, George A. Smith, and John Taylor. Of course, each respondent was limited to five listings. Several respondents made notes indicating their perplexity about Joseph Smith. Admittedly, he was a towering and inspiring figure, but was he an intellectual?

27. Obviously, I could not attempt in this brief essay to judge the quality of these writings. Certainly I would not contend that all of the writings of these "intellectuals," if such they be, have (or had) solid intellectual worth. Some would no doubt contend that they stand out mainly because of the barren surroundings.

28. Joseph Smith Jr., *History of The Church of Jesus Christ of Latter-day Saints*, B. H. Roberts, ed., 7 vols. (Salt Lake City: Deseret Book, 1930).

29. Davis Bitton, "B. H. Roberts as Historian," *Dialogue* 3 (winter 1968): 26.

30. James E. Talmage, *The Articles of Faith: A Series of Lectures on the Principal Doctrines of the Church of Jesus Christ of Latter-day Saints* (Salt Lake City: Deseret News, 1899); and James E. Talmage, *Jesus the Christ: A Study of the Messiah and His Mission According to Holy Scriptures both Ancient and Modern* (Salt Lake City: Deseret News, 1915).

31. Sterling M. McMurrin, *The Patterns of our Religious Faiths* (Salt Lake City: University of Utah, Extension Division, 1954); Sterling M. McMurrin, *The Philosophical Foundations of Mormon Theology* (Salt Lake City: University of Utah Press, 1959); and Sterling M. McMurrin, *The Theological Foundations of Mormon Theology* (Salt Lake City: University of Utah Press, 1965).

32. Lowell L. Bennion, *Religion and the Pursuit of Truth* (Salt Lake City: Deseret Book, 1959).

33. Hugh Nibley, *The World and the Prophets* (Salt Lake City: Deseret Book, 1954).

34. Louis Midgley, "Hugh Nibley: A Short Bibliographical Note," *Dialogue* 2 (spring 1967): 119.

35. Compare Edward Shils, "Intellectuals," *International Encyclopedia of The Social Sciences,* 17 vols. (New York: Macmillan, 1968), 7:410.

36. Daniel Bell, *The End of Ideology: On the Exhaustion of Political Ideas in the Fifties* (Rev. ed., New York: Free Press, 1965), 17. One cannot deny that some articulate intellectuals abuse their positions and betray doctrinaire and uncompromising attitudes. Intellectuals are susceptible (as we all are) to insidious forces, and may deliberately ridicule the well-meaning and obfuscate the issues. Intellectuals may also lax their relevance by refusing to serve society in a constructive way or to get involved in the "muck and mire" of contemporary organizations and movements.

37. See Eric Hoffer, *The Ordeal of Change* (New York: Harper and Row, 1963), 46; and Stanford Gwilliam, "The Critic in Zion," *Dialogue* 2 (winter 1967): 149–54.

38. By this they presumably mean accepting a position in the government, the Church, or a large business corporation. As ethical purists they dislike working with imperfect institutions. But can they really know society and its problems without participating actively in its processes?

39. Compare Hofstadter, *Anti-Intellectualism in American Life*, 393, 417.
40. One non-Mormon historian friend has suggested in a letter to the writer that the Roman Catholic attempt to consolidate orthodoxy coincided with intellectual decline in Italy—and still more in Spain where orthodoxy was more complete. The Protestant Reformation, on the other hand, brought an intellectual awakening to Elizabethan England. Thomas O'Dea in *American Catholic Dilemma: An Inquiry into the Intellectual Life* (New York: New American Library, 1962) intimates that the conservative and defensive theology of American Roman Catholicism has tended to produce sterility, while the more liberal Catholic theology in France, the Netherlands, and Germany has produced intellectual brilliance.
41. Hofstadter, *Anti-Intellectualism in American Life*, 429.
42. Moses Rischin, "Beyond the Great Divide: Immigration and the Last Frontier," *Journal of American History* 55 (June 1968): 49. Also: "The most striking changes of all were in the historiography of the Mormons (Latter-day Saints) of Utah, which only recently had seemed divided between the unsympathetic and sometimes malicious accounts of outsiders and the inexorably dull, painfully defensive annals of the Saints themselves. The new generation of Mormon historians related religion to economic institutions, politics, and immigration, all with remarkable objectivity." Earl Pomeroy, "The Changing West," in John Higham, ed., *The Reconstruction of American History* (New York: Harper and Row, 1962), 78.

Chapter 12

On Writing Latter-day Saint History

TODAY I WOULD LIKE TO SUGGEST some guidelines for those of you who are involved in writing the history of The Church of Jesus Christ of Latter-day Saints in the Pacific. As the Church becomes more international, it will become increasingly important to write the history of Latter-day Saints in their homelands. By reconstructing these people's lives, we give their heirs a sense of their LDS heritage as well as provide real models for their own lives, models with whom they can identify.

Reasons to Study Mormon History

BEFORE I OFFER SUGGESTIONS about writing local histories, I suppose I should start out by explaining why the study of Latter-day Saint history in general is important. Let me suggest four reasons. First, the study and writing of our history will help us better understand the Lord. For example, it will tell us more about the settings and circumstances of his revelations. It will provide examples of how the Lord works through men and women and what he expects of us. It will tell us more about the Saints' relationship with the Lord

---

First published as "On Writing Latter-day Saint History," in *Celebrating the LDS Past: Essays Commemorating the 20th Anniversary of the 1972 Founding of the LDS Church Historical Department's "History Division"* (Provo, Utah: Joseph Fielding Smith Institute for Church History, Brigham Young University, 1992), 1–9. Reprinted in *Voyages of Faith: Explorations in Mormon Pacific History*, Grant Underwood, ed. (Provo, Utah: Brigham Young University Press, 2000), 1–9.

during the progress and problems of the Church and of its membership, so we can learn how and why changes have taken place.

Second, the study and writing of history will help strengthen Church unity by building in all of us a sense of community and pride in our past. It will give us a sense of who we are, where our cultural and spiritual roots lie, as well as where our biological and social roots originate. It will give us a sense of appreciation for our Latter-day Saint ancestors. Studying Church history is like studying the scriptures—it gives us a society against which to compare or contrast our own. We can compare ourselves with members of other religious or social cultures, but it is not the same as looking at people who have lived with the restored gospel. The Jews were a covenant people, and they made mistakes. The Nephites and the Lamanites were a covenant people, and they made mistakes. Our Latter-day Saint ancestors were a covenant people, and they made mistakes. We have the advantage of being a covenant people who follow all these cultures, and we can learn from the way they honored their covenants and from their failures. This will help us see our problems in perspective and remind us to be humble about our own achievements.

Third, studying history helps give us a knowledge of the past so that we can be informed when discussing our religion with others. It will give us accurate information to counter distorted histories and misunderstandings about the Church; it will provide accurate information to counter the arguments of apostates and others who border on apostasy. In short, it will help us be informed as we discuss the Restoration with those not of our faith.

And fourth, we study and write history because the Lord commands it. On 6 April 1830, the very day the Church was organized in this dispensation, the Lord commanded the Prophet Joseph Smith to arrange for the keeping of a record of the Church's history (D&C 21:1). Joseph appointed Oliver Cowdery to do this, and thus Oliver served as the first Church Historian and Recorder. Eleven months later, on 8 March 1831, John Whitmer was commanded by revelation to "write and keep a regular history" of the Church (D&C 47:1). In a later revelation, Whitmer was instructed to "continue in writing and making a history of all the important things which he shall observe and know concerning my church" (D&C 69:3). Other revelations attest to the Lord's insistence that the Church's documents be preserved and that histories be written. With the encouragement of the prophets, the Church has fully complied with these commandments. From Oliver Cowdery's first history (later published in the *Latter Day Saints' Messenger and Advocate*), to the most recent works of the general authorities, the Historical Department of the Church, and others, Latter-day Saint historians have prepared and published histories of events and personalities from each stage of the Church's development that are important to the Church and its members.

Added to this record of following the Lord's admonitions about keeping the Church's history, President Spencer W. Kimball has counseled us to keep our personal and family histories. These instructions apply to all members, in whatever part of the world they reside and under whatever government they make their living. Church and family history is a record of our brotherhood and sisterhood in Jesus Christ—a history that brings us home to an understanding of the Lord's kingdom and how we fit into it.

The Value of Local Histories

When the Historical Department of the Church was organized in 1972, we looked over our written history and identified areas that had been neglected and that needed further attention. We realized very quickly that we should give encouragement to studies of ethnic groups and their experiences in the Church; studies of Latter-day Saints in their local settings; studies of ordinary men, women, and family groups; studies of local leaders; and studies of the workings of Church programs at the local level.

Now I am going to suggest something that may seem to be heretical—something that may seem ridiculous. I am going to suggest that it is more important to study and write local history than it is to study and write general history. What I am suggesting is that it is more important for you to do Hawaiian history than general American history, New Zealand history rather than history of the British Commonwealth, and so on. This is true of Church history as well. It is more important to do stake and ward history than general Church history. It is more important to do the history of your family than the history of the family in general. As I say, this seems ridiculous, but I firmly believe that one who concentrates on Hawaii's history can make more progress toward understanding the aspirations, experiences, and achievements of mankind than one who has elected to study the history of the United States.

Only at the local level can the historian come to grips with reality in its most elemental forms. Focusing on the local allows the historian more intimate knowledge than studying the general. Too much history has been written from a detached perspective, from the important documents, from the ivory towers as it were. History needs to come from the grassroots, from where the people live. Many of the significant administrative steps the Church has taken had their beginning at the grassroots level. Local innovations and suggestions were brought to the attention of Church leaders who then felt inspired to use them as the basis for Church wide programs such as the welfare program, the Primary, the Young Women's program, the Relief Society, and so on. While many Church members have felt that there is little room for individual initiative in a Church directed by God and with prophets at its head, positive achievements have taken place when Church members did not wait to be "command[ed] in all things" but did "many things of their own free will" (D&C 58:26–29).

As the Church grows, the saga of the locality—of the ward, the stake, the region, and the individual Latter-day Saint—takes on greater significance. Traditionally, our general Church history is too abstract and too impersonal. When history comes from the grassroots, from where the people live and worship, the individual can identify personally with the general Church experience.

Suggestions for Church Historians

As you go forward with your work, let me offer a number of suggestions that might be helpful in compiling and writing the history of the Church in the Pacific. First, give due importance to the work of the sisters. Let's not have histories that give lists of bishops but omit lists of Relief Society presidents. Let's include descriptions of the activities of the women's organizations as well as those of the priesthood. It is incorrect to start out with the notion that since men hold all the important policy-making positions, they are the ones who determine the course of events. Although the priesthood holders have certain key leadership offices, the brethren are not exclusively responsible for everything that happens in the Church. We must avoid a male interpretation of Mormon history. Those who spend a substantial amount of time going through the materials in the Church Archives find themselves gaining a new appreciation of the important and indispensable role of women in Church history—not to mention gaining new insights from viewing Church history through the eyes of women. The historical studies of what Latter-day Saint women have done thus far reveal them to be strong individuals with tremendous varieties of temperaments, talents, and sensitivities. Further biographical studies of these women will help our sisters in charting their own lives without feeling constrained to mold themselves into existing stereotypes. Real models should be more useful than simply ideals.

Second, in our writing we should give due emphasis to the Church's intellectual, social, and cultural accomplishments. There is a tendency for us to remember the tangible, the material, and the visible simply because we can see them and because they have had greater survival value. We have tended to measure the accomplishments of earlier members by such durable achievements as the construction of canals and dams, temples and meetinghouses, homes and cooperative stores. But our forebears also made contributions in thought, in poetry, in music, in games and dancing and recreation, in human relations, and in education. These contributions are more difficult to discover and to trace but they are nevertheless there, and we should give them sufficient attention.

Third, in our writing we must acknowledge that not every program and organization proceeded smoothly. This is illustrated by Lance D. Chase's talk on the Hawaiian Mission crisis of 1874.[1] Our histories should make us aware of some of the problems, obstacles, objections, and difficulties Church members have faced. It would be especially instructive to know the particular problems of applying Church procedures and programs in the Pacific because of the differing cultural and social backgrounds among the people.

Fourth, we should give due attention to the so-called "ordinary" members of the Church. An ideal example of this is Carl Fonoimoana's paper on his grandfather Opapo.[2] We should be concerned with both the obscure and the famous, the deacons as well as the general authorities. Actually, one may get a more accurate reflection of the impact of the Gospel on the lives of members by studying the humble, the unambitious, or the devoted ward worker. The "ordinary" member provides a richer field for understanding the functioning of the Church in the lives of people. The unexpected variety of people, the complexity and the uncoached elements of their character, demonstrate the richness of the gospel plan and the manner in which it can serve all men and women.

Fifth, we need to recognize the complexity of people, especially in biographical and family histories. We get a mistaken view of humanity by watching certain television shows. A half-hour show alone, or even an hour-long show, cannot develop a full-rounded personality in that time; the writer can exploit only one facet of a person's character. And so he or she presents one person as compassionate, another as cruel, still another with the single motive of wanting more money, and a fourth who wants to take to bed every pretty woman he meets. But people are not that simple. The person who finds it hard to resist an opportunity to take advantage of another may be hardworking and kind to the unfortunate. The person who cannot resist an opportunity to make money may love his or her family, may be generous, and may have courage. A whole series of qualities—good and bad—may exist in the same person. And sometimes these qualities are contradictory. Historians are obligated to give some indication of this diversity, this complexity, this contradictory nature of historical persons. I am not suggesting anything that might serve to malign beloved ancestors or leaders. It is, of course, distressing to think that the composer of a beautiful song was less than a completely beautiful person, or that the author of a lovely poem may have been stingy and small. I am merely suggesting that we acknowledge that everybody has weaknesses. If we are conscious that the people we respect have faults as well as achievements, we may come to believe that personal achievements may be possible even with our own defects.

My sixth point is that we should tell a straightforward story, not bogging down the narrative with attempts to moralize. Latter-day Saint writers have a tendency to moralize. Maybe we got into that habit by having to give talks in church or perhaps by hearing the constant moralizing of parents, seminary teachers, and missionaries. The secret of good historical writing is to stick to the point and to cut text whenever you can. There is a tendency for us, especially those who are new at history, to look upon our writing as something of a miracle, to be amazed that we are able to put words on paper at all. When they are on paper, out of our own brain if not straight from heaven, we look upon them as sacred. We cannot bear to sacrifice one of them. The best historians, having cultivated the ability to write, have learned to cut with fortitude. Each of you, as you write, will hit upon a quotation, a thought, that seems so exceptional that to cut it is worse than having a tooth extracted. It is then that you must accept the advice of another reader that you respect. If editorializing takes us away from the story we are trying to tell, it should be cut.

Finally, I hope you will, through your interviews and writing, convey the lovable spirit of Pacific peoples: their faith, their sense of humor, their playfulness, their physical prowess, their love of nature, their generosity, their practicality, and their happy disposition. Caucasian missionaries who return from this area tell of this special spirit—and speak of it longingly, as if one cannot find it duplicated in the continental states. We need not just rely on the reports of the so-called white missionaries, but the stories, the tales, the characterizations of the Pacific peoples themselves—illustrations of this spirit from their own lives. For this purpose we need to interview bishops, Relief Society presidents, Sunday School teachers, and others. Relatively speaking, we do not have much in the Church Archives reflective of the Pacific perspective, either in past records or current ones.

Conclusion

I think of Solomona Pi'ipi'ilani. We don't know exactly when he was born—sometime around 1800. This brother first received the gospel from George Q. Cannon in 1851 and was soon afterward ordained an elder. He was a fluent speaker in his native Hawaiian tongue, a close and careful reasoner, a thorough student of the scriptures, and a conscientious man. He was among those who gathered to Palawai, on the island of Lanai, in 1854. When Laie was purchased in 1865 and established as a gathering place for the Saints, he was among the first to gather and labor on the plantation there. In 1879, his wife having died, he decided to emigrate to Utah, and he took his granddaughter along. He acquired a home in the Salt Lake Nineteenth Ward and made a modest living. He went to the Endowment House to make his temple covenants and was one of the first Hawaiians to receive his endowments. When Iosepa in western Utah was established as a gathering place for Hawaiians and Polynesian emigrants in 1889, he gathered there, obtained a city lot, built a home, and supplied it with the needed comforts. He managed to save enough to send for a grandson who stayed with him at Iosepa, his granddaughter having died. Over a forty-year period, he was a stalwart. He had a thorough knowledge of the Bible and the Book of Mormon, and he made regular trips to the temple in Logan, Utah, to do temple work on behalf of his kindred dead. Finally, around the ripe old age of ninety-one, he died, still in Iosepa. At his funeral, President Joseph F. Smith described him as one of the most worthy, faithful, and true-hearted Latter-day Saints he had ever known.

There must be dozens of others about whom we could say similar things. One sign of the vitality of the restored gospel is its capacity to produce strong people—people of faith and commitment and talent. I think of Mele Vea (also known as Mary Ashley), a native Tongan who later lived in Fiji. She was baptized a member at age fourteen and became a woman of tenacious faith, a pioneer of the Church both in Tonga and Fiji. I think of Helen Sekaquaptewa, the great Hopi woman whose life is eloquently told in *Me and Mine*;[3] Faith Okawa Watabe, an American-born Japanese woman whose marriage linked her to the "pioneer" Watabe family of the Church's first real expansion into Japan; Lucile Bankhead, the faithful Black member whose long wait for temple blessings was finally rewarded by the glorious announcement of 9 June 1978. Finally, there was Jonatana H. Napela, a Hawaiian judge on Maui, who met George Q. Cannon in 1851 and was frequently mentioned in his diary. Napela was baptized and ordained an elder, was a fine speaker and reasoner, and was a person of standing and influence in the community. He was also a charming and intelligent man who helped the ministry in many ways, assisted with translating the Book of Mormon, healed the sick, and in other ways showed the spirit of Jesus.[4]

Let me close by saying to those who are interested in studying Mormonism in the Pacific that we wish you well in all your endeavors to write history. We offer also our facilities to help you to the extent that we can. What you are proposing to do is important to you, to your wards and stakes and regions, and to the Church. May the Lord bless you in your efforts and all of us who are engaged in similar endeavors.

Chapter Twelve Notes

1. See Lance D. Chase, "The Hawaiian Mission Crisis of 1874: The 'Awa Rebellion Story," in *Voyages of Faith: Explorations in Mormon Pacific History*, Grant Underwood, ed. (Provo, Utah: Brigham Young University Press, 2000), 59–70.
2. See Carl Fonoimoana, "Opapo: The Power of His Faith," in *Voyages of Faith*, 305–9.
3. Helen Sekaquaptewa, *Me and Mine: The Life Story of Helen Sehaquaptewa*, as Told to Louise Udall (Tucson: University of Arizona Press), 1969.
4. For a detailed study of Napela, see Joseph H. Spurrier, *Sandwich Island Saints: Early Mormon Converts in the Hawaiian Islands* (Oahu, Hawaii: J. H. Spurrier, 1989), 233–63.

Chapter 13

The Marrow in the Bones of History

New Directions in Historical Writing

As a person who has tried to write things that might be accepted by scholarly publications and university presses—and who has at this very moment two book-length manuscripts being considered by two of the presses represented at this convention—let me confess how really humble I feel. Just last Sunday the Mormon Church held its semi-annual conference in the Mormon Tabernacle just a few steps to the west, and during the services they elected their first Native American to the position of general authority of the Church. He was George Patrick Lee, a full-blooded Navajo, and incidentally a graduate of Brigham Young University, our host institution. When called upon to speak to the vast assemblage of those present in the Tabernacle, plus those in the Salt Palace, plus the thousands, perhaps millions, listening over the radio and TV, this gentle young man, small of stature and bashful, walked the long distance up to the podium, looked long and hard at the audience, took a deep breath, and then said: "Brothers and Sisters, I finally realized how General Custer must have felt [when he rode into that valley on the upper Big Horn!]"[1]

Well, I do feel apprehensive, even though I really should feel at home. I was just looking over this group during Bob Thomas's address of welcome, and it suddenly dawned on me that I know a

---

Previously unpublished paper presented at the Western University Press Banquet, Empire Room, Hotel Utah, Salt Lake City, 12 October 1975.

good many of you, and I suppose the reason is that I have published with several of you. I started to make out a list and was surprised to discover that I had published books with no less than six of the university presses involved in this conference: University of Nebraska Press, University of Washington Press, University of Wyoming Press, University of Utah Press, Utah State University Press, and Brigham Young University Press. In fact, it now occurs to me that this may be the reason you invited me to be with you this evening. How could you avoid asking a person who had been such a persistent customer? Many of you publish journals as well, and I started counting up and discovered that I had published articles in no less than fourteen different scholarly journals that are published by university presses and other professional publishers west of the Mississippi.

As the result of experiences I have had, particularly when I was editor of the *Western Historical Quarterly*, I came to realize the enormous amount of work and care that presses and publishers devote to each of the books they turn out. I once had a relative who worked at Disneyland and he was good enough one time to take me into the catacombs beneath that Kingdom of Magic. On the surface, at Disneyland, were thousands of innocent people absorbed in an illusion of reality. But the true magic, as I found out, was among the hidden studios, passageways, machinery, electric trams, and thousands of employees who lay beneath their feet and behind the false fronts. I came up from the underground thinking that the real magic was something that was deliberately hidden—something nobody would ever see. I have the feeling that it would be excellent training for each author and prospective author to spend a few months working at a publisher's office so that he would realize just how much goes on behind the scenes backstage—you might say—how much is involved in the production of a monograph or book.

And yet despite their essentially silent and unappreciated contribution, people who work for publishers somehow generate and maintain an immense fund of good humor. "We shall lose no time in reading your manuscript," wrote a wry university press editor. And so I wondered: Did it mean they would get to it right away, or that they would not read the manuscript because they thought it would be a waste of time? Farther down in the letter it became clear he was just having fun. "Sir," he wrote, "I believe that you could write like Faulkner if you had a mind to!" Yes, I thought, if I had a mind to I could! And then, as I went through the marginal comments on the manuscript, I found one last punch. I had included a long quotation—a quotation too long, as I would now realize. The editor wrote: "Sir, this should be modified to the point of deletion!"

I need to mention one thing more. As Gail Bell knows, I had the opportunity this summer of visiting the Far East. And as you might suspect in Hong Kong I ran into one of those fly-by-night publishers that seem to frequent that colony. As soon as he found out I had authored some books he was anxious to make a deal. How much would be the author's share, I asked. Well, you get fifty cents a book, he said.

"Great," I said. "How many copies would you run?"

"Hold on," he said, "the translator gets twenty cents."

"All right, I'll settle for thirty cents."

"Yes, but the agent gets ten cents."

"Well, I will still make twenty cents."

"There's a tax, you know; and remember that the publisher has to make a profit."

"Then what do I get out of it?"

"It's a great honor, sir, and it won't cost you more than ten cents a copy."

Dr. Thomas made a great deal of my being a "noted author"—well known. The other day one of my colleagues, whose work takes him to several offices a day, told me that 90 percent of the people at Church headquarters do not know the name of the Church Historian. He made a point by asking if they knew the name of the Church Historian. Apparently he asked twenty people during the day, and he discovered only two who could give him the correct name. There were three persons, he said, who could only think of Joseph Fielding Smith. Another thought it was Howard W. Hunter, who was my predecessor, and still another thought it was

Bruce McConkie. Three persons didn't know the Church had a historian, and the remainder got that puzzled look and said they knew there was one but couldn't think of his name. I told him this didn't surprise me. Arrington, after all, is a pretty hard name to remember. But then he added a clincher. He said he had run into Grace, my wife, who had gone to the genealogical library to do research. "Gosh, Grace," he said to her, "I really can't believe what my survey said about Leonard's identity problem." And according to him she replied, "Leonard who?"

Since you are gathered here in the heart of the Mountain West, in what geographers, sociologists, and literary people like Wallace Stegner call Mormon country, let me take five minutes to talk about the role of this region in American literary history.

There was enormous interest in this region in the nineteenth century. On the one hand, there was interest in the marvels of Mormon colonization and settlement, in the miracle by which the desert was made to blossom like the rose. People were fascinated with irrigation, with the Mormon village, with Mormon cooperative activity, and of course with Mormon family life. A whole genre of literature was produced which reported back on their experiences and observations on this exotic culture. These might be classified under the general heading of the Salt Lake City travel accounts. More than two hundred books of this nature, some by the literary greats of the century, were produced and circulated.

On the other hand, the Mormons, isolated from the East and Victorian England, also attracted attention because of the rumored existence of Destroying Angels or Danites, and the practice of plural marriage. More than one hundred novels and a dozen major works of humor were published in the nineteenth century in which the Mormons were the principal theme and characters. The authors of these novels, which we might call "Mormon Westerns," saw the Mormons as a nest of snakes in America's Garden of Eden. Indeed, the fascination of outsiders for the Mormon community was like that of children when they look into a snake pit; or similar to that of a woman with her eye glued to the telescope focused on a neighboring apartment who keeps repeating, "Isn't it disgusting!" The image was one of hateful intolerance, but the fascination was such that an enormous literature was produced. No local group in America had ever been the object of such interest and concern. And the image of the Mormons conveyed in these works, which were written by persons, many of whom had never met a Mormon, was almost completely unfavorable. Inevitably, the Mormons were portrayed as seething cauldrons of sexual passion, cruelty, and fanaticism. Consider the following:

1. The first appearance of Sherlock Holmes was in an anti-Mormon story, *A Study in Scarlet*.[2] Arthur Conan Doyle created the character to deal with a vengeful group of Mormons. Holmes was such a successful character that the host of stories featuring him then followed and the clever detective was established.
2. Joaquin Miller made his national and international reputation largely on an anti-Mormon novel he wrote in England in 1871 entitled *First Fam'lies in the Sierras*.[3] Miller's novel was so successful that he later wrote a play from it, *Danites of the Sierras*, which played on Broadway for several months. A rewritten play based on the same theme, *The Mormon Maid*, appeared in 1917 as one of the first motion picture films.
3. The book which really "made" Mark Twain nationally was *Roughing It*, first published in 1871, and the section which created the most excitement and interest, still often quoted, was that relating to his visit in Salt Lake City.[4]
4. The first novel of Metta Victoria Fuller Victor, who later wrote scores of books for the Beadle series of dime novels, was an anti-Mormon polygamy novel, first published in 1855.[5] Other feminine writers who included commentary, mainly antipathetic, about Mormons in their works on suffrage, temperance, and better home life included: Harriet Beecher Stowe, Mary Livermore, Kate Field, Etta Luce Gilchrist, Mrs. J. H. Hudson, and Cornelia Paddock.
5. His hilarious lectures on the Mormons caused Artemus Ward to become recognized as America's greatest humorist—he was the Bob Hope or the Will Rogers of his day. And his famous

London "Mormon" lecture was attended by Queen Victoria, cabinet ministers, and other leading figures. Oscar Wilde treated Mormonism, as did the humorist Bill Nye and Marietta Holley.

6. What Carl Van Doren calls the first really fine novel of the West was the anti-Mormon novel *John Brent*, written by Theodore Winthrop and published in 1861.[6] Winthrop is still regarded highly as an American novelist. Other Western novels have followed in profusion. The most prolific writer of them, Zane Grey, wrote his first Western, *Heritage of the Desert*, on an anti-Mormon theme.[7] His second, and most successful of all, *Riders of the Purple Sage*, was also an anti-Mormon book.[8] This one has been produced several times as a motion picture.

Most other western novelists have tried at least one anti-Mormon book: Hoffman Birney, Forrester Blake, Dane Coolidge, Mayne Reid, Percy Bolinbroke St. John, Noah Brooks, Bernard DeVoto, and many others.

7. Prosper Merimee, who wrote the story around which Bizet's opera *Carmen* was based, was the man who first interpreted the Mormons to the French. His sixty-page article appeared in the leading French magazine of the time. John Stuart Mill, Oscar Wilde, Charles Mackay, John Greenleaf Whittier, Charles Dickens, Bayard Taylor, Albion Tourgee, John Russell, the father of Bertrand Russell—these and many others paid their respects to the Mormons with major works or important comments.

Mormonism's leadership, its experiments in social and economic reform, and its capacity for bold and unified endeavor intrigued the intellectually curious, many of whom made pilgrimages to Utah. These distinguished visitors saw the Mormons developing a separate culture and civilization in the heart of the Rockies and wrote what they saw with a mixture of fascination and condescension. In any case, Salt Lake City was on the must list for world travelers.

Let us begin with a "fact of life." A recent report of the Organization of American Historians states that there has been an erosion in confidence and interest in history in recent years. Students do not find that it is relevant or helpful or exciting. It is too dull, they declare, and has little personal value. The OAH report revealed that the study of history across the nation is often downgraded in favor of a broad "social studies" approach, issue-oriented rather than chronological. Vaguely related subjects such as geography, political science, economics, sociology, and cultural anthropology are deemed interchangeable with history for purposes of teacher certification, and so history is being taught in many instances through the social sciences, where the economic, political, social, behavioral, and geographic ramifications are emphasized. The result of this search for relevance, this submergence into the formless glop of social studies, states the OAH report, is a kind of social stew which leads people away from self-pride and self-understanding—and breeds boredom and reinforces ignorance.

I do not want here to argue that history, for its own sake, is relevant—that it obviously provides perspectives on the present, gives pride in one's family, community, and national heritage, and that it provides a sense of time and place that are indispensable for every man and woman.

Rather, I should like to discuss what seems to me one of the greatest traps of going the social science way, and one of the foremost reasons for our contemporary boredom with history; namely, the realization that historians and the publishers of historical works must publish exciting and relevant history. Too often our histories have been what might be called documentary histories. They attempt to give an account of the important events of the past without critical analysis or interpretation. They depend, essentially, on institutional records and policies which have been compiled into a narrative by a busy graduate student or safe public relations man. Such histories have dealt primarily with the externals of events which transpired, and have not concerned themselves with the internals—the underlying motives or thoughts of those who made the actions happen. Our local and regional histories, for example, have dealt primarily with changes in the structure of local institutions—with organizations, businesses, governmental agencies, educational institutions and programs, industries and economic enterprises. One reason for the popularity of such studies is the survival and availability of the records of the organizations and programs. Personal records are hardly available to anyone outside of given families, and these are widely scattered. Thus, using organizational records rather than diaries and personal accounts, scholars, at least in the field of Western American history, have tended to describe the "outside" of the events.

There is, of course, another kind of history. The first to define it clearly was Aristotle. "The artistic representation of history," he wrote, "is a more scientific and serious pursuit than the exact writing of history. For the art of letters goes to the heart of things, whereas the factual report merely collocates details." In the second quotation, Aristotle writes, "The aim of art is to represent not the outward appearance of things, but their in-ward significance; for this, and not the external mannerism and detail, is true reality."

In other words, art, including the art of writing history, is mimesis or the imitation of life. The ultimate goal is to learn what goes on in the mind of the individual. R. G. Collingwood has called this the history of the inside of the event. This history seeks to determine and expose the thoughts in the minds of the persons "by whose agency the events came about." The historian does this by creatively re-thinking the thoughts of the participants in the context of his knowledge, analyzing them, and forming his own judgment of the validity of their explanations. He invests the narrative with meaning by consciously selecting from the sources what he thinks important, by interpolating in the reports of the participants and observers things which they do not explicitly say, and by rejecting or amending what he regards as due to misinformation or mendacity. Above all, he puts his sources in the witness-box, and by cross-examination extorts from them information that in their original statements they withheld, either because they did not wish to give it or because they did not realize they possessed it. In other words, the historian must read contemporary accounts with a question in his mind, and seek to find out, by inference and otherwise, what he wants to find out from them. Every step in his research depends on asking a question—not so much whether the statement is true or false, but what the statement means. Obviously, since his informants, by and large, are dead, the historian must put the questions to himself. The historian, as with scholars in other disciplines, must engage in the continuous Socratic questioning that Plato described so well (in the quotation used at the beginning of the article) as "a dialogue of the soul with itself."[9]

Eric Auerbach, who follows this line of reasoning, sees progress and development in literature, including historical literature, as going through a series of phases, each of which gets us closer to real life. Whether or not this does indeed represent the trend in literature, it is unquestionably the trend in historical writing. We are moving farther and farther toward the goal of getting at the inside of those who make history—their rationalizations, their motivations, and their aspirations. This movement in the field of historical writing takes three forms:

1. The publication of diaries, letters, and papers.
2. The publication of biographies and family histories.
3. The publication of community and institutional biographies which get at the "inside" of developments.

Since these are trends in historical writing, they will be manifest in the months and years to come in the type of manuscripts which will be submitted to university presses.

Let me now switch and suggest what our own center for research and writing on Mormon history is doing to meet this problem.

The Historical Department of the Church was organized in January 1972. Our research and writing staff consists of eighteen persons, including an editor. We are working on the sesquicentennial history of sixteen volumes, biographies, the Mormon Heritage Series, monographic volumes, task papers, and oral histories. If you have ideas on books that ought to be written, and that you'd like to publish, that relate to any aspect of the Mormons and their history, call this to our attention and we'd be glad to consider it.

Since the primary source of our "inside" history is diaries, we are interested in the scope and location of diaries. For several years Davis Bitton, of the University of Utah, has been compiling a "Guide to Mormon Diaries." Each diary or journal is described as to its physical format and location. Then there is an abstract that explains the chronological coverage of the document, the geographical location or locations of the author, and the main kinds of activities he was involved in. Usually he included a short passage or two as a sample of the style. The hope is that this guide will enable future history students and researchers to find those diaries likely to contain information relevant to their different topics.

There are something like diaries of six thousand persons. Mormons keep records rivaling the Puritans and the Quakers.

One observer has called our work "The New Mormon History," and I do not react against the characterization. Breaking with past tendencies, we have sought to base our "new history" on primary sources, we have given important attention to the role of women and children as well as men; we have toyed around with psychohistory; we have written about artists, teachers, and philosophers as well as colonizers and frontiersmen and ecclesiastical leaders; we have written about the critics and the unorthodox as well as the mainstreamers and the orthodox; we have sponsored a prosopographical study or group biographies; we have pioneered with some community biographies; we have done interpretive studies of Mormon intellectual history; we have been proud to describe people as they are, warts and all, and our history has been written primarily by professionals. The result, we believe, is history that is at once exciting, fun to write and fun to read, and, because it deals with the timeless problems of the human condition, we believe it has a relevancy that is not limited to time and place. We hope it will show style as well as accuracy, selectivity as well as honesty, humor as well as scholarship.

We have been working on a biography of Brigham Young and we have been delighted with the things which we have found that will not only enliven the book with human interest material, but will also give intimate glimpses heretofore unsuspected in that great western leader. For example, while he could be politic in negotiations, Brigham Young had no great Christian forgiveness for his enemies:

> Bro. Brigham arose and [made] some pointed and appropriate remarks. He called upon the Lord to bless this place for the good of the saints, and curse every Gentile who should attempt to settle here with sickness, rotenness, and death. Also to curse the Land of Missouri that it might sease to

> bring forth grain or fruit of any kind to its inhabitance and that they might be cursed [with] sickness, rotenness and death that their flesh might consume away on their bones and their blood be turned into Maggots and that their torments never sease. . . . He also cursed Mr. Miller the Indian Agent who came upon the Boat and and said if there was any [liquor] unloaded here he would spill it . . . and said if he had done it he would have tap[p]ed his vains for him if he had died the next moment for doing so.[10]

If the indoor sport of Utahns now is to criticize "the feds," at that time it was to curse the Missourians. In later years Brigham had such colorful comments edited from his speeches before publication.

Isaiah Moses Coombs's journal reveals that "It was hard to feel kindly towards the federal officials. 'If I could have my way I would have the whole infernal lot sent out of the territory with a flea in each ear. Forgive me, posterity, for such rough language.'"[11]

One July 24 celebration toast included the following:

> All mobocrats, anarchs and lovers of lies
> May their portion be with mosquitoes and flies
> And all who uphold them and live their ease
> May their portion be with bedbugs and fleas.[12]

One of ways of trying to defeat the plagues of crickets or grasshoppers was to burn them. But "to very little effect, as the hoppers would sit on a bush until it would burn within 2½ inches of them, gritting their teeth apparently, and swearing they would not go until they got ready, which proved to be a fact."[13]

Brigham Young, as well, takes on a new quality in the simple, naïve writing of Mary Goble Pay, daughter of English converts who brought her across the plains in the late-starting handcart companies. Death had taken two children along the way and as the family arrived in Salt Lake City, 11 December 1856, their mother was dead in the wagon. Mary's words tell the story with an eloquence unsurpassed by all the writer's craft:

> Bishop Hardy had us taken to a home in his ward and the brethren and the sisters brought us plenty of food. We had to be careful and not eat too much as it might kill us we were so hungry. Early next morning Bro. Brigham Young and a doctor came. The doctor's name was Williams. When Bro. Young came in he shook hands with us all. When he saw our condition—our feet frozen and our mother dead—tears rolled down his cheeks.[14]

Two decades later, Brigham Young was visiting in St. George when the temple was nearing completion. A celebration was held in which the Saints paid their respects to President Young on his birthday, and later there was a special meeting for "old folks." After the meeting President Young called Charles Walker over to him and asked for a copy of "The Temple Song" that Brother Walker had composed. In his diary (a rich and colorful document of the period) Brother Walker told of a precious experience that he would never forget:

> After meeting I went home and got the song and took it to him. He treated me very kindly and asked me to sit beside him and take dinner with him. I spent the time very pleasantly and found him to be very polite, genial, and sociable, and I felt quite at home in Chatting over the work on the Temple, old times, and other general topics. In bidding him goodbye He took my hand in both of his and said, God bless you, Br Charley, and God has blessed you, hasnt He? It seemed that in an instant all the blessings I had ever recei[v]ed were before Me. My emotion was too much to answer him, and I chokeingly said, I have learned to trust in the Lord.[15]

If the purpose of history is the reconstruction of the past, these first-person, intimate accounts we are using are the sine qua non of history, the one thing necessary to the re-creation of how it really was. It was in the family, in each canvas tent, or leg shelter, or adobe home, or frame shelter, or Georgian castle that our roots were planted. Granted, we cannot ignore the wider picture, the momentous decisions which determined the circumstances under which families lived: the debates in Congress, the decisions in the oval office, the wars and depressions, earthquakes and revolutions. Still, what goes on in the minds of people are the moving events of history.

It is of the honest, intimate accounts of the lives of all the people that the history of the people is written. These records are the marrow in the bones of history. They are the conveyors of our heritage—our past, and our present. They are the roots which hold us, individually and collectively, to our source, roots which hold the nourishment on which we subsist during the winters of our disorientation until we again find ourselves in the productive summers of our souls.

Chapter Thirteen Notes

1. George P. Lee, "My Heritage Is Choice," in *Official Report of the 145th Semi-Annual Conference of The Church of Jesus Christ of Latter-day Saints* (Salt Lake City: The Church of Jesus Christ of Latter-day Saints, 1975), 149.
2. A. Conan Doyle, *A Study in Scarlet* (New York: George Munro's Sons, 1895).
3. Joaquin Miller, *First Fam'lies in the Sierras* (London: George Routledge and Sons, 1875).
4. Mark Twain, *Roughing It* (Hartford, Conn.: American Publishing, 1872).
5. Metta Victoria Fuller Victor, *Mormon Wives: A Narrative of Facts Stranger than Fiction* (New York: Derby and Jackson, 1956).
6. Theodore Winthrop, *John Brent* (Boston: Ticknor and Fields, 1862).
7. Zane Grey, *The Heritage of the Desert: A Novel* (New York: Harper and Brothers Publishers, 1910).
8. Zane Grey, *Riders of the Purple Sage: A Novel* (New York: Harper and Brothers Publishers, 1912).
9. R. G. Collingwood, *The Idea of History* (New York: Oxford University Press, 1956), 215, 235–37, 269, 273–75.
10. Mary Haskin Parker Richards Journal, 14 May 1848, L. Tom Perry Special Collections., Harold B. Lee Library, Brigham Young University, Provo, Utah (hereafter Perry Special Collections).
11. Isaiah Moses Coombs Journal, 18 September 1870, Perry Special Collections.
12. Toast by Levi Hancock, 24 July 1851.
13. Abraham A. Kimball Journal, p. 89, Perry Special Collections.
14. As quoted in Barbara B. Smith and Blythe Darlyn Thatcher, *Heroines of the Restoration* (Salt Lake City: Bookcraft, 1997), 196.
15. Charles Lowell Walker diary, 11 June 1976, in *The Diary of Charles Lowell Walker*, A. Karl Larson and Katharine Mile Larson, eds., 2 vols. (Logan: Utah State University Press, 1980), 1:427.

Chapter 14

The Writing of Latter-day Saint History
Problems, Accomplishments, and Admonitions

THE CHALLENGE OF WRITING religious history is an old one.[1] The ancient Hebrews incorporated history into their scriptures, and Luke the physician is but one of the historians whose writings were canonized in the Christian New Testament. That the same facts could look quite different when viewed through a variant set of religious glasses was made clear, if it had not been so before, by the writing of St. Augustine's *City of God*. The monastic and ecclesiastical histories of the Middle Ages tended to set forth the drama of salvation, while secular histories, when they finally began to appear, were little more than chronicles or annals of rulers and battles. Histories of families, guilds, towns and nations gave emphasis to the political and economic realities of life but did so with little analysis. Indeed, history was more a branch of literature than of science. To worshipful and believing Christians, history was a vast pool from which could be drawn moral lessons, faith-promoting stories and examples of faith and dedication.

The problem is that facts never speak for themselves. Chronicles and testimonies and stories mean different things to different people. The inevitability of diverse opinions on the meaning of

---

First published as "The Writing of Latter-day Saint History: Problems, Accomplishments and Admonitions," *Dialogue* 14 (autumn 1981): 119–29.

historical events became clear early in Christian history. Could the real bearers of the Christian message be not the successors to the bishop of Rome, but those who were being persecuted by the established Church—the Waldensians, for example? This version of "a saving remnant" was picked up by the Reformers in the sixteenth century, and the Reformation brought about a great confrontation of different versions of Church history: Catholics vied with Protestants, and Protestants with Protestants. The writers in all camps faced questions about assumptions about interpreting events, about the metahistorical meaning behind the events. And there were practical, immediate questions. How open should the record be? Should the historian include activities by his religious leaders that did not edify? Was this not putting weapons in the hands of the enemy? Would it not destroy the great lesson-teaching capacity of history? Could the historian really establish without question the dealings of God in the affairs of men?

Some of the histories, from all sides, treated the leading personalities as two-dimensional figures, actors in a morality play of right and wrong. Cochlaeus portrayed Martin Luther as a shallow, immoral rake who did not have a religious bone in his body.[2] The disgraceful immorality in the monasteries, on the other hand, served the Protestants nicely as a counter-theme and drew upon a widespread anti-clerical prejudice. Although imposing in bulk and useful in compiling scattered sources, the ponderous tomes of the *Magdeburg Centuries* (1559–74) and the *Ecclesiastical Annals* (1588–1607) were but inflated pamphlets in their predictable partisanship. History was a weapon, and both sides—indeed, all sides—made use of it.

But some of the problems would not go away. What did the historian do with sources, with primary documents, that did not fit readily into the interpretation he had already decided upon? And what did one do with documents that turned out to be spurious, as the techniques of textual criticism were brought to bear? We will be better able to understand the mind-set of the sixteenth century if we imagine the historian to be a novelist who feels justified in leaving out anything that doesn't fit his purposes. As the creator of a story, he decides what goes in and what stays out. Confident of their right to decide the content of their works, historians may not have seen themselves as inventing a story, making it up from nothing, but they were positive that God had affirmed the great teaching function of history and that their primary task was to conform to what was consistent with His will.

In this context there appeared a new approach: the secular treatment of religious history. Those aspects of religious history that were properly religious and hence controversial, even emotional and unprovable, were quietly ignored in order to write about such things as changes of administration, the publication of works, the issuing of concordats and other documents, Church councils and colloquies, proselyting and conversions, and the establishment of new congregations. This history was administrative, geographic, economic, political. Above all, it was external. It dealt with those matters that could be established clearly and beyond doubt. Sleidan's *Commentaries on the State of Religion and Public Affairs under Emperor Charles V* (1555), the finest work of this kind, "set the tone and methodology of German and European Reformation history at least until the nineteenth century."[3]

Although political and dynastic bias could affect such external treatments, it was possible to rally substantial agreement on such externals as councils and movements of peoples. What the approach left out—and this is a serious indictment of something that pretends to be religious history—was religion.

Long before the restoration of the gospel in 1830, therefore, a series of questions about the relationship of history to religion had been raised. Was the primary purpose of such history to be faith-promoting? Should it ignore or leave out items that did not fit the purpose? Should the less-than-admirable activities of religious leaders be mentioned? What reliance should be placed on interested testimony? Should the archives of churches be open to research? What does one do when anecdotes purveyed by earlier historians, especially if they filled a moral and faith-promoting purpose, lack credence in the light of later examination and possibly contradictory evidence? Are historians well advised to abandon that which they can get hold of only in part and with the greatest difficulty, namely, the spiritual and supernatural, in order to deal with mundane topics like changing administrations, the construction of chapels, and the establishment of new congregations? Is it possible for a nonbeliever to write accurate and reliable history about religion? For that matter, is it possible for a believer to write accurate and reliable history about his church? And should the denomination paying the piper—employing the historian—call the tune? Every one of these questions had been raised and wrestled with before the organization of the Church of Jesus Christ in 1830.

Writing LDS History, 1830–90

When the Church was organized on 6 April 1830, the Lord commanded, by revelation, that "a record [be] kept among you" (D&C 21:1). In a subsequent revelation the responsibility of the historian was made more explicit: he was to "write and keep a regular history" (D&C 47:1). At first, Oliver Cowdery was appointed to supervise their history-gathering efforts. His ecclesiastical responsibilities as Second Elder and, later, as Counselor in the First Presidency, being of a demanding nature, he was soon replaced by John Whitmer. Although he did compile a short chronicle of early activities, Whitmer proved not to be valiant, and George W. Robinson was appointed in his stead. When Willard Richards was appointed Church Historian in 1842, it became an established practice that an apostle serve as Church Historian; that tradition continued through such illustrious officials as George A. Smith, Wilford Woodruff, Albert Carrington, Orson Pratt, Franklin D. Richards, A. William Lund, Joseph Fielding Smith and Howard W. Hunter.[4]

Thus, from the very day of the organization of the Church there was a Church Historian charged with the responsibility of keeping records and writing history. At the same time, at every stage in the history of the Church, others—private individuals independent of Church headquarters—joined in the task of making contributions to the writing and understanding of LDS history. Some of these made substantial contributions.

The first systematic attempt to prepare a history of the growing Church began in 1839 when Joseph Smith and his clerks and associates began the preparation of a multi-volume documentary record called the "History of Joseph Smith."[5] The manuscript for this history had progressed to 5 August 1838, when Joseph Smith was murdered on 27 June 1844. The scribes and clerks continued to assemble material and write in the years that followed.

In the meantime, however, the manuscript of "History of Joseph Smith" was published serially in *Times and Seasons* (1842–44, covering the years 1805–32); *Latter-day Saints' Millennial Star* (1842–45, covering years 1805–44); and the *Deseret News* (1851–58, covering the years 1834–44).[6] The process of preparing these for publication in a multi-volume bound work began in 1900, when George Q. Cannon was assigned by the First Presidency to begin the compilation. But his death in 1901 interrupted the task and it was reassigned to Brigham H. Roberts who, from 1906 to 1912, prepared "History of Joseph Smith" for publication. Unfortunately, Roberts subtitled this *History of the Church, Period I*: "History of Joseph Smith, the Prophet, by Himself," thus creating a misunderstanding that exists to this day. The entire work was compiled and written by Church-employed scribes and clerks, using diaries of Joseph Smith, his clerks and associates, and other documents. Having been instructed to use the pronoun "I" because it was Joseph Smith's history, the clerks continued that practice even after the Prophet's death. The initial portions of the history (1805–38) presumably benefited from the perusal of the Prophet, but the remainder, covering the years 1838 to his death in 1844, were compiled and written after his death and could in no sense have had the benefit of his suggestions and corrections. Roberts's edition even included some of his own corrections, deletions, and emendations, sometimes without explanation.[7]

After the "History of Joseph Smith" was completed (in 1856) to the death and burial of Joseph Smith (actually to 8 August 1844), the clerks in the office of the president of the Church continued it as the "History of Brigham Young." As in the case of the Joseph Smith history, this was an "annals" approach to Church history, and documents from a wide variety of sources were used to tell not only the history of Brigham Young but the history of the Church over which he presided.[8] To this date, the only portion of this history, which consists of forty-eight volumes of about one thousand pages each, that has been published is that from 1844 to 1848, issued under the editorship of B. H. Roberts in 1932 as Volume VII of *History of the Church* under the subtitle "Apostolic Interregnum."[9] Hopefully, additional volumes of the massive Brigham Young history will eventually be edited for publication. The volumes are in good quality up to about the year 1858, after which they partake more of the nature of a scrapbook of information. There appears to have been less attention to possible publication in compiling the work after 1858 than had been true during the compilation of the "History of Joseph Smith," the "Apostolic Interregnum," and the first ten years of Brigham Young's presidency.

The most systematic and professional attempt to collect, preserve, and write LDS history was launched in 1891 with the appointment of Andrew Jenson as Assistant Church Historian.[10] Jenson collected and wrote biographies of the founders and subsequent officers of the Church, published as *Latter-day Saint Biographical Encyclopedia*;[11] prepared a superbly useful encyclopedia of Church history, published in 1941 as *Encyclopedic History of the Church*;[12] directed the preparation of a 700-volume scrapbook record of the day-to-day activities of the Church, with excerpts from available sources, both published and unpublished, called the Journal History of the Church; and published numerous articles in professional and Church-sponsored periodicals on subjects as varied as "Danes on the Isle of Man," "History of the Las Vegas Mission," "Orderville: An Experiment in a Communistic System, called the 'United Order,'" and "Day by Day with the Utah Pioneers." He also wrote a full history of the Scandinavian Mission, which has stood well the test of time. Jenson's work established the Church Historian's Office as the indispensable and effective source of Latter-day Saint history.

Survey Histories, 1879–1930

During Andrew Jenson's lifetime of labor in the Church Historian's Office, other historians, not with Church sponsorship but with Church cooperation, began to write narratives that were to some extent analytical and interpretive. The two principal contributors to Mormon historiography in the nineteenth century were Edward W. Tullidge and Hubert Howe Bancroft. With some access to documents in the Church Archives, Tullidge wrote *The Life of Brigham Young; or Utah and Her Founders, The Women of Mormondom, Life of Joseph the Prophet, History of Salt Lake City,* and *History of Northern Utah and Southern Idaho.*[13] These tend to be adulatory and are heavily documentary, but they are nevertheless valuable sources for early Utah history, and to a lesser extent, for early Mormon history.[14]

Bancroft, in his *History of Utah, 1540 to 1886*, tells the story of the Mormons during the pre-Utah period as well as the history of Utah after the Mormons settled there.[15] Much of the volume was written by Alfred Bates, one of Bancroft's employees. Bancroft was supplied with a great deal of material by the Church and its members, and his interpretation was regarded as generally favorable to the Church, with the anti-Mormon allegations carefully couched in the footnotes.[16]

In the same tradition followed Orson F. Whitney, an apostle and Assistant Church Historian.[17] Whitney's four-volume *History of Utah*, written in sesquipedalian prose, is a compelling narrative of Utah's history, from a Mormon point of view.[18] During the same years that Whitney served as Assistant Church Historian (1902–6), a colleague of equal rank was Brigham H. Roberts. An old fashioned orator (as was Whitney) with a searching mind and majestic style, Roberts entered upon the writing of a comprehensive history which would counteract the unfavorable image of Mormonism resulting from the long antipolygamy crusade of the 1880s, the controversy over his own election to the House of Representatives in 1899, and the testimony given in the trial of Senator Reed Smoot for seating in the Senate in the early years of this century. Courageous and indefatigable, Roberts wrote a full history which appeared in serial form in the *Americana* magazine from 1909 to 1915. With some updating, this was published with additional material as a six-volume set in connection with the Church's centennial observance in 1930 under the title *A Comprehensive History of the Church: Century One.*[19] Roberts's work, while still worth reading, is not a "definitive" work. Many documents since uncovered have altered some of his interpretations, and his preoccupation with the conflict between the Church and the federal government, and other personal biases are evident in his reconstruction of a number of critical episodes in Mormon history. Moreover, the volume fails to say much about cultural, social, and economic history, and covers only incompletely the years after 1915. It is an epic work, but not completely satisfactory for 1981 readers.[20]

The Professionalization of LDS History, 1920–72

While no historian would wish to denigrate or detract from the enormous significance of the histories by Tullidge, Bancroft, and Elders Whitney and Roberts, it is nevertheless essentially true that "objective," "scholarly," and "systematic" treatises on the Mormons and their culture began in this century as a product of students' work toward the Ph.D. in history and the social sciences.[21] One notes, in particular, the sociological dissertations of Ephraim Ericksen, Joseph A. Geddes, Lowry Nelson, and Thomas F. O'Dea; the economic histories of Feramorz Y. Fox and (if I may be so immodest) Leonard Arrington; and the history dissertations of Andrew Love Neff, L. H. Creer, Joel Ricks, Thomas C. Romney, Milton R. Hunter, Richard D. Poll, S. George Ellsworth, Philip A. M. Taylor, Merle E. Wells, Eugene E. Campbell, Kent Fielding, Warren Jennings, Klaus Hansen, Carmon Hardy, Robert Flanders, and Jan Shipps. These are not all of the Mormon-related dissertations written from 1920 to 1972, but they are representative of the large volume of scholarly works written during that period. There are a few other works, such as those of Juanita Brooks, which are fully as scholarly as the doctoral dissertations mentioned. Less defensive than the earlier writers, these authors have been fully professional in identifying and using sources, more persistent in seeking additional information, and more willing to advance honest answers for hard questions.

During the 1960s Elder Joseph Fielding Smith, Church Historian and Recorder, recognized the need for a professionalization of the Church Library and Archives and instructed his Assistant Church Historian, Earl Olson, to join and "be active in" professional library and archival societies.[22] Thus began, particularly after 1963, the employment of professional librarians and archivists, the systematic cataloguing of record books and manuscripts, the adoption of proper security measures and the planning for adequate facilities in the new Church Office building, the construction of which was first announced in 1960. When Elder Smith became president of the Church in 1970, he appointed Elder Howard Hunter, of the Council of the Twelve, as Church Historian and Recorder, with the understanding that Elder Hunter would further these efforts toward "professionalization." As Elder Hunter's assistant historian, Earl Olson continued to upgrade the Historian's Office.

Meanwhile, a group of professional Mormon historians and some of their colleagues in the social sciences who were "kindred souls" in historical interest met in San Francisco in December 1965 to form the Mormon History Association. The aim of the association was "to promote understanding, scholarly research, and publication in the field of Mormon history." The association has made annual awards to the authors of the best books and articles, has held meetings each year where scholars can share their research and writing, and sponsors a scholarly journal, *The Journal of Mormon History*, founded in 1974. The association also undertakes special projects, such as the editing of special issues of other journals. Steadily growing in size, now including in addition to all historians working on Mormon subjects several hundred interested amateurs or "buffs," the association has been a powerful motivating and coordinating force in promoting Mormon history.

Simultaneous with the formation of the Mormon History Association was the launching of *Dialogue: A Journal of Mormon Thought*. Historians have contributed regularly to the pages of *Dialogue*, which remains a major and welcome outlet for Mormon historical scholarship. Partly because of the competition offered by *Dialogue*, *Brigham Young University Studies*, usually referred to simply as BYU *Studies*, was reinvigorated and began to feature historical essays. An enlarged summer issue, composed primarily of historical articles built around a common theme, has appeared annually since 1969, and "The Historian's Corner" was inaugurated as a regular feature in 1970. In 1974 LDS women in the Boston area founded *Exponent II*, stimulating historical scholarship with respect to women in the LDS experience. Two years later a young group of Mormon intellectuals founded *Sunstone*. All of these carry articles on Mormon history.

Activities of the History Division, 1972–80

In 1972, with the imminent completion of the Church Office Building, of which the four-story East Wing would be dedicated to Church library, archives, and historical endeavors, Church Historian Howard Hunter recommended the organization of the Historical Department. Approved by the First Presidency and Council of Twelve Apostles in March 1972, the department was managed by Elder Alvin R. Dyer, an apostle and former member of the First Presidency. Donald T. Schmidt was appointed Church Librarian; Earl Olson, Church archivist; and Leonard Arrington, Church Historian, with James B. Allen and Davis Bitton as Assistant Historians. Some time later, Florence Jacobsen was appointed Church Curator. With the exception of Elder Dyer, who served as the ecclesiastical overseer of the department, and Florence Jacobsen, who served on a "dollar a year" basis, the appointees and their staffs were Church employees, paid for their time and expertise.

The principal departure from past tradition was the creation of the History Division which, under the direction of Leonard Arrington, was staffed with a dozen professional historians assigned to conduct research and writing projects on behalf of the Church. With ecclesiastical sanction, these and other historians, at Brigham Young University and elsewhere, were given full access to the Church Archives and commissioned to write accurate and reliable treatises on a variety of assigned topics. They have published 2 one-volume histories of Mormonism—the first, a 638-page narrative history primarily for Latter-day Saints; the second, a 400-page topical history, was written primarily for sale to libraries and non-

Mormon readers. History Division historians have published four biographies, and four others are on the way; two histories of Church auxiliaries and departments, with one more on the way; and edited two book-length collections of documents, one of which has been published and the other on the way. All in all, History Division staff members, during the period 1972–80, published fifteen books, with six others on the way; approximately one hundred professional articles, with twenty on the way; and published approximately 250 articles in Church magazines, with others on the way. The division also sponsored a Task Paper Series in which thirty-three occasional papers were published. Division historians have written articles for several encyclopedias, assisted religion editors of several newspapers and magazines, and spoken before many learned societies.

In terms of subject matter, the History Division has made important contributions to the history of LDS women, the history of priesthood quorums and Church administration, the history of auxiliaries, and the histories of ethnic and national groups. We have done community histories, ward and stake histories, and advanced our knowledge of the roles of many individuals in Church history. One of our most significant contributions to Mormon historiography was the inauguration of an oral history program. Established in 1972, the program later received a large grant from the James Moyle Genealogical and Historical Association, and has since been called the James Moyle Oral History Program. To date the program, currently directed by Gordon Irving, has recorded some 1,500 interviews with 750 persons, representing about 3,000 hours on tape. The bulk of the interviews have been conducted in English, but possibly 15 percent have been conducted in other languages, including Spanish, Portuguese, Danish, and German. Interviews for the program have been done not only in Salt Lake City and Provo, Utah, but also in several parts of Canada, South America, Europe, Asia, and the South Pacific. Those interviewed have included General Authorities of the Church, administrators of Church programs, mission presidents and missionaries, officers of auxiliary organizations, old-timers with interesting stories to tell, and articulate members with particular insights that are worth preserving. The task of documenting LDS history is one that will lie continually before us, and as time and resources are available Director Irving intends to continue to document the past and the present so as to preserve a record for the future.

The History Division, I want to emphasize, at no time took the attitude that it should reserve to itself the research and writing of Mormon history. On the contrary, the division assisted other historians, both Mormons and non-Mormons, by preparing research aids and indexes, by sharing research findings, and by commenting upon manuscripts submitted for "checking." The division gave encouragement to many scholars by granting special fellowships and agreeing to serve as co-sponsor of their books. These include several volumes of the projected "History of the Latter-day Saints, 1830–1980," which have been prepared and approved and hopefully will be published under separate titles in the years to come by Deseret Book Company, BYU Press, and other university and commercial publishers. They also include *The Expanding Church* by Spencer Palmer;[23] the biography of Heber C. Kimball by Stanley Kimball, published by the University of Illinois Press;[24] the biography of Jedediah M. Grant by Gene S. Sessions, recently accepted by the University of Illinois Press;[25] and *Voices of Women* by Ken and Audrey Godfrey and Jill Mulvay Derr, now being published by Deseret Book Company.[26] Several other volumes are in process of preparation.

I hope you will agree with me, on the basis of this recital and the personal knowledge many of you have of our work, that the History Division serves well the interests of the Historical Department, the Church, and of Latter-day Saints generally during the period of its existence from 1972 to 1980. Perhaps because of this success, on the assumption that even more can be done in an academic setting, the First Presidency and Quorum of the Twelve, in July 1980, transferred the staff of the History Division from the Historical Department to constitute the newly created Joseph Fielding Smith Institute for Church History at Brigham Young University. President Spencer W. Kimball stated in announcing the transfer:

> The stature, objectivity and effectiveness of our fine professional historians will be enhanced by association with the church's university, where they can perform their scholarly tasks in a university atmosphere with increased interchange with professional colleagues and the teaching process.[27]

The Reconciliation of Faith and History

I MENTIONED AT THE START of this paper some of the challenges of writing religious history.[28] On the one hand the historian must convey the facts of history honestly and straightforwardly. The historian must strive against the conscious or unconscious distortion of events to fit the demands of current fashions; he must renounce wishful thinking. On the other hand, the religious historian wishes also to bear testimony of the reality of spiritual experience. We all know by now that the pretense of "objectivity" can mask a hypocritical dodge to cover up unspoken, perhaps even incorrect, assumptions.

Some tension between our historical training and our religious commitments seems inevitable. Our testimonies tell us that the Lord is in this work, and for this we see abundant supporting evidence. But our historical training warns us that the accurate perception of spiritual phenomena is elusive—not subject to unquestionable verification. We are tempted to wonder if our religious beliefs are intruding beyond their proper limits. Our faith tells us that there is moral meaning and spiritual significance in historical events. But can we be completely confident that any particular judgment or meaning or significance is unambiguously clear? If God's will cannot be wholly divorced from the actual course of history, can it be positively identified with it? Although we see evidence that God's love and power have frequently broken in upon the ordinary course of human affairs in a direct and self-evident way, our caution in declaring this is reinforced by our justifiable disapproval of chroniclers who take the easy way out and use divine miracles as a short circuit of a causal explanation which is obviously, or at least defensibly, naturalistic. We must not use history as a storehouse from which deceptively simple moral lessons may be drawn at random.

At the same time, I hope that LDS historians will be known for the sense of reverence and responsibility with which they approach their assignments. There should be a certain fidelity toward and respect for the documents. There should exist a certain feeling for human tragedy and triumph. LDS history is the history of Latter-day Saints, in their worship and prayer, in their mutual relationships, in their conflicts and contacts, in their social intercourse and in their solitude and estrangement, in their high aspirations, and in their fumbling weaknesses. We must be responsive to the whole amplitude of human concerns—to human life in all its rich variety and diversity, in all its misery and grandeur, in all its ambiguity and contradictions.

Part of that human life, we must insist, is its religious dimension. The Latter-day Saint historian will not do his subject justice, will not adequately understand the people he is writing about, if he leaves out the power of testimony as a motivating factor in their lives. In his "Second Century Address" at Brigham Young University in 1976, President Kimball gave us wise counsel. "As LDS scholars," he said, "you must speak with authority and excellence to your professional colleagues in the language of scholarship, and you must also be literate in the language of spiritual things."[29] The great histories of our people, most of which remain unwritten, will reflect both the rigor of competent scholarship and the sensitivity able to recognize, as the New Testament records, that "the wind bloweth where it listeth" (John 3:8).

May we as historians lengthen *our* stride as we strive to develop these capacities, which will then enable us to write histories worthy of the marvelous work and a wonder that is our heritage.

Chapter Fourteen Notes

1. I acknowledge the help of my colleagues in the Joseph Fielding Smith Institute for Church History, Brigham Young University, in the preparation of this paper. I am particularly grateful for the help of Davis Bitton, Senior Historian, Historical Department of The Church of Jesus Christ of Latter-day Saints and Professor of History at the University of Utah, Salt Lake City.
2. Johannes Cochlaeus, *Commentaria de Actis et Scriptis Lutheri* (1549).
3. A. G. Dickens, *The German Nation and Martin Luther* (New York: Harper and Row, 1974), 202.

4. See Leonard J. Arrington, "The Search for Truth and Meaning in Mormon History," *Dialogue: A Journal of Mormon Thought* 3 (summer 1968): 56–66. The essay is reprinted in chapter five of this volume.
5. On this and the following paragraph, see "Writing the History of Joseph Smith," in Howard C. Searle, "Early Mormon Historiography: Writing the History of the Mormons, 1830–1858" (Ph.D. diss., University of California at Los Angeles, 1979), 200–336. See also Dean C. Jessee, "The Writing of Joseph Smith's History," *BYU Studies* 11 (summer 1971): 439–73.
6. Searle, "Early Mormon Historiography," 220. See also Dean C. Jessee, "The Reliability of Joseph Smith's History," *Journal of Mormon History* 3 (1976): 23–46.
7. See Davis Bitton, "B. H. Roberts as Historian," *Dialogue* 3 (winter 1968): 25–44; and David J. Whittaker, "Historians and the Mormon Experience: A Sesquicentennial Perspective," paper presented at the Sidney Sperry Symposium on Church History, Brigham Young University, 26 January 1980, typescript generously furnished by the author.
8. See Searle, "The History of Brigham Young," 337–57.
9. See also Elden J. Watson, ed., *Manuscript History of Brigham Young, 1801–1844* (Salt Lake City: Smith Secretarial Service, 1968); and Elder J. Watson, ed., *Manuscript History of Brigham Young, 1846–1847* (Salt Lake City: E. J. Watson, 1971).
10. Keith W. Perkins, "Andrew Jenson: Zealous Chronologist" (Ph.D. diss., Brigham Young University, 1974); Louis Reinwand, "Andrew Jenson, Latter-day Saint Historian," *BYU Studies*, 14 (autumn 1973): 29–46; and *Autobiography of Andrew Jenson: Assistant Historian of The Church of Jesus Christ of Latter-day Saints* (Salt Lake City: Deseret News, 1938).
11. Andrew Jenson, *Latter-day Saint Biographical Encyclopedia: A Compilation of Biographical Sketches of Prominent Men and Women in The Church of Jesus Christ of Latter-day Saints*, 4 vols. (Salt Lake City: Andrew Jenson History, 1901–36).
12. Andrew Jenson, *Encyclopedic History of The Church of Jesus Christ of Latter-day Saints* (Salt Lake City: Deseret News, 1941).
13. Edward W. Tullidge, *Life of Brigham Young; or, Utah and her Founders* (New York: 1876); Edward W. Tullidge, *The Women of Mormondom* (New York: 1877); Edward W. Tullidge, *Life of Joseph the Prophet* (New York: Tullidge and Crandall); Edward W. Tullidge, *The History of Salt Lake City and its Founders* (Salt Lake City: Edward W. Tullidge, Publisher and Proprietor, 1886); Edward W. Tullidge, *Tullidge's Histories. Volume II: Containing the history of all the northern, eastern and western counties of Utah, also the counties of southern Idaho* (Salt Lake City: Press of the Juvenile Instructor, 1889).
14. See William F. Lye, "Edward Wheelock Tullidge, The Mormons' Rebel Historian," *Utah Historical Quarterly* 28 (January 1960): 56–75; Ronald W. Walker, "Edward Tullidge: Historian of the Mormon Commonwealth," *Journal of Mormon History* 3 (1976): 55–72.
15. H. H. Bancroft, *History of Utah, 1540–1886* (San Francisco: The History Co., 1889).
16. John Walton Caughey, *Hubert Howe Bancroft: Historian of the West* (Berkeley: University of California Press, 1946); S. George Ellsworth, "Hubert Howe Bancroft and the History of Utah," *Utah Historical Quarterly* 22 (autumn 1954): 99–124, and Ellsworth, "A Guide to the Manuscripts in the Bancroft Library Relating to the History of Utah," *Utah Historical Quarterly* 22 (July 1954): 197–247.

17. Woodruff Christian Thomson, "Orson F. Whitney, Mormon Writer" (Master's thesis, University of Utah, 1949).
18. Orson F. Whitney, *History of Utah: Comprising preliminary chapters on the previous history of her founders, accounts of early Spanish and American explorations in the Rocky Mountain region, the advent of the Mormon pioneers, the establishment and dissolution of the provisional government of the State of Deseret, and the subsequent creation and development of the territory* (Salt Lake City: G. Q. Cannon and Sons Company, 1892–1904).
19. B. H. Roberts, *A Comprehensive History of The Church of Jesus Christ of Latter-day Saints, Century One*, 6 vols. (Salt Lake City: Deseret Book, 1930).
20. Truman G. Madsen, *Defender of the Faith: The B. H. Roberts Story* (Salt Lake City: Bookcraft, 1980); and Davis Bitton, "B. H. Roberts as Historian," *Dialogue* 3 (winter 1968): 25–44.
21. In what follows, see Leonard J. Arrington, "Scholarly Studies of Mormonism in the Twentieth Century," *Dialogue* 1 (spring 1966): 15–28; and Leonard J. Arrington, "The Search for Truth and Meaning in Mormon History," *Dialogue* 3 (summer 1968): 56–66. These essays are reprinted in chapters five and ten of this volume.
22. In what follows see especially Leonard J. Arrington, "Historian As Entrepreneur: A Personal Essay," *BYU Studies* 17, no. 2 (winter 1977): 193–209. The essay is reprinted in chapter one of this volume.
23. Spencer J. Palmer, *The Expanding Church* (Salt Lake City: Deseret Book, 1978).
24. Stanley B. Kimball, *Heber C. Kimball: Mormon Patriarch and Pioneer* (Urbana: University of Illinois Press, 1981).
25. Gene A. Sessions, *Mormon Thunder: A Documentary History of Jedediah Morgan Grant* (Urbana: University of Illinois Press, 1982).
26. Kenneth W. Godfrey, Audrey M. Godfrey, and Jill Mulvay Derr, *Women's Voices: An Untold History of the Latter-day Saints, 1830–1900* (Salt Lake City: Deseret Book, 1982).
27. "New Institute at Y. to Assume Role of Church History Division," *Church News* (5 July 1980).
28. In what follows I have benefited from reading the essays in C. T. McIntire, ed., *God, History, and Historians: An Anthology of Modern Christian Views of History* (New York: Oxford University Press, 1977); Robert N. Bellah, *Beyond Belief: Essays on Religion in a Post-Traditional World* (New York: Harper and Row, 1970); and George Santayana, *The Life of Reason* (New York: Scribner's Sons, 1936).
29. Spencer W. Kimball, "Second-Century Address," *BYU Studies* 16 (summer 1976): 446.

Leonard James Arrington (1917–99)
A Bibliography

By David J. Whittaker

THIS BIBLIOGRAPHY CORRECTS and extends three previously published lists: the first in *Dialogue: A Journal of Mormon Thought* in 1978, the second in *New Views of Mormon History: A Collection of Essays in Honor of Leonard J. Arrington* in 1987, and the third in the *Journal of Mormon History* in 1999.[1] Efforts to make this bibliography as complete as possible lead to the decision not to include notices about Leonard in public prints or professional publications. Thus no attempt has been make to include information on (1) his various civic and professional associations, (2) his numerous awards, both professional and honorary, (3) his numerous research grants and fellowships, and (4) his service as an editor (active or as a guest) or his service on various editorial boards of professional organizations or periodicals. While a large number of his addresses are included here, no attempt has been made to identify all his talks or interviews.

The Leonard J. Arrington Historical Archive, containing his personal, professional and family papers, is now housed in the Special Collections, Merrill Library, Utah State University, Logan,

---

David J. Whittaker is Curator, Western and Mormon Manuscripts, L. Tom Perry Special Collections, Harold B. Lee Library, and Associate Professor of History, Brigham Young University, Provo, Utah.

Utah. The collection has been organized into Twelve Series (319 linear feet) and has a guide of about two hundred pages, which is available online at www.usu.edu.library. Some items have been returned to the Arrington family, and Leonard's personal journals are restricted until 2010.

Abbreviations

AH	*Agricultural History*
AHR	*American Historical Review*
AW	*Arizona and the West*
BYU Studies	*Brigham Young University Studies*
BHR	*Business History Review*
Dialogue	*Dialogue: A Journal of Mormon Thought*
EHR	*Economic History Review*
Ensign	*The Ensign* (Salt Lake City)
Era	*The Improvement Era* (Salt Lake City)
HLQ	*Huntington Library Quarterly*
IY	*Idaho Yesterday*
JAH	*Journal of American History*
JEH	*Journal of Economic History*
JMH	*Journal of Mormon History*
New Era	*The New Era* (Salt Lake City)
PHR	*Pacific Historical Review*
PNQ	*Pacific Northwest Quarterly*
PUASAL	*Proceedings of the Utah Academy of Sciences, Arts & Letters*
SUP News	*Sons of Utah Pioneers News* (Salt Lake City)
UHQ	*Utah Historical Quarterly*
WHR	*Western Humanities Review*
WHQ	*Western Historical Quarterly*

Dissertation

"Mormon Economic Policies and Their Implementation on the Western Frontier, 1847–1900." University of North Carolina at Chapel Hill, 1952. Revised and published as *Great Basin Kingdom* in 1958.

Books, Pamphlets, and Monographs

Adventures of a Church Historian. Urbana: University of Illinois Press, 1998. 254 pp. Leonard's autobiography.

The Alta Club, 1975–1998. Salt Lake City: Publishers Press for the Alta Club, 1998. Also in this volume is the reprint of O. N. Malmquist's *The Alta Club, 1883–1974.*

Bankers Extraordinary: A History of First Security Corporation, 1928–1973. 365 pp. Submitted to First Security Corporation, 1973. It has not been released to the public.

Beet Sugar in the West: A History of the Utah-Idaho Sugar Company, 1891–1966. Seattle: University of Washington Press, 1966. 234 pp.

The Big Kanyon Lasting Legacy: Parley's Park. Salt Lake City: 1998. A compilation of historical facts about the Parleys Canyon area near the Salt Lake Valley. 120 pp.

Brigham Young: American Moses. New York: Alfred A. Knopf, 1985. 544 pp. Paperback reprint, Urbana: University of Illinois Press, 1986. Winner of the first David Woolley Evans and Beatrice Cannon Evans Biography Award for a distinguished biography of a significant personality who lived in Mormon Country during the past 150 years.

Brigham Young University: The First One Hundred Years, Volumes 3 and 4. Provo, Utah: Brigham Young University Press, 1976. 644 and 789 pp. Coeditor with Ernest L. Wilkinson.

Building the City of God: Community and Cooperation Among the Mormons. Salt Lake City: Deseret Book, 1976. 512 pp. 2nd ed., Urbana: University of Illinois Press, 1992. With Feramorz Y. Fox and Dean May. Received the Best Book Award for 1976 from the Mormon History Association.

Celebrating Cache Valley's Entrepreneurs. Logan: Special Collections of Utah State University Library, Arrington Lecture Series, 1998. 36 pp.

The Changing Economic Structure of the Mountain West, 1850–1950. Logan: Utah State University Monograph Series, Vol. 10, No. 3, June 1963. 64 pp. Reprinted in the Bobbs-Merrill Reprint Series in History.

Charles C. Rich, Mormon General and Veteran Frontiersman. Provo, Utah: Brigham Young University Press, 1974. 386 pp. First volume in the Studies in Mormon History series.

The Commercialization of Utah's Economy: Trends and Developments from Statehood to 1910. Logan: Utah State University, 1964. 40 pp. Paper for the Annual Meeting, Utah State Historical Society, Salt Lake City, 12 September 1964.

David Eccles: Pioneer Western Industrialist. Logan: Utah State University Press, 1975. 294 pp.

The Defense Industry of Utah. Logan: Department of Economics, Utah State University, 1965. Utah State Planning Program, Economic and Population Studies. 50 pp. With George Jensen.

Faith and Intellect as Partners in Mormon History. Logan: Special Collections of Utah State University Library, Leonard J. Arrington Mormon Lecture Series, Volume 1, 1996. 34 pp.

Farm Boy at the University of Idaho, 1935–39. Hyde Park, Utah: Historian's Press, 1996. 32 pp.

Federally-Financed Industrial Plants Constructed in Utah During World War II. Logan: Utah State University Monograph Series, Vol. 16, Number 1, March 1969. 72 pp. With Anthony T. Cluff.

From Quaker to Latter-day Saint: Bishop Edwin D. Woolley. Salt Lake City: Deseret Book, 1976. 592 pp. Wooley was a long-serving bishop of Salt Lake City's 13th Ward.

From Small Beginnings: A History of Steiner Corporation, American Linen Supply Company and their Affiliates. Salt Lake City: Publishers Press, 1991. 243 pp.

From Wilderness to Empire: The Role of Utah in Western Economic History, Monograph No. 1, Institute of American Studies, University of Utah. Salt Lake City, 1961. 20 pp.

Great Basin Kingdom: An Economic History of the Latter-day Saints, 1830–1900. Cambridge: Harvard University Press, 1958. 534 pp. Published in paperback in the Bison Books series, Lincoln: University of Nebraska Press, 1966. Reprinted in paperback with new author's preface, Salt Lake City: University of Utah Press and the Tanner Trust Fund, 1993. 534 pp. Reissued as a "New Edition" by the University of Illinois Press, 2005, with an Introduction by Ronald W. Walker. This book won the Award of Merit of the American Association of State and Local History and was given the annual award of the Pacific Coast Branch, American Historical Association, as the best first book by a Western historian published in 1958–59. The book is among those selected for the White House Library.

Growing Up in Twin Falls County, Idaho: A Pictorial History. Hyde Park, Utah: Historian's Press, 1996. 108 pp.

Harold F. Silver: Western Inventor, Businessman, and Civic Leader. Logan: Utah State University Press, 1992. 250 pp. With John R. Alley Jr.

History of Idaho. 2 volumes. Moscow : University of Idaho Press; Boise: Idaho State Historical Society, 1994. 961 pp. Issued in a one-volume, paperback edition in 1995.

A History of Salt Lake Rotary Club No. 24. Salt Lake City: Rotary Club, 1981. 58 pp.

The Hotel: Salt Lake's Classy Lady, The Hotel Utah, 1911–1986. Salt Lake City: Publishers Press, 1986. 101 pp. With Heidi S. Swinton.

An Illustrated History of the History Division of the LDS Church, 1972–82. Salt Lake City: Historian's Press, 1994. 59 pp. Privately distributed.

I'm Glad My House Burned Down: The Personal Story of Grace Fort Arrington. Salt Lake City: Privately printed, 1977. 189 pp. Edited with Rebecca F. Cornwall.

Impact of Defense Spending on the Economy of Utah. Logan: Department of Economics, Utah State University, 1967. Utah State Planning Program, Economic and Population Studies. 84 pp. With George Jensen.

In the Land of the Tar Heels: "Jimmie" in Raleigh and Chapel Hill, North Carolina, 1939–43, 1949–50, 1952: An Illustrated History. Hyde Park, Utah: Historian's Press, 1996. 38 pp.

In the Utah Tradition: A History of The Governor's Mansion. Salt Lake City: Publishers Press for the Governor's Mansion Foundation, 1987. 166 pp. With Heidi S. Swinton.

Introduzione alla Storia Economica delgi Stati Uniti. Genoa, Italy: Libraria Mario Bozzi, 1959. 272 pp. Pages 241–60, "The American Economy in the Age of the Atom and Automation," appears in English translation as Appendix E in Rebecca F. Cornwall, *From Chicken Farm to History: The Life of Leonard Arrington, 1917–1977.* Salt Lake City: Privately distributed, 1978. 406–21.

Editor. *Journal of Mormon History* 13 (1986–1987): 1–144.

Kate Field and J. H. Beadle: Manipulators of the Mormon Past. Salt Lake City: Center for Studies of the American West, University of Utah, 1971. 20 pp. Semi-annual American West Lecture, 31 March 1971.

Life in Happy Valley, Early Years in Logan and Our First Sabbatical, 1946–58: A Pictorial History. Hyde Park, Utah: Historian's Press, 1996. 46 pp.

Madelyn Cannon Stewart Silver: Poet, Teacher, Homemaker. Salt Lake City: Publishers Press, 1998. 331 pp.

Magic Valley Pioneers: A Photographic Record of N. W. and Edna Corn Arrington. Salt Lake City: Historian's Press, 1991. 110 pp.

The Mormon Experience: A History of the Latter-day Saints. New York: Alfred A. Knopf, Inc., 1979. 404 pp. Published simultaneously in England by Allen and Unwin. Listed by the History Book Club. Awarded the Mormon History Association Best Book Award, 1980. Issued in paperback by Vintage Books of Random House, 1980. 2nd ed., Urbana: University of Illinois Press, 1992. 414 pp. Paperback. With Davis Bitton.

Mormons and Their Historians. Salt Lake City: University of Utah Press, 1988. 200 pp. With Davis Bitton.

The Mormons in Nevada. Las Vegas: *Las Vegas Sun*, 1979. Originally appeared serially in *The Sun*, 15 and 29 April, 13 and 27 May, 10 and 24 June, 8 and 22 July, 5 and 19 August, and 2 and 16 September 1979.

Mothers of the Prophets. Salt Lake City: Deseret Book, 1987. 213 pp. With Susan Arrington Madsen.

Orderville, Utah: A Pioneer Mormon Experiment in Economic Organization. Logan: Utah State Agricultural College Monograph Series, Vol. 2, Number 2, March 1954. 44 pp.

Editor and author of three chapters ("Preface," vii–viii; "Joseph Smith," 3–40; "Brigham Young," 43–72; "Harold B. Lee," 343–71). In *The Presidents of the Church.* Salt Lake City: Deseret Book, 1986.

The Price of Prejudice: The Japanese-American Relocation Center in Utah During World War II. Twenty-fifth Faculty Honor Lecture, Logan: Utah State University, 1962. 48 pp. Reprinted in 1962, Logan Faculty Association, Utah State University with photographs (73 pp.); and again in 1997: Delta, Utah: The Topaz Museum (73 pp.), with an afterward by Jane Beckwith.

Rescue of the 1856 Handcart Companies Charles Redd Monographs in Western History, No. 11. Provo, Utah: Brigham Young University Press, 1981. 59 pp. Revised ed., 1993. 63 pp. With Rebecca F. Cornwall.

"The Richest Hole on Earth": A History of Bingham Copper Mine. Logan: Utah State University Monograph Series, Vol. 11, No. 1, October 1963. 103 pp. Reprinted by Utah State University, 1969. With Gary B. Hansen.

St. George Tabernacle and Temple: The Builders. St. George, Utah: Dixie College, 1993. 24 pp. Presented as the Juanita Brooks Lecture on the occasion of the dedication of the renovated LDS Tabernacle at St. George, Utah, 21 July 1993.

Saints Without Halos: The Human Side of Mormon History. Salt Lake City: Signature Books, 1981. 158 pp. With Davis Bitton.

"Service Above Self:" A History of Logan Rotary Club, 1919–1969. Logan, Utah: J. P. Smith Printing, 1969. 42 pp. With the collaboration of earlier historians A. N. Sorenson and M. P. Hovey.

A Soldier in North Africa and Italy, 1943–1946: A Pictorial History. Salt Lake City: Historian's Press, 1995. 69 pp.

A Study of the Impacts of Research and Development-Based Manufacturing in Utah. Prepared under contract C-394 with the National Science Foundation and subcontract No. 1 with Utah State University. Mimeographed by George Washington University, Washington, D.C., November 1965. 127 pp. With Reed R. Durtschi, Bartell C. Jensen, Charles T. Stewart, Don W. Thomas, and Thomas C. Anderson.

Sunbonnet Sisters: True Stories of Mormon Women and Frontier Life. Salt Lake City: Bookcraft, 1984. 161 pp. With Susan Arrington Madsen.

Tar Heels, Hoosiers, and Idahoans: A History of the Noah and Edna Arrington Family to 1933. Salt Lake City: Privately printed, 1976. 167 pp. With Rebecca F. Cornwall.

Tracy-Collins Bank & Trust Company: A Record of Responsibility, 1884–1984. Salt Lake City: Eden Hill, 1984. 252 pp.

Utah's Audacious Stockman: Charlie Redd. Logan: Utah State University Press; Provo: The Charles Redd Center for Western Studies, BYU, 1995. 282 pp.

Voices from the Past: Diaries, Journals, and Autobiographies. Provo, Utah: Brigham Young University Press, Division of Continuing Education, Campus Education Week, 1980. Co-edited with Thomas G. Alexander, Donald Q. Cannon, Richard H. Cracroft, and Neal E. Lambert.

W. W. Clyde, The Builder (Salt Lake City: Devonshire Press, 1999). 305 pp.

Water for Urban Reclamation: The Provo River Project. Utah Agricultural Experiment Station Bulletin, Utah Resources Series 29. Logan, Utah: Utah State University Press, 1966. 35 pp. With Thomas G. Alexander.

William Spry: Man of Firmness, Governor of Utah. Salt Lake City: Utah State Historical Society and the University of Utah Press, 1971. 236 pp. With William L. Roper.

Years of Achievement and Pleasure in Logan, 1958–72: An Illustrated History. Hyde Park, Utah: Historian's Press, 1996. 70 pp.

Articles (Professional and Non-Professional) and Chapters in Books

"Abundance from the Earth: The Beginnings of Commercial Mining in Utah." *UHQ* 31 (Summer 1963): 192–219.

"Achievements of Latter-day Saint Women." *Era* 73 (April 1970): 61–62.

"Agricultural Price Control in Pioneer Utah." *AH* 30 (July 1956): 104–13.

"Alice Merrill Horne, Cultural Entrepreneur." In *A Heritage of Faith; Talks Selected from the BYU Women's Conferences*, edited by Mary E. Stovall and Carol Cornwall Madsen, 121–36. Salt Lake City: Deseret Book, 1988. With Harriet Horne Arrington.

"All is Well." In *Mormon Pioneer Memorial Monument*, unpaged [pp. 5–13]. Salt Lake City, 1974.

Entries in *American National Biography*, 24 volumes, edited by John A. Garraty and Mark C. Carnes. New York: Oxford University Press, 1999: "Alfred Cumming," 5: 847–48; "Edwin Dilworth Wooley," 23: 847; and "Brigham Young," 24: 152–55.

"Anchors Aweigh in Utah: The U.S. Naval Supply Depot at Clearfield, 1942–1962." *UHQ* 31 (Spring 1963): 109–26. With Archer L. Durham.

"Arizona in the Great Depression Years." *Arizona Review* 17 (December 1968): 11–19.

"Attitude of the Mormon Church Toward Mining, 1847–1900." *PUASAL* 31 (1954): 173–74.

"Background" to "The Order is Love" by Carol Lynn Pearson, *New Era* 1 (April 1971): 19–20. Also the "Introduction" to *The Order is Love* by Carol Lynn Pearson (Provo, Utah: Trilogy Arts, 1971), 7–9.

"Banking Enterprises in Utah, 1847–1880." *BHR* 29 (December 1955): 312–34.

"Basic Economic Institutions of Pioneer Utah." *SUP News* 2 (August–September 1955): 6–7.

"The Beginning of Better Days: Joseph Gave Women New and Higher Status." *This People* 13 (Summer 1992): 53–54.

"Black Pioneer Was Union Fort Settler." *The Pioneer* 28 (September–October 1981): 8–9.

"Blessed Damozels: Women in Mormon History." *Dialogue* 6 (Summer 1971): 22–31. Presidential address to the Western History Association, given in Omaha, Nebraska, on 10 October 1969. Awarded Second Prize in *Dialogue*'s annual competition for the best article in the field of Mormon social literature.

"Blessed Relief Society Sisters." In *Blueprints for Living, Perspectives for Latter-day Saint Women*, edited by Maren M. Mouritsen, 2: 14–24. 2 vols. Provo, Utah: Brigham Young University Press, 1980.

"Brigham Young: American Moses." *Utah Holiday* 14 (April 1985): 48–56.

"Brigham Young and the Great Basin Economy." In *Seminar on Brigham Young 1962*, 79–96. Provo, Utah: Brigham Young University Extension Publications, 1963.

"Brigham Young and the Great Basin Economy." In *Lion of the Lord: Essays on the Life and Service of Brigham Young*, ed. Susan Easton Black and Larry C. Porter, 291–311. Salt Lake City: Deseret Book, 1995.

"Brigham Young and the Transcontinental Telegraph Line." *Era* 54 (July 1951): 510–11, 529.

"Brigham Young." In *Research Guide to American Historical Biography*, edited by Robert Muccigrosso, 3: 1674–80. 3 vols. Washington, D.C.: Beacham Publishing, 1988.

"Brigham Young Leads the Mormons into the West." In *The Underside of American History*, 5th edition, ed. Thomas R. Frazier, *Volume 1: To 1877* (New York: Harcourt Brace Jovanovich, 1987), 381–404. With Davis Bitton. Reprint of Chapter Five of *The Mormon Experience* (1979).

"Brother Brigham: The Human Side." *This People* 11 (Spring 1990): 26–32.

"Building a Commonwealth: The Secular Leadership of Brigham Young." Address for Statehood Day, St. George, Utah, 4 January 1977. *UHQ* 45 (Summer 1977): 216–32. With Ronald K. Esplin.

"Building Blocks of the Kingdom, 1830–1980." *Sidney B. Sperry Symposium: A Sesquicentennial Look at Church History*, 26 January 1980 (Provo, Utah: Church Education System and Brigham Young University Press, 1980), 15–26.

"Cache Valley's Bicentennial Heritage." Address to Banquet for the George Washington Bicentennial Ball, Logan, Utah, 20 February 1976, published in Douglas D. Alder, ed., *Cache Valley: Essays on Her Past and People* (Logan: Utah State University, 1976), 1–12.

"Camp in the Sagebrush: Camp Floyd, Utah, 1858–1861." *UHQ* 34 (Winter 1966): 3–21. With Thomas G. Alexander.

"Can the Family Farm Survive?" In *The Future of Agriculture in the Rocky Mountains*, edited by E. Richard Hart, 65–71. Salt Lake City: Westwater Press, 1980. Address presented at the Conference on Western Agriculture sponsored by the Institute of the American West, Sun Valley, Idaho, 25 October 1979.

"Celebrating Idaho's Historians." *IY* 34 (Winter 1991): 2–9.

"Celebration of a Century of Accomplishments." Presented at the Utah State University Centennial Symposium, Logan, Utah, 15 April 1987, and published in *Proceedings, Centennial Centerpiece Opening Conference* (Logan: Utah State University, 1987), 47–52.

"Centrifugal Tendencies in Mormon History." In *To the Glory of God: Mormon Essays on Great Issues,* edited by Truman G. Madsen and Charles D. Tate Jr., 163–77. Salt Lake City: Deseret Book, 1972.

"Charles Mackay and His 'True and Impartial History' of the Mormons." UHQ 36 (Winter 1968): 25–40.

"The Christ-Bearer: Columbus Knew His Mission." *This People* 13 (Spring 1992): 18–19.

"Christmas: An Opportunity to Serve the Lord." In *The Magic of Christmas: A Collection of Stories, Poems, Essays, and Traditions by Favorite LDS Authors,* 96–100. Salt Lake City: Deseret Book, 1992.

"Christmas Eve in Front of the Open Oven Door." In *A Celebration of Christmas,* 41–44. Salt Lake City: Deseret Book, 1988.

"Christmas is Memories: Mormon Journals from Bygone Years Tell a Poignant Story." *This People* 9 (Winter 1988): 20–24.

"Church History and the Achievement of Identity." *Commissioner's Lecture Series* (Provo, Utah: BYU Press for the Church Education System, The Church of Jesus Christ of Latter-day Saints,1972). 7 pp.

"Church Leaders in Liberty Jail." *BYU Studies* 13 (Autumn 1972): 20–26.

"Church of Jesus Christ of Latter-day Saints." In *Encyclopedia Britannica,* 1973 Book of the Year, 587–88.

"Church of Jesus Christ of Latter-day Saints." In *Encyclopedia Britannica,* 1979, 1980, 1981, 1982, 1983, 1985, 1987, 1988, 1990 Year Book, s.v. Religion.

"Church of Jesus Christ of Latter-day Saints." In *Encyclopedia Britannica,* 1991 Book of the Year, s.v. "Religion: Protestant Churches," 294; 1992, 263–64; 1993, 265–66; 1995, 269; 1996, 291; 1997, 303; 1998, 307.

"Coin and Currency in Early Utah." UHQ 20 (January 1952): 56–76.

"Colonizing the Great Basin." *Ensign* 10 (February 1980): 18–22.

"Coming to Terms with Mormon History: An Interview with Leonard Arrington." *Dialogue* 22 (Winter 1989): 39–54.

"The Commercialization of Utah's Economy: Trends and Developments from Statehood to 1910." In *A Dependent Commonwealth: Utah's Economy from Statehood to the Great Depression,* edited by Dean May, 3–34. Provo, Utah: Charles Redd Center in Western Studies, BYU, Charles Redd Monographs in Western History, No. 4, 1974.

"Community and Isolation: Some Aspects of 'Mormon Westerns,'" *Western American Literature* 8 (Spring–Summer 1973): 15–31. With Jon Haupt.

"Comparison of Income Changes in the Western States, 1929–1960." *Western Economic Journal* 1 (Summer 1963): 205–17. With George Jensen.

"Contributions of the Latter-day Saints to Western Agriculture." *Benson Institute Review* 13 (Winter 1989): 7–13. Published by the Ezra Taft Benson Agriculture and Food Institute, BYU.

"Cooperative Community in the North: Brigham City, Utah." UHQ 33 (Summer 1965): 199–217.

"Crisis in Identity: Mormon Responses in the Nineteenth and Twentieth Centuries." In *Mormonism and American Culture*, edited by Marvin S. Hill and James B. Allen, 168–84. New York: Harper and Row, 1972.

"Crusade Against Theocracy: The Reminiscences of Judge Jacob Smith Boreman of Utah, 1872–1877." HLQ 24 (November 1960): 1–45.

"Daniel Cowan Jackling." In *Dictionary of American Biography*, Supplement Six, 1956–1960, edited by John A. Garraty, 316–17. New York: Charles Scribner's Sons, 1980.

"David Eccles: A Man for His Time." JMH 25, no. 2 (Fall 1999): 1–10. Originally prepared for the dedication of the David Eccles College of Business, University of Utah, 6 October 1991.

"Days of Praise and Thanksgiving." *This People* 11 (November 1990): 47–48.

"Delights of Church History." In *Know Your Religion Speeches: California, 1972–73* (Los Angeles: BYU California Center, 1973), 1–16.

"The Deseret Agricultural and Manufacturing Society in Pioneer Utah." UHQ 24 (April 1956): 165–70.

"The Deseret Telegraph." *This People* 10 (Spring 1989): 53–55.

"The Deseret Telegraph—A Church-Owned Public Utility." JEH 11 (Spring 1951): 117–39.

"*Dialogue*'s Valuable Service for LDS Intellectuals." *Dialogue* 21 (Summer 1988): 134–36.

"'A Different Mode of Life': Irrigation and Society in Nineteenth-Century Utah." AH 49 (January 1975): 3–20. With Dean May.

"'Divinely Tall and Most Divinely Fair': Josephine Donna Smith—'Ina Coolbrith.'" *Utah Libraries* 13 (Spring 1970): 8–14.

"Doing to Learn: Idaho Future Farmers in the 1930s." IY 43 (Summer 1999): 25–31.

"Early Mormon Communitarianism: The Law of Consecration and Stewardship." WHR 7 (Autumn 1953): 341–69. Reprinted without footnotes in *Mormonism and American Culture*, edited by Marvin S. Hill and James B. Allen, 37–58. New York: Harper and Row, 1972.

"Eccles, Marriner Stoddard." In *Dictionary of American Biography*, Supplement 10, edited by Kenneth T. Jackson, 204–6. New York: Charles Scribner's Sons, 1995.

"Economic Development In Early Utah." In *Historical Atlas of Mormonism*, edited by S. Kent Brown, Donald Q. Cannon, and Richard H. Jackson, 100-1. New York: Simon and Schuster, 1994.

"Economic History of a Mormon Valley: [Utah Valley, Utah]." PNQ 46 (October 1955): 97–107.

"An Economic Interpretation of the 'Word of Wisdom,'" BYU *Studies* 1 (Winter 1959): 37–49.

"Economic Policy Crisis In Utah—1869." PUASAL 18 (1951): 123ff. Abstract.

"The Economic Role of Pioneer Mormon Women." WHR 9 (Spring 1955): 145–64.

"The Economic Value of Utah's Travel and Recreation Business: The Perspective of 117 Years." *Proceedings of the Third Annual Utah Travel Institute*, held in Salt Lake City, 1 February 1964, pp. 13–15.

"The Economics Past and Future of Utah." *Salt Lake Tribune*, Empire Edition, 17 February 1979.

"Eleventh President: Harold B. Lee (1899–1973)." In Preston Nibley, *The Presidents of the Church* (13th ed., rev. and enl., Salt Lake City: Deseret Book, 1974), 427–57.

"Emmeline B. Wells: Mormon Feminist and Journalist." In *Forgotten Heroes: Inspiring Portraits from Our Leading Historians*, A Society of American Historians' Book, edited by Susan Ware, with a Foreword by David McCullough, 121–28. New York: The Free Press, 1998.

Entries in *Encyclopedia of Mormonism*, 5 vols., edited by Daniel H. Ludlow. New York: Macmillan Publishing Company, 1992: "Economic History of the Church," 2: 613–22; (with Dean L. May) "History of the Church: 1844–1877," 2: 435–41; "Pioneer Economy," 3: 1083–84; and "Brigham Young," 4: 1601–9.

Entries in *Encyclopedia of the American West*, 4 vols., edited by Charles Phillips and Alan Axelrod. New York: Macmillan reference USA, 1996: "Danites," 2: 432–33; "Orson Pratt," 3: 1323–24; "Charles Coulson Rich," 3: 1370.

Editor of "Experiment in Utopia: The United Order of Richfield, 1874–1877," by Feramorz Y. Fox, UHQ 32 (Fall 1964): 355–80.

"The Faithful Young Family: The Parents, Brothers, and Sisters of Brigham." *Ensign* 10 (August 1980): 52–57. With JoAnn Jolley.

"Farm Boy Genius: What You Didn't Know About Philo Farnsworth's Mormonism." *This People* 11 (Summer 1990): 61–62.

"The 'First' Irrigation Reservoir in the United States: The Newton, Utah, Project." UHQ 39 (Summer 1971): 207–23. With Thomas C. Anderson.

"Foreword." In *Brigham Young University: The First One Hundred Years,* edited by Ernest L. Wilkinson, 4 volumes, 1: vii–xii. Provo, Utah: Brigham Young University Press, 1975–1976.

"Foreword." In *Christmas: A Joyful Heritage*, by Susan Arrington Madsen, ix–xiii. Salt Lake City: Deseret Book, 1984.

"Foreword." In *Latter-day Patriots: Nine Mormon Families and Their Revolutionary War Heritage*, by Gene Allred Sessions, xi–xii. Salt Lake City: Deseret Book, 1975.

"Foreword"." In *Mormon Democrat: The Political and Religious Memoirs of James Henry Moyle*, edited by Gene A. Sessions, , iii–iv. Salt Lake City: The James Moyle Genealogical and Historical Association, 1975.

"Foreword." In *Political Deliverance: The Mormon Quest for Utah Statehood*, by Edward Leo Lyman, ix–x. Urbana: University of Illinois Press, 1986.

"Foreword." In *Builders of the Kingdom*, by Merlo J. Pusey, ix–xi. Provo, Utah: Brigham Young University Press, 1981.

"Foreword." In *The Life and Thought of Orson Pratt*, by Breck England, ix–xi. Salt Lake City: University of Utah Press, 1985.

"Foreword." In *The Story of the Latter-day Saints*, by James B. Allen and Glen M. Leonard, vii–viii. Salt Lake City; Deseret Book, 1976.

"Foreword." In B. H. Roberts, *The Truth, The Way, The Life, An Elementary Treatise on Theology: The Masterwork of B. H. Roberts*, edited by Stan Larson, xi–xii. San Francisco: Smith Research Associates, 1994.

"Foreword." In *Differing Visions: Dissenters in Mormon History*, edited by Roger D. Launius and Linda Thatcher, ix–xi. Urbana: University of Illinois Press, 1994.

"Foreword." In *Eliza and Her Sisters*, by Maureen Ursenbach Beecher, vi–ix. Salt Lake City: Aspen Books, 1991.

"Foreword." In *We'll Find the Place: The Mormon Exodus, 1846–1848*, by Richard E. Bennett, xi–xii. Salt Lake City: Deseret Book, 1997.

"Foreword." In *The Mormons' War on Poverty: A History of LDS Welfare, 1830–1990*, by Garth L. Mangum and Bruce D. Blumell, vii–xi. Salt Lake City: University of Utah Press, 1993.

"Foreword." In *Utah: A Portrait*, by William B. Smart and John Telford, xi–xv. Salt Lake City: University of Utah Press, 1995.

"Foreword." In *A Believing People: Literature of the Latter-day Saints*, edited by Richard H. Cracroft and Neal E. Lambert, xv–xvi. Provo, Utah: Brigham Young University Press, 1974.

"Foreword." In *A School of Destiny*, by Ernest L. Wilkinson and W. Cleon Skousen, vii–x. Provo, Utah: Brigham Young University Press, 1976.

"Foreword." In *Ships, Saints, and Mariners, A Maritime Encyclopedia of Mormon Migration, 1830–1890*, by Conway B. Sonne, ix–x. Salt Lake City: University of Utah Press, 1987.

"The Founding of the LDS Church Historical Department, 1972." *JMH* 18 (Fall 1992): 41–56.

"The Founding of the L.D.S. Institutes of Religion." *Dialogue* 2 (Summer 1967): 137–47. Dr. Arrington graduated from the LDS Institute of Religion, Moscow, Idaho, in 1939, and he taught occasionally at the Institute of Religion at Utah State University.

"From Apache-hunting to 'Hosting' America: The Economic Development of Arizona, 1863–1950." *Arizona Review* 18 (August–September 1969): 1–5.

"From Panning Gold to Nuclear Fission: Idaho's Economic Development, 1860–1960." *IY* 3 (July 1962): 2–10.

"From Subsistence to Golden Age: Cache Valley Agriculture, 1859–1900." *UHQ* 57 (Fall 1989): 340–69. With Linda Wilcox.

"Gather Ye Together . . . Upon the Land of Zion." *The Instructor* 102 (April 1967): 148–49.

"General Editor's Preface." In *Letters of Brigham Young to His Sons*, edited by Dean C. Jessee, vi–vii. Salt Lake City: Deseret Book in collaboration with the Historical Department of The Church of Jesus Christ of Latter-day Saints, 1974.

"George Albert Smith." In *Dictionary of American Biography*, Supplement Five, 1951–1955, edited by John A. Garraty, 639–40. New York: Charles Scribner's Sons, 1977.

"George S. Eccles" and "Marriner S. Eccles." In *Encyclopedia of American Business History and Banking and Finance, 1913–1989*, edited by Larry Schweikart, 98–113. New York: Facts-on-File, 1990.

"George S. Tanner: A Teaching Pioneer." In *Teachers Who Touch Lives: Methods of the Masters*, edited by Philip L. Barlow, 79–91. Bountiful, Utah: Horizon Publishers, 1988.

"Grass Roots Entrepreneurship in the Frontier West: The Allens of Cache Valley and the Coreys and Wattises of Weber Valley." In *Community Development in the American West: Past and Present Nineteenth and Twentieth Century Frontiers*, edited by Jessie L. Embry and Howard A. Christie, 183–200. Charles Redd Monographs in Western History, No. 15. Provo, Utah: Charles Redd Center for Western Studies, BYU, 1985.

"*Great Basin Kingdom* Revisited." *Dialogue* 26 (Summer 1993): 173–83.

"Have the Saints Always Given as Much Emphasis to the Word of Wisdom as They Do Today?" *Ensign* 7 (April 1977): 32–33.

"Historian as Entrepreneur: A Personal Essay." *BYU Studies* 17 (Winter 1977): 193–209.

"Historical Development of International Mormonism." *Religious Studies and Theology* 7 (January 1987): 9–21.

"Historical Roots of the Mormon Settlement in Southern Alberta." In *The Mormon Presence in Canada*, edited by Brigham Y. Card, Herbert C. Northcott, John E. Foster, Howard Palmer, and George K. Jarvis, 3–18. Edmonton, Alberta: University of Alberta Press, 1990. Based on an address given at the Mormon Presence in Canada Conference, University of Alberta, Edmonton, Canada, 6–9 May 1987.

"History Is Then and Now: A Conversation with Leonard J. Arrington, Church Historian." *Ensign* 5 (July 1975): 8–13.

Chapters in *The History of a Valley: Cache Valley, Utah-Idaho*, edited by Joel E. Ricks. Logan, Utah: Cache Valley Centennial Commission, 1956: chapter 7, "Life and Labor Among the Pioneers," 140–69; chapter 8, "Railroad Building and Cooperatives, 1869–1879," 170–204; chapter 9, "Transition to the Modern Era, 1880–1910," 205–39; chapter 10, "Economy in the Modern Era," 240–74.

"History of the Church in the Pacific Northwest." *Task Papers in LDS History*, No. 18. Salt Lake City: Historical Department, The Church of Jesus Christ of Latter-day Saints, 1977. 28 pp.

"H. L. A. Culmer: Utah's Renaissance Man." *Pioneer* [publication of Sons of Utah Pioneers], (January–February 1994), 23.

"'In Honorable Remembrance': Thomas L. Kane's Services to the Mormons." *Task Papers in LDS History*, No. 22. Salt Lake City: Historical Department of The Church of Jesus Christ of Latter-day Saints, 1978. Based on an address delivered at the Centennial Service, Kane Memorial Chapel, Kane, Pennsylvania, 2 June 1978. Reprinted in *BYU Studies* 21 (Fall 1981): 35–52.

"The Horn Silver Bonanza." In *The American West: A Reorientation*, edited by Gene M. Gressley, 35–54. Laramie: University of Wyoming Publications, Vol. 32, 1966. With Wayne K. Hinton.

Howard D. Lamar, ed., *The Reader's Encyclopedia of the American West* (New York: Thomas Y. Crowell, 1977). Leonard Arrington is credited with the following entries: John Milton Bernhisel, p. 90; George Q. Cannon, p. 161; Patrick Edward Connor, p. 254; William Godbe, p. 445; handcart companies, p. 485; William Henry Hooper, p. 511; William Jennings, p. 598; Latter-day Saints, pp. 646–52; Logan, Utah, pp. 673–74; Ogden, Utah, p. 859; Joseph Smith Jr., pp. 1112–24; Joseph Fielding Smith, p. 1124; Eliza Roxey, Snow, pp. 1126–27; James E. Talmage, pp. 1155–56; John Taylor, p. 1161; uranium mining, pp. 1207–8; Utah, pp. 1208–11; Wilford Woodruff, p. 1287; Brigham Young, pp. 1299–1300; Mahonri Macintosh Young, p. 1301; and Zion's Cooperative Mercantile Institution, p. 1306.

"How Do You Know if You Have Received the Holy Ghost?" *New Era* 2 (October 1972): 40–41.

"How the Mormons Settled Idaho LDS Communities." *The Prospector* no. 4 (1970), unpaged. This is the junior historical magazine of the Idaho Historical Society, Boise, Idaho.

"How the Saints Fed the Indians." *Era* 57 (November 1954): 800–1, 814.

"How They Settled the Upper Snake Country." *This People* 12 (Holiday 1991): 61–62.

"The Human Qualities of Joseph Smith, the Prophet." *Ensign* 1 (January 1971): 35–38. Appears in Spanish translation in *Liahona* (Salt Lake City) 17 (July 1971): 7–10.

"Idaho and the Great Depression." *IY* 13 (Summer 1969): 2–8.

"Idaho's Benson Family." *Idaho Heritage* No. 9 (1977): 18–19.

"Il Nuova Capitalismo negli Stati Uniti." Serially in *Il Genovese* (Genoa) 12 July–6 September 1959.

"The Industrial Structure of the Mountain West, 1850–1950." In *Proceedings of the Thirty-Sixth Annual Conference of the Western Economic Association at Seattle, Washington, August 24–25, 1961* (Salt Lake City: University of Utah Press, 1962), 19–23.

"The Influenza Epidemic of 1918–19 in Utah." *UHQ* 58 (Spring 1990): 165–82.

"The Influenza Epidemic of 1918–1919 in Southern Idaho." *IY* 32 (Fall 1988): 19–29.

"'In Honorable Remembrance': Thomas L. Kane's Services to the Mormons." *BYU Studies* 21 (Fall 1981): 389–402.

"Inland to Zion: Mormon Trade on the Colorado River, 1864–1867." *AW* 8 (Autumn 1966): 239–50.

"In Praise of Amateurs." *JMH* 17 (1991): 35–42.

"In Quest of Betterment: The Lee Roy and Priscella Arrington Family." In *Nearly Everything Imaginable, The Everyday Life of Utah's Mormon Pioneers*, edited by Ronald W. Walker and Doris R. Dant, 469–81. Provo, Utah: Brigham Young University Press, 1999.

"The Institution of Private Property in Early Utah." *PUASAL* 29 (1952): 55. Abstract.

"The Intellectual Tradition of Mormon Utah." *PUASAL* 45, Part 2, (1968): 346–65. An address to the Utah Academy in St. George, Utah, on 13 September 1968, upon receiving the Charles H. Redd Award.

"The Intellectual Tradition of the Latter-day Saints." *Dialogue* 4 (Spring 1969): 13–26.

"An Interview with Leonard Arrington and Davis Bitton." *Sunstone* 4 (July–August 1979): 38–41.

"Intolerable Zion: The Image of Mormonism in Nineteenth Century American Literature." *WHR* 22 (Summer 1968): 243–60. With Jon Haupt. This article was awarded the Mormon History Association Prize as best article on Mormon history published in 1968–69.

"Introduction." In Charles S. Walgamott, *Six Decades Back* (Moscow: University of Idaho Press, 1990): ix–xviii.

"Introduction" to *Atlas of Utah*, Wayne L. Wahlquist, ed. (Ogden and Provo, Utah: Weber State College and Brigham Young University, 1981), 1–2.

"Introduction" to "A World Divided in an Age of Space: A Symposium." *WHR* 15 (Summer 1961): 201–2. This symposium was held in October 1960 at Utah State University, Logan, Utah. It was part of the semiannual meetings of the Utah Academy of Sciences, Arts & Letters. Dr. Arrington was chairman of the Social Sciences section at the meeting.

"Introduction" to *Rails from the West: A Biography of Theodore D. Judah*, by Helen Hinckley (San Marino, Calif.: Golden West Books, 1969), v–vi.

"Introduction" to William G. Hartley, *Kindred Saints: The Mormon Immigrant Heritage of Alvin and Kathryne Christenson* (Salt Lake City: Edwin Hill, 1982), vii–ix.

"Iron Manufacturing in Southern Utah in the Early 1880s: The Iron Manufacturing Company of Utah." *Bulletin of the Business Historical Society* 25 (September 1951): 149–68.

"Irrigation in the Snake River Valley: An Historical Overview." *IY* 30 (Spring–Summer 1986): 3–11. Originally presented to the Irrigation in Idaho Conference, Boise, Idaho, 26 March 1986.

"James Gordon Bennett's 1831 Report on 'The Mormonites,'" *BYU Studies* 10 (Spring 1970): 353–64.

"The John Tanner Family: He Gave the Church Two Fortunes—His Wealth and a Family that has Built the Kingdom Ever Since." *Ensign* 9 (March 1979): 46–51.

"Joseph F. Smith: From Impulsive Young Man to Patriarchal Prophet." *The John Whitmer Historical Association Journal* 4 (1984): 30–40. Originally duplicated by Historical Department of The Church of Jesus Christ of Latter-day Saints, 1973. 25 pp. Address prepared for the Joseph Smith Family Reunion, 19 August 1973.

"Joseph Fielding Smith: Faithful Historian." *Dialogue* 7 (Spring 1972): 21–24.

"Joseph Smith and the Lighter View." *New Era* 6 (August 1976): 8–13.

"Joseph Smith, Builder of Ideal Communities." In *The Prophet Joseph: Essays on the Life and Mission of Joseph Smith*, edited by Larry C. Porter and Susan Easton Black, 115–37. Salt Lake City: Deseret Book, 1988.

"La Lotta Contro i Cicli Economici e l'Inflazione negli Stati Uniti." *Le Compere de San Giorgio* (Genoa) 8 (February 1959): 3–8.

"Launching Idaho's Beet Sugar Industry." *IY* 9 (Fall 1965): 16–27.

"Latter-day Saint Women on the Arizona Frontier." *Henry Eyring Speakers' Series* (Tucson, Ariz.: LDS Institute of Religion, 1973), 1–17.

"Latter-day Saint Women on the Arizona Frontier." *New Era* 4 (April 1974): 42–50.

"The Latter-day Saints and Public Education." *Southwestern Journal of Social Education* 7 (Spring–Summer 1977): 9–25.

"The Latter-day Saints in the Far West, 1847–1900." In *The Restoration Movement: Essays in Mormon History*, edited by F. Mark McKiernan, Alma R. Blair, and Paul Edwards, eds., 257-71. Lawrence, Kans.: Coronado Press, 1973. With D. Michael Quinn. Reprinted, Independence, Mo.: Herald House, 1979.

"LDS Girls in the Pioneer West." *New Era* 12 (July 1982): 16–22.

"The LDS Hawaiian Colony at Skull Valley." *Era* 57 (May 1954): 314–15, 365–67.

"The LDS Hawaiian Colony at Skull Valley, UT, 1889–1917." *Proceedings, First Annual Conference, Mormon History in the Pacific, August 1–2, 1980*, 33–38. N.p.: Mormon Pacific Historical Society, August 1980.

"LDS Settlement of Eastern Utah: A Story of Faith, Courage, and Tolerance." In *Carbon County: Eastern Utah's Industrialized Island*, edited by Philip F. Notarianni, 109-29. Salt Lake City: Utah State Historical Society, 1981. Address delivered at the Utah State Historical Society Lecture Series, Price, Utah, 23 April 1980.

"Learning About Ourselves through Church History." *Ensign* 9 (September 1979): 6–8.

"L'Economia Americana nell 'Era Atomica." *Civilta degli Scambi* (Bari) 4 (June 1959): 13–16.

"L'Economia Americana nell 'Era Atomica e dell'Automazione." In *Annali dell 'Universita degli Studi di Napoli*, 35–47. Naples, Italy: Instituto di Storia Economica e Sociale, 1960.

"The Legacy of Early Latter-day Saint Women." *John Whitmer Historical Association Journal* 10 (1990): 3–17. Originally presented at the Annual Banquet, John Whitmer Historical Association, Lamoni, Iowa, 23 September 1989.

"The Lehi Beet Sugar Factory." *Beehive History* 10 (1984): 16–21.

"Leonard Arrington Responds." *This People* 7 (November 1986): 38–39.

"Life in these United States." *Reader's Digest* (November 1953): 16. Leonard contributed a short story to this monthly series.

"The Logan Tabernacle and Temple." *UHQ* 41 (Summer 1973): 301–14. With Melvin A. Larkin.

"The Looseness of Zion: Joseph Smith and the Lighter View." BYU Devotional Address, 19 November 1974, published in *Speeches of the Year: BYU Devotional and Ten-Stake Fireside Address*, 1974 (Provo, Utah: Brigham Young University Press, 1975), pp. 291–300. Also in *Task Papers in LDS History*, No. 7 (Salt Lake City: Historical Department, LDS Church, 1976); and *New Era* 6 (August 1976): 8–13.

"The Looseness of Zion: The Lighter Side of Mormon History." *Montana: Magazine of Western History* 40 (Spring 1990): 73–78.

"Lorenzo Hill Hatch: Pioneer Bishop of Franklin." *IY* 17 (Summer 1973): 2–8. With Richard L. Jensen.

"Louisa Lula Greene Richards: Woman Journalist of the Early West." *Era* 72 (May 1969): 28–32. Reprinted in *Chronicles of Courage* 5 (1994): 142–47.

"Lucy Mack Smith." In *LDS Women's Treasury*, 69–87. Salt Lake City: Deseret Book Co., 1997. With Susan Arrington Madsen.

"Making a Living: The Economic Life of Chesterfield." In *Chesterfield: Mormon Outpost in Idaho*, edited by Lavina Fielding Anderson, 21–32. Provo, Utah: Brigham Young University Press for the Chesterfield Foundation, Bancroft, Idaho, 1982. With Richard L. Jensen.

"The Many Uses of Humor." *Last Lecture Series* (Provo, Utah: Brigham Young University Press, 1974). 33 pp.

"MHA in the Past." *The Mormon History Association Newsletter* no. 92 (Spring 1994): 1–2.

"Missionaries in Church History." *New Era* 3 (June 1973): 62–65.

"Missionary at West Point." *This People* 9 (Fall 1988): 13, 15.

"Mississippi Mormons." *Ensign* 7 (June 1977): 46–51.

"The Missouri and Illinois Mormons in Ante-Bellum Fiction." *Dialogue* 5 (Spring 1970): 37–50. With Jon Haupt.

"Modern Lysistratas: Mormon Women in the International Peace Movement, 1899–1939." *JMH* 15 (1989): 88–104.

"A Mormon Apostle Visits the Umatilla and Nez Perce in 1885." *IY* 31 (Spring/Summer 1987): 47–54.

"Mormon Beginnings in the American South." presented at the American Historical Association Convention, Atlanta, Georgia, 29 December 1975, published in *Task Papers in LDS History*, No. 9 (Salt Lake City: Historical Department of The Church of Jesus Christ of Latter-day Saints, 1976). 21 pp.

"The Mormon Cotton Mission in Southern Utah." *PHR* 25 (August 1956): 221–38. This article was awarded the Louis Knott Koontz prize of the Pacific Coast

Branch, American Historical Association, as the best article published in PHR in 1956–57.

"The Mormon Debt Problem of the 1890's." PUASAL 29 (1952): 56. Abstract.

"Mormon Economic Organization: A Sheaf of Illustrative Documents." UHQ 28 (January 1960): 41–55. With Ralph W. Hansen.

"The Mormon Experience in Idaho." *New Perspectives* 11 (December 1994): 2–6. Address given to faculty and students at Ricks College on 6 April 1994.

"Mormon Family Life in Nineteenth-Century Western America." *World Conference on Records: Preserving Our Heritage* (Salt Lake City: The Church of Jesus Christ of Latter-day Saints, 1980), Vol. 3, Part 1, Series 331. 10 pp.

"Mormon Finance and the Utah War." UHQ 20 (July 1952): 219–37.

"The Mormon Heritage of Vardis Fisher." *BYU Studies* 18 (Fall 1977): 27–47. With Jon Haupt.

"Mormon History: A Dialogue with Jan Shipps, Richard Bushman and Leonard Arrington." *Century II* 4 (Spring–Summer 1980): 27–39.

"Mormon Origins in New York: An Introductory Analysis." *BYU Studies* 9 (Spring 1969): 241–74. With James B. Allen.

"The Mormon Settlement of Cassia County, Idaho, 1873–1921." *IY* 23 (Summer 1979): 36–46. Address delivered at Burley, Idaho, 18 October 1978. This was prepared for the Snake River Series under a grant from the National Endowment for the Humanities.

"The Mormon Tithing House: A Frontier Business Institution." BHR 28 (March 1954): 24–58.

"The Mormon Utopia." *Halcyon: A Journal of the Humanities* 10 (1988): 131–42.

"Mormon Women for Peace." *This People* 12 (Spring 1991): 13–14.

"Mormon Women in Nineteenth-Century Britain." *BYU Studies* 27 (Winter 1987): 67–83. Reprinted in *Coming to Zion*, ed. James B. Allen and John W. Welch (Provo: BYU Studies, 1997), 278–99.

"Mormondom in Centennial Idaho." *This People* 11 (Fall 1990): 40–42.

"Mormondom's Financial Records: They Reflect the Life and Times of Its People." *This People* 12 (Summer 1991): 46–47.

"Mormonism: From Its New York Beginnings." *New York History* 61 (October 1980): 387–410. Also published in *Dialogue* 13 (Fall 1980): 120–35. Originally presented at the Mormon History Association annual meeting, Canandaigua, New York, 3 May 1980.

"Mormonism: Views from Without and Within." *BYU Studies* 14 (Winter 1974): 140–53.

"The Mormons and the Indians: A Review and Evaluation." *The Record* 31 (Friends of the Library, Washington State University, 1970): 4–29.

"Mormons in Twentieth-Century New Mexico." In *Religion in Modern New Mexico*, edited by Ferenc M. Szasz and Richard W. Etulain, 101–23. Albuquerque: University of New Mexico Press, 1997.

"Mule Cars in Pioneer Utah." *Pioneer* 40 (November–December 1993): 18–19.
"Mule Cars in Pioneer Utah." *SUP News* 4 (July 1957): 15–16.
"N. Eldon Tanner, Man of Integrity." *Dialogue* 15 (Winter 1982): 8–10.
"New Deal Economic Programs in the Northern Tier States, 1933–1939." In *Centennial West: Essays on the Northern Tier States*, edited by William L. Lang, 227–43. Seattle: University of Washington Press, 1991. With Don C. Reading.
"The New Deal in the West: A Preliminary Statistical Inquiry." *PHR* 38 (August 1969): 311–16.
Entries in *The New Encyclopedia of the American West*, ed. Howard R. Lamar (New Haven: Conn.: Yale University Press, 1998) [Revision of 1977 *Reader's Encyclopedia of the American West*]: John Milton Bernhisel, p. 94; ; George Q. Cannon, pp. 162–63; Patrick Edward Connor, p. 252; William Godbe, p. 432; Handcart Companies, p. 467; William Henry Hooper, p. 493; William Jennings, p. 572; Latter-day Saints, pp. 621–26; Logan, Utah, p. 648; Ogden Utah, p. 810; Provo, Utah, pp. 924–25 (with Thomas G. Alexander); Joseph Fielding Smith, p. 1060; Reed Smoot, p. 1061 (with Thomas G. Alexander); Eliza Roxey Snow, pp. 1062–64; James E. Talmage, pp. 1091–92; John Taylor, p. 1096; Uranium Mining, pp. 1145–46; Utah, pp. 1146–49; Wilford Woodruff, pp. 1232–33 (with Thomas G. Alexander); Brigham Young, pp. 1246–47; Mahonri Macintosh Young, p. 1248; and Zion's Cooperative Mercantile Institution, pp. 1252–53.
"New Deal Programs and Southwestern Agriculture." In *Southwestern Agriculture: Pre-Columbian to Modern*, edited by Henry C. Dethloff and Irwin M. May, 275–92. College Station: Texas A & M University Press, 1982.
"1992—Year of Anniversaries." *This People* 13 (Fall 1992): 71–72.
"The 1921 Depression: Its Impact on Idaho." *IY* 15 (Summer 1971): 10–15. With Gwynn W. Barrett.
"Objectives of Mormon Economic Policy." *WHR* 10 (Spring 1956): 180–85.
"Of Latter-day Saint Men, Women, and Books." *Sunstone Review* 1 (May 1982): 26–28.
"Oliver Cowdery's Kirtland, Ohio, 'Sketch Book,'" *BYU Studies* 12 (Summer 1972): 410–26.
"On Writing Latter-day Saint History." In *Celebrating the LDS Past: Essays Commemorating the 20th Anniversary of the 1972 Founding of the LDS Church Historical Department's "History Division,"* 1-9. Provo, Utah: Joseph Fielding Smith Institute for Church History, Brigham Young University, 24 January 1992.
"On Writing Latter-day Saint History." presented to the Mormon Pacific History Association Conference, Laie, Hawaii, 1 August 1980. In *Proceedings, First Annual Conference, Mormon History in the Pacific, August 1–2, 1980* (N.p.: Mormon Pacific Historical Society, August 1980), 1–5. Reprinted in *Cele-*

brating the LDS Past: Essays Commemorating the 20th Anniversary of the 1972 Founding of the LDS Historical Department's "History Division" (Provo: Joseph Fielding Smith Institute for Church History, Brigham Young University, 1992), 1–9.

"Origin of the Welfare Plan of The Church of Jesus Christ of Latter-day Saints." *BYU Studies* 5 (Winter 1964): 67–85. With Wayne K. Hinton. Reprinted in *The Exodus and Beyond: Essays in Mormon History*, eds., Lyndon W. Cook and Donald Q. Cannon (Salt Lake City: Hawkes Publishing Co., 1980), 203–22.

"The Other Jack Dempsey: Boxing's Greatest Champ Never Forgot His Mormon Roots." *This People* 10 (Summer 1989): 63–65.

"Panaca: Mormon Outpost Among the Mining Camps." *Nevada Historical Society Quarterly* 18 (Winter 1975): 207–16. With Richard Jensen. Originally duplicated by Historical Department of The Church of Jesus Christ of Latter-day Saints, 1973. 16 pp. Address prepared for the annual banquet of the Nevada State Historical Society, Las Vegas, 19 October 1973.

"Paying the Tenth in Pioneer Days." *The Instructor* 98 (November 1963): 386–87, 390.

"Perpetuation of a Myth: Mormon Danites in Five Western Novels, 1840–90." *BYU Studies* 23 (Spring 1983): 147–65. With Rebecca F. Cornwall.

"Personal Reflections on Mormon History." *Sunstone* 8 (July–August 1983): 41–45. Paper presented at the Mormon History Association annual meeting, Omaha, Nebraska, 6 May 1983.

"Persons for All Seasons: Women in Mormon History." *BYU Studies* 20 (Fall 1979): 39–58. This appeared in modified form, translated into Dutch, as "Moeders, Zusters, Dochters: Aspecten van de Vrouw in de Mormoonse Gcschiedenis." *Horizon: Tijdschrift over de Mormoonfe Geneenschap* (Wilrijk, Belgium) 2 (May 1983): 58–66.

"Philo T. Farnsworth, Inventor of Television." In *Acceptance and Dedication of the Statue of Philo T. Farnsworth, Presented by the State of Utah*, 33–48. Washington, D.C.: United States Government Printing Office, 1991. The dedication took place on 2 May 1990.

"Pioneering Communications Technology in Utah." *Pioneer* 43 (Spring 1996): 30–31.

"Planning an Iron Industry for Utah, 1851–1858." *HLQ* 21 (May 1958): 237–60.

"A Practical Prescription: Pioneer Medicine Combined Faith with Works." *This People* 10 (Fall 1989): 59–60.

"The Prayer for a Miracle." *Turning Points* (Salt Lake City: Bookcraft, 1981), 53–55.

"President Harold B. Lee: Eleventh President of the Church." In Joseph Fielding Smith, *Essentials of Church History*, 26th ed. Revised and enlarged, (Salt Lake City: Deseret Book Co., 1973), 555–60.

"Price Control in Early Utah." *PUASAL* 29 (1952): 55. Abstract.

"The Promise of Eagle Rock: Idaho Falls, Idaho, 1863–1890." *Rendezvous, Idaho State University Journal of Arts and Science* 18 (Spring 1983): 2–17. Prepared for delivery as part of the program "Idaho Small Town Experience." sponsored by the Idaho State Historical Society and Association for the Humanities in Idaho, 22 April 1981.

"Property Among the Mormons." *Rural Sociology* 16 (December 1951): 339–52.

"The Provo Woolen Mills: Utah's First Large Manufacturing Establishment." *UHQ* 21 (April 1953): 97–116.

"The Quest for Interpretation in Local Studies." In *Working Together: A Regional Approach to Community Traditions and History in Idaho*. Published by the Idaho Humanities Council and Idaho State Historical Society, 1983, pp. 8–10.

Entries in *The Reader's Companion to American History*, ed. Eric Foner and John A. Garraty (Boston: Houghton Mifflin, 1991): Mormons, 748–50; Joseph Smith, 998–99; Brigham Young, 1185–86.

Editor of "Reappraisals of Mormon History." A 120-page "Special Section" in *Dialogue* 1 (Autumn 1966): 21–140.

"Recalling a Twin Falls Childhood." *IY* 25 (Winter 1982): 31–40. Originally delivered in Twin Falls, Idaho, 25 March 1981, as part of the program "Idaho Small Town Experience," sponsored by the Idaho State Historical Society and Association for the Humanities in Idaho.

"Reclamation in Three Layers: The Ogden River Project, 1934–1965." *PHR* 35 (February 1966): 16–34. With Lowell Dittmer.

"Reflections on the Founding and Purpose of the Mormon History Association, 1965–1983." *JMH* 10 (1983): 91–103.

"Religion and Economics in Mormon History." *BYU Studies* 3 (Spring–Summer 1961): 15–33.

"Religion and Planning in the Far West: The First Generation of Mormons in Utah." *EHR* 11, Series 2 (August 1958): 71–86. With Philip A. M. Taylor.

"Religion and Planning in the Great Basin, 1847–1900." *Proceedings of the Thirty-Second Annual Conference of the Western Economic Association, 1957* (Salt Lake City: University of Utah Press, 1957), Volume 32, 37–41. Reprinted in the Bobbs-Merrill Reprint Series in Economics.

"Religious Sanction and Entrepreneurship in Pioneer Utah." *PUASAL* 30 (1953): 130. Abstract.

"Reverence and Responsibility." *Sunstone* 21 (June–July 1998): 80. Excerpt from last chapter of *Adventures of a Church Historian.*

"The Role of the Council of the Twelve During Brigham Young's Presidency of The Church of Jesus Christ of Latter-day Saints." *Task Papers in LDS History*, No. 31 (Salt Lake City: Historical Department of The Church of Jesus Christ of Latter-day Saints, 1979). With Ronald K. Esplin.

"Role of the Mormon Church in the Economic Development of the Mountain West, 1847–1900." *PUASAL* 33 (1956): 193–94. Abstract.

"Rural Life Among Nineteenth-Century Mormons: The Woman's Experience." *Agricultural History* 58 (July 1984): 239–46. Paper presented to the Rural Life Conference, Florida A&M University, Tallahassee, Florida, 23 September 1983.

"The Sagebrush Resurrection: New Deal Expenditures in the Western States, 1933–1939." PHR 52 (February 1983): 1–16. Presidential address to the American Historical Association, Pacific Coast Branch, San Francisco, California, 16 August 1982.

"Sakajawea's Mormon Connection." *This People* 12 (Autumn 1991): 53–54.

"Scholarly Studies of Mormonism in the Twentieth Century." *Dialogue* 1 (Spring 1966): 15–32. Includes a chronological listing of Ph.D. dissertations on Mormon history.

"The School of the Prophets." PUASAL 35 (1958): 145–46. Abstract. See also *Encyclia* 60 (Part 2, 1983): 141–42.

"Science, Government, and Enterprise in Economic Development: The Western Beet Sugar Industry." AH 41 (January 1967): 1–17.

"The Search for Truth and Meaning in Mormon History." *Dialogue* 3 (Summer 1968): 56–66. This article was awarded the Mormon History Association Prize as best article on Mormon history published during the year 1967–68. Reprinted in *Personal Voices: A Celebration of Dialogue*, ed. Mary Lithgoe Bradford (Salt Lake City, Signature Books, 1987), 63–79; and in *The New Mormon History: Revisionist Essays on the Past*, ed. D. Michael Quinn (Salt Lake City: Signature Books, 1992), 1–11.

"Sentinels on the Desert: The Dugway Proving Ground (1942–1963) and Deseret Chemical Depot (1942–1963)." UHQ 32 (Winter 1964): 32–43. With Thomas G. Alexander.

"The Settlement of the Brigham Young Estate, 1877–1879." PHR 21 (February 1952): 1–20.

"Seven Steps to Greatness." *BYU Studies* 16 (Summer 1976): 459–70.

"Seven Steps to Greatness: Overview of the History of Brigham Young University." Commencement Address to the Graduates of Brigham Young University, 18 April 1975, published in *Task Papers in LDS History*, No. 3 (Salt Lake City: Historical Department of The Church of Jesus Christ of Latter-day Saints, October 1975). 25 pp. Also in *BYU Studies* 16 (Summer 1976): 459–70.

"The Six Pillars of Utah's Pioneer Economy." presidential address to Utah Academy of Sciences, Arts & Letters, St. George, Utah, 25 March 1977, *Encyclia: Journal of The Utah Academy of Sciences, Arts & Letters* 54 (Part 1, 1977): 9–24.

"Smith, Joseph Fielding." In *Dictionary of American Biography*, Supplement 9, ed. Kenneth T. Jackson (New York: Charles Scribner's Sons, 1994), 736–38.

"Spencer W. Kimball, Apostle of Love." *Dialogue* 18 (Winter 1985): 10–13.

"The Spirit of Mormon History." Published weekly in the *Church News Section* of the Salt Lake City *Deseret News*, 1, 8, 15, 22, and 29 March, 5, 19, and 26 April, and 3 May 1980.

"Stopping a Run on a Bank: The First Security Bank of Idaho and the Great Depression." *IY* 14 (Winter 1970–71): 2–11. With Gwynn W. Barrett.

"Supply Hub of the West: Defense Depot Ogden, 1941–1964." *UHQ* 32 (Spring 1964): 99–121. With Thomas G. Alexander.

"Talking Things Over." *Pioneer* 41 (September–October 1994), 20–23.

"Taming the Turbulent Sevier: A Story of Mormon Desert Conquest." *WHR* 5 (Autumn 1951): 393–406.

"Taxable Income in Utah, 1862–1872." *UHQ* 24 (January 1956): 21–47.

"They Kept 'Em Rolling: The Tooele Army Depot, 1942–1962." *UHQ* 31 (Winter 1963): 3–25. With Thomas G. Alexander.

"'This is the Place': The Mormon Trek to Utah." In *The American Destiny: An Illustrated Bicentennial History of the United States*, 10 vols. (New York: The Danbury Press, 1976), 5: 94–114.

"To Zion: Brother Brigham's Last Trek." *Pioneer* 41 (July–August 1994), 8–11.

"The Transcontinental Railroad and Mormon Economic Policy." *PHR* 20 (May 1951): 143–57. Reprinted in Thomas C. Cochran and Thomas B. Brewer, ed., *View of Growth: The Industrial Era* (New York: McGraw-Hill Book Company, 1966), 50–60.

"The Transcontinental Railroad and the Development of the West." *UHQ* 37 (Winter 1969): 3–15. Reprinted in *The Exodus and Beyond: Essays in Mormon History*, ed. Cook and Cannon (1980), 97–106.

"Tribute to Merrill D. (Sam) Beal." In *Sixty Years of Educational Endeavors in Idaho: Memoirs of Merrill D. Beal*, i–ix. Pocatello: Idaho State University Press, 1984.

"The U and I Sugar Company in Washington." *PNQ* 57 (July 1966): 101–9.

"The U.S. Army Overlooks Salt Lake Valley: Fort Douglas, 1862–1865." *UHQ* 33 (Fall 1965): 326–50. With Thomas G. Alexander.

"Utah and The Depression of the 1890s." *UHQ* 29 (January 1961): 3–18.

"Utah." In the *Encyclopedia Americana* (30 vols.; New York, Americana Corporation, 1964) 27: 825–38. Revised and updated in 1969 edition.

"Utah, the New Deal, and the Depression of the 1930s." *Weber State College Monograph Series* (Ogden, Utah, 1983). Originally presented as the Dello G. Dayton Memorial Lecture, Weber State College, Ogden, Utah, 25 March 1982.

"Utah Women Helped to Achieve Statehood." *Pioneer* 43 (Winter 1996): 30–31.

"Utah's Ambiguous Reception: The Relocated Japanese Americans." In *Japanese-Americans: From Relocation to Redress*, edited by Roger Daniels, Sandra C. Taylor, and Harry H. L. Kitano, 92–97. Salt Lake City: University of Utah Press, 1986.

"Utah's Ambiguous Reception: The Relocated Japanese Americans." In *Japanese Americans: From Relocation to Redress*, rev. ed., ed. Roger Daniels, Sandra C. Taylor, and Harry H. L. Kitano (Seattle: University of Washington Press, 1991), 92–97.

"Utah's Biggest Business: Ogden Air Material Area at Hill Air Force Base 1938–1965." UHQ 33 (Winter 1965): 9–33. With Thomas G. Alexander and Eugene A. Erb Jr.

"Utah's Coal Road in the Age of Unregulated Competition." UHQ 23 (January 1955): 35–63.

"Utah's Emerging Metropolis: The Wasatch Front." In *Utah's Urban-Rural Revolution: Sixth Annual Agriculture and Industry Conference, Salt Lake City, February 6, 1962*, 9–20 plus tables. Logan: Utah State University, 1962. With George Jenson.

"Utah's First Line of Defense: The Utah National Guard and Camp W. G. Williams, 1926–1965." UHQ 33 (Spring 1965): 141–56. With Thomas G. Alexander.

"Utah's Great Drought of 1934." UHQ 54 (Summer 1986): 245–64.

Entries in *Utah History Encyclopedia*, edited by Allan Kent Powell (Salt Lake City: University of Utah Press, 1994): "Banking and Finance in Utah," 27–31; "Coin and Currency," 103–5; "Colonization of Utah,"106–8; "David Eccles," 151–53; "Marriner Stoddard Eccles," 152; "Charles Redd," 457–58; "George Albert Smith," 502; and "The Sugar Industry in Utah," 534–35.

"The Utah Military Frontier, 1872–1912: Forts Cameron, Thornburgh and Duchesne." UHQ 32 (Fall 1964): 330–54. With Thomas G. Alexander.

"Utah's Pioneer Beet Sugar Plant: The Lehi Factory of the Utah Sugar Company." UHQ 34 (Spring 1966): 95–120.

"Utah's Small Arms Ammunition Plant During World War II." PHR 34 (May 1965): 185–96. With Thomas G. Alexander.

"Utah's Spectacular Missiles Industry: Its History and Impact." UHQ 30 (Winter 1962): 2–39. With Jon G. Perry.

"Vistas in Church History." *The First Annual Church Educational System Religious Educators Symposium*, held 19–20 August 1977, at Brigham Young University (Salt Lake City: Church Educational System, The Church of Jesus Christ of Latter-day Saints, 1977), 17–21.

"Voices from the Past: Autograph Books." *This People* 9 (Spring 1988): 15–16.

"Western Agriculture and the New Deal." AH 64 (October 1970): 337–53. Presidential address to the Agricultural History Society at its annual luncheon held in Los Angeles on 17 April 1970.

"When the Mormon Church Invested in Southern Nevada Gold Mines." *Nevada Historical Society Quarterly* 41 (Fall 1998). Slightly revised, it was reprinted in *Dialogue* 35 (Summer 2002): 73–87. With Edward Leo Lyman.

"Where Does the Term 'Jack-Mormon' Come From?" *Ensign* 4 (March 1974): 25.

"Why Did the Latter-day Saints Experience Persecution?" *Era* 73 (August 1970): 49–53.

"Why I Am a Believer." *Sunstone* 10 (January 1985): 36–38. Presented at the annual Sunstone Symposium, Hotel Utah, Salt Lake City, Utah, 26 August

1983. Reprinted in *A Thoughtful Faith: Essays on Belief by Mormon Scholars*, ed. Philip L. Barlow (Centerville, Utah: Canon Press, 1986), 225–33; and as "Myth, Symbol and Truth." In *Faithful History: Essays on the Writing of Mormon History*, ed. George D. Smith (Salt Lake City: Signature Books, 1992, 303–10.

"Willard Young: The Prophet's Son at West Point." *Dialogue* 4 (Winter 1969): 37–46.

"William A. ('Bill') Hickman: Setting the Record Straight." *Task Papers in LDS History*, No. 28 (Salt Lake City: Historical Department of The Church of Jesus Christ of Latter-day Saints, 1979). With Hope A. Hilton.

"The Writing of Latter-day Saint History: Problems, Accomplishments and Admonitions." *Dialogue* 14 (Autumn 1981): 119–29.

"Women as a Force in the History of Utah." *UHQ* 38 (Winter 1970): 3–6. This constitutes the "Introduction" to the special issue on the same topic.

"World's Largest Military Reserve: Wendover Air Force Base, 1941–1966." *UHQ* 31 (Fall 1963): 324–35. With Thomas G. Alexander.

"Zion's Board of Trade: A Third United Order." *WHR* 5 (Winter 1950–51): 1–20.

"Zion's Manuscript Newspapers." *This People* 10 (Winter 1989): 63–64.

Reviews

American Business History, by Louis Galambos. *JEH* 28 (September 1968): 469–70.

The American West in the Twentieth Century: A Short History of an Urban Oasis, by Gerald D. Nash. *JAH* 61 (June 1974): 233–34.

The "Americanization" of Utah for Statehood, by Gustive O. Larson. *The American West* 8 (November 1971): 56.

AZn: A History of the American Zinc Company, by James D. Norris. *JAH* 57 (June 1970): 191–92.

Beckoning Frontiers: Public and Personal Recollections, by Marriner S. Eccles. *WHR* 5 (Autumn 1951): 407–10. With Evan B. Murray.

The Bonanza West: The Story of the Western Mining Rushes, 1848–1900, by William S. Greever. *Northwest Historical Quarterly* 54 (October 1963): 177–78.

The Charles Ilfeld Company: A Study of the Rise and Decline of Mercantile Capitalism in New Mexico, by William J. Parish. *UHQ* 30 (January 1962): 92–94.

Claus Spreckels: The Sugar King in Hawaii, by Jacob Adler. *AH* 41 (July 1967): 319–20.

Colorado in the Great Depression, by James F. Wickens. *PHR* 51 (May 1982): 233–34.

The Company Town in the American West, by James B. Allen. *AHR* 72 (January 1967): 721–22.

The Economics of Agriculture, by R. L. Cohen. *Southern Economic Journal* 17 (October 1950): 209–10.

The 1838 Mormon War in Missouri, by Stephen C. LeSueur. *Missouri Historical Review* 82 (January 1988): 240–43.

The Farm Boy and the Angel, by Carl Carmer. *Dialogue* 5 (Summer 1970): 97–98.

The First 100 Years: A History of the Salt Lake Tribune, 1871–1971, by O. N. Malmquist. *Ensign* 1 (October 1971): 66–67.

Forging New Rights in Western Waters, by Robert G. Dunbar. AH 59 (April 1985): 353–55.

History of Wyoming, by T. A. Larson. AH 41 (April 1967): 196.

Hutterian Brethren: The Agricultural Economy and Social Organization of a Communal People, by John W. Bennett. EHR 25 (May 1972): 385–86.

Intermountain Railroads: Standard and Narrow Gauge, by Merrill D. Beal. AW 6 (Spring 1964): 84–85.

In the Direction of His Dreams: Memoirs, by Lowry Nelson. WHQ 18 (January 1987): 72–73.

John Doyle Lee: Zealot-Pioneer Builder-Scapegoat, by Juanita Brooks. *Montana, The Magazine of Western History* 14 (April 1964): 114.

The Lamp in the Desert: The Story of the University of Arizona, by Douglas D. Martin. AW 3 (Spring 1961): 91–94.

The Lion of the Lord: A Biography of Brigham Young, by Stanley P. Hirshson. *BYU Studies* 10 (Winter 1970): 240–45. Includes listing of manuscript material in LDS Church Archives on Brigham Young.

Massacre at Mountain Meadows: An American Legacy and A Monumental Crime, by William Wise. *BYU Studies* 17 (Spring 1977): 382–84.

Mining Frontier of the Far West, 1848–1880, by Rodman W. Paul. *Mississippi Valley Historical Review* 50 (September 1963): 312–13.

A Mormon Chronicle: The Diaries of John D. Lee, 1848–1876 (two volumes), edited by Robert Glass Cleland and Juanita Brooks. PHR 25 (August 1956): 405–7.

The Mormon Conflict, 1850–1859, by Norman F. Furniss. *Mississippi Valley Historical Review* 47 (December 1960): 509–11.

The Mormon Establishment, by Wallace Turner, and *The Latter-day Saints: The Mormons Yesterday and Today* by Robert Mullen. *Dialogue* 1 (Winter 1966): 118–22.

The Mormon Village: A Pattern and Technique of Land Settlement, by Lowry Nelson. PHR 22 (May 1953): 181–82.

Nauvoo: Kingdom on the Mississippi, by Robert Bruce Flanders. WHR 20 (Autumn 1966): 356–57.

Nevada Land, Water and Politics in the Nineteenth Century, by John M. Townley. AH 56 (April 1982): 470–71.

Nevada's Twentieth-Century Mining Boom: Tonapah, Goldfield, Ely, by Russell R. Elliott. JAH 53 (March 1967): 843–44.

On the Mormon Frontier: The Diary of Hosea Stout, edited by Juanita Brooks (two volumes). *Utah Alumnus* 41 (April 1965): 12–14.

Our National Park Policy: A Critical History, by John Ise. *AG* 36 (January 1962): 53.

The Progress of Economics: A History of Economic Thought, by Warren B. Catlin. AHR 68 (July 1963): 1013–14.

Rebel of the Rockies: A History of the Denver and Rio Grande Railroad, by Robert G. Athearn. BHR 37 (Autumn 1963): 293–94.

Reclaiming the American West: An Historiographical Guide, by Lawrence B. Lee. AH 56 (April 1982): 479–80.

The Reminiscences and Civil War Letters of Levi Lamoni Wight: Life in a Mormon Splinter Colony on the Texas Frontier, edited by Davis Bitton. *Southwest Historical Review* 74 (April 1971): 565–66.

Restless Strangers: Nevada's Immigrants and Their Interpreters, by Wilbur S. Shepperson. AHR 78 (February 1973): 167–68.

The Rockies, by David Lavender. AHR 74 (February 1969): 1075.

Rocky Mountain Carpetbaggers: Idaho's Territorial Governors, 1863–1890, by Ronald H. Limnbaugh. JAH 69 (March 1983): 981–82.

Silver and the First New Deal, by John A. Brennan. IY 14 (Fall 1970): 31.

Snake River Country, by Bill Gulick, photographs by Earl Roberge. IY 15 (Winter 1972): 36.

Social Economy and the Price System: An Essay in Welfare Economics, by Raymond T. Bye. *Southern Economic Journal* 17 (April 1951): 483–84.

This Crested Hill: An Illustrated History of the University of Idaho, by Keith C. Petersen. IY 32 (Summer 1988): 35–36.

Union Pacific Country, by Robert G. Athearn. UHQ 40 (Winter 1972): 89–90.

Utah: A Guide to the State, 2nd ed. revised and enlarged, by Ward J. Roylance. BYU *Studies* 22 (Fall 1982): 502–4.

Wyoming: A Political History, 1868–1898, by Lewis L. Gould. *Journal of the West* (10 January 1971): 185.

Addresses and Duplicated Papers

"Achievements of the 'Second Generation' of Mormon Women." Presented at the Eighth Annual Women's Conference, Brigham Young University, 18 February 1983.

"Achievements of Utah Women." Paper presented at the annual luncheon of the Utah Federation of Women's Clubs, Salt Lake City, 27 January 1979.

"Achievements of Utah's Pioneer Businessmen." Duplicated by Historical Department of The Church of Jesus Christ of Latter-day Saints, Salt Lake City, Utah. 13 pp. Address to Salt Lake City Rotary Club, 25 July 1972.

"Across the Great Plains." Presented at Brigham Young University Devotional, 22 July 1980.

"Advice to the Graduates." Convocation Address, College of Family, Home, and Social Sciences, Brigham Young University, 17 April 1987. 7 pp.

"Agriculture and Mormonism: The Historical Perspective." Address at Centennial Agricultural Week, Brigham Young University, 30 March 1976. 19 pp.

“Blessed Relief Society Sisters.” Prepared for Parley’s First Ward (Salt Lake City) Relief Society, 24 August 1976. 15 pp.

“The Book of Mormon as an Influence in the Life of People.” Duplicated, 28 pp., 1975.

“A Brief History of the Salt Lake Valley.” Delivered to the National Conference of Organ Builders in Salt Lake City, 8 October 1984. 16 pp.

“Cassandra in Pursuit of Clio; or, Why Economists Become Historians.” Duplicated by Department of Economics, Utah State University, Logan Utah, 1964. Luncheon Address to the Pacific Coast Branch, American Historical Association, Los Angeles, California, 27 August 1964. 20 pp.

“Cedar City: The Building of a Community.” Cedar City: Southern Utah State College and Iron Mission Days Committee, 1978. With Dean L. May. Originally prepared for 125th anniversary of the settlement of Cedar City, Utah, 11 November 1976.

“Cliometrics, The New Economic History.” Presented in the Economics Seminar, Utah State University, 8 July 1988.

“‘Clothe These Bones’: The Reconciliation of Faith and History.” Address delivered at a Retreat of the History Division, The Church of Jesus Christ of Latter-day Saints, Ensign Peak, Salt Lake Valley, 23 June 1978. 16 pp.

“The Confiscation of Church Properties Under the Edmunds-Tucker Act of 1887.” Duplicated by Historical Department of The Church of Jesus Christ of Latter-day Saints, 1973. 12 pp. Address prepared for Idaho Education Week, August 1973.

“David Eccles: A Man for His Time.” Address given at dedication of the David Eccles College of Business, University of Utah, Salt Lake City, 6 October 1996. 14 pp.

“Early Idaho Personalities.” Presented at the annual banquet of the Idaho State Historical Society, Rexburg, Idaho, 5 March 1979.

“The Economic Development of Utah.” Duplicated by Department of Economics, Utah State University, Logan, Utah, 1965. Address at the Annual Fellowship Banquet, Utah Academy of Sciences, Arts & Letters, Logan, Utah, 16 April 1965. 15 pp.

“Economic Policies of the Mormon Church, 1847–1961.” Duplicated by Department of History, Brigham Young University, Provo, Utah, 1961. Address to Phi Alpha Theta and History Majors at Brigham Young University, 17 May 1961. 26 pp.

“The Economic Role of Pioneer Mormon Women.” Presented at lecture series sponsored by Economics Department, Utah State University, Logan, Utah, 30 June 1982.

“Economics of Cache Valley Agriculture, 1859–1900.” 17 April 1980. Duplicated by Ronald Jensen Historical Farm, Logan, Utah. With Linda Wilcox.

“Faith and Intellect in the Mormon Church.” Series of lectures given at Brigham Young University, Hawaii, 24–29 May 1994. Topics included Joseph Smith,

Brigham Young, Parley and Orson Pratt, Emmeline B. Wells, B. H. Roberts, J. Reuben Clark, Lowell Bennion, Henry B. Eyring, Hugh Nibley, Chieko Okazaki, and others. A book-length manuscript based on these lectures was in preparation at the time of Leonard's death: "Faith and Intellect in Mormon History: The Lives of Latter-day Saint Leaders of Thought" (224 pp.). The introductory essay was presented as the inaugural Leonard J. Arrington Lecture (given 7 November 1995) in a series sponsored by the Special Collections, Merrill Library at Utah State University, and was published in 1996 as *Faith and Intellect as Partners in Mormon History* (34 pp.).

"Fresh Insights into the Character of Brigham Young." Presented at the annual banquet of the Utah Valley Historical Society, a chapter of the Utah State Historical Society, Provo, Utah, 14 November 1978.

"Grass Roots Entrepreneurship in the Frontier West: The Allens of Cache Valley and the Coreys and Wattises of Weber Valley." Presented at Charles Redd Lecture Series, Brigham Young University, Provo, Utah, 23 September 1982. Published in 1985.

"Great Basin Queendom." Address to the Salt Lake Retrenchment Society and the Utah Endowment for the Humanities, in Richfield and Salt Lake City, Utah, 18 and 25 September 1975. 21 pp.

"The Great Drouth in Utah, 1934." The Seventh David E. Miller Lecture on Utah and the West, University of Utah, Salt Lake City. Given 17 April 1985.

"H. L. A. Culmer—First President of Salt Lake Rotary." Address to Salt Lake Rotary Club, Salt Lake City, 22 July 1975, duplicated.

"Highlights of Utah's Industrial History." Duplicated and distributed by the Utah Manufacturers Association, January 1971. Address given at the annual membership luncheon of the Utah Manufacturer's Association.

"History of Boise Stake." Duplicated by Historical Department of The Church of Jesus Christ of Latter-day Saints, 1973. 22 pp. Address prepared for Idaho Education Week, August 1973.

"History of Bonneville Stake, Salt Lake City." Duplicated by Historical Department of The Church of Jesus Christ of Latter-day Saints, 1973. 18 pp. Address prepared for High Priests and Wives, Bonneville Stake, 27 April 1973.

"History of Livestock in the Great Basin." Address to the Society for Range Management, Salt Lake City, 11 February 1985.

"History of the Church in Utah Valley, Utah." Delivered to Provo Utah Central Stake sesquicentennial celebration, 22 June 1980.

"A History [of sorts] of the Practice of Medicine in Utah." Address to annual banquet of Western Anaesthesiologists, Salt Lake City, 21 February 1976, duplicated. 18 pp.

"History of Twin Falls Stake." Duplicated by Historical Department of The Church of Jesus Christ of Latter-day Saints, 1973. 26 pp. Address prepared for Idaho Education Week, August 1973.

"History of University West Stake, Salt Lake City." Duplicated by Historical

Department of The Church of Jesus Christ of Latter-day Saints, 1973. 16 pp. Address prepared for High Priests and Wives, University West Stake, 8 March 1973.

"Horton David and Louisa Leavitt Haight." Presented at the Haight Family Reunion in Oakley, Idaho, 28 June 1980.

"How Relief Society Minutes Help Us in Writing Church History." Duplicated typescript, Historical Department of The Church of Jesus Christ of Latter-day Saints, Salt Lake City. 8 pp. Address to Relief Society Conference, 5 October 1972.

"'I Have the Grit in Me': Brigham Young, From His Private and Public Papers." Presented at the Western History Association annual convention, San Antonio, Texas, 16 October 1981.

"The Importance of the Humanities." Prepared for the Nevada Humanities Council, Lake Tahoe, 22 July 1976. 11 pp.

"International Mormonism: Historical Development and Present Challenges." Presented at History Week, Brigham Young University, Provo, Utah, 23 Match 1982. 27 pp.

"John Tanner, His Children, and their Families Who Came West." Prepared for the John Tanner Family, 13 September 1976. 26 pp.

"Joseph Earl Arrington." Address prepared for the reception in recognition of the establishment of the Joseph Earl and Genevieve Thornton Arrington Collection of Nineteenth-Century Americana at the Harold B. Lee Library, Brigham Young University, Provo, Utah, 10 July 1980.

"Joseph F. Smith: From Impulsive Young Man to Patriarchal Prophet." Duplicated by the Historical Department of The Church of Jesus Christ of Latter-Day Saints, 1973. Address prepared for the Joseph Smith Family Reunion, 19 August 1973.

"Joseph Fielding Smith: The Training of a Prophet." Duplicated typescript, Historical Department of The Church of Jesus Christ of Latter-day Saints, Salt Lake City, 1972. 11 pp.

"Latter-day Saint Men at West Point." Duplicated, 1975.

"L'Intervento Statale nella Vita Economica degli Stati Uniti." 1959, mimeographed, Bocconi University, Milan.

"The Looseness of Zion: The Lighter Side of Mormon History." Presented to the Phi Alpha Theta Luncheon of the Western History Association, Salt Lake City, Utah, 13 October 1983.

"The Marrow in the Bones of History: New Directions in Historical Writing." Address for Western University Press Association, Salt Lake City, 12 October 1975. 14 pp.

"The Meaning of July 24 in Pioneer Utah History." Presented at Salt Lake Rotary Club, 22 July 1980.

"Memories and Traditions." Presented to the Old Main Society at Utah State University, 1982.

"A Mormon Apostle Visits the Umatilla and Nez Perce, 1885." Presented to the Conference on Missionary Influences on Northwest History, Whitman College, Walla Walla, Washington, 25 July 1986. 12 pp. Published in 1987.

"Mormon Colonization of the Great Basin Kingdom." Address delivered at the Days of '47 luncheon, Salt Lake City, 24 July 1978. 12 pp.

"Mormon Contributions to the Development of Arizona." Presented at a sesquicentennial celebration sponsored by the LDS Institute of Religion at Tucson, Arizona, 16 April 1980.

"Mormon Contributions to Western Agriculture." Duplicated by the Ronald Jensen Historical Farm. Presented at Ronald Jensen Historical Farm, Utah State University, Logan, Utah, 17 April 1980. With Scott Kenney.

"Mormon Economic Idealism." Duplicated by the LDS Student Association, University of Utah, Salt Lake City, 1968. 10 pp. Address at the LDS Institute of Religion, Salt Lake City, Utah, 25 October 1968.

"The Mormon Experience in Idaho." Summer School Lecture, Idaho State University, Pocatello, Idaho, 15 June 1976. 25 pp.

"The Mormon Experience in Illinois." Address delivered to a stake fireside, Urbana, Illinois, 15 April 1978. 18 pp.

"Mormonism and the Arts: An Historical Appreciation." Duplicated by Historical Department of The Church of Jesus Christ of Latter-day Saints, 1973. 29 pp. With D. Michael Quinn. Address prepared for Mormon Arts Festival, Tempe, Arizona, 1 February 1973.

"The Mormon Utopia." Presented to the American Utopias Lectures at Northern Nevada Community College, Elko, 22 October 1986.

"Mormon Women in Nineteenth Century Britain." Presented to students in Religion Courses, Nottingham University, Nottingham, England, 4 March 1986. Published in 1987.

"Patterns of Economic Organization in the Early West." Presented at lecture series sponsored by Economics Department, Utah State University, Logan, Utah, 28 June 1982.

"A Pioneer Mormon Bishop and His Ward: Edwin D. Woolley and the Salt Lake City Thirteenth Ward." Duplicated by Historical Department of The Church of Jesus Christ of Latter-day Saints, 1973. 24 pp. Address prepared for Mormon History Association Meeting, Fort Worth, Texas, 12 October 1973.

"The Pioneer Mormon Cooperative Village." Presented at lecture series sponsored by Economics Department, Utah State University, Logan, Utah, 29 June 1982.

"Pioneer Mormon Midwives." Duplicated by Historical Department of The Church of Jesus Christ of Latter-day Saints, 1973. 21 pp. Address prepared for Idaho Education Week, August 1973.

"Reflections on Economics and the Church." Address to the Conference on Economics and Mormon Culture, Brigham Young University, 7 October 1975, duplicated. 14 pp.

"Reflections on Pioneer History." Duplicated by Historical Department of The Church of Jesus Christ of Latter-day Saints, 1973. 8 pp. Address prepared for the annual luncheon of Daughters of Utah Pioneers, Salt Lake City, 6 October 1973.

"Remarks for Great Basin Kingdom Symposium." Logan, Utah, 4 May 1988. 11 pp.

"The Scholarly Approach to Church History." Presented to the Honor Students of Brigham Young University, 13 February 1986. 14 pp.

"The Secularization of Mormon History and Culture." Duplicated by Department of Economics, Utah State University, Logan, Utah, 1965. Paper for the Annual Meeting, Western History Association, Helena, Montana, 22 October 1965. 20 pp.

"Significance of the Mormons in American History." Duplicated by Historical Department of The Church of Jesus Christ of Latter-day Saints, 1973. 21 pp. Address prepared for the LDS Institute at Stanford University, 1 March 1973.

"The Spirit of Mormonism: The Restoration after 150 Years." Presented at a sesquicentennial stake fireside in Los Angeles, 12 April 1980.

"Their Share and More: The Story of the Salt Lake Emigration Stake." Prepared for Bicentennial Lecture Program, Emigration Stake, 30 September 1976. 32 pp.

"The Testament of Martin Harris." Presented at Aaronic Priesthood Commemoration, The Martin Harris Grave Site, Clarkston Cemetery, Clarkston, Utah, May 1982. Duplicated.

"Traditions." Prepared for the graduation banquet at Brigham Young University, 19 April 1984. 10 pp.

"The U.S. Army in Cedar Valley: Camp Floyd, Utah, 1858–1861." Duplicated by Department of History, Brigham Young University, Provo, Utah, 1963. Prepared for the Special Tour of the Western History Association, meeting in Salt Lake City, 19 October 1963. 6 pp. With Thomas G. Alexander.

"Utah and the Economic Program of the Roosevelt New Deal." Presented at lecture series sponsored by Economics Department, Utah State University, Logan, Utah, 2 July 1982.

"Utah's Copper Industry." Presented at a symposium on mining sponsored by the Utah State Historical Society, 31 October 1987.

"Utah's Pioneers Were Prospectors Too." Presented at the Utah Mining Association annual convention, Park City, Utah, 11 September 1981.

"The Utah War." Duplicated by Historical Department of The Church of Jesus Christ of Latter-day Saints, Salt Lake City, 1973. 23 pp.

"Vignettes from the Lives of The Great Economists." Presented at lecture series sponsored by Economics Department, Utah State University, Logan, Utah, 2 July 1982.

"Women in Pioneer Utah." Delivered in Las Vegas, Nevada, and in Delta, Salt Lake City, Cedar City, Logan, and other Utah communities. 18 pp.

Books and Articles About Leonard J. Arrington

Anderson, Lavina Fielding. *Doves and Serpents: The Activities of Leonard Arrington as Church Historian, 1972–1982*. Salt Lake City: Privately distributed to family and friends, 1982. 288 pp. Based on a larger, unpublished manuscript by the same title. 1281 pp.

Bitton, Davis, and Maureen Ursenbach Beecher, eds. *New Views of Mormon History: A Collection of Essays in Honor of Leonard J. Arrington*. Salt Lake City: University of Utah Press, 1987. 480 pp.

Cazier, Stanford. "Honoring Leonard Arrington." *Dialogue* 22 (Winter 1989): 55–60.

Cornwall, Rebecca F. *From Chicken Farm to History: The Life of Leonard Arrington, 1917–1977*. Salt Lake City: Privately distributed to family, 1978. 478 pp.

"Idaho Future Farmer Has Outstanding Project." *American Farm Youth* 1 (April 1935): 14.

Jolley, JoAnn. "Leonard J. Arrington: Mormon History's Leading Man." *This People* 1 (Sesquicentennial Issue 1980): 14–19.

Journal of Mormon History 25, No. 1 (Spring 1999) included a number of memorials to Leonard, including the texts from the 15 February 1999 Memorial Service (10–33), the expanded tributes of Ronald K. Esplin (103–12) and Ronald W. Walker (113–30), and an extensive series of personal tributes by those who knew and interacted with Leonard (33–103).

May, Dean. "In Memoriam: Leonard James Arrington." *Sunstone* 22 (June 1999): 8–11.

Nash, Gerald. "Leonard J. Arrington." In *The New Encyclopedia of the American West*, edited by Howard R. Lamar, 56. New Haven: Yale University Press, 1998.

Stack, Peggy Fletcher. "LDS History was 'Ecstasy' for Arrington." *Salt Lake Tribune* 30 May 1998): D1–D2.

Swinton, Heidi. "Leonard Arrington: And That's the Way It Was." *This People* 7 (November 1986): 30–39.

Wells, Merle, W. "Leonard James Arrington, July 2, 1917–February 11, 1999." *IY* 43 (Sprint 1999): 3–4.

"Western History Association Prize Recipient, 1984: Leonard J. Arrington." *WHQ* 16 (January 1985): 17–26. Awarded at the Western History Association annual meeting, St Paul, Minn., October 1984.

Whittaker, David J. "Leonard James Arrington: His Life and Work." *Dialogue* 11 (Winter 1978): 23–47.

Obituaries/Notices/Funeral

Alexander, Thomas G. "In Remembrance: Leonard J. Arrington." *Newsletter of the Western History Association* (Spring 1999): 5.

———. "Leonard James Arrington." *Organization of American Historians Newsletter* 27 (May 1999): 23–24.

Beecher, Maureen Ursenbach. "Leonard J. Arrington: Reflections on a Humble Walk." *Dialogue* 32 (Spring 1999): 1–5.

Concurrent Resolution, Idaho State Affairs Committee, Recognizing the Accomplishments of Leonard James Arrington. Passed by the First Regular Session of the Fifty-fifth Idaho Legislature, 16 March 1999. SCR 134.

"Death of a Moses." *Ogden Standard Examiner,* Saturday (13 February 1999).

"Exhibit Honors Former Educator." *Utah Statesman* (26 February 1999): 3.

"Historian of Mormonism Dies" (AP Release), *The Daily Herald* (Provo, Utah) Friday (12 February 1999): A-7.

"In Our Opinion: Leonard J. Arrington." *Deseret News* (17 February 1999): A-10.

Lyman, Edward Leo. "In Memoriam: Leonard J. Arrington, Western Historian." *Nevada Historical Society Quarterly* 41 (Fall 1999): 221–22.

Lythgoe, Dennis. "LDS Historian Remembered as Witty, Articulate." *Deseret News,* Sunday (14 February 1999): E-3, E-5.

Obituary, *Deseret News, Church News Section* (Week ending 20 February 1999): 12.

Obituary, *Deseret News*, Saturday (13 February 1999): D-9.

Obituary, *Herald Journal* [Logan, Utah], Sunday (14 February 1999): A-4.

Obituary, *Los Angeles Times*, Saturday (13 February 1999): A-27.

Obituary, *Salt Lake Tribune,* Saturday (13 February 1999): E-2.

Official Declaration, Michael O. Leavitt, Governor of Utah, honoring Leonard J. Arrington "for his lifetime contributions to the State of Utah as a scholar, historian and friend." 25 March 1999.

"Proclamation" issued by The Office of Dirk Kempthorne, Governor, State of Idaho, recognizing Leonard James Arrington for his contributions to the people and the state of Idaho, 16 March 1999. Reprinted in *JMH* 25, no. 2 (Fall 1999): xiv.

Prucha, Francis Paul. "Obituary: Leonard James Arrington." *Western Historical Quarterly* 30 (Summer 1999): 263.

Saxon, Wolfgang. "Leonard J. Arrington, 81, Mormon Historian." *New York Times,* Saturday (13 February 1999): B-19.

Stack, Peggy Fletcher. "Leonard Arrington, LDS Historian, Intellectual Dies." *Salt Lake Tribune,* Friday (12 February 1999): B-1, B-5.

Swensen, Janet. "Leonard Arrington, Dean of LDS Historians, Dies at 81." *Deseret News,* Friday (12 February 1999).

———. "Hundreds bid farewell to Leonard Arrington; Pres. Hinckley praises 'Dean of Mormon History.'" *Deseret News,* Wednesday (17 February 1999): A-12.

Epilogue Notes

1. David J. Whittaker, "Bibliography of Leonard James Arrington," *Dialogue: A Journal of Mormon Thought* 11 (Winter 1978): 33–47; David J. Whittaker, "Leonard James Arrington: A Bibliography," in *New Views of Mormon History: A Collection of Essays in Honor of Leonard J. Arrington*, edited by Davis Bitton and Maureen Ursenbach Beecher (Salt Lake City: University of Utah Press, 1987), 439–69; and David J. Whittaker, "Leonard James Arrington (1917–1999): A Bibliography," *Journal of Mormon History* 25 (Fall 1999): 11–45.

Index